Praise for *Cl*

"[A] compulsive portrait of one of rock's most enigmatic figures. Sandford is an utter iconoclast compared to the usual [Clapton] profiler; he paints an intriguing tale."
—*Guitar Magazine*

"Well-written, full of insight and spiced with telling little details."
—*Q*

"A creditable portrait [and] a particularly good read."
—*Daily Mail* (U.K.)

"For a spikier read consult Sandford's book: not a hatchet-job, but unafraid to look sternly on Clapton's dodgier moments."
—*Mojo*

CLAPTON

Edge of Darkness

Christopher Sandford

UPDATED EDITION

DA CAPO PRESS

CIP data is available.

First Da Capo Press edition 1999

This Da Capo Press paperback edition of *Clapton* is an unabridged
republication of the edition first published in London in 1994, with ten textual
emendations, updated appendices, and a new epiloque by the author. It is
reprinted by arrangement with Victor Gollancz Ltd.

Published by Da Capo Press, Inc.
A Member of Perseus Books Group

Manufactured in the United States of America

To Monty Dennison

Contents

Acknowledgements

First, Eric Clapton. Whatever one thinks of him – and this book perhaps strays from the conventional view – Clapton has stirred powerful emotions with his music; powerful and often overwhelming. In writing his biography I came to have a quite genuine and deep sympathy for him.

I am indebted to scores of people for providing insights, ideas and opinions, and for putting their memories of Clapton at my disposal. First and foremost, those who played with Clapton or knew him professionally: Chuck Berry, Pete Brown, Chris Dreja, Georgie Fame, Chris Farlowe, Hughie Flint, Dick Heckstall-Smith, Paul Jones, the late Alexis Korner, Tom McGuinness, Dave Markee, Jim McCarty, Ben Palmer, Greg Phillinganes, Chris Rea, George Terry and Bobby Whitlock. Jack Bruce and John Mayall, while not giving formal interviews, both made a number of remarks about Clapton after I had identified myself to them as his biographer. I have included their comments in the text.

I am also grateful to: Elaine Akalovsky, Pattie Boyd, Geoff Bradford, Duncan Caine, Linda Chandler, Sylvia Clapton, Peter Cockwill, Ray Connolly, Jenny Dolan, Richard Drew, Christopher Elson, Godfrey Evans, Martin Forbes, Goronwy Gealy, Bob Geldof, Jeff Griffin, Anthony Haden-Guest, Pete Hogman, Neal Hunter, David Jacobs, Kenny Jones, Steve Judson, Tom Keylock, Graham Lancaster, Gary Lawson, Cecilia Lewis, Colin Longmore, Anne McDowell, Pamela Wynn Mayall, Kay Munday, John Murray, Nick Parkinson, Gary Patterson (for Robert Stigwood), Andy Peebles, Anthony Phillips, John Platt, Jenny Pocock, Sally Prescott, Dave Rees, Tim Rice, Cliff Richard, Harry Shapiro, Don Short, Philip Solly, Peter Strachan, the late Ian Stewart, Dick Taylor, Chris Thacker, Rob Townsend, David Whitlock, Tom Wolfe and Matthew Wood.

On an institutional note, source material on Clapton and his family was provided by: the Canadian High Commission and National Archives; Companies House; the US Department of Justice – Information Management Division; the General Register Office; Hollyfield School; the Performing Rights Society; and the New York, Seattle and British Libraries. I should acknowledge the help of Cynthia Facha of the California Department of Corrections.

I also interviewed a number of people who prefer not to be named. Where sources asked for anonymity – usually citing friendship with Clapton or his manager – every effort was made to persuade them to go on the record. Where this was not possible, I have used the phrase 'a witness' or 'a musician' as appropriate. I apologize for the frequency with which I have had to resort to this formula.

Finally, personally, I should again thank: Peter Barnes, Tony Brown, Noel Chelberg, Monty Dennison, Jackie Francis, Focus Fine Arts, Malcolm Galfe, Jo Jacobius, Johnny Johnson, Terry Lambert, Amina McKay, Jim Meyersahm, Elise Moore-Searson, John Prins IV, Nancy Roller, my father Sefton Sandford, Sue Sims-Hilditch, Hilary Stevens, Katrina Whone and Richard Wigmore, an editor of genius.

This book was written in accommodation rented at top speed from my friend Peter Scaramanga. My thanks to him and his family.

C. S.

1

The End of Something

When else but in 1968 could four thousand souls, dressed in ruffles and Chelsea boots, in Op-Art and flares, their chests festooned with McCarthy, Amnesty and I'm Backing Britain slogans, with buttons and badges lined up across their shirts like campaign ribbons, have sat submerged in the great vat of the Albert Hall, listening to rock musicians play snatches from *West Side Story*?

After the group left the stage, a bearded, balding man, the compère John Peel, came forward to the lip. He stood against the red backdrop in his blue shirt, mumbling after some technical delay, 'Now . . . for the last time . . . ever. The *Cream*.' The noise seemed literally to detonate, the music exploding off the speakers as, stage right, a figure in black jeans, red Nudie shirt and cowboy boots announced 'White Room'. The song began, a percussive assault of bass, drums and rhythm guitar, a mundane chord structure salvaged by a solo of histrionic novelty. Next, in 'Politician', a number so lumbering it seemed in danger of stalling, Clapton shuffled, shrugged and, turning his back, played two passages of such banality that, offstage, the man who co-wrote the song failed to recognize it.

From there things deteriorated. 'I'm So Glad' and 'Sitting On Top Of The World' perfectly illustrated the hybrid that Cream had become: a blues-rock group of competing virtuosi with jazz pretensions. The humour of the originals was lost in the rapacity to improvise. During the second number all three members played solos simultaneously. The song ended in a crash of mangled drums, the bass player, an elfin figure with the look of an animated troll, burying his face in his hands.

At this stage, half-way through the concert, it became apparent that, 'White Room' aside, it was one of those nights – perhaps 30 per cent of the total – when Cream seemed not to be working. The rock audience being infinitely forgiving, only later were the reasons advanced: *ennui*, tiredness (this being the group's 200th performance), and that, in the words of one of them, 'We all heard things in our heads – whole orchestras, in my case – we couldn't reproduce on stage.' Whatever the cause, the effect was that Cream compensated by playing at massive, seat-shaking volume.

The next number was 'Crossroads'. Clapton's guitar moved across the beat, a pleasurable inoffensive noise, yet a physical one – like shuffling one's feet through a pile of leaves. The solo came two and a half minutes in: a high, keening sound weaving eccentrically over the bass, on and on, at a pace beyond the reach of any other white guitarist, or, as Peel put it later, 'If you thought Eric Clapton was human, listen to this.' The song ended in a choric scene of chaos and delirium: fans became ecstatic and had to be restrained by bouncers. Even the drummer looked animated. Clapton, a lean pale figure, totally impassive, stood there biting his lip, the only sober person in a roomful of drunks. 'Ginger Baker,' he announced, 'Toad', a rambling double-bass–drum odyssey, during which the hall thinned appreciably, underscored by crashing guitar. The house lights came up, the group waved, walked off, returned – Clapton last – and played requests. After the second encore a chubby dark-haired man in a black sweater jumped on stage and, swinging his arm, showered the guitarist in confetti. Clapton smiled for the only time that evening. 'I was amazed,' he said later. 'I didn't think anybody would remember us . . . It was really a fine evening for me. I felt very excited.'

Later still, during a party at his manager's house in Stanmore, he added, 'Personally, it bored me shitless.'

A quarter of a century passes. The buttons and badges are replaced by women with Aids ribbons and, belted and shivering, men in streaming suits shuffling through the ice and fog, the night falling with February speed. Outside, the coaches ('EC BLUES', 'ROTHERHAM R&B', and one intriguingly marked 'LOST') make their approach over the steely patch of Kensington Gore. The crowd, men and women in their forties, seem glad to see each other. A sense of reunion greets the slender, pale figure who lopes unannounced on stage.

At a glance he looks miraculously unchanged. There are the same narrow eyes, the same mouth, the same chin now adorned by the grey splinters of a beard. His glasses and rigorously clipped hair give him the look of an amiable chemistry don. For forty minutes Eric Clapton proceeds to give a Ph.D. lecture on the blues. Alone with his pianist he plays Robert Johnson and Memphis Slim, Freddie King and Leroy Carr, picking an acoustic guitar on his red upholstered chair less than a dozen feet from the spot where, an age ago, he performed 'Crossroads'. When Clapton plays now he does so with a gentle rocking motion, pumping his leg, announcing each song in his flat, ironic voice. You get the impression he could play at least a parody of the blues all night, and, for an uncomfortable hour, it seems as though he will.

Things improve with the arrival of the band – drums, guitar, harmonica and, more pertinently, a bass player who knew Otis Redding and Wilson Pickett. After a merely boisterous version of 'Blues, Leave Me Alone', Clapton sings 'Key To The Highway', reminding the crowd that, whatever his reputation, his success as a solo artist lies in his voice, jigging from one foot to another like a child unbearably excited. In the chorus his mouth reaches the microphone before the rest of him, giving him the look of a man struggling into a high wind. The number ends to polite applause.

The next songs need to be announced: 'Meet Me In The Bottom', 'Goin' Away Baby' and – 'because he just died' – a version of Albert King's 'Born Under A Bad Sign'. After two hours of derivative, if competently played covers, some of the numbers are not so much seized on as accepted. The first call for 'Layla' is heard. ('Next year,' snaps Clapton.) The garish purple and blue lights and constant inducements to 'have a good time' seem barely to animate the crowd, elements of which, in the more melodic passages, actually do rattle their jewellery. A few women are allowed up to lean on the stage, still clutching their handbags. At the end of a number Clapton bends towards them in his suit and brown shoes. 'I *love* this music,' he says joylessly, drawing his upper lip away from his teeth, almost a snarl. Slowly it becomes apparent that Clapton's love of the blues, where impatience, frustration and irony always lurk below the surface and now threaten to break out more openly, is incompatible with the demands of the 'good time' concertgoer. The first couples are already forcing themselves down the soiled red aisle when Clapton, draining a glass from his conjuror's prop table, lighting a cigarette, says dramatically, '*This* is what I'm all about.' He plays a version of 'Nobody Knows You (When You're Down And Out)', a song of such abject content, such mawkishness, much maudlin self-pity, that truly it seems, to Clapton, fate still adopts an attitude of implacable malice.

The next day, in front of an audience of fifteen thousand in Los Angeles, he collects six Grammys.

2

A Little Learning

Born on Friday 30 March in mid-century, son of a soldier, after a troubled childhood he developed into a pioneer of modern word-music – specializing, as he always said, in 'feeling, not thinking' – indulged in a long, harrowing courtship of a woman about whom he wrote his best work, married and divorced her, fell prey to alcohol and drugs, recovered, his art dwindling as his reputation increased. His followers took him for the real thing long after he realized that nothing real was left. The key to his life, he once told an interviewer, lay in his relationship with his mother.

Admirers of Eric Clapton will have no difficulty in recognizing the life details of Paul Verlaine; a man prematurely considered a 'genius', who re-created himself at thirty, emerging as a simple rhyming poet, the nonconformist embracing conformity. When he died at fifty-one, in a prostitute's arms, Verlaine was forgotten by the critics but widely admired by those for whom he recalled the Romantic tradition. Being a distillation of all that came before him, he supplied a classical education without the need to acquire it oneself. One of Verlaine's greatest strengths was as a monument to the past.

Art Hickman's name is rarely mentioned in the roll-call of modern musicians, but he it was who developed Swing. Hickman and his pianist Ferde Grofe began arranging for reed and brass choirs in the 1920s, a tradition continued by, among others, Bix Beiderbecke and Duke Ellington. From 1927 to 1931 Ellington was resident at the Cotton Club, New York, where his use of tone colour, his mingling of out-and-out jazz with Swing rhythms, not to mention his penchant for whimsical lyrics, advanced the style to an art form. The Big Band era had begun. For a decade the young on two continents came under the spell of Benny Goodman, of

Charlie Barnet, Artie Shaw, of Jimmy and Tommy Dorsey, subdividing into those promised to pure jazz and the lesser option of Glenn Miller and Guy Lombardo.

Among the former was a young Canadian trooper, native of Montreal, Edward Walter Fryer, who both sang and played piano in the style of Grofe. Fryer, who also had a talent for drawing, arrived in England with the 14th Canadian Hussars in 1942. An army colleague, Neal Hunter, describes him as an 'essentially uncomplicated, but sensitive guy, off to himself most of the time. I remember Ed reading all day. It sort of set him apart. That and the fact that he played that high, tinkling piano.'

What Hunter was hearing was boogie-woogie, a genre then stigmatized as 'race' music, a blues piano style derived from Swing involving repeated figures played by the left hand and blues improvisations by the right. A superficially simple style to play, boogie-woogie was a technical precursor of skiffle; its charm was its accessibility. Opinions vary as to whether, within the vast province of the word, Fryer was a 'good' pianist. All that is known is that he played enthusiastically, seeming to have no life outside his music, his books and his drawing, and that his shortcomings as a soldier were not to be numbered.

In 1944, between postings to the military base at Bushy Park, Teddington, and other encampments around Guildford, Fryer met and befriended a local teenager named Patricia Clapton, born in London on 7 January 1929. Pat's father Reginald – an articled clerk – died in 1933, and her mother Rose subsequently married a plasterer and bricklayer called, with striking symmetry, Jack Clapp. The extended family – Jack, Rose, Pat and her elder brother Adrian – settled at 1, The Green, Ripley, a community lying between Guildford and Woking of which the late Paul Getty (who moved nearby) once said, 'You could imagine it being used by Hollywood as the typical English village.' The house itself was modest: one of four terraced cottages flanked by the open heath and Newark Lane, it was a four-roomed redbrick dwelling with an outside lavatory and a miniature garden, enclosed by a broken picket fence. Having attended the local secondary school and grown, by 1944, into a young woman of striking looks – dark hair, pale and full-lipped – Pat increasingly inhabited the Ship and, such as they were, dances in the local halls. It was at one of the latter that she met Edward Fryer.

It is perhaps difficult to convey the alarm with which Jack and Rose Clapp must have greeted the news that their fifteen-year-old was pregnant. They were not merely surprised – they were shocked. Not only, it emerged, was Fryer already married, but Pat's own views concerning motherhood were, at best, ambivalent. As news of her condition spread, local youths, translating their values into action, shouted and spat at the girl in the street. Graffiti that disparaged Pat's morals appeared on The Green's walls. A resident of nearby Rose Lane, still living in the area, confirms that it was 'without a doubt, the talk of the town. A lot of it was viciously cruel. *That*'s hindsight. At the time we just saw a noisy girl who'd done what our mothers warned us not to.'

The winter of 1944–5 was bleak. While the war situation fluctuated, relations between Pat, her brother (who that year joined the Royal Signals), Rose and Jack deteriorated – there were near-daily rows about the baby. Fryer having announced his intention to return to Montreal, where he was discharged from the army on 4 September, the prospect of raising a child in so small a home – where money was never abundant – can only be guessed at. After a false start in mid-month, the baby was born in the front room of The Green early on 30 March 1945; delivered by Rose and the local midwife as Pat, barely sixteen, lay on the floor behind the black-out curtains. The boy, registered on 6 April, was christened Eric Patrick. Although the Clapps' neighbour recalls 'some sort of discussion about the surname' he was immediately called Clapton (a word derived from the Old English 'clop' or rock, denoting bulky, heavily built or sturdy of character).

Historically, the boy shared a birthday with Verlaine, Goya and van Gogh. Astrologically (as he himself later became inclined), born under the sign of Aries, he could be expected to be adventurous, impulsive and energetic, self-reliant and self-centred, while the presence of Scorpio suggested a secretive side and tendency to withdraw. According to a musician who later worked with him, 'He is heavily ruled by Mars in Pisces, which means that he's far more liable to break down and is much more emotional than we see on the surface.'

On the day Eric Clapton was born the war entered its final phase: the frontier town of Emmerich, on the Dutch–German border, fell to Canadian troops; advanced British tank divisions approached Münster and occupied Westphalia; an official report from Supreme Allied Command claimed the battle for Germany to be 'developing with such overpowering velocity that often the positions of armoured columns ranging in the enemy interior [are] known only to Allied air patrols'. On 30 March the US 7th Army captured Heidelberg. The Russians invaded Austria and took Danzig. A new Czech government was formed.

On the home front, aspects of normal life returned, albeit slowly, to Ripley. The Surrey *Comet* for March 1945 advertises Judy Garland in *Meet Me In St Louis*; Lord John Sanger's COLOSSAL EASTER ATTRACTION (featuring 'Rosa – The Little Marvel On One Wheel') returned after an absence of five years; the Royal Canadian Ordnance Dance Band, in which Edward Fryer had periodically performed, played foxtrots in the Lion Hotel. There was a feeling, even as US aircraft took off from Bushy Park to attack Bremen and Hamburg, that victory – finally – was at hand.

The price for this was extreme. Matthew Wood, born in Woking a few days before Clapton, with whom he later attended school, speaks of the accumulation of shared experience among those growing up in the late 1940s and early 1950s: the constant shortage of food; the bargain Utility clothes; the sense that, through the Marshall Plan and other schemes, the country was living beyond its means. '[Clapton and I] had only six weeks of actual war,' says Wood. 'The consequences lasted for ten years. Britain in those days was quite uniquely grim: rationing, shortages, power cuts, strikes. It seemed to rain the whole time. No wonder we all went mad in the Sixties.'

Patricia Clapton remained with her son for two years. For a time she courted a local man six years her senior, Sid Perrin, an extrovert sports-man and raconteur who helped push the infant's pram across Ripley Green. Despite a suggestion that she and Perrin might marry (they did live together thirty years later), in 1947 Pat announced her engagement to a second Canadian soldier, Frank McDonald. Again the village expressed its displeasure. A brick wall adjoining the Methodist Church, abutting the Clapps', became daubed with graffiti: GET LOST PC YOU BITCH. By morning the last two words had been erased by an unknown passer-by who still agreed with the main thesis. 'The locals were hard on me,' Pat later told a journalist, 'but those were the days before the phrase "love child" had been heard of.'

When his mother left Ripley, Eric Clapton was raised by his grand-parents. Though never formally adopting the child, Jack and Rose Clapp were his *de facto* guardians until 1963 (when, against their better judge-ment, they co-signed a contract admitting Clapton to the Yardbirds). As late as 1965 he was living with them while working professionally as a musician. An understanding of their values is critical to understanding Clapton as he grew up. A shy, reticent man, Jack Clapp, sitting shirt-sleeved in the parlour over his 'thousand on a raft' (beans on toast), was quick to assert what he considered to be his best qualities: realism, perseverance and self-effacement. He was, says Matthew Wood, 'the prototype of the honest English working man. If you had one word to describe Jack, it would be "decent". He had a profound, intuitive sense of what was right.'

Rose Clapp, once a widow at twenty-seven, was a pragmatic, calm, on the whole cheerful woman, crisp in conversation, who saw her lifetime's role as to support her family. Thirty-nine when her grandson was born, she happily reverted to a routine of nappies and baths, of tears, feeds and walks on the green, the fiction, maintained until 1950, of being 'Mum'. It was Rose who contrived the boy's baptism at St Mary Magdalen; who pushed him every afternoon in her daughter's pram down Ripley high street (where asides, though not in their previous number, continued to be muttered); who bought him his black Labrador, Prince; who later encouraged him to paint and draw; who arranged in January 1950 for him to enter the Church of England First School.

The building, then adjacent to St Mary Magdalen, was a redbrick structure, infinitely decayed, covered in lichen and moss and admitting rain through its timber roof. Something gloomy about the interior communicated itself to the pupils, one of whom remembers it as 'a depressing, unheated place, at one end of which lessons would desultorily take place, while at the other Wootton pie was served at lunchtime'. Two months short of his fifth birthday, Clapton became one of sixty children arriving each morning in his uniform of grey shorts, blue shirt and pullover, and grey socks, studying English, maths, geography, art and scripture. From the first week he was recognized as talented in drawing and writing, 'hopeless' (according to Wood) at arithmetic and, above all other qualities, almost morbidly shy.

Some time in the first days of the new decade Rose Clapp had told her grandson the true story of his parentage. While she later explained that '[he] had to understand why I, or my husband, signed certain forms as his guardians and not parents' there was also, one source insists, pressure from Clapton's peers: a fellow pupil clearly recalls 'tongues wagging in the playground about Eric being "different". That was how it was put. The word bastard wasn't mentioned, but I can imagine it might have been by certain parents. People were blunter about things in those days.'

Clapton attended the school from 1950 to 1956, when he transferred to St Bede's Secondary Modern in nearby Send. By the age of ten, as stated by his contemporaries, a definite set of characteristics had emerged: he was quiet, moody, polite (doffing his school cap to elderly villagers), withdrawn, chary. Silent with most humans, he had a strong affinity with animals – his pet Labrador and snails, a pony grazing periodically on the green. All his drawings were of inanimate objects. A member of the First Ripley troop of Boy Scouts, even there he tended to hold himself apart. Asked at that age what he wanted to be, he answered, 'A doctor – so that I'd stop people from going to heaven.' On another occasion he amended this to the single word 'artist'.

At St Bede's, Clapton was subject to the following school curriculum:

–To
  * Ensure that Christian principles permeate all aspects of life
  * Encourage a general enjoyment in the art of learning
  * Foster an enjoyment of books and reading
  * Develop skills in solving problems
  * Instill a sense of personal responsibility for behaviour.

Imperfectly grasped as it was, there is evidence that at least one of the above informed Clapton's youth. He had a definite sense of responsibility. Until at least the age of eleven he was scrupulously, even abnormally well-behaved. Clapton's only known friend, a local boy of the same age named Guy Pullen, describes him as a 'distant kid who was definitely a one-off, didn't join in. He wasn't a normal country boy.' On his eleventh birthday, avenging some schoolyard feud, Clapton declined to invite Pullen to his party. Another boy who did attend remembers 'Rick [as he was known] sitting in the front room, brooding, receiving presents without the slightest hint of pleasure. You could say he was a loner.' He also resolutely refused to join in any sport with the occasional exception of boxing matches staged in the back garden of Pullen's home.

All this changed for the worse in 1956 when Clapton's mother visited from her home in Canada, bringing with her her six-year-old son by McDonald. The effect on Clapton was dramatic. From being merely moody he became morose. For the benefit of Pullen and other youths Pat was introduced as 'Rick's sister', a fiction that could scarcely have commended itself to their parents. Clapton was made vividly aware of his renewed status as 'odd', a condition radically affecting his behaviour at school. As he later told the journalist Philip Norman: 'From that moment they say I was moody and nasty and wouldn't try. We had to go through this whole thing of pretending she was my sister. At school

I used to hang around with all the weeds. I was always getting hit – on the hand with a ruler, or the side of the head.'

The change occurred at a particularly sensitive time. Throughout the 1950s British schoolchildren were confronted with the Eleven-Plus, an ordeal rendering three-quarters of them intellectual failures. Secondary moderns, originally intended as a practical alternative for those thought unsuitable for a grammar-school education, instead became stigmatized as repositories for children generally expected to leave school at fifteen with few, or no, qualifications. In 1956, shortly after Pat and her son returned to Canada, Clapton failed the exam and on 4 September that year arrived at St Bede's, later transferring to Hollyfield School, a gloomy Victorian manor-house whose chief distinction lay in the teaching of art. From being an affable if timid eleven-year-old, at thirteen Clapton had become a scrawny, belligerent adolescent with narrow eyes and down-turned mouth, much given to complaining, someone for whom all crises was major crises.

His hobbies from then on were solitary: drawing, coarse fishing, cycling. He abandoned boxing and developed a lifelong aversion to physical confrontation of any kind. At home Clapton's companions were his dog, snails and budgerigars. During meals (thousand on a raft, his favourite mock turtle soup) he ate silently, with excessive concentration, the parlour penetrated by the marshy tang of the green. At school he was known by the stock nickname 'Loony'.

Hollyfield was a co-educational establishment of seven hundred pupils aged from eleven and a half to eighteen. Its modesty as a place of academic excellence was offset by the opportunity it afforded to study art, a subject, according to the school's 1958 prospectus, 'having particular educational value in terms of a pupil's development as a "whole person"'. 'That was its great thing,' says an ex-Hollyfield student, Richard Drew. 'Although you were still a failure compared to grammar or public school, you were expected to work. It was quite radical in that respect – there was a culture of allowing you to improve yourself. Anyone with the slightest interest in drawing, painting or design was encouraged.' The same prospectus quotes these skills as 'providing a very good training for those who wish to go on to art schools and colleges in order to take up design or teaching as a career', as a substantial number of Hollyfield graduates did.

Clapton's first term at the school was uneventful. His form-master Peter Strachan remembers him as 'moodily quiet', dour, yet prepared to exert himself in class. In mid-1958 Strachan was shown a Surrey

Education Committee report on Clapton in which the description of 'Home Circumstances' left no doubt of the boy's history. 'We were aware that he was illegitimate, had had a rough time and had a chip on his shoulder. The staff all read the file. Most of his friends would have known through word-of-mouth and, even if they didn't, Clapton would have *assumed* they did. He was incredibly sensitive.' Another student, Philip Solly, confirms that 'We knew about it, and he knew that we knew.'

Clapton largely missed the opportunity to improve himself academically. Instead he concentrated on drawing, painting and on developing a marked if tortuous sense of humour. 'He was a practical joker,' says Solly, 'a stink-bomb, exploding cigar, whoopee-cushion type – but with a malicious edge. He pushed it to the point of cruelty', a fact for which psychological explanation – revenge for the privations of Clapton's youth – was readily available. In 1958, like thousands of British teenagers, he discovered *The Goon Show* and added a manic aspect to his character, goosestepping in the schoolyard, using a saucepan for sound effects. His 'looniness' became proverbial. At thirteen he was one of a half-dozen pupils whose lack of size, sporting prowess and ready wit made them vulnerable to bullying: 'I was the one that used to get stones thrown at me because I was so thin and couldn't do physical training . . . One of those types. I was always the seven-stone weakling. I used to hang out with three or four other kids who were all in that same kind of predicament. The outcasts. They used to call us "the loonies".'

All this made Clapton uniquely receptive to the revolution called rock and roll. Although the phrase first reached England through the film *Blackboard Jungle* in 1955 it was three years before the first wave of identifiable role-models – Little Richard, Buddy Holly, Jerry Lee Lewis – crossed the Atlantic. The impact on Clapton was electric. Rock, essentially simple with its twelve-bar format and seductive lyrics, appealed to one generation's desire to be different from another. As Philip Solly says, 'to anyone vaguely frustrated, which most of us were, it was a godsend. All of a sudden you had a way out.' Clapton and 'the loonies', he confirms, were among the school's first converts, experimenting with accents, adopting mannerisms, hastening to *Oh Boy* and *Drumbeat* on television and to *Uncle Mac's Hour* on radio.

It was through the last, which occasionally played a Sonny Terry bop or Memphis Slim boogie, that Clapton first discovered the blues. By 1959 Elvis Presley was in the army, Lewis and Richard semi-retired, Chuck Berry was under arrest and Buddy Holly dead. There was a feeling, as another British teenager, Keith Richards, puts it, that 'the initial wham had gone out of rock and roll'; like Richards, Clapton began to enquire into its roots; like him he responded with the zeal of a convert. Initially associated with slavery and work gangs, the blues' primary appeal was verbal: it spoke of angst, apathy and discomfort, of pain, prejudice – and, above all, of sex. Heavily sardonic in style, its lyrics were at best ironic, at worst cloyingly self-indulgent. The blues spoke to the wistful, the woebegone, the self-conscious. To Eric Clapton.

I felt through most of my youth that my back was against the wall and that the only way to survive was with dignity, pride and courage. I heard that in certain forms of music and I heard it most of all in the blues, because it was always an individual. It was one man and his guitar versus the world. It wasn't a company, or a band or a group. When it came down to it, it was one guy who was completely alone and had no options, no alternatives other than just to sing and play to ease his pains. And that echoed what I felt.

Again and again Clapton would return to the theme: of being separate, alone, one man versus the world, constantly comparing the Negro's predicament to his own. Edward Fryer, too, had played the blues. Clapton might not have known his father (he only ever saw a photograph) but he reflected his values in much that he heard and admired.

Among those he came to absorb were Robert Johnson (whose use of the guitar as a vocal instrument would become Clapton's own motif), W. C. Handy, Bill Broonzy, Sun House, Blind Lemon Jefferson, Blind Willie Johnson, Blind Boy Fuller, Sonny Terry (also blind), Roosevelt Sykes, Brownie McGhee and, of urban or electric bluesmen, Leroy Carr, Memphis Slim, Otis Spann, Otis Rush, Jimmy Reed, Willie Dixon, Albert King, B. B. King, Freddie King, Howlin' Wolf and Muddy Waters.

The result was that in summer 1958 Rose and Jack Clapp were persuaded to buy their grandson his first guitar.

The model, a £14 Spanish Hoya acoustic, accompanied Clapton to Hollyfield. By the end of the autumn term he was heard to create 'excruciating' sounds in the room immediately below where the staff assembled for tea, causing Peter Strachan to suggest he 'For God's sake, learn to play properly.' A second master, Goronwy Gealy, also remembers Clapton as 'permanently carrying the instrument around, a slightly querulous look on his face, as if daring you to challenge him'. If anything, this underestimates his attachment to the guitar. Strachan, Gealy and others at Hollyfield, and those, like Pullen, who knew him in Ripley confirm that, from fourteen, Clapton's horizons altered. He related to the instrument the way other children relate to sporting equipment or clothes. The guitar was an extension of his nervous system. In the course of twelve months he learned to play Dixon and Broonzy with style and Muddy Waters without fault. By early 1959 Clapton could reproduce Waters's 'Honey Bee' with its distinctive buzzing tone, sitting alone in the front parlour at midnight: ' "Testing, testing." I can hear it now,' says Rose. ' "Rick, are you coming to bed? Your father's got to work in the morning." '

'Devil music,' rumbled Jack.

Eric Clapton received no formal musical education. His training was purely imitative, derived from Waters, the Kings and Buddy Guy, a Chicago guitarist who in 1958 won the 'Battle of the Blues' at that city's Blue Flame Club. Richard Drew, present when Clapton first played Guy's and Magic Sam's 'All Your Love', states that 'it was a case of practise, practise and practise again. Obviously he had a gift, but he wasn't an overnight sensation. For a year you saw him playing on the bus, in class, under the stairs – anywhere.' He ends by adding, 'It rather set him apart, which was obviously what Eric wanted.'

Clapton's sense of being apart increased from that moment. Pullen, speaking of this era to Ray Coleman, confirmed, 'He was basically a loner . . . He had the tightest jeans, the longest hair, a dirty face, and eventually he sat alone on the village green playing this guitar to himself . . . He was certainly the odd one out.' Previously content to sulk or, if provoked, offer a wolflike leer, Clapton was now openly hostile. The reach and range of his jokes extended, punctuated by his use of a BSA air rifle. 'From fourteen,' says Philip Solly, 'he was a pest – dirty, lewd, aggressive – with no time for anyone else.' According to Solly, Clapton's main preoccupations were 'in strict order, music, art, and a fascination with both war and blood and guts generally', the last of which found expression in a poem published in the Hollyfield magazine that summer:

THE BATTLE CRY

'Forward into battle, men!'
The cry rings loud and clear,
And on the field a thousandfold

Are armed with sword and
spear.

The foe approach with cunning
eye,
The blood of men to seek,
But underneath the bright
breastplate
A heart beats humble and meek.

The sword is drawn, the spirit
roused,
The charge is swift and harsh.
Cold steel and iron clash one on
one
And men die upon the marsh.

And now the fight is really on,
And death is everywhere,

But men who fight for glory's
sake
Have neither fear nor care.

The dark black marsh is stained
with red,
The men are growing few,
The blades strike home,
The spears are launched,
The arrows swift and true.

At last the fight is over,
The enemy have fled,
But many of the warriors
Lie on their black Death Bed.

Other than art, Clapton's sole interest to survive the onset of adolescence was cycling. In 1959–60 he was attached to the Kingston Wheelers, occasionally racing against other clubs in Malden, Morden and Feltham, more often hastening up and down the Portsmouth Road on his own, rushing, slowing, determined even in this pursuit to be alone. At Hollyfield Clapton progressed to the art department, a building separate from the main school, known colloquially by its street number, 35, adjacent to Surbiton hospital. Richard Drew, a year senior to Clapton, has a picture of him, 'cycling uphill, a set expression on his face, dressed in jeans and a maroon jacket. From the age of fifteen he had a hedgehog haircut which he used to adjust in the side-mirror of his bike.'

For two years Clapton worked in the upstairs studio at 35, a room deliberately contrived in the style of a garret, easels and canvases littered in front of the high art-deco window. He and his fellow student Clive Blewichamp were the reprobates of the class. At break they huddled smoking under the domed ceiling of the attic, brooding over van Gogh or practising the guitar. Clapton's appreciation of the instrument now began in earnest. It was in 1960 that Philip Solly remembers him 'getting off the bus from Ripley, already snapping his fingers and crooning a song he'd written about himself called "Lord Eric"'. Further uphill stood Surbiton's sole specialist music shop, 'A magical place,' says Solly, 'with saxes and violins displayed in glass cases like an old-fashioned chemist's.' There were also guitars. Of the twenty-seven classes for which Clapton was scheduled every week, Richard Drew estimates he attended twelve: 'At least half the time he was skiving, writing songs, or doing both simultaneously.'

He did, however, pass both O and A level art. Philip Solly (like Clapton, achieving the minimum pass in the latter) remembers him 'not only doing no work, but despising anyone who did. He really had an attitude about it.' On the other hand, Solly agrees, Clapton was sufficiently talented not only to paint and draw to GCE standard but, in summer 1961, to be admitted to Kingston Art College.

He arrived there in September, in his own words 'not [having] enough certificates, but [the authorities liking] what they saw. They did an interview and I got into the art school for one year on probation ... At that point I was sixteen, getting into the Bohemian thing and listening to music and not really working very much.' In deference to his grandparents, Clapton did enrol for a class in commercial graphics. Again, says Drew, 'That was a mistake. Whereas the fine art crowd tended to be beatniks, in graphics you were expected to work. Clapton was totally unsuited for it.'

Armed with his Green Line bus pass he began to extend the distance between himself and his family, discovering Twickenham, Richmond and finally the capital itself. From 1961 to 1963 Clapton was an habitué of the 2Is coffee bar, sundry pubs and cafés and both Ray's and Dobell's music shops, in the latter of which imports of Johnson, Broonzy, Reed and Waters could be bought. Content to play and listen to music, he made little effort to adopt other aspects of the musician's lifestyle. Despite a one-night stand – his first – with an older woman, Clapton had no love life to speak of. As a teenager he was known to see a Ripley girl named Sandra Ploughman while not, says Pullen, 'exactly [being] the local Romeo'. At both Hollyfield and Kingston Clapton joined in discussions about sex – muttering, making speculative remarks – while giving no evidence of personal experience. He quoted occasional advice from the Surrey *Comet*'s 'For Women' column, drawing Drew's or Blewichamp's attention to some mildly risqué anecdote or homily, somehow increasing, rather than the reverse, his sense of detachment from the facts of life. (As late as his seventeenth birthday he remarked approvingly on an artist's model's 'public hair'.) Yet another Kingston student, Chris Dreja, later to work with Clapton professionally, believes him to have had 'virtually no sex life as a teenager. The aggressive, macho side of the blues didn't appeal. What Eric liked was being different.'

A girl who knew Clapton at college, Jenny Dolan, adds that his 'mournful, little-boy's look', while attractive to the maternal instinct, was otherwise lacking in appeal. He was, she says, known locally as 'Ewik'.

In June 1962 Clapton was expelled when his first year's work, adequate in style, was found lacking in quantity. This surprised him. According to an interview he gave later, Clapton 'felt my work at art school was very promising compared with the other students. Most of them in that department were mathematicians more than artists. What I was doing was creative and imaginative. I was shocked.' He none the less, vainly trying to reverse the decision, sought conscientiously but ineffectually to increase his output; ironically, he produced more paintings in his last month at Kingston than in the previous eight.

Clapton's year at art school, unrewarding in itself, advanced the qualities he would take into adulthood: self-reliance, separateness – a sense of being alone or apart, of being persecuted and put on. It also, not coincidentally, nourished his love of the blues. The trips to London introduced him to a second tier of musicians – Junior Wells, J. B. Hutto, Hound Dog Taylor – for whose work Dobell's was the sole British outlet. He expanded his own repertoire and in late 1962 persuaded his grandmother to buy him a Kay 'Red Devil' electric guitar, a relatively cheap imitation of the Gibson ES335 marketed in America. Jenny Dolan confirms that 'whatever else, Eric took the music incredibly seriously . . . forever playing, and always with that woebegone look'. Clapton also possessed a reel-to-reel Grundig tape recorder with which, night after night, he honed his technique. According to Rose Clapp's son Adrian, '[Clapton] swore and cursed till he could copy the sounds exactly, from as many records as he could get hold of. He ended up with seven or eight of those reels full of his practising, with the sound of the house's two budgerigars tweeting in the background.'

What his uncle was hearing was the birth of the blues-based style, later informed by rock and jazz, that became Clapton's hallmark. No longer merely competent, he began to simulate, in some cases to emulate, the liquid tones of Johnson and B. B. King. He experimented with tunings and strings. The seventeen-year-old emerging from art school (like a surprising number of adolescents, including John Lennon, Pete Townshend, Keith Richards, Jimmy Page and Ray Davies) was already technically proficient. Now practical experience was completing his education as fast as he could get it.

That left the matter of a job. At Christmas 1961 Clapton had supplemented his allowance as a relief postman. The following summer he was recruited by his grandfather as a builder, travelling with Jack to Aldershot and Camberley, setting up a 'caterwauling' with his radio while he worked. He retained his Green Line bus pass. At weekends Clapton returned to London, witnessing the first stirrings of British rhythm and blues at the Marquee and Ealing jazz clubs. According to Alexis Korner, then resident at the latter, 'within the group [Korner's own Blues Incorporated] there was room for anyone with the gall to stand up and blow'. Among those who did were an Economics student from the London suburbs called Jagger, and Clapton himself; Dick Heckstall-Smith, a member of Blues Incorporated, was present the first time 'this pale, sulky kid came on stage, not with his guitar but a hand mike. He sang two numbers and fled. I wasn't exactly knocked out.'

On the other hand, Clapton was sufficiently competent to play both 'Alberta' and 'San Francisco Bay Blues', occasionally performing the latter in the Crown, Kingston, or singing unaccompanied on Richmond Green – a kind of staging-house between Ripley and London. He became known for a particularly emotive version of 'Nobody Knows You (When You're Down And Out)', a song to which he returned twice later in his career. According to Keith Richards, another Ealing habitué, Clapton 'fully appreciated the dramatic side of the blues', its sense of futility, of doom, of life closing down.

It was more than appreciation. It was already an attachment. Clapton loved the blues, absorbing the message, emulating the music, muttering and strumming among the autumn leaves like the 'loony' he had long been designated. After an initial enthusiasm for building ('An excellent worker,' said Rose. 'His perfectionism showed in the way he laid tiles'), a crisis was reached in Clapton's career. In late 1962 he considered returning to the Post Office, even to applying himself to commercial graphics. Reginald Brill, former principal at Kingston, had retired that summer to become warden of Little Hall, an endowed hostel in Lavenham – on the edge of Constable country – for displaced Surrey art students. While retaining Clapton's portfolio, which he thought 'promising', an initial enquiry was not followed up. No further drawings were submitted. Instead Clapton returned to the building-site and to Ealing, playing Broonzy, Waters, Terry and McGhee, in whose variations the theme – one man versus the world – was constantly restated. A stickler for practice, Clapton, according to Korner, was 'already as competent as most pros' and 'aware, to put it mildly', of his ability. That winter he refused invitations to join both a local Kingston-based dance band, the Bluebeats, and the exotic Thunder Odin's Big Secret. He did, however, consent to play in an acoustic duo with a jazz fanatic named Dave Brock.

Meanwhile a twenty-one-year-old guitarist had applied to, and just as readily been rejected by, a quartet in the Station Hotel, Richmond. When Tom McGuinness, with tastes roughly comparable to Clapton's, realized the extent of that group's ambitions – stretching to straight pop or swing jazz – he was heard to complain to his girlfriend that 'no one else understands the blues'. His girlfriend was Jenny Dolan. According to her, at least one person, recently expelled from Kingston, had just such comprehension. She arranged for an introduction.

McGuinness first set eyes on Clapton on 2 January 1963. The former, a proficient musician himself, was quickly aware that 'technically, Eric was superior' – a view Clapton endorsed – though 'nothing yet like the later legend'. According to McGuinness:

The idea that he was a purist is nonsense. Eric loved the blues, but he wasn't above other types of music. The Beatles were just happening then and I remember him green with envy at *that* band. He was also partial to Jerry Lee Lewis and Little Richard. I heard him praise Fats Domino. It was the image of the blues that attracted him. He was an incredibly mixed-up teenager. He really *did* think that it was him against the world. On the other hand, he could play the guitar.

The result was that, complemented by a singer, drums and piano, the Roosters (named obscurely after Willie Dixon) were formed that February.

The group lasted for six months, playing a medley of rock and roll, dance hits and occasional blues. 'It was a composite,' says McGuinness. 'Within the band there were two ravers, a Little Richard fan, an authentic blues pianist – and Eric. Something for everyone.' The pianist in question, Ben Palmer, remembers Clapton as having 'one quality that stood out: he loved to take solos. That was a big thing then – having the guts to let rip in front of an audience. Eric never hesitated . . . He was quite different in that respect to the shrinking character offstage.' Palmer also states Clapton to have had 'a marked sense of timing . . . He seemed to know exactly when and when not to cut loose. There was something uncanny about it.'

If anything this underestimates Clapton's intuitive grasp of dynamics, his ability to structure a song, to play both rhythm and lead, above all to solo. His guitar was an oratorio in which he sang and played all the parts. While by no means as fluent as he became later Clapton was, according to Palmer, 'at least twenty per cent better than the rest of us', semi-professional rather than semi-amateur. Being 'semi-professional' was important to Clapton, though even that phrase exaggerated an arrangement still restricted to £5 per player per night. Barely aspiring to the Ricky-Tick circuit in Guildford, New Malden and Windsor, with occasional forays to Leeds and Manchester – Clapton returning home to sleep – the Roosters expired when Palmer, even in front of an audience as modest as thirty, admitted to crippling stage-fright.

Clapton then made the first in a series of perverse career moves when at the Scene, Piccadilly, he learnt that a Liverpudlian named Brian Casser, trading as Casey Jones, was recruiting guitarists. Neither Casser's stage persona (heavily in the mould of Screamin' Lord Sutch and Arthur Brown) nor repertoire (Elvis hits, ballads) should have endeared itself to the blues fanatic – a man so introverted he looked 'physically startled' when the Roosters' vocalist shook his hair. According to McGuinness, 'Eric suddenly announced that Casser, arguably the world's worst singer, wanted us to join . . . I think what appealed to him was the sense of being a professional, earning enough to throw in the bricklaying job with Jack.' On 2 October 1963 Clapton began the strangest episode in a career not unknown for eccentricity. Over the space of four weeks he, McGuinness and two hired musicians stood in matching suits while, stage centre, Casser bounced on trampolines or swallowed fire. (In a still more bizarre twist, Clapton was called on to back the cabaret singer Polly Perkins, reincarnated thirty years later as a star of the soap opera *Eldorado*.) The end came when Clapton, with his lifelong aversion to confrontation, failed to appear one night in London. That was typical, says McGuinness. 'There was no sense of commitment, other than onward and upward.' (Or as Clapton himself put it, 'It was all good experience.') He returned to Ripley and to Friday night sessions at the Crown, Kingston.

In the space of a year Clapton had developed and extended his repertoire; learnt the basics of performing live; been noticed by Korner and John Mayall; and, away from the scrutiny of his grandparents, established a liking for the beer, spirits and more exotic traits of the musician. He was known to swallow purple hearts and period-pain pills. He smoked. Although he was unaccompanied by a girlfriend he none the less, says Palmer, 'had an eye open in that direction'. References to sex increased.

When a Kingston teenager named Anne McDowell met Clapton in October 1963 she found him to be 'blunt to the point of crude' in his ambitions, ambitions which as far as McDowell was concerned went unfulfilled. At night he still returned to Ripley, where he discovered the Ship and Half Moon pubs, whose regulars remember him as 'a rather intense young man who, even at eighteen, kept himself to himself'.

Clapton's debut as a professional musician came at the moment when imported rhythm and blues, informed by skiffle and such interim figures as Cliff Richard and Adam Faith, had coalesced into a recognizable pop movement. On 5 October 1962, as Clapton hovered between art, building work and folk-blues, the Beatles' first single, 'Love Me Do', was released, followed in February 1963 by a British tour. The effect of the group was immediate. Not only did the Beatles, if not ringing bells in the far universe, appeal to hundreds of thousands, millions of adolescents; they persuaded teenagers everywhere of the material possibilities of music. Among the first to benefit were the Rolling Stones (first signed in April 1963), and a group then known as the Detours, playing a repertoire of Jimmy Reed and Howlin' Wolf, later to become the Who. Clapton's formation of the Roosters unconsciously recognized that, for the first time since the war, a definable youth culture, with a matching need for role models, had made music a viable commercial option.

Closely linked to it was the rise and rapid accessibility of the electric guitar. First developed by the Gibson company in 1935 and advanced by the inventor Leo Fender, the latter's Telecaster became the first instrument specifically designed for use with amplification. The Stratocaster followed in 1954, a wide-bodied model associated with Buddy Holly and the Shadows' guitarist Hank Marvin. Clapton (who was heard to praise the latter's 'Apache', released in late 1960) experimented with both instruments. Before his nineteenth birthday he bought a red Telecaster, the guitar with which he made his professional breakthrough, before switching to the Gibson Les Paul – as patronized by Freddie King – in 1965. If Clapton's turning to music had stemmed from his awareness and appreciation of the blues, it also owed something to recent technology. In 1963, for the first time, motive met with opportunity.

Gratified, Clapton returned to sessions in Kingston, on Richmond Green and in the nearby Station Hotel. The last, made famous by the Rolling Stones' Sunday residency, became a focal point that autumn. Clapton, who by his own admission 'used to live there', was a fixture both at the hotel and the import record shop then at the foot of Richmond

Hill, dressed in his overcoat and flowing brown scarf, completely abandoned to his own self-image, which, as Brian Jones remarked, was so 'grotesquely comic' it rose above ridicule. McGuinness agrees that Clapton's sense of 'identifying with a cause' was morbidly, almost satirically intense. Within 'a general framework of self-flagellation' he did, however, increase his technical knowledge of the blues, in particular of Freddie King, whose 'I Love The Woman' he could dimly be heard playing on Ripley green. Clapton's reputation in his home town as irrevocably odd grew. According to Guy Pullen, '[In 1963] we used to sit in Rose's house – he had his first electric guitar . . . He'd sit there and sing . . . da . . . di . . . di . . . di. And then ask: "Is that all right?" Well, I wouldn't know. I knew nothing about music.'

The reverse applied to Clapton himself, who, according to Ben Palmer, 'was something of an encyclopaedia when he left the Roosters . . . always quoting lyrics and the most esoteric song titles.' While others in the group returned to steady jobs (or, in Tom McGuinness's case, to playing semi-professionally) Clapton, first on the northern club circuit, then at home in Ripley, made it known that he intended to remain a working musician, a point vividly conveyed to McGuinness that autumn: 'I always remember Eric turning to me in Liverpool and saying in his most sober tones, "We're professionals now." That meant a lot to him.'

3

'Who's Upset Eric?'

The great awakening of British blues grew, in time, to include a second wave of acts – Graham Bond, Spencer Davis, the Animals – seeking to merge the southern boogie tradition of Jimmy Reed and Muddy Waters with more contemporary lyrics. Among those trying and failing to follow in the Rolling Stones' tracks was the Metropolis Blues Quartet, essentially a vehicle for vocalist Keith Relf (so influenced by Mick Jagger he even played maraccas) and Paul Samwell-Smith on guitar. Securing a residency at the Richmond Crawdaddy Club (in reality the rear room of the Station Hotel) and adopting the name Yardbirds, in vague homage to Charlie Parker, the group grew to a quintet, recruiting Tony Topham, Jim McCarty and a former Hollyfield student, Chris Dreja. Relf and McCarty came to dominate the group, the 'real musicians', in Dreja's words, constantly rehearsing, practising, lobbying their manager for work. 'All goes to show,' wrote Relf, 'that we have to organize now to hold this band together. NOW.'

His sense of togetherness did not, however, extend to Topham, who, at sixteen, was constantly under pressure to return to art school. In October 1963 he did so. Immediately Relf approached McCarty with the opinion that the 'moody sod' heard weekly at the Crown, Kingston, would be ideal as a replacement. Relf may have had other motives than Clapton's mere musicianship. According to McCarty, 'Keith sold him to us as a kind of James Dean figure. The idea was that Eric would pull the women.' After a perfunctory rehearsal in the Great Western pub Clapton was offered the job and accepted, Rose and Jack Clapp formally co-signing the contract in Relf's home that November.

Chris Dreja, switching to rhythm guitar alongside Clapton's lead, retains strong memories of his colleague.

Eric was a chameleon. At school he used to change appearance – new hairstyle, different clothes, gain or lose weight – about once a month. Never the same look twice. The same in the Yardbirds . . . There were incredible mood swings – first he hated you, then loved you, then hated you again – all for no reason. *Hugely* defensive. He also had a remarkable ability to turn negatives into positives. That sense of hurt was what gave him his motivation.

Jim McCarty:

It took me a year to get to know him. Eric was cocky – a very arrogant guy with a nasty sense of humour. Because he was so insecure he played on other people's insecurities, like criticizing my drumming. He could be incredibly scathing, taking the piss out of Paul [Samwell-Smith] and Chris. On the other hand, he was totally dedicated, always hanging out at Dobell's and those import shops. He seemed to take it more seriously than we did.

Both men agree that Clapton's fickleness – his ability to hover between manic humour and depression – owed much (as the guitarist himself insisted) to the circumstances of his upbringing: 'The classic [emotionally] abused child syndrome,' says Dreja. 'There was an almost tangible sense of suffering.' Having risen unaided to professional status himself, Clapton saw no reason why things should be easier for others. He particularly resented Dreja and Samwell-Smith, both of whom he suspected of a dilettante attitude to the music that, for him, remained 'life or death'. The latter especially irritated him. Samwell-Smith, with his Home Counties accent and stable family background, struck Clapton as the worst kind of traitor to the blues. Compounding the problem was the question of musicianship. Samwell-Smith (reverting to bass after being told by Clapton, 'Don't play any more lead guitar solos') would, by his own cheerful admission, 'frequently screw up a chord structure, only for Eric to go ape . . . It was as though you'd personally insulted him.' On still other occasions Clapton would ask Relf or McCarty to assure him, in the latter's words, 'that he was the latent genius he obviously thought himself', displaying the 'weird mix of ego and insecurity' for which the group still remember him.

The Yardbirds first entered a recording studio on 1 November 1963, recording an acetate of Jimmy Reed's 'Baby What's Wrong', John Lee

33

Hooker's 'Boom Boom' and Billy Boy Arnold's 'Honey In Your Hips'.*
Exactly six months earlier an itinerant hustler named Andrew Loog Oldham had sold the Rolling Stones to Decca on the basis of that label's
prior failure to sign the Beatles; now, proving the cyclical nature of
the industry, the Yardbirds' manager Giorgio Gomelsky, who preceded
Oldham in discovering the Stones, himself approached Decca and was
turned down. Eventually the group were contracted to EMI (the Beatles'
own company), for whom they recorded a debut single, 'I Wish You
Would', in early 1964.

The four songs and the single's B-side, 'A Certain Girl', show Clapton
to have already had a style beyond the range or grasp of other teenage
guitarists. Possessed of his new Fender Telecaster (and, more often than
not, Dreja's Gibson) he could emulate the three-finger triad 'shake'
perfected by Waters on 'Honey Bee', experimented with single-string
solos and, as McCarty notes, 'took to the studio like a bird to the air'.

Much of this stemmed from Clapton's own ability, his instinctive feeling
for what would and would not work in a particular song. There was also
the matter of mimicry. Much of Clapton's apparent spontaneity as a
soloist was, says Dreja, the result of continual rehearsal: 'That's the part
people don't see ... Instead of appearing from nowhere, ringing the
guitar like a bell, it was the result of hour after hour, day after day, of
listening to records. That was the *real* difference between Eric and us.
Whereas we had some sort of life outside the music, he didn't.' There
was, none the less, a 'sweetness' about Clapton's playing that Dreja
attributes to 'pure God-given talent, as anyone could tell'.

Anyone except the Yardbirds' audiences. Private rehearsal was one
thing, the demands of the college and club circuit were a more intimidating prospect. In late 1963 the group began a near-continual provincial
tour. The playing on these occasions was primitive: onstage for thirty
minutes, frequently as part of a package not excluding vaudeville and
cabaret acts, the Yardbirds restricted themselves to manic, occasionally
off-key renditions of Berry and Bo Diddley, and were known to play
Beatles' numbers on request. Clapton, in the words of one reviewer,
tended to 'rather wild and undisciplined sheets of power-chord rhythm
guitar', windmilling his right arm over his head, a gesture originally
credited to Pete Townshend and Keith Richards. 'Onstage,' says Dreja,

* The songs were also included in a session held at R. G. Jones Studios, Morden, in
February 1964.

34

'we were a pop group – anything the customer wanted. Giorgio saw to that.'

Gomelsky also, to his credit, promoted an American Blues Festival that autumn, showcasing Muddy Waters in the unlikely settings of Guildford and the Fairfield Hall, Croydon. Attached to the tour was a sixty-three-year-old hellraiser called Ford, also known as Miller, also known as Sonny Boy Williamson. Williamson remained in England all winter. Towards the end of November – McCarty pinpoints it as at or about the time of the Kennedy assassination – Gomelsky made the introduction to his prize, though still uncelebrated group. A number of joint appearances followed. On 7 and 8 December 1963 the Yardbirds appeared onstage with Williamson in Richmond, the second evening recorded and eventually released commercially in 1965.

Inconclusive as evidence of his latent genius, *Sonny Boy Williamson And The Yardbirds* at least afforded Clapton the chance to play the blues. His solo on 'Take It Easy Baby' almost echoed the original. Elsewhere, in a radical restructuring of the Yardbirds' set, there were covers of *King Biscuit Time* favourites of the forties. In 'Smokestack Lightnin'' (recorded, but not released on the album) Clapton and Relf engaged in the sort of extended, free-form interplay the former would perfect in Cream. 'They became the two real stars,' says Dreja. 'Eric always needed someone to feed off, and in the Yardbirds it was Keith.'

In this and other ways the guitarist and singer began to separate from the rest. Musically, Clapton and Relf were more attuned to Williamson (or, as the former says, '[The Yardbirds] didn't know how to back him. It was frightening. He'd say, "We're going to do 'Don't Start Me Talkin' or 'Fattening Frogs for Snakes' and of course, some of the members of this particular band had never heard these songs."') Socially, Clapton took to Relf, and to a lesser extent McCarty, as the more 'ethnic' characters in the group. When Williamson arrived drunk on stage or collapsed into the drum-kit it was they who laughed loudest. Sonny Boy, announced Clapton, was expressing himself. All behaviour – lateness, rudeness, churlishness, conceit – was excused in the light of his 'having suffered'. Having devoted himself to principles, to blues in the abstract, Clapton now had a flesh-and-blood archetype – a man who knew Robert Johnson and hoboed with Sunnyland Slim – to identify with. To the others Williamson merely seemed odd.

Clapton himself increased his attachment to the blues. He continued to patronize Dobell's and the import shops. He still practised, alone or with Relf, every afternoon. While the other Yardbirds sported jeans and grew their hair, Clapton appeared with a burr cut wearing an Ivy League jacket or a bowling-shirt bought in Shaftesbury Avenue. On other occasions it was the baggy funeral suit like the one favoured by William-son. The 'pulling of women' foretold by Relf began in earnest. In early 1964 Clapton was seen with one, two, sometimes half a dozen girls in a day. 'None of them lasted,' says McCarty. 'After the Pill came out, a certain kind of chick didn't have to be "talked into it" any more. You couldn't help yourself.' Clapton's mood swings also increased, leading to a series of triangular relationships in which he befriended one musician specifically while offending another.

Samwell-Smith quickly realized that to play professionally with Clapton was no commendation to his good books socially. Throughout his career, certain musicians would command Clapton's respect; to some, because he saw in them the embodiment of a cause, he even had devotion. Very few would become his friends. In 1964, having disabused Samwell-Smith of any claims he might have to musical ability, Clapton started on him personally. 'I took an instant dislike to him,' he admitted to Ray Coleman. 'He had such a very tweedy image. Then, he came from sub-urban *Twickenham* and he lived with his mum and dad and it was all so perfectly *normal* and *good*. He was such a good boy! I was much more into developing myself by hanging out with people who were more likely to be rebels, come from broken homes and were generally neurotic . . . I mean, Paul liked the *Shadows*! I didn't.' (Clapton, a professed fan of 'Apache', continued to live with his grandparents in suburban Ripley, not known to possess any Bohemian advantage over Twickenham.) Samwell-Smith, McCarty and Dreja agree that Clapton suffered from a 'humour breakdown' when discussing music or image. His love of one was matched only by his longing for the other.

Clapton was, however, brave in the face of adversity – in the sense of not inflicting it on others. By his nineteenth birthday he seems to have been reconciled to the circumstances of his upbringing. (Not proud of, but reconciled.) After London performances the Yardbirds would be driven home in Relf's father's transit van. Despite initial grumbling at the distance involved, the itinerary included Ripley. McCarty remembers being invited in by Jack and Rose, the latter of whom 'obviously doted on Eric', if betraying anxiety at the presence of 'four long-haired hoodlums in her front room'. Tea would be served. Clapton seems to have had no sense of awkwardness or embarrassment at being seen in so 'suburban' a setting. This sense of ambiguity, of hovering between worlds, was to become his trademark. Throughout that spring Clapton commuted from smoke-filled halls in Soho to leafy Ripley, from all-night blues sessions to dinner with the Drejas – whom he impressed as a 'scrupulously polite boy from the provinces'.

On 13 March 1964 the Yardbirds were again recorded live, during their residency at the Marquee, Oxford Street. The resulting LP proved, in Tom McGuiness's words, 'an incredible advance' on the standards of the Roosters just a year before. Both 'Respectable' and Berry's 'Too Much Monkey Business' showed remarkable attention to the originals. 'Louise' was an affectionate parody. Best of all was 'Good Morning Little School-girl', an otherwise trite number in which Clapton played a break of swooping novelty – the moment, says Dreja, 'Eric proved to us, as well as himself, he really *was* different.' *Five Live Yardbirds* was released to little effect in December 1964. 'Schoolgirl' appeared as a single in October, peaking at number 44. (This despite a launch campaign devised by Gomelsky and his colleague Hamish Grimes, consisting of blue-skirted teenagers chasing the group down Ham high street, and their manager's insistence as late as 1965 that 'The Yardbirds are another Rolling Stones' – to which *The Times* retorted, 'The Rolling Stones wrote "Satisfaction".') The single was backed by 'I Ain't Got You', salvaged by Clapton with an eccentrically darting solo. According to the critic Don Short, 'It was then that some people did compare the Yardbirds to the Stones. Because of Eric.'

The theme was taken up in the correspondence pages of the press. In a *Record Mirror* poll in April 1964 the Yardbirds were voted third best group behind the Stones and Manfred Mann. A letter in *Melody Maker* that May opened: 'Let Me Proclaim The Gospel. The Yardbirds Are Coming. The chart isn't big enough for the Stones and the Yardbirds. The Rolling Stones will have to go.' While full consensus was never reached, there was in reality no contest. The truth is that, on the basis of commercial success alone, the Yardbirds were a full year behind their counterparts. While *The Rolling Stones* spent fifty-one weeks in the charts, the Yardbirds were reduced to mugging with schoolgirls in the street.

Gomelsky actively encouraged the comparison. The Yardbirds, like their peers, had graduated from the Station Hotel to the Marquee and the Flamingo; like them they recorded at Olympic studios, favouring the same raw material; like them ('Schoolgirl' notwithstanding) their public image was not wholly endearing. In a letter in January 1964 Gomelsky catalogued the virtues of his protégés: they were 'mean', they were moody, they were, in Grimes's phrase, blueswailing; they were full of ideas. Yet nothing happened. Their singles flopped and they never progressed beyond the club and cinema circuit.

Among the reasons was the relative ineptitude with which the Yardbirds played the blues. They never had the intuitive grasp, still less the enthusiasm, of the Stones. Clapton was another factor. Obviously the most naturally gifted of the group, he was the least commercially minded. He was genuinely embarrassed by Gomelsky's efforts to create a pop phenomenon. At photo sessions he was invariably the one oddly dressed; while the others appeared in suits and ties Clapton emerged in a letter-sweater or an Austin's jacket. In interviews he was determinedly morose. 'How can we describe ourselves?' he answered *Melody Maker*. 'We're a *sort* of rhythm and blues group, I suppose, when you come down to it.' A member of the group remembers him 'weeping inconsolably' in Gomelsky's office after a meeting in which the manager had informed the group they were a success. Clapton was married to suffering, and to have gone with joy would have felt like adultery.

When reports began to circulate of their guitarist's unhappiness, the others were unsympathetic. 'There was a sense of one-for-all and all-for-one,' says Dreja, 'in which Eric, to put it mildly, didn't participate. Right from the start he made it clear he didn't really approve of us. There was a sense in which he seemed older, or at least more serious.' (Clapton was younger than any of the group except Dreja himself.) Gradually, over the spring and early summer of 1964, Clapton began to establish himself as a separate entity. He sometimes appeared for sessions, and sometimes not. His moods increased. While Dreja happily lent Clapton his Gibson 335, Samwell-Smith proved more reluctant to part with his own guitar. A fight ensued and for a week the two spoke only through intermediaries.

Meanwhile, on the basis of his playing on 'I Wish You Would' and a dozen appearances at the Marquee, Clapton's reputation had grown. Chris Farlowe, then recording with the Thunderbirds, remembers 'a very quiet, oddly dressed character who used to stand stock-still, sometimes playing with his back to the audience – unheard of in those days'. Georgie Fame, whose *Fame At Last* aptly chronicled the peak of his own celebrity, notes that 'the word went round' that Clapton, in this and other ways, was different: original; unique, even. Whereas other guitarists 'were basically apeing Chuck Berry' or 'doing a million notes a second' Clapton had genuine feel. He had flair. Much of this derived from the reticence of his playing; he seemed to know, says Dick Heckstall-Smith, 'exactly when to lead and when not to . . . All the great players have that faculty. They know the gaps are as important as the notes.' Both Dreja and McCarty agree that, whatever one thought of him, 'Clapton was already on the road to genuine virtuosity.' He knew it himself.

Whatever their limitations, the near-nightly appearances with the Yardbirds only accelerated the process. The atmosphere on these occasions was primal, the acoustics crude, the group amplified to the threshold of pain as girls bayed and fans brawled on the floor. The Yardbirds played, in full: 'Boom Boom', 'I'm A Man', 'I Ain't Got You', 'A Certain Girl', 'Slow Walk', 'You Can't Judge A Book By The Cover', 'Who Do You Love', 'Louise', 'Here 'Tis', 'Pretty Girl', 'Respectable', 'Too Much Monkey Business' and 'Good Morning Little Schoolgirl' – fifty minutes of raw, frenetic energy in which the guitarist, stage right, stood motionless in his tab collar and Levis. The star of these shows, as much for his presence as his still inchoate playing, was Clapton. A year after turning professional he was a stage veteran. The eye turned to him wherever he appeared. He was aware, he once admitted, of the pressure this exerted; of the thought that as he played, so did the group. When Dreja or Samwell-Smith failed they disappointed themselves and the band: when Clapton failed he ruined the night for hundreds. Not only was he not inhibited by this – he relished it. 'Being aware,' says Dreja, 'of his talent, he began to concentrate more and more on his playing and less and less on being a star – with the inevitable result that he became one.' That he strove so consciously to be anonymous is the best evidence that by instinct Clapton wanted the opposite. In the space of six months, the fans' hunger for leadership had found expression in the pale morose teenager with the downturned mouth and hooded eyes. Though he did nothing to encourage this, Clapton, says McCarty, 'was far from distraught' at the outcome, forever reminding the Yardbirds of his volume of fan mail, his status as 'guitar god' and 'most popular picker' on the circuit. (Widely credited with having brought the Fender Telecaster into the open, Clapton in private acknowledged the influence of Geoff Bradford, a man who had refused the Rolling Stones in 1962, and who developed the model into the lead, as opposed to rhythm, instrument it became.)

The Yardbirds' management invested both time and ingenuity in singling Clapton out. Early in 1964 Gomelsky coined his nickname (as the guitarist said: 'He did it as a good pun – he kept saying I was a fast player, so he put together the slow-handclap phrase into "Slow-hand" as a play on words'), still among the most enduring epithets in the business. That was as nothing compared to the work of Hamish Grimes: he compèred the group's performances and composed a series of increasingly tremulous epigrams ('Fabulous Blueswailing . . . Twitch Inspiring . . . Crawdaddyfying . . . Recordyfying Yardbirds') to promote the band in general and Clapton in particular. Both manager and publicist appreciated the values of their star property: he was 'mean, morose, talented and above all *mysterious*,' says Dreja. 'Giorgio and Hamish latched on immediately.' Less than a year after joining the Yardbirds, Clapton, the least publicity-conscious of any of them, was their *de facto* leader.

At this stage, approaching his twentieth birthday, Clapton left home. In autumn 1964 he, Relf and, on occasion, Dreja shared a flat off the South Circular Road, Kew, though 'flat' overestimates what was essentially a two-roomed studio with a shared facility. At some stage that winter Dreja, patiently accepting Clapton's rotational sense of friendship, again fell into the guitarist's favour. For a period of three months the two were inseparable, even sharing the small rear bedroom. Again, says Dreja, 'that was typical . . . For weeks he didn't talk to you, then it was the other extreme. Eric always had one close male friend, so much so that, when he ditched you, it hurt. It was like an affair.'

That left the business of women. Here, unlike his music, Clapton's abilities hugely outstripped his ambitions. Early in 1964 he professed undying (though, Dreja suspected, unreciprocated) love for Ronnie Spector, then touring Britain with the Ronettes. He made lurid observations about certain actresses. Nor was Clapton, according to a man then associated with the Yardbirds, averse to 'soft' pornography, 'stuff full of masturbatory fantasies – innocent by today's standards – such as schoolgirls standing around in their knickers'. Clapton's practical experience also increased. As he later informed *Rolling Stone*: 'When I was with the Yardbirds I did [sleep with women] all the time. It was an obviously novel thing to try and do. You come out of school, you get into a group and you've got thousands of chicks there. I mean, you were at school and you were pimply and no one wanted to know you. And then there you are – on stage, with thousands of little girls screaming their heads off. Power!' According to Janella Gibbs, a teenager close to Clapton in 1964, 'He always thought of me as the one that got away, the one he didn't sleep with. I wanted to go out with him but I couldn't deal with all the other girls. Even then he was inundated with women.'

On the question of emotional involvement, or commitment, Clapton was more guarded. His attachments were strictly temporary. McCarty remembers 'a large number of women who were told they were the love of Eric's life for twenty-four hours', after which boredom, or a sense of trepidation, set in. Among the more exotic cases was a Frenchwoman, in England to study the language, with a tendency to unusual frankness in naming the sexual parts. Clapton 'loved it', said Relf, 'when she referred to her *poussée* as though it were a vintage wine'. But even he looked startled when, in a drunken conversation about the meaning of life, the woman loudly proclaimed her desire for 'a penis'. It was Relf who explained that in England the word was pronounced happiness.

Dreja was also present – in the next bed – when Clapton arrived at Kew one night with a partner. At three in the morning, 'I suddenly heard Eric talking – it was all about "Life is short" and "Let's enjoy it while we can", incredible stuff. It wasn't as though the girl needed talking into it. She was already in his bed.'

The concept of a shy, essentially introverted character, unprepossessing in appearance, enjoying almost unlimited female company may seem an eccentric one, but it was not peculiar to Clapton. All of the Yardbirds benefited from the phenomenon described by McCarty as 'the kind of chick [not having] to be talked into it any more'. What separated Clapton from the others was his almost morbid fear of involvement with the other party. One of the most striking things about his personality was his urgent need to achieve a sense of belonging by binding himself to a tradition, to a culture, rather than to individuals. The same process – allowing for sex – was at work in the way that he treated both men and women. No one got too close to Clapton. One of his major limitations as a musician was his incapacity for detachment from the supposed values of the men he worshipped. The same sense of intensity, of being unable to make light of experience, meant that any relationship was conducted on the basis of minimizing the potential risk to himself.

The other side of Clapton was represented by his love of slapstick. He retained a taste for clockwork mice, for custard pies, for pails of water. On excursions in Relf's van Clapton would awake from an apparent coma to engage in the kind of comic monologue characteristic of the Goons. He was particularly adept at accents. Another feature, says Dreja, was his ability to 'pick up on somebody's quirks' – a facial gesture, a peculiar walk

– and mimic them, somehow conveying the opposite of good humour in doing so. While Ray Coleman believed 'this [contrasted] vividly with his characteristics as a loner', McCarty and Dreja were less convinced. 'If anything,' says the latter, 'it was a put-down. A pie in the face from Eric meant "stay away".'

Samwell-Smith and Dreja continued to bear the brunt of such antics. There were daily rows about the image and commercial leanings of the Yardbirds (Samwell-Smith wanting them greatly enhanced, Clapton the opposite); in time they deepened and became personal. By late 1964 the guitarist was unable to mention his colleague's name calmly: references to Samwell-Smith's 'tweedy' persona increased. The obvious irony was that Clapton himself retained a large degree of tweediness. As Chris Welch of *Melody Maker* (who interviewed him that autumn) put it: 'Everyone thought Eric was mysterious and aloof, but really he was just shy, talking in a well modulated Home Counties accent.' Others noted the disparity between Clapton's love of the blues, with their hint of decadence and genuine depravity, and his intermittent residence in his grandparents' home in Ripley. With Samwell-Smith, as with Dreja, he protected his feelings by attacking what he admired, passing off self-loathing as loathing of others.

He extended his sense of separateness, of being aloof from the group, both in the way he looked and played. Throughout 1964 the Yardbirds each drew a salary of £20 a week. Clapton, who took a relaxed view of his financial responsibilities, contributed little to his own upkeep. The money went on records and clothes. At Austin's in Shaftesbury Avenue he thought nothing of spending a week's wages on a Madras jacket or American jeans. While this advanced the image Clapton had of himself, it exacerbated tension with Dreja and Relf, more mundane souls for whom the running of the Kew flat was paramount. The former still recalls 'picking up certain bills' in his colleague's absence. Clapton's parsimony was not restricted to his immediate circle. A musician named Pete Hogman, singer with Jimmy Powell and the Five Dimensions, had a disagreement with the guitarist about money. 'It ended up with me hitting Eric over the head with his own Telecaster.'

Put to more conventional use, the instrument brought Clapton to a still wider audience. Reviews of the Yardbirds' performances singled him out. His stated function as the champion of blues purism also made its mark on the press. Clapton's obvious proficiency and development of techniques such as feedback won him a generation of fans among his own peers. As Pete Townshend told *Rolling Stone* in 1968: 'When I was at school I lived with this guy [Richard Barnes] who used to go and see Eric Clapton. And he would come back saying, "Look, you've got to do this! Clapton does this great thing where he goes *ba-ba-ba-bam* on the guitar for hours and hours and everyone goes crazy and lights flash on and off and it's great." So I used to go *ba-ba-ba-bam* and attempt to do this from what I'd heard from him. Luckily enough, the influence, which could have been very obvious and direct if I'd actually gone to see Clapton, was very effective coming second-hand.' Brian Jones, then in the throes of losing creative control of the Rolling Stones to Keith Richards (who says he, too, idolized Clapton), also noted in private, 'Eric's influence – the way he put blues and jazz solos into pop – was phenomenal.' And in New York a session musician playing with the Isley Brothers, Jimmy (*sic*) Hendrix, was heard to mutter that 'the English cat' had talent.

On 18 September 1964 the Yardbirds began a package tour with Billy J. Kramer, Cliff Bennett and the Nashville Teens (later joined, when that combination proved insufficiently potent, by Jerry Lee Lewis). For two months Clapton appeared at the Granada, Walthamstow, the Northampton ABC and Southend Odeon, forty shows in as many nights, crammed into Relf's transit or, for appearances in Dublin and Cork, the overnight ferry. Relations within the group, already stretched, deteriorated to breaking-point. In Grantham there was a row about rehearsals (of which Clapton was strongly in favour), in Bedford another dispute about money. Slowly, over the space of the autumn, hints about Clapton leaving were heard. In October 'Schoolgirl' was released to minimal effect. Gomelsky, it was assumed, because of a series of sanguine pronouncements about the group, had no idea how unhappy some of its members were. A close study of his actions behind the scenes shows that this was not true. Privately he had a dark view of the prospects and likely fate of the Yardbirds. Strongly persuaded by the commercial success of the Rolling Stones, Gomelsky now insisted that the group appear 'edgy' on stage (of which Clapton needed no great persuasion), while delegating overall musical control to Samwell-Smith (of which he did). 'Eric began to get gloomier and gloomier,' says McCarty. 'While the rest of us fooled around, he was off by himself brooding. It was as if he knew something we didn't.'

What the audience saw on these occasions was a frenzy of tightly played pop in which the Yardbirds stood static, unsmiling, taking deep ironic bows after each rendition. Gomelsky's fascination with the Stones was obvious, though he retained equal affection for the Beatles (a group, he insists today, 'who were the models all along'). That winter he entered into negotiation with Brian Epstein for the Yardbirds to appear on the Beatles' Christmas show. Gomelsky's elation at his coup was short-lived. At the very moment of the group's commercial breakthrough, Clapton was informing his manager that he needed a month off. Asked to elaborate, he cited only 'family reasons'.

Immediately the Yardbirds left the stage at the Hammersmith Odeon, where the crowd grew ecstatic and threw jellybeans, Clapton was travelling with his grandparents to Germany. Once there he was reunited with his mother, living with her husband Frank McDonald in barracks outside Dortmund. According to a later interview given by Pat, '[Clapton] looked at me, I looked at him – the knowledge was there but we both found it painful.' A corporal also present in the barracks, Terry Leslie, remembers meeting the family and shaking the hand of an 'obviously unhappy' nineteen-year-old, wearing the sort of tortured look he associated with 'someone contemplating murder'. Clapton's gloomy outlook increased when, in order to obtain entry to the sergeants' mess, he was given a crewcut on McDonald's orders. The Yardbirds were astounded when their star player, the exemplar of hirsute cool, returned to Kew looking like a military recruit. A generation raised on Freud will have no difficulty in identifying the sense of paranoia felt by Clapton: having been abandoned by his mother, the reunion occurred only to add to his feeling of persecution. 'He was incredibly upset by it,' says Dreja. 'That [haircut] was like a humiliation' – though this, too, he believed, 'added to Eric's sense of being different – he kept it short for months afterwards'.

In the first weeks of 1965 the group returned to the circuit with Gene Vincent, the Kinks and the Small Faces. In Richmond they met a twenty-year-old local guitarist playing erratic but occasionally inspired blues, qualities that applied equally to the musician himself. As soon as he met Jeff Beck, Dreja registered the words 'wayward' and 'genius', a prediction time would amply fulfil. From that moment the Yardbirds generally, and Relf specifically, began a campaign to induct Beck into the group. By then, says McCarty, 'we all knew a change was coming. The situation with Eric was intolerable.'

Things deteriorated when, at a session at IBC studios described by McCarty as 'tense', Gomelsky announced the group would record their third single, a 'gassing number', he put it, written by a teenage crooner,

Graham Gouldman, present at IBC to demonstrate the song's bongo-and-harpsichord arrangement. When Clapton first heard 'For Your Love' he was appalled. Not only was the song the very antithesis of the blues, it featured the Yardbirds barely (the harpsichord being played by Brian Auger) and Clapton not at all. A counter-suggestion of Otis Redding's 'Your One And Only Man' was rejected. Clapton did, however, play on the single's B-side, 'Got To Hurry', an instrumental credited obscurely to 'Rasputin' (Gomelsky's sobriquet) though written by the guitarist himself. When 'For Your Love' was released in March 1965 it reached number three in the charts. Gouldman went on to form Hot Legs and 10CC (the latter of which Clapton always disparaged); the Yardbirds were elated; Gomelsky himself was 'ecstatic'.

Was Clapton? In private he continued to seethe at management in general and the Gomelsky–Samwell-Smith axis in particular. In public he complained, not without justice, of the impracticability of his performing a guitarless hit single. Not that 'For Your Love' made money for the Yardbirds, each of whom continued to draw a weekly wage from Gomelsky. 'It was like the responsibilities of success – constant gigging, appearances, interviews – without the privileges,' says Dreja. 'I remember Eric asking, "We've sold our souls – for what?"' When *Five Live Yardbirds* was released that winter, to generally favourable reviews ('Raucous interplay . . . great guitar . . . feral energy of the ensemble') it, too, failed to materially benefit the group. In February the flat at Kew was vacated and Clapton returned to Ripley.

On 3 March 1965 the Yardbirds played the Corn Exchange, Bristol. Backstage there was a dispute involving members of the group and their manager. In a memo circulated that morning Gomelsky extended what Clapton called 'a political thrust towards the top of the charts' by insisting on stricter attention to the details of collective success: 'Time is money,' he wrote. 'If you're late for rehearsals you will be fined . . . Punctuality in the studio is a must . . . If you have any queries about this, report to Paul Samwell-Smith or come to my office immediately.' Clapton's indignation at being thus 'babied', a month short of his twentieth birthday, was matched only by his pique at Samwell-Smith's promotion. A showdown took place with Gomelsky, either at the latter's office, flat, or over the phone. Clapton himself told Coleman, 'I went to Giorgio's office and said, "I don't like it and I'm going to leave." Instead of being upset, Giorgio said, "Good. Okay, well, we're not really surprised'; while Gomelsky, believing 'Eric had a problem with the music, [wasn't] happy with Keith's singing and the fact that "For Your Love" didn't need a lead guitarist' attributes the same outcome to a later interview; Samwell-Smith himself remembers, 'in the middle of making [For Your Love], Giorgio getting a phone call from Eric, very dignified, saying he was leaving. Nobody was surprised.'

Whatever the cause, the effect was inevitable. Both Dreja and McCarty believe 'the end had to come . . . The memo might have done it for Eric, but it was only the last straw. The guy could be insufferable.'

Obeying the rule which then restricted such decisions to 'musical differences', the following appeared in *Melody Maker*:

CLAPTON QUITS YARDBIRDS – 'TOO COMMERCIAL'

Eric Clapton, lead guitarist with the Yardbirds, has left the group because he says: 'They are going too commercial.'

He has been replaced by Jeff Beck and leader Keith Relf told the *Melody Maker*: 'It's very sad because we are all friends. There was no bad feeling at all, but Eric did not get on well with the business. He does not like commercialization.

'He loves the blues so much I suppose he did not like it being played badly by a white shower like us.'

Relf's last statement conveyed less irony than he thought. Among Clapton's many frustrations with the Yardbirds were their reluctance to play the 'pure' blues he so craved; their very inability to do so. His own love of the music was a romantic attachment. Clapton's self-professed dreams were of the integrity of the American Negro, of the 'heroic quality' of that race's grace under pressure. Such dreams changed the outlook for him, recalling his own youthful trauma. A demanding obsession like the blues calls for a sacrifice in human values, and it failed to develop in Clapton such compensating virtues as diplomacy or a willingness to compromise. Dealing with four colleagues, in at least one of whom the desire to 'get laid' seemed to exceed any artistic ambition, must have been galling for someone who continued to see himself as 'one man with his guitar versus the world'.

His immediate horizons were limited to suburban Oxford. In the eighteen months since leaving the Roosters, Clapton had maintained a correspondence with his former pianist, Ben Palmer. The latter, reluctant to play in front of an audience, had settled on a life of wood-carving and sculpture, eventually settling at a studio in north Wales. In 1965

Palmer was living above stables in Parktown, Oxford. He retained his sizeable collection of records, some exceeding in 'purity' even Clapton's exacting standards. By the second week of March the two were living together, doing what Clapton did best – rehearsing, listening to albums – existing, in Palmer's words, 'on a diet of beans and Algerian red'. This prosaic truth was different from the later myth surrounding the period: that, in order to perfect his playing of the blues, Clapton had 'sold his soul', or at least entered into some unholy contract of the type legendarily made by Robert Johnson. Not so, says Palmer: 'The reason Eric improved as a player was constant practice. He played the guitar before lunch, before tea, before dinner.'

The Yardbirds, meanwhile, enjoyed the services of Jeff Beck for eighteen months. They had transatlantic hits in 1966 with 'Shapes Of Things' and 'Over Under Sideways Down', appeared in Antonioni's *Blow Up*, employed their sometime producer Jimmy Page and disbanded in 1968. They remain, with Graham Bond, the Pretty Things and the Kinks, in the second rank of British R&B, their entry in reference books invariably including the footnote of having 'discovered Eric Clapton'. In 1965 they made a half-hearted attempt to keep in touch: 'For a while,' says Dreja, 'there was a faint possibility Eric could have rejoined. He still talked to Giorgio, though primarily about money. The others got occasional phone calls.' Dreja himself, who admits to no hard feelings, never spoke to Clapton again. Jim McCarty was present with Samwell-Smith in September 1983 when Clapton played a benefit concert at the Albert Hall. 'Eric approached us backstage and immediately started hassling Paul, *still* moaning about that "Time is money" memo. After eighteen years – incredible.' When Clapton met McCarty at a party later in the eighties he appeared not to recognize him.

More significantly, when Keith Relf died in May 1976, Clapton (at home in England) failed to attend the funeral. This, says Dreja, was 'typical ... When Eric moved on, he moved for good.' As part of this process of reinventing himself, Clapton periodically felt the need to rewrite the past. Old arrangements were rescinded, intimate friends forgotten. No one came too close to Clapton. His time in the Yardbirds began a lifelong habit of attaching himself to musicians for limited periods. Clapton specialized in relationships specifically dependent on his giving or withdrawing his friendship. The idea was that he alone retained control. 'He had an unnerving ability to turn,' says Dreja. 'At any moment he had one "best friend", whom he stuck to like glue. Then the best

47

friend would change. Eric had that child's thing of "I'm not playing with you any more." It was my loss, but I always had the feeling a relationship with Clapton was only a milestone on the road to being dropped.'

Dreja was not the only victim of Clapton's view of friendship. In April 1965 the guitarist was living with Palmer, occasionally 'becoming overbearing' in his insistence they form a group, and sporadically returning to Ripley. Despite lobbying Gomelsky for residuals – few, if any, of which were ever forthcoming – and briefly returning to playing impromptu for cash, the financial situation remained bleak. Speaking of this era in 1985, Clapton remembered 'taking some money off a girl in Oxford who was very nice to me. I was broke. I was just a scoundrel . . . I enjoyed having no ties for a while.' It was at about this time that he met a woman in the White Horse pub in Broad Street, to whom he 'expressed major doubts' about returning to the music business professionally. A second witness also confirms that 'Eric had something of a crisis of confidence, running down the "pop scene" and the way it was trivialized in the press.' Clapton did, however, give an interview to *Rave* in which, among the 'Chart Chicks' and Kenny Ball reviews then redolent of the title, he noted, 'For me to face myself I have to play what I believe is pure and sincere and uncorrupted music', a statement seized on by a thirty-one-year-old blues aficionado recently arrived in the London suburbs.

John Mayall's career to then had remained frustratingly in chrysalis. Having discovered music as a teenager, Mayall performed National Service, fronted a group called Powerhouse Four, specifically to back touring American bluesmen, moved to Blackheath from his native Cheshire, continuing to play semi-professionally while working by day as an advertising executive. Mayall's reputation, according to one musician who knew him, was as a 'total eccentric . . . John used to leap on stage naked to the waist like a geriatric Mick Jagger. When he sang you couldn't believe it – he sounded as bluesy as your grandmother. What John had was enthusiasm.'

On 11 April Mayall sounded Clapton and found him willing to join his group the Bluesbreakers, the very title of which he believes 'decidedly impressed' the guitarist.

Inclusive in the arrangement (which kept Clapton's wage at £20 a week) was an offer of room and board. Mayall, his schoolteacher wife and their four children made the journey to Ripley. Clapton, having returned there from Oxford, now finally vacated the family home. 'It was traumatic,' says Pamela Mayall. 'Eric was *very* reluctant to go. Although he'd moved out before, this was the first time everything went with him. There was a big scene on the doorstep with Rose.' She also remembers her youngest children being 'fascinated with the outside loo, running in and out of it shrieking when they saw what it was. Embarrassing.'

At the Mayalls' home in Lee Green, Blackheath, Clapton was given the small spare bedroom and unlimited access to his host's record collection. At first there was understandable reluctance to enter too closely into the family's lives. Who, after all, was he? A known loner with a talent for alienating people. For a week Clapton remained in his attic room, periodically seen on a landing or at the door, giving Mayall and his wife a filmy side glance as he entered. Towards the end of April there was an excursion to London Zoo. It was there, says Pamela, that the relationship 'evolved' – though even that underestimates a process that bordered on reincarnation. 'Eric was transfixed,' she says. 'He loved that zoo, particularly the chimpanzees . . . After the first visit he was always pleading to go back. I was astonished. Here was this grown-up pop idol asking for a "treat" like one of the kids. It was endearing, but it was strange.'

Clapton then met his fellow Bluesbreakers Hughie Flint and John McVie. Both had heard and been impressed by 'Got To Hurry', which Mayall (spluttering with rage when the jukebox at first erroneously played 'For Your Love') also admired. Like the Yardbirds, the group's initial opinion of Clapton was guarded. Flint remembers him as 'very quiet, very reserved, very aloof. It may have been nerves or it may have been something else.' Like the Yardbirds, they soon encountered the capricious side of Clapton's nature. 'It was basically Eric and John,' says Flint. 'Then there were periods when he switched to McVie or me, usually to have a go at Mayall.' Among Clapton's numerous complaints (again analogous to the Yardbirds) were both money and the technical deficiencies of his leader's singing. Still living at Mayall's house, he began, in his later recollection, to 'gang up on him behind his back, muttering about him not being a good enough singer, being too flamboyant . . . In any situation, I've always found *something* that isn't right.'

He continued to seethe with cumulative rage at the Yardbirds. Flint was not alone in finding 'something almost warped' in the way Clapton referred to his previous group, to their shortcomings as musicians and individuals. Mayall, too, believed it was akin to 'running down an ex-lover to your new wife . . . It was like: "You're the only one. The others didn't count."' Discussing the Yardbirds with Flint, Clapton went as far as to say they were 'virtual idiots – he wanted to play Chicago blues while all they were into was being pop stars'. In his first six weeks with Mayall, Clapton repeatedly stressed the need for 'purity'; his devotion to *The Best Of Muddy Waters*, his kinship with the blues.

He clung to the music with a cold, rational deliberation. Clapton's morale was boosted by the misfortune of others and depressed by their contentment. Disaster is fascinating, prosperity boring. The blues provided a glimpse of real torment – of poverty, madness, despair – without the need to be tormented oneself. They gave expression to Clapton's sense of hurt, a sense almost entirely restricted to his own perception. The truth is that he came to maturity at a time of unparalleled prosperity (twelve years old when, as Macmillan said, 'most of us have never had it so good', eighteen when an unemployment rate of 2 per cent was considered average), when the boom of the late 1950s had pumped money into every level of the community, not excluding adolescents. Clapton himself, in a not untypical case-study, was being housed, fed and paid to comment on the vagaries of society. Yet society continued to tolerate and even encourage him. The cloud of real suffering was always passing over him, but fell only on others. His identification with the Kings, with Handy, Broonzy and Johnson was at best peripheral, at worst abjectly cynical. Already, by 1963, Clapton was being adequately paid to do what he loved. His continued attachment to the blues owed less to *angst* and more to a logical career choice. It was, as he put it to Flint, a living.

Though never launching a formal bid, Clapton in time became the group's effective leader. Watching from the sidelines, Flint became aware that 'Eric was fanatically ambitious for the Bluesbreakers, if equally so for himself.' As Clapton later put it: 'I had a sense of impending fame . . . [which] I used to my advantage. The reason John acquiesced was the pressure I put on him in terms of what material we could do.' That spring and early summer the Bluesbreakers' repertoire veered towards the Otis Rush, Buddy Guy and Freddie King titles recently discovered in Mayall's attic. In June they taped three songs of which 'Telephone Blues', released as a B-side in October, impressed even Clapton's grandmother. Ralph Gleason believed that 'if this was a parody, it was an uncommonly affectionate one'. Another critic suggested that Clapton's popularity was due in large part to 'record-buying adolescents', in the search for 'gratification and ego', which had grown so rampant in the 1960s, having lost much of their capacity for feeling, and that Clapton, with his intensity, verve and apparent sense of destiny, restored the consciousness of other ends that made life worth living. Clapton may not have been born to the blues, but he played them with both the zeal of the convert and the fervour of the missionary.

Mayall, already middle-aged, craving the prestige of success without the commercial focus to achieve it, increasingly deferred to his guitarist. Not only did Clapton transform the Bluesbreakers' material, his stage act developed and extended. Already, by midsummer, he was walking the free-improvisation tightrope. In 'Telephone Blues' and 'I'm Your Witchdoctor' Clapton engaged in the sort of blues-rock exploration, clichéd now, which, as Flint says, 'No one, literally *no one* was then doing.' As with the Yardbirds, so with the Bluesbreakers. Musically and personally, Clapton began to separate from the others: 'A knockout,' stated *Melody Maker*; 'Eric Clapton is the best blues guitarist in Britain', while on certain billings his name appeared above that of the group. This, says Mayall, inevitably led to 'a sense of remoteness', one tolerated in the interests of group success. 'It was like Manchester United and George Best – to some extent you remodelled the team around the star player.'

Critics contended that Clapton's strengths were primarily as a tactician rather than a strategist. He was adept at absorbing and playing the blues without the vision to create them himself. There was, as Gleason said and Clapton would admit, an element of merely parodying an art form. It says much for the state of British music in 1965 (the year Joan Baez and Julie Andrews topped the charts) that imitation was confused with invention. In the Bluesbreakers and later groups, Clapton achieved some remarkable successes. Many of the songs he performed were enlightened and imaginative, others garish and vulgar. Some were clever, others too clever by half. But he was able to take a clear-eyed view of the market: by bringing a style once stigmatized as 'race' or even 'nigger' music to a largely white, predominantly urban audience, Clapton astutely tapped the vein being exploited, in their different ways, by the Byrds, Paul Butterfield and Buffalo Springfield, to say nothing of the Beatles and Stones. He was perhaps less of a visionary and more of a pragmatist than people thought.

He became suspicious, prone to manipulating people's hostilities more readily than appealing to their goodness. His feeling of hurt, of being singled out for unusual punishment, never left him. Clapton's sense of betrayal by his mother provided his second connection to the blues: on stage or in the studio he could express himself in the way of Johnson or Waters, translating their own – more material – sense of loss to the audience. The ensuing money and female adoration were a bonus. He began to develop, or extend, a personality wholly devoid of security while not lacking in ego. Clapton was brash but never confident. Naturally thin-skinned, he was easy to offend and, by his own later admission, 'took things too seriously'. His look of unmitigated doom was animated by eyes that appeared to be hungry for approval.

In May 1965 Clapton first met a musician whose contrariness exceeded his own. After two performances at the Albert Hall ('weirdly compelling songs' wrote *Melody Maker*, for fans in bell-bottoms and Coke-bottle glasses) Bob Dylan arrived at Levy's Recording Studio in London's West End. He was in time to join the session which produced 'If You Gotta Go Go Now' – to which Dylan's prime contribution was to belch in counterpoint to the music – an unpromising start to a relationship that extended into a fourth decade. Alone that night Clapton informed Flint that Dylan had 'no future' in pop music.

He was also, the drummer says, 'already bored' with life in a group. The touring, the travel, the constant need to conform to the demands of a teenage audience displeased Clapton. They depressed him. Within weeks he was muttering about the direction taken by the Bluesbreakers, and by Mayall in particular. That summer Clapton moved from Blackheath, dividing his time between Ripley, a writer's flat in Redcliffe Gardens and a commune above a warehouse at 74 Long Acre, Covent Garden. The last included Ben Palmer, a puppeteer named Ted Milton and the actor John Hurt. According to a local teenager, Kay Munday: 'it was chaotic . . . a big open-plan place in which half a dozen people would always be sprawled around drunk. They virtually lived in the Freemasons Arms. At four in the afternoon you'd see Clapton asleep. His main tipple was cheap red wine. Then he'd get up and play the guitar, hunched over it and mumbling. That was his whole life, then – drink, sleep and music. You never saw him eat.'

Clapton's Bohemian leanings developed in spite of Mayall – almost unique among blues musicians in retaining rigid control over details of his own life. On the road the three sidemen travelled separately from their leader. Forced into a bus or van, even there Mayall insisted on segregation; he had his own bed installed in the aisle. A system of fines and punishments was devised to discourage lateness. Mayall, a teetotaller, thought nothing of abandoning a drunken musician on the roadside. On Fridays Clapton, Flint and McVie were each handed an envelope containing £20, minus those sums deducted as penalties. In hotels Mayall turned in early with his blues records and pornography collection. Only Clapton was allowed access to either.

When Mayall issued an edict regarding 'dress sense' there was talk of Clapton confronting him, much of it from Clapton himself. Flint remembers this as a 'dramatic moment', McVie and himself empowered by a musician at last willing to challenge Mayall's overbearing leadership. The crisis passed only when Clapton, in yet another reversal, deemed it 'groovy' to wear a white linen jacket and tie. This isolated McVie and Flint, the latter of whom believes 'it was all a game for Eric, offering or withdrawing his support . . . First he was for Mayall, then against him, then for him again. You never knew where you stood.' At a party at the SODS club attended by Brian Jones and his bodyguard Tom Keylock, Clapton was heard to murmur about the technical limitations of his two colleagues in contrast to Mayall, whom he considered 'a gas'. A month later, at the launch of Immediate Records, Clapton was back to his previous tack: John, he loudly complained, was a drag. At a photo session that night the others smiled while Clapton, alone, stared in studied three-quarters view at his feet.

'His main problem,' says Flint, 'was the music. Eric's moods came from a feeling of frustration. We couldn't play the blues as well as the masters – and, for that matter, neither could he.' Both Mayall and McVie confirm that the group had more musicality than raw ability: there was a sense of providing tasteful, mature, if over-reverent covers of standards, investing them with a significance greater than that intended in the originals. Sensing the group's ambitions extended only to affectionate imitation, Clapton was appalled. His moodiness, his feeling of frustration and *ennui*, increased. Early on, he seems to have recognized that in terms of talent, the Bluesbreakers barely if at all exceeded the standard of the Yardbirds. The discovery caused him to swing violently between bouts of depression and manic excess. After one performance at Uxbridge he was heard to remark that 'even [Howlin'] Wolf would have got off on that'. The next night he informed Flint that this was the 'shittiest blues band in the world'. Clapton could never give unstinting praise without an equivalent volume of criticism. His fickleness was, in its way, a deliberate statement, testifying to his complicated mixture of self-disparagement and self-esteem, and his conviction that only 'purity' of expression counted.

Between bouts of drinking and deep inertia he still had normal moments, sometimes extending to a week, but from midsummer Clapton basically lost interest. Boredom, frustration, even the influence of Milton and Hurt, may have contributed: but what really motivated Clapton was the knowledge that, musically, the Bluesbreakers would always be average. Once he realized that, says Flint, 'apathy set in'. As well as Clapton the dedicated purist there was a Clapton who had a childlike capacity for petulance and an egoist's interest in his own promotion. At Welwyn Garden City the group performed as a trio* when their guitarist failed to turn up. At the Marquee Clapton appeared only to fall asleep on stage. On yet another occasion he pulled McVie aside with the confession, 'This is a wank.' Family and friends still occasionally asked him if he was happy and Clapton was only able to temporize. 'I feel like a puppet in a freak-show,' he told them.

So began the most improbable journey which even Clapton ever undertook. In late August 1965 Flint was collecting his drum-kit from the stage door of the Twisted Wheel, Manchester, when he noticed his guitarist in the shadows. After a 'hissed conversation' it became apparent that Clapton was leaving the Bluesbreakers to 'form a band in Australia' and that he, Flint, was invited to join. Under no circumstances was he to inform Mayall.

After the shock had died down Flint, a practical man in his mid-twenties, asked about wages. To this 'hopelessly middle-aged' question Clapton gave a look of withering scorn. As to an itinerary, 'Eric just shrugged and said that plans were fluid. That was how he put it. I thought it was a crazy idea and said so. Eric had this dreamy smile as if the whole thing was a wind-up. I thought it was a joke. Two days later Mayall came in and said, "Clapton's left."'

The original plan, devised in a drunken torpor at Redcliffe Gardens, was for Clapton – much given to Utopian ramblings – to hire a double-decker bus, driving it through Asia, stopping to play whenever and whatever he liked, arriving eventually in Australia, where he intended to 'fish, get laid and play cricket'. That was the plan. Incredibly, not one of Clapton's roommates objected. Indeed, they encouraged the idea. The only practical concession was to abandon the bus (although enquiries were made at a depot in Victoria) in favour of a second-hand Ford Fairlane, daubed red for the occasion; fittings were added on Clapton's orders. Next there was an argument with the Bluesbreakers' bookkeeper about

* Deputizing for one song was a local teenager named Mick Taylor, later to join both the Bluesbreakers and, on Mayall's recommendation, the Rolling Stones.

money. Finally Mayall himself intervened, threatening to 'sue Clapton to oblivion' for desertion. Overnight the dour, taciturn guitarist was transformed into a vagabond, outlaw and free spirit. Now Clapton was ready to go on tour.

His happiness, almost his survival, as a musician depended as much as anything on the people who surrounded him. Samwell Smith, Dreja, and to a lesser extent Flint and Mayall had all felt the ironic edge of Clapton's tongue. Kay Munday confirms that 'he was the moodiest bugger, bar none, ever. If Eric didn't like you, that was it.' Clapton's companions on leaving the Bluesbreakers were Ben Palmer, a singer named John Baily, Bob Ray on bass, the saxophonist Bernie Greenwood and Ted Milton's brother Jake on drums. According to one of them, 'It should have been a laid-back, Overland Express kind of trip. Instead it was a disaster . . . Eric was uptight and the constant booze and dope kept everyone off balance. Here was this incredible collection of poets, musicians and hangers-on, all raving and jabbering at each other in the middle of Europe. It almost came to blows at the beer festival in Munich. No one had money for a hotel and after a week in the car it smelt of something worse than cheese.'

The Glands, as they became, eventually arrived in Athens in the third week of September. Any doubts concerning the direction and future career of the group were removed by the sight of the local promoter, known only as such, who met them in his cane-cutter shirt and high heels, carrying a swagger stick and teasing his lacquered hair. He was, he said, prepared to hire the Glands on a *per diem* basis: 5000 drachmae a performance, plus room and board, the repertoire to include a sprinkling of Top Twenty tunes, with touches of Elvis and Chuck Berry, plus – at the promoter's specific insistence – a finale of *South Pacific*.

For three weeks – as, in London, a succession of guitarists joined Mayall to play the blues – Clapton stood in the Igloo taverna, ad-libbing Kinks hits, while tourists whistled and called for 'Young At Heart'. 'It was awful,' says Palmer. 'Right away, we knew we'd made a mistake. Here were these blues fanatics playing as a Greek bar band . . . Eventually Eric and I managed to inject a few Buddy Holly and Little Richard numbers. Even that went down like a lead balloon.' A second member of the Glands calls it 'the worst farce imaginable. Within a week Eric was on the phone to Mayall asking for his job back.'

Things deteriorated when, a car crash having killed their own leader, a second group at the taverna co-opted Clapton on guitar. From being merely drawn he became depressed. Compounding the problem was the promoter – a loud, fractious figure whose devotion to Clapton seemed not entirely entrepreneurial. 'He was always trying to get Eric upstairs,' says a witness. 'I can see him with his arm around Eric's shoulder inviting him up for a drink. By then the whole scene was out of hand. What started out as a beautiful dream ended up a nightmare. It was like a Fellini film.'

For this and other reasons the Glands made the decision to disband. According to Clapton's later memory: 'The owner of the club took a liking to me and said that I should stay . . . So I actually had to escape, and I lost an amp which I left in the club . . . I had a mad dash to the station where I caught the Orient Express and came back home.' If anything this underestimates an imbroglio that included the serving of deportation orders on Baily and Greenwood, the furtive removal of the group's equipment to the station and Clapton extracting his own guitar from the promoter on the grounds of 'needing to buy strings'. He and Palmer then caught the return train while Baily and Greenwood did, briefly, appear in Australia.

The *sangfroid* with which Mayall greeted Clapton's return was notable. According to Flint: 'Eric rang up one night in the studio. John wandered in and announced calmly, "Clapton's back." It seemed like a natural progression. First he was there, then gone, then back again. No one looked surprised.' Mayall's reception of his guitarist may not have been entirely selfless. In the two months Clapton was gone the Bluesbreakers engaged a half-dozen surrogates. McVie had also left – fired by Mayall for, in Flint's words, 'turning up pissed once too often'. His replacement, himself on the rebound from the Graham Bond group, was Jack Bruce. 'Right away,' he says, 'I got in a groove with Eric. There was a great thing between us then. Positive electricity, I'd call it.'

The amended line-up returned to the circuit in time for the release of the Bluesbreakers' single 'I'm Your Witchdoctor'. Described by *Melody Maker* as a 'knockout up-tempo number . . . Hums along with some gas parts of unison with vocal and the blues guitar of Eric Clapton . . . Deserves to be a hit', it did, briefly, appear in the lower reaches of the Top 100. The paper's critic if anything belittled Clapton's contribution to 'Witchdoctor', a technical *tour-de-force* in which the notes were sustained progressively longer at each chorus. By year's end it became the centre-piece of a Bluesbreakers set comprising 'Crossroads', 'Have You Heard', 'Parchman Farm', 'Stormy Monday', 'Ramblin' On My Mind', 'Little

Girl', 'Telephone Blues', 'Hoochie Coochie Man', 'Steppin' Out' and 'What'd I Say' – an hour of tightly choreographed blues in which Clapton stood mute with his Gibson Les Paul as Mayall, apelike, twisted his trunk and prodded the piano.

According to Flint, Clapton suffered attacks of anxiety for fear that his playing was 'pandering to the commercial', and compensated by appearing bored or irritable. There was something other-worldly about his stage persona. Frequently closing his eyes or turning his back to the crowd, smoking a series of cigarettes, Clapton not only defied the conventional rock guitarist's pose – he reversed it. While players like Townshend, Alvin Lee or Keith Richards engaged the audience, gritting their teeth or manhandling their equipment, Clapton merely stood or, in exceptional circumstances, proffered a sphinxlike smile. He differed in this respect not only from men like Beck and Page – to say nothing of Chuck Berry and Albert Collins – he transposed the work of his idols. There was nothing reticent about B. B. King or Buddy Guy. Collins himself used a 100-foot guitar lead that allowed him, when playing live, to stroll into the audience, into the bar, or outside into the car park. Perhaps only Robert Johnson fully conformed to the ideal: a brooding, ascetic figure rarely heard to speak, he was constantly quoted by Clapton as a role model. Even then, there may have been a touch of over-compensation. Johnson was known to shake and bob his head on the few occasions he played to an audience. When, that November, a member of the Bluesbreakers suggested to Clapton he 'loosen up' on stage, the guitarist swung at him with a suitcase. He had to jump into the street to save himself.

That autumn the Bluesbreakers entered Wessex Studios, Soho, to record 'Lonely Years' and 'Bernard Jenkins' under the production of Mike Vernon. The primitive force of these sessions – the instruments were played through a single microphone – further advanced Clapton's reputation. Not only was he the best blues guitarist in Britain, he personally *linked* British rhythm and blues. No other player could have performed, albeit with reservations, in groups as diverse as the Yardbirds and Bluesbreakers and been credible in each. 'He was untouchable then,' says Flint. 'Nobody else, including Mayall, had listened to the amount of blues Eric had. His whole life was playing and rehearsing ... It was like a brilliant tennis player, improvising all the shots – first of all he's spent a lifetime learning the basics.' When Jack Dupree, a sometime boxer and barrelhouse pianist,

57

invited Clapton to record with him that winter he announced himself 'shitstruck' by a guitarist he quickly endorsed as 'king of the blues'.

During his second spell with Mayall, from November 1965 to June 1966, Clapton's fame grew. He was greeted warmly by Keith Richards and without insult by Brian Jones. The Beatles asked to see him. While failing to attract the same pre-teen audience as themselves, Clapton became a cult to certain proto-hippies, art students and beatniks. Nineteen sixty-six saw the breaking of the first wave of the Baby Boom. Thousands of people born in 1946 and 1947 discovered pop music in the wake of the Beatles, a statistical fact from which a second tier of acts – the Stones, the Kinks, the Who, even exotics like Mayall – could hardly fail to benefit. They did benefit. Working musicians like Korner and Chris Farlowe, previously content to play for themselves, were rung person-to-person by booking agents and summoned to Chelsea for photo sessions. Nonentities like Vic Flick and the Applejacks were given recording contracts. Rage, amounting to delirium, swept over Britain. Musicians everywhere were instructed by their managers – many of them schooled in vaudeville – to exaggerate their performance to the point of burlesque. What Andrew Oldham calls 'the histrionic side of pop' was fully exploited. Clapton's own appeal lay elsewhere. Critics in England were impressed by the fact that he was taken seriously abroad. He was adopted by culturally ambitious people and experienced the fate of a symbol. Clapton, it was agreed, was different.

By 1966 it was the one point where Clapton's opinion and his critics' met. He *was* different. Standing at the stage door of the Marquee one night that winter, a London copy-typist named Sally Prescott turned to her companion as the Bluesbreakers emerged on the pavement: 'The rest of the group came out, followed by Eric with a face like thunder. I looked round and said, "Here comes God Himself." He really looked that uptight. Clapton must have heard it because I got a special dirty look as he went past. My friend said, "That's a good name for him, God. He looks like the Almighty."'

The epithet, taken up by *Melody Maker* and the other papers, caught on. At the Bluesbreakers' first appearance in the New Year fans shouted 'God', 'Give Him a solo' and 'We want God'. 'Clapton is God' slogans were daubed on walls at London railway stations. A particularly dramatic example appeared on the Paddington viaduct. Clapton's own reaction ranged from passive ('It just began to become fashionable – a lot of people grabbed hold of my name and started using it – people were starting to write "Clapton is God" all over the place without knowing what they were talking about. Very funny. Very strange') to gratified ('My vanity was incredibly boosted') to resigned ('There's nothing you can do about it'). In private he continued to insist that he was, if not God, then at least 'the best guitarist in the world'.

Meanwhile Clapton's contemporaries were graduating from Kingston Art College and disappearing, around late 1965, into bank jobs or minor positions in graphic design.

'You can imagine how it set him apart,' says Flint. 'All of a sudden it was "Eric Clapton and the Bluesbreakers" or "Eric Clapton and His Band". There was a lot of muttering, particularly after the trip to Greece. McVie* complained that it was one rule for Eric and another for the rest.'

In January 1966 Clapton was still short of his twenty-first birthday. His first reaction to deification suggested something like tolerance. In fact it was the same ironic acceptance of his talent he displayed in the Yardbirds. Clapton loved being apart from the crowd. In later years he developed seclusion to a virtual art form. Whatever the drawbacks of being singled out (and it was hard, in 1966, to see one), Clapton enjoyed the undoubted attention and recognition it brought him. Later the mood changed. In full maturity it must have been galling to Clapton to be forever associated with his past; 'then came a feeling of bitterness and sensitivity,' he told Ray Coleman. Later still, in his thirties and forties, Clapton allowed and even encouraged critics to revive the nickname. That left him, let alone them, in a quandary: Clapton seemed to be insisting that his later work had the freshness and quality of the Bluesbreakers, yet the values of that group – roughness, naïveté, enthusiasm – had gone. Clapton reluctantly acknowledged the problem, and understood it meant that while the pretext for his later fame was musical, its obvious basis was nostalgia.

There were other rewards. Clapton travelled widely in his later days with the Bluesbreakers – France, Germany, Belgium, Holland, Switzerland – excursions, if undertaken in anything but luxury, in which his reputation ensured him VIP status throughout. A member of the group recalls 'Eric . . . indulging in a personal orgy at some venues. He'd have girls waiting, literally queuing up, backstage. At the door it was, "You,

---

* McVie rejoined the Bluesbreakers when Jack Bruce, exchanging his denims for a white polo neck sweater, was recruited by Manfred Mann.

you, and, ah, you at the back.' I never saw him without at least two women.'

The same source is adamant that Clapton, 'because of the mournful little-boy-lost look' he retained, was equally attractive to male fans. Though no evidence ever emerged of a physical relationship, he was known to consort with the Beatles' manager Brian Epstein. Another musician saw them in an out-of-hours drinking club in Mayfair, where Epstein's demeanour suggested 'he found Clapton more than usually attractive'. On another occasion a woman named Cecilia Lewis overheard them on the stairs of the Ad Lib club, discussing financial aspects of the music business: at the word 'royalties' a barely perceptible flicker of professional interest came over Clapton, passing immediately as he left for the bathroom. Lewis remembers 'an almost slavish look of attention' on Epstein as he waited patiently for his guest to return.

Early that April the Bluesbreakers assembled at Decca's studio two in West Hampstead and, over three days, cut the basic material for a record described as 'the first bona fide British rock album'. *Blues Breakers With Eric Clapton* was released on 22 July 1966. While failing to disturb the *Billboard* Top 100 in the US it enjoyed seventeen weeks in the British charts, reaching number six. Hughie Flint calls it among the most depressing experiences of his life.

The trouble began when Clapton informed Mike Vernon and his engineer Gus Dudgeon that he intended to play 'exactly as I like' – which turned out to be loud, fast and unbound by the normal demands of studio etiquette. A row ensued, Dudgeon being joined by Flint and a muttering McVie in asking that the guitarist at least perform at reduced volume. Clapton's response was to list for Dudgeon's benefit the numerous effects – feedback, distortion and sustain – only achievable on his terms. There was also, Flint believes, 'a degree of machismo about it, wanting to drown us out by being loudest'. Finally the engineer was taken aside by Mayall and told to 'do whatever it is God wants'. Dudgeon recorded Clapton at maximum volume and straight through an amplifier. McVie and Flint were left barely audible.

The resulting album settled all doubt in the public's mind about Clapton's genius. Unsurprisingly, it was his performance that dominated the album. The influences on *Blues Breakers* were obvious – Buddy Guy, Freddie King, Robert Johnson – but the aggressive approach and raw, quavering solos were uniquely Clapton's. His abandonment of the Tele-caster in favour of the Les Paul contributed to a fuller, bass-heavy sound at odds with the anaemic twang achieved in the Yardbirds, not to mention the Roosters. Ben Palmer speaks of the 'dramatic advance' made by Clap-ton in the space of three years, a point echoed by Tom McGuinness, who insists, 'I considered myself on level pegging with Eric in 1963. Not in 1966. The sheer variety of *Blues Breakers* was what got to me.' The emotiveness of a blues like 'Have You Heard' was matched by the rock-style leads on 'Key To Love' and 'Steppin' Out'. On 'Double Crossin' Time' (a reference to Bruce's defection to Manfred Mann) Clapton's playing was both simple and astute, a description applying generally to the record as a whole. While contemporary reviews were mixed – 'joyless', one critic called it – the album was subsequently discovered as a classic. In a long notice, *The Times* asserted the view that it was Clapton's carefully matured intention to 'open up the whole scene' to a wider audience, encouraging 'a thousand closet performers to exchange their cricket bats and broomsticks for the real thing'. *Blues Breakers* became a Bible for would-be guitarists everywhere, virtually reinventing the Gibson com-pany overnight and hauling the instrument into the forefront of contem-porary pop. Jeff Griffin, a veteran BBC producer, calls this 'the very moment the Guitar Hero was born'.

With its stark sound, uncompromising sleeve-notes and surrealist cover, *Blues Breakers* was one of a quintet of albums – alongside *Aftermath*, *Pet Sounds*, *Blonde On Blonde* and *Revolver* – to establish a recognizable rock music culture that summer. (The subject of inordinate debate as to its 'meaning' or symbolism, the cover photograph was the result, says Flint, 'of a long, boring shoot on a cold afternoon. No wonder we all looked miserable.' As to Clapton's enigmatic display of the *Beano*: 'Again, nothing was planned. Eric went everywhere with it in his pocket. The photographer caught him off-guard.') Along with these, *Blues Breakers* helped define the future direction of rock, emphasizing studio sophistry and technique over the interminable package-tours and singles. It also made Eric Clapton a star. Previously admired by art students and those who spray-painted walls, by July 1966 he was on level creative terms with, if not Lennon–McCartney and Jagger–Richards, at least George Harrison and Brian Jones. Reviews of *Blues Breakers* ('It's Eric Clapton who steals the limelight and no doubt several copies of the album will be sold on his name') singled him out; requests for interviews increased; even Mayall, a man not given to excessive promotion of his colleagues, allowed Clapton's name to appear in the title* – none of which seemed conspicuously to gratify him.

'CLAPTON: LONELY MAN WITH POWER IN HIS GUITAR' ran a typical headline that spring. The subsequent profile revealed a musician at the end of his famously short tether:

> He readily puts down English artists and says that he'll get out of England when he can. 'I don't think there will be room for me here much longer. None of my music is English – it is rooted in Chicago. I represent what is going on in Chicago at the moment . . .
>
> 'I feel that the English are rooted in rock and roll, and Tommy Steele. The stuff coming out of England now makes me puke. I'll be the first to put Chris Farlowe down.'
>
> Clapton is convinced it will be his scene over there [the US]: 'I deal in realism. Nothing but realism, and the nastier the better. The buyers and sellers of records in England are not concerned with it, which is why I'm being driven out.'

The overall impression was of almost manic paranoia, of the delusion of being 'driven out' at a time when Clapton was among the most-admired artists in Britain. Also notable was the embracing of 'realism', the disparagement of at least one musician to whom Clapton was conspicuously friendly in private. Whatever the cause – the tension with McVie and Flint, the problems with Mayall, the continuing sense of being undervalued – the result was a man motivated by notions of grandeur. According to Mayall, 'you only had to mention Chicago' to receive positive impressions. While much of this was mere dreaming, the self-conscious allusions of an English adolescent to abroad, it also stemmed from Clapton's undoubted sense of frustration, of being tied to a singer he regarded as little more than a joke, his feeling that Mayall would always remain a novelty act. When a young poet and lyricist met Clapton that spring he was told that life in the Bluesbreakers was 'nothing better than a circus'.

Pete Brown was also present at Clapton's twenty-first birthday party. Arriving at Mayall's house that night he saw the rear view of a 'hairy, almost simian figure' sitting reading a newspaper, which he failed to lower at Brown's entry. Slowly the figure turned. The simile was an apt one:

---

* Mayall's generosity did not, however, extend to paying Clapton more than the standard session fee.

it turned out to be Clapton dressed in a gorilla suit. An evening of 'lightweight debauchery' ensued, the guitarist being joined by a diminutive teenage singer known as Marie or, more popularly, Lulu. At one stage in the proceedings she and Clapton were seen descending the stairs. It was plain that, a minute or two earlier, they had emerged from one of the four upper bedrooms or the bathroom. There was not a shred of evidence pointing to one of these starting-points over another, though Brown detected 'a sense of intimacy' in the way they joked and laughed. Clapton had by then removed the gorilla suit. He sat talking to Brown, Mayall and Mayall's wife, Pamela, the last of whom remembers it as 'a funny evening, Eric alternately madly happy or depressed, dancing around like a child, then falling into catatonic silence'. He also delivered a monologue on the next day's general election, which Clapton rightly, and apparently approvingly, predicted would be won by Labour.

It was in the following week that Ginger Baker, drummer with the Graham Bond Organization – from which he had fired Jack Bruce – played informally with the Bluesbreakers, declaring himself 'knocked out' not only by Clapton's technique but his understanding – here Baker's voice grew emphatic – of *when to shut up*. The two agreed to stay in touch.

Discussions between Clapton, Baker and, at the former's insistence, Bruce in fact began that April. Early in the month the singer Paul Jones was approached by Joe Boyd, a producer at Elektra Records, to help compile British contributions to a blues anthology entitled *What's Shakin'*.* Jones in turn approached Jack Bruce. Further names were discussed – Steve Winwood, Peter York – until Jones casually mentioned Clapton and Baker. There was a pause. Bruce went pale. 'How much do you know?' he asked. 'The band's meant to be a secret.'

'What band?'

'Mine – with Eric and Ginger.'

He spoke sharply, as if the question had been a stupid one.

'You're forming a band?'

'As you must know.'

Jones denied it. Reassured, Bruce contacted Clapton; Baker failed to appear. The ensuing session took place in the Beatles' studio at Abbey Road. Over the space of a weekend the group recorded 'Steppin' Out', 'I Want To Know' and 'Crossroads' – the last, according to Jones, 'having

* The first album on which Clapton's name appeared in America.

obviously been worked on by Eric and Jack'. Clapton appeared in a fractious mood. No matter how much he flattered him, no matter how hard he tried, Jones knew he was not getting the best from his guitarist. Clapton's playing on 'Steppin' Out' was a mere parody. 'Crossroads' was better, though it too suffered by comparison to the later version. Only Jones's composition, 'I Want To Know', did the session justice. The song later surfaced on the compilation LP *History Of Eric Clapton* with, its composer notes drily, 'dramatically enhanced guitar'.

Jones found Clapton a remote, abstracted figure, quick to take offence, uneasy even with Bruce. To Clapton, a display of truculence and ill humour, not least to his friends, was neither surprising nor illogical. Rather, he saw it as the best way to achieve his lifelong desire: to stand out, to be apart. A musician present at Abbey Road believes 'he got a kick out of that, of making people think they'd offended him. Because of his reputation, there was incredible paranoia about "Who's upset Eric?" The truth was that no one had. It was all a game for our benefit.'

The same witness believes – an assumption borne out by the facts – that Clapton was 'fully aware' of his status, enjoyed it, and hastened whenever possible to promote the legend. At Abbey Road there were repeated references to 'God' and 'the greatest guitar player alive', none of which Clapton rushed to refute. There was a sense of indulging an admittedly talented but temperamental child, one continually bringing his achievements to others' attention. His greatest asset was the awe in which fellow musicians held him. Usually, as at Abbey Road, the sheer weight of Clapton's reputation was enough to draw praise for his performance. No one came away from the session with the impression of having been in the company of a genius: in fact, most had trouble even specifying what was special about Clapton's playing. But years later many of them were still talking about how 'brilliant' his work was. 'It's incredible,' says Jones. 'Eric barely turned up, but he's still the only thing people remember.'

The other side of Clapton's character – the demotic, genial, unassuming person known to fans and reporters – was revealed that summer. The Bluesbreakers were supported at a concert at Rutlish Grammar School by a local dance-band named the Torque. Chris Rea, the group's guitarist, was storing his equipment backstage when he felt a tap on the shoulder. It was Clapton. 'He stood there,' says Rea, 'talking about guitars and technique and how much he admired my playing. It turned out he'd lost his plectrum. I gave him mine.' Clapton's intensity fascinated

Rea. Intensity barely existed in British pop music at the time; it was all, as the latter says, about 'chicks, pills and weekends in Brighton'. For twenty minutes Clapton discussed amplifiers and tunings. He mentioned feedback and sustain. By then, says Rea, 'the compère was literally onstage, announcing the Bluesbreakers . . . Clapton went on with a kind of shrug, as if apologizing for ending the conversation. Whatever it meant, I took it as a huge compliment.' ('I don't doubt it,' says an ex-member of the Bluesbreakers. 'But the end result was that Eric got his plectrum.')

Capable of childlike innocence, of impulsive kindness, of doing favours for people in no position to return them, Clapton retained an impressive ego, a broad streak of insecurity and, says the journalist Don Short, 'the ability to play the press like a violin. He used to tell you what he thought you wanted to hear, then ask your opinion. It's very flattering.' Clapton himself was aware of the masks he wore and apparently removed at will. Keenly conscious of his role as a tortured genius, he played the part with an intense and poignant consistency that gave his performance the quality of high art. The same week he was charming Chris Rea backstage he wrote of himself to a musician, 'The dark side is not yet destroyed.'

His senses both of ego and insecurity led Clapton to challenge Mayall more freely. Flint remembers the spring of 1966 as 'a war of attrition . . . Eric and John squabbling in public as well as private, an uneasy alliance punctuated by moments of real nastiness'. Pete Brown recalls 'an immense amount of moaning about the way Mayall acted on stage. All three of them were fed up.' Gradually, over the late spring and summer, encouraged by Bruce and Baker, Clapton began to realize he could just as easily have Mayall's success without having Mayall. As he put it later: 'I first thought: I can do this! I can do what *he*'s doing. And when John Mayall let me sing one song on his album, I thought, I can sing as well . . . God, I should get my own band!' Clapton went home to Ripley after a concert in Guildford, talking excitedly in the Ship of a 'blues trio' he intended to form. To the obvious question 'Who's in it?' he winked and said, 'Me, me and more me.'

In fact discussions about the group's line-up proved lengthy and elaborate. Winwood was an early candidate; a meeting took place in Paul Jones's presence in which 'Steve was definitely asked but declined on account of Spencer Davis'. A second singer was also interviewed in the Ad Lib club, where he fell asleep as a form of refusal. There was an idea that Graham Bond or Jones himself might join. Even Pete Hogman, whose previous relations with Clapton consisted of having hit him over the head with his guitar, was asked and, just as soon, declined.

Clapton thought it safe to make such offers because he was certain that, with the possible exception of Winwood, no one would take them seriously. There was a feeling of engaging in hazy advance publicity for the group rather than forming it. Hogman states that 'whatever one thought of Eric as a musician, the idea of him starting a band was incredible . . . Everyone thought of him as John's sidekick,' a view evidently shared by Mayall himself. 'Eric had never shown leadership qualities,' he says. 'I was aware he was friendly with Jack and Ginger, but no one thought of those two in a group. They hated each other.'

If anything, that underestimates a relationship that had, on occasion, turned violent. Dick Heckstall-Smith remembers 'amazing nights with Graham [Bond] when Ginger literally flung drumsticks at Jack's head . . . It was a full-time job refereeing them. I've never, in forty years as a musician, known anything like it.' When, in April 1966, Baker approached Clapton with the tentative idea of a band, Bruce would have been among the very last names he had in mind. Clapton insisted: 'Jack had once played [with Mayall] and we got on very well . . . A natural first choice for any group I might dream of forming.' Baker, with much muttering and intimations as to the future, duly set out for Bruce's home. 'I knocked at the door,' he recalls. 'Jack was surprised . . . We sat down and had a cup of tea. I told him what was going on and said, "Do you want to come with us?" He said, "Yeah," and that was it.' The prospective trio met at Baker's house in Birchen Grove, Neasden. Later that same night a twelve-year-old named Gary Lawson was riding his bicycle over adjacent wasteland when he heard 'startlingly loud' music from Baker's window: 'Half a dozen kids stood there gaping. It sounded like nine or ten people inside playing different instruments. I couldn't believe it when the three of them came out and said, "We're it."'

That left the question of management. Both Rik Gunnell of the Bluesbreakers and Giorgio Gomelsky were mooted. Bruce and more volubly Baker proposed Robert Stigwood, previously involved with Graham Bond. Stigwood, a thirty-year-old Australian exotic more naturally at home in theatrical than rock music promotion, signed each of the three to personal contracts. At the line marked 'title of artiste' Clapton, in Bruce's words, 'came right out and said it . . . "We're the Cream – that's the name of the band."'

Reflecting on this period of his life in 1988 Clapton admitted: 'I was only turning twenty-one . . . You have this dichotomy of a guy who was a serious blues musician and was also a very wild young man. There was this adolescent side of me that wanted to get out and see the world . . . I was feeding on a lot of other directions, and I started to look on the whole Mayall thing as a dead-end street.' In a second interview he informed Steve Turner of *Rolling Stone*, 'I wanted to be a star.'

Cream's ambitions were, at least at first, more modestly stated: according to Pete Brown, the original plan was for 'Eric to play straight Chicago blues with a rhythm section'. There was talk of restricting the group's appearances to small clubs. Both Bruce and Baker had leanings towards jazz-rock with, in the former's words, 'a touch of exoticism thrown in'. In cold terms, Cream had certain Dadaist–surrealist pretensions. Clapton's fondness for primates – on which he seems to have had a fixation – was eventually expressed by the presence of a mangy, notably unhygienic stuffed gorilla onstage.

Incredibly, none of this was communicated to Mayall, who opened *Melody Maker* on 11 June 1966 to the following:

ERIC, JACK AND GINGER TEAM UP

A sensational new 'Group's Group' starring Eric Clapton, Jack Bruce and Ginger Baker is being formed.

Top groups will be losing star instrumentalists as a result. Manfred Mann will lose bassist, harmonica player, pianist and singer Jack Bruce; John Mayall will lose brilliant blues guitarist Eric Clapton; and Graham Bond's Organization will lose incredible drummer Ginger Baker.

According to Flint, 'when John read that he went ballistic . . . Eric was summoned and told, in words of one syllable, what he could do with Cream. He may have been going anyway, but Mayall still fired him.'

While Clapton returned to Ripley the Bluesbreakers hired Peter Green, a guitarist previously involved with Peter Bardens and Rod Stewart. Green and McVie left the group in 1967 to form Fleetwood Mac. Flint also quit and, again proving the circular nature of all music, joined Clapton's ex-colleague Tom McGuinness in a country-rock duo briefly famous in the early seventies. Later still the two were joined by the putative Cream vocalist Paul Jones in the Blues Band. Today Flint works as a porter in an Oxford college, happy, he says, 'to carry the bags and sign the occasional album'. He last saw Clapton in February 1986, when the guitarist was 'friendly in a noncommittal sort of way . . . I got the impression he's uncomfortable with anyone who reminds him of the past.'

Mayall himself is more blunt: 'There was always a chameleon thing with Eric, a sense of impermanence. When he joined the band we were very, *very* close on a social level. A year later he walked out.' The unpleasantly tense ending of the relationship was exacerbated by the ferocious argument that ensued about money. A member of the Bluesbreakers and a journalist close to the group both remember retrospective demands made by Clapton on the basis of the *Blues Breakers* album's success. Years later Mayall and his guitarist were reconciled, though not before, in Flint's words, 'Eric showed his ruthless streak by leaving us flat. As far as he was concerned, we were just a career move.'

4

Slouching Towards Bethlehem

The joke requiring an Englishman, an Irishman and a Scotsman, designed to convey those national types, might have been expressly intended for Cream. On bass Jack Bruce, whose tangled, uncut hair emphasized the look his face sometimes wore of belonging to a fractious, unruly child, an articulate yet withdrawn soul with a tendency to brood; Baker, the very embodiment of Gaelic excess, a registered heroin addict and alcoholic whose technical ability promoted him from mere timekeeper to featured musician; and Clapton, a man assuming, by his own admission, the role of 'the sane Englishman with his guitar'. The internal dynamics of the group were arguably what gave it its quality. Unarguably, they also meant that Cream was, at best, a short-term proposition.

The greatest of the group's strengths, and not the least of its weaknesses, lay in its diversity of interest. Bruce, whose career to then was probably the most eclectic of the trio, had roots in modern jazz, free jazz, R&B, blues and pop. Speaking of the group's origins a year later he denied Cream were purists, adding 'it was me who [wanted] us to be commercial, because I had been with a commercial group'. He none the less – both then and later – was the most professionally intense of the three, constantly writing, rehearsing, eschewing the lifestyle of the others, investing the music with a seriousness previously associated with Clapton himself.

Baker (serious when it came to his own self-promotion) almost defined the part of the modern back-line rock star: wild, exuberant, given to violent swings between delirium and despair, the inevitable target of which was Bruce. Baker's own tastes included jazz, ancient and modern, blues and rock; as early as 1963 he developed an innovative, fluid drum style, subsequently much imitated, based less on military precision than on danceable, R&B-type rhythms. Among the many musicians in Baker's debt were Keith Moon, John Hiseman and Mitch Mitchell. According to Pete Brown, 'As a drummer, no one could touch Ginger ... as a human being, not that many tried to. It was an incredible scene between him and Jack, though all three of them were over-sensitive. There was a minimum of one feud at any given time.'

Rehearsals, meanwhile, continued in June 1966 in Baker's home and at a nearby Scout hall in Willesden. Slowly, over the course of a month, the group developed a basic repertoire of 'Crossroads', 'Spoonful', 'I'm So Glad', 'I Feel Free', 'Traintime' and 'Toad', the last two of which featured Bruce and Baker respectively. Clapton's role was more muted. He stood on the bare-boarded stage with his Les Paul, the crackling monitor and single anaemic amplifier giving no hint of the sonic assault to come. One of the three spectators at Willesden was Ben Palmer. 'Having read the announcement in *Melody Maker*, I rang Eric and said something like, "Let me know if you ever need a driver." Next thing I was being introduced to Stigwood, who appointed me road manager. It was like that in the early days ... Cream was just a shambles to start with – no money, no material and not a clue as to who they were', a confusion, Palmer believes, extending to the group personally as well as creatively. 'The other two were up and down like yo-yos, while Eric just stood there, fag in mouth, mumbling. He was still on his Dadaism kick and wanted to play in a transparent top hat with a frog in it. *Eric Clapton*. They actually did appear with a stuffed ape for a couple of gigs.'

Robert Stigwood, meanwhile, contemplating his own significant investment in Cream, turned to Chris Welch of *Melody Maker*, also present at Willesden, and asked in a quavering voice if the group were 'any good'.

'They will be.'

Cream's first public outing was at the Twisted Wheel, Manchester, on 29 July 1966. Stigwood, at Clapton's repeated insistence, had obtained a second-hand black Austin Princess, in the rear of which the group sat listening to the Rolling Stones' *Aftermath* on a portable record player. At the stage door Palmer, seeking refreshment after the long drive, was stopped by a familiar voice.

'Would you mind setting the gear up?'

'Gear?'

'The amps and such like. Prepare the stage. It shouldn't take long.'

'How long?'

'Say twenty minutes.'

Two back-bending hours later Palmer was unloading the last of the

100-watt speakers when Clapton returned, grunted, nodded to Bruce and Baker, and walked on. To lukewarm applause the group played their six-song set – then began it again. The trend was repeated the next night at the jazz and blues festival in Windsor. The audience was enthusiastic but not exuberant. Certain numbers, 'Toad' included, were accepted rather than seized on. Expanded to twice its normal length, 'Traintime' lost much of the tension of the original; 'abject self-indulgence' one critic called it, though even he may have confused prolix repetition with a need to fill the required sixty minutes. As Clapton later admitted, 'We found that we ran out of numbers so quickly that we had to improvise. So we just made up twelve-bar blues and that became Cream. That became what we were known for. I liked it up to a point, but it wasn't what I wanted.' Palmer, present backstage, confirms that 'the freewheeling, jazzy thing was actually foisted on them. There was a point where they ran out of material and had to improvise. Simple as that.' Cream left the stage after Baker's fifteen-minute drum odyssey, unsmiling but, as Stigwood says, £400 richer.

What the 10,000 crowd enduring the rain at Windsor were witnessing was the birth of a hybrid described as 'jazz-rock', 'blues-pop' and by Stigwood himself as 'commercial jazz'. Like the Yardbirds before them, Cream championed the use of volume, came to reinvent if not define British rock and, in common with the Beatles and Stones, advanced the idea of the album over the single. Their fundamentally simple, riff-based song structures allowed for extensive improvisation; at any moment one or more of the trio would be called on to embellish the basic tune. Added to genuine technical ability, a shrewd sense of stage presentation and lighting, an awareness of psychedelia and Stigwood's rabid promotion, and Cream should have been the overnight success their manager so craved. Instead for nine months they did nothing.

Part of the reason lay in the continuing confusion surrounding the group's intentions. Throughout the summer and autumn of 1966 they played a mix of theatres, lounges and outdoor festivals, Stigwood's stated preference for 'major gigs' countered by Clapton's for intimate clubs. Palmer is adamant that Cream's early career was, at best, capricious. The three members and himself nightly ploughed the Great North Road, the Princess's rolling gait (greatly aggravated when Baker tinkered with the steering) somehow giving the impression of a ship listing in heavy seas. In London Cream played to a record number at the Marquee; in Liverpool, Sutton and Stockport to merely half-full halls, where cat-whistles could be heard in the intervals between songs. The group's relative lack of impact took shape in different ways: at an early concert in Leeds Clapton was refused entry at the stage door on the basis of the commissionaire 'not knowing who you are'; at a second appearance in London he was prominently billed as Jeff Beck; while, when Mike Vernon arrived to record the Bluesbreakers' second LP later that year, he was 'staggered' to hear that Clapton had ever left. A journalist who travelled with Cream in September and October says that it was 'an incredibly loose arrangement, always one step from disaster. Within the group it was invariably two against one: Eric and Ginger versus Jack, Bruce and Clapton against Baker. When I asked Eric about it he said, "I like to surprise people. It keeps them getting dependent on me."'

This sense of impermanence, of confusion in the internal dynamics of Cream, extended to the group's material. Between appearances in Brighton and Portsmouth the trio arrived at Chalk Farm Studio to record their debut single. At some stage that night the phone rang in Pete Brown's London flat. It was Bruce, 'announcing he'd written this pseudo-Bay-Area blues, and could I come up with some words?' The result was 'Wrapping Paper', a record Brown describes as 'appallingly produced' and Clapton as the last hangover of the group's 'totally dada, weird' persona. Released on 7 October, the song reached number 34 in the chart. A fan hearing the group for the first time would have discerned semi-psychedelic intent along the lines of the Jefferson Airplane or Lovin' Spoonful.

Sessions were also arranged to produce a debut album. *Fresh Cream*, released in December, perfectly illustrated the divergent tastes the group represented: routinely played rock vying with, at Clapton's insistence, radically restructured blues standards. The primal energy of *Blues Breakers* was replaced by a richer guitar sound, solo-free and heavy with improvisation, underscored by thunderous rhythm. Clapton's use of feedback on 'Sweet Wine' preceded both Lennon and Jimi Hendrix, variously credited with perfecting the technique. There was an accompanying version of 'Traintime' (the group as a whole, and Clapton in particular, says Brown, had a fixation on roads and railways: 'there was a sense of the drifter, the vagabond and the gypsy') for which Clapton insisted the ailing composer Skip James receive a royalty.

Fresh Cream reached the upper half of both the British and American charts without threatening to set either market alight. The album suffered from Pete Brown's absence (undergoing withdrawal from drugs and alcohol); Stigwood's at best limited abilities as producer; and the constant struggle between Bruce and Baker to include their own material. ('Ginger would argue it was a co-operative and we'd have to do two or three of his songs, as a kind of obligation,' Clapton told Ray Coleman. 'We did them, but it was no way to keep a healthy atmosphere.') Cream's second single, meanwhile, 'I Feel Free', gave them their first Top Twenty hit and a chance to perform on *Top of the Pops*, dressed ludicrously as convicts.

In late 1966 Clapton met and befriended a model named Charlotte Martin. Within a month they were living together in a loft in the Pheasantry, Chelsea, rapidly assuming the characteristics of a commune. Also present in the three bare-floored rooms, furnished with Moroccan tapestries and drapes, were Pete Brown, the illustrator Martin Sharp, a journalist (later caricatured in *The Bonfire of the Vanities*), Anthony Haden-Guest, and Germaine Greer. As he had in Covent Garden, Clapton created a light and free-form atmosphere in which, none the less, his status as head of the household was constantly asserted. After strumming the chords of 'Spoonful' or 'Four Until Late', pausing to avail himself of a bottle of wine, Clapton would arrive in the kitchen to demand that Martin cook him dinner or iron a shirt. 'It was all agreeably laid-back,' says Haden-Guest, 'until such time as Eric wanted something. Then hell broke loose.' Brown also describes Clapton as 'something of a shit' to women. 'He'd wander around with a hazy smile, drinking and playing Indian music on a tape-recorder ... There were a lot of Australian hangers-on, whose presence Eric usually tolerated. Once a week, he'd throw everyone out and start yelling at Charlotte, berating her for not looking after the place. He treated females badly.' (Greer's comment is not recorded.)

Provided with both time and opportunity to do so, Clapton indulged his love of change, of dissembling, of physical disguise. Already in 1966, his hair permed into a Hendrix bouffant, he sported a collection of fashion rings, bracelets, breathtakingly taut trousers and shirts, beneath which medallions gleamed and clanked, whose sail-like collars extended earthwards to his nipples. He experimented with incense and joss-sticks. He even had his Gibson Les Paul/SG (a small-bodied cutaway model bought that January) painted in psychedelic colours by two Dutch designers, Simon and Marijke, protégés of the Beatles. Backstage at *Saturday Club*, when Clapton was invited by a journalist for a drink, he replied, verbatim, 'Booze is out, man', a notable reversal for one previously fond of pints of bitter and cheap Algerian red. (Clapton's abstinence, if such it was,

was short-lived: on the plane to America six weeks later, the same journalist saw him 'put at least five points on Remy Martin stock single-handed'.)

In this and other ways Clapton was unusually influenced by a twenty-three-year-old, veteran of Little Richard, the Isley Brothers and Wilson Pickett, arrived in London the previous September. Within a week Jimi Hendrix had made fans of Lennon, McCartney and Jeff Beck; even Jagger was 'completely awestruck'. On 30 September Hendrix's manager met Bruce and Baker, who invited the guitarist to Cream's performance the following night at London Polytechnic. On cue Clapton announced 'the cat from Seattle', the lights flared and Hendrix, to polite applause, walked on. 'I'll never forget Eric's face,' says Chas Chandler. 'He just went off to the side and stood and watched.' John Platt (later biographer of the Yardbirds) was also present: 'Hendrix played a version of "Killing Floor" while Clapton just stood there. It was like, "How the hell did he do *that*?" At the curtain-call he had his arm around Jimi's shoulder while Bruce and Baker skulked at the back.'

Everything changed for Clapton from that moment. Obviously a talented instrumentalist with a flair for adapting the blues, his career to then had been one of affectionate imitation, informed by equal amounts of seriousness and wit, with little or no effort to reinvent the guitar beyond its original scope. Hendrix, with his use of fuzz boxes and wah-wah, his knowledge of distortion, harmonics and sustain, was new, ingenious, original. He combined the lyrical approach of Clapton's playing with the more aggressive edge of Pete Townshend. Hendrix was the subject under discussion when Clapton met Townshend at the theatre that November. Both agreed that 'the cat from Seattle' was in danger of merging their own separate techniques into one integral whole, including elements – rock, pop, blues, soul, jazz – previously thought distinct. The truth is that, in Clapton's case, all he had perpetrated to date had been entirely if cleverly derivative. There was no 'unknown quality' such as abounded in Hendrix and the original bluesmen. Clapton played guitar in the way Nabokov or Conrad wrote English. There was a sense of enthusiasm, even of love for the adopted language, but always with the hint of a foreign accent. Hendrix, with his more intuitive grasp of dynamics, of structure, of interlocking rhythm and lead (of the cultural roots of the blues) was gloriously unbound by the need for 'purity' of expression. That was the irony: while Clapton and the other white converts insisted on the seriousness of the genre, its archetypes joked, preened or, in Hendrix's case, set fire to their guitars on stage.

As a result, Clapton's perspective began to alter. After seeing Hendrix at the Bag O'Nails on 11 January 1967 (also present were Townshend, Lennon, McCartney, Jagger and sundry Hollies, Small Faces and Animals), Clapton began a long, animated monologue on the possibilities of expanding his own repertoire. As he later put it in *Rolling Stone*: 'It opened [me] up a lot because I was still at that time pretty uptight by the fact that we weren't playing 100 per cent blues numbers, and to see Jimi play that way I just thought, Wow! – that's all right with me . . . It just opened my mind up to listening to a lot of other things and playing a lot of other things.' Hendrix's influence was also at work in the way Clapton presented himself in public: gone was the shy, almost morbidly withdrawn ascetic, replaced by a man whose topaz rings and clanking necklace ensured that, in Pete Brown's words, 'had he drowned, we would have sent in salvage experts to raise him'. He developed his stage act to incorporate at least a parody of Hendrix's exhibitionism. He experimented with feedback and distortion. That winter he learnt what a thousand guitarists would learn later: how incredibly forgiving is the average rock audience. It needs only to hear the vaguest facsimile of a hit record, suitably dramatized. At a group meeting on 13 January all three members of Cream agreed that, from henceforth, style – lights, volume, garishly hued guitars and uniforms – would be equally important as substance. 'That's when the pop thing began,' says Brown. 'After that second meeting with Hendrix. Next time I saw Clapton he was wearing three bracelets and a kimono.'

The Black v. White, America versus Britain debate now raged in earnest. CLAPTON YEARS AHEAD OF HENDRIX, ran a typical headline in *Melody Maker*: others ranged from WILD THING to SEATTLE CAT LICKS THE CREAM and ERIC: IT'S ALL OVER NOW. The comparison, fastened on by the press, completely missed the point. Other than both playing electric guitar, the two had virtually nothing in common. Clapton, a cosseted boy, turned to the blues from a sense of romantic association; Hendrix was genuinely deprived. Hendrix, because of his early experience in soul, attached greater importance to rhythm than Clapton, who saw the guitar as a virtuoso solo instrument. Clapton wanted to perpetrate the myth of 'one man versus the world'. Hendrix, by his own cheerful admission, wanted 'money, chicks – and lots of them'.

There was another, more oblique contrast. At unguarded moments throughout the 1970s (after his return to public and before his present incarnation of amiable vulnerability) Clapton evoked a roll-call of right-wing prejudices. Women, trades unions and socialists were all commented on disparagingly. From a concert stage in Birmingham he delivered a long and (he later explained) drunken harangue on social harmony, at one point asking: 'Do we have any foreigners in the audience tonight? If so, please put up your hands ... I think we should vote for Enoch Powell.' In later defending the remark, and in repeated comments in private, Clapton attracted the inevitable charge of racism. While opinion varied – 'The least prejudiced person in Britain,' says Ben Palmer; 'His [1976] speech grew of pure, unalloyed evil,' according to the writer C. L. R. James – so Clapton's own attitude fluctuated wildly. If it was true he liked to giggle and make 'coon' jokes in private he may have been doing no more than following the British post-war tradition with which he grew up. (The first West Indian couple to settle in Ripley in 1953 were subject to silent looks and at least one case of verbal harassment.) If, as he pointed out, most of the people Clapton admired were black, most of those he vilified were black too. In terms of political correctness, he lived dangerously. His very respect for Hendrix, his subsequent apeing of the American's technique – at once both more sensual and refined than his own – was tinged with emotions more primal than mere curiosity. 'Everybody and his brother think that spades have big dicks,' Clapton explained in 1968. 'And Jimi came over and exploited that to the limit, the fucking tee. Everybody fell for it. I fell for it.'

The same sense of ambiguity, of simultaneously being attracted and repelled by black culture, was the hallmark of Clapton's playing. Much of his soloing, seized on by adoring fans oblivious of the originals, was merely a fusion of B. B. and Freddie King. Clapton was, on the other hand, the only white musician ever to emulate the Kings' flowing phrases. Early in 1967 he had developed a distinctive sustain technique (itself an adaption of B. B. King's 'ringing bell') designated by Clapton his 'woman tone'. Achieved by removing the treble from the guitar's controls – another device initiated by Hendrix – it was first heard in the intense yet sparing solo on 'I Feel Free'. Clapton's use of the Les Paul SG, with its natural blues properties, further developed this rich, bass-heavy sound, a preference for light, flexible strings encouraging his rapacity to solo. Gifted with a natural fluidity and lightness of touch, even this part of Clapton's repertoire was imitative:

What I like about my playing [he said in 1985] are still the parts that I copied. If I'm building a solo I'll start with a line that I know is definitely a Freddie King line and then, though I'm not saying this happens consciously, I'll go on to a B. B. King line. I'll do something to join them up, so that part will be me.

Finally, given that much of Cream's material consisted of relatively simple structures, relying on distinctive or aggressive execution, Clapton was forced, as much as chose, to adapt his technique. In any song lasting, as theirs did, twenty or thirty minutes, there was obvious scope for individual embellishment. As Jack Bruce says: 'It was a case of the three of us pushing each other, without which not all of the songs would have stood up.' In Cream, as at other times in his career, there was a sense that Clapton made virtuosity out of necessity.

If Bruce and Baker were at this stage fully committed to the group, Clapton already had doubts. Given the absence of interviews this seems a subjective opinion, but then it is silence that counts. After Cream's Windsor debut, Chris Welch was approached by Stigwood at a party at the latter's house: 'Jack and Ginger were very happy, but sitting on the floor in the corner was Eric looking glum and miserable, and Stigwood said, "Could you go over and speak to him? Find out what's wrong." It turned out through a very mumbled conversation that he wasn't happy with what Cream were doing right from the start.' Stigwood himself remembers 'a lot of discussion' at the time of the group's launch. Pete Brown is blunter: 'Eric would have been genuinely happy playing sitar' (an instrument he listened to constantly at the Pheasantry) 'in front of six people in a club. He was scared shitless of fame, mainly because it exposed him to the critics. Eric was always thin-skinned. On the other hand, he loved the goodies that Cream brought. The need for success vying with contempt for those who bestow it – the classic English radical's dilemma.'

In the event, since his colleagues saw only an emotional recluse with a matching tendency to egoism, Clapton was treated by Bruce and Baker (and musicians are good at this) as one of *them*. 'Them' conveyed a sense of being fickle, cold, changeable, dour and different. While they fought over songwriting or volume settings on stage, Clapton brooded and read the *Beano*. At other times the drummer or bassist opened the dressing room door to receive an upturned pail of water. Clapton also led the most involved domestic life of the three. When Charlotte Martin briefly transferred her affections to another musician it seemed to be of a piece with an exotically turbulent existence. Clapton responded by moving a blonde model into the Pheasantry. There were nights, Haden-Guest confirms, 'of light-to-middling excess'. John Dunbar, husband of Marianne Faithfull, even swears that 'Eric was caught in bed with Mick [Jagger].' There was also a young Spanish waiter, now remembered only as Raoul, in whose company he was sometimes seen. According to Ben Palmer's wife Jo, 'He wasn't very good at treating women as adults,' preferring 'the fat-bottomed girls who follow bands about'. The woman Clapton married also noted him as a chauvinist.

A snapshot of Clapton as Cream was formed appeared in *Melody Maker* on 15 October 1966:

Eric Clapton – guitarist extraordinaire – came to the door in his ballooning white bell-bottom trousers and a striking purple-looking shirt, with one of his vast collection of military jackets hanging on his shoulders.
'Hello, man,' came the greeting . . .

Having fallen in and out of love with America ('I don't want to go other than just to see the place and find out what's happening') without yet setting foot there, Clapton discoursed gloomily on Cream's prospects in Britain:

I don't believe we'll get over to [the public]. People will always listen with biased ears, look through unbelieving eyes, and with preconceived ideas, remembering what we used to be, and so on. The only way to combat this is to present them with as many facets of your music as possible.

Clapton did so. Cream's next single, 'Strange Brew', a weird amalgam of the old (Albert King's 'Crosscut Saw' and 'Lawdy Mama') and new (Hendrix), welded traditional blues guitar with revolutionary sound effects. This was the year Clapton discovered wah-wah – the use of a foot-pedal to create the onomatopaeic sound. Added to vaguely exotic lyrics, recorded at nerve-jarring volume, 'Brew' and its B-side, 'Tales Of Brave Ulysses', established for ever Cream's status as purveyors of superior if simplistic blues-rock, elaborately played, pretentiously wrapped, with lyrical ambiguity sufficient to allow the listener to identify with the message.

Clapton's habitual asceticism did nothing to prevent him enjoying the fruits of Cream's success. Early that year the Robert Stigwood Organization* took offices at 85 New Cavendish Street, Marylebone, where, in Pete Brown's words, 'a kind of court developed with Robert screaming on three phones, sending writs, and simultaneously interviewing a new chauffeur'. He formed his own record company, Reaction, a four-act label distributed through Polydor. (Reaction also issued material by Hendrix, the Who and the Bee Gees.) Stigwood, not indifferent to his own interests, was fiercely defensive of his charges. Cream received among the highest booking-fees of any British act, not excluding the Beatles and Stones. Initially available for £400 a night, their rate had tripled within six months. Stigwood also negotiated tirelessly with Polydor. The result was that, by spring 1967, Cream enjoyed at least the illusion of being rich. Clapton had only to sign for something in one of the numerous bistros or boutiques whose name was enhanced by his patronage to possess it. Food, drink and more exotic substances were delivered to the Pheasantry gratis. A new guitar became an impulse item. On 20 October 1967, Stigwood incorporated Marshbrook Limited on his client's behalf. Initially a deposit for performance fees and royalties (its stated object 'to carry on the business of producers, licensers, licensees, performers, agents, consultants, distributors, contractors, publishers and dealers in radio and television shows, cinematographic film, plays, dramas, operas, pantomimes, revues, concerts, song, sketches and entertainments and productions of all kinds'), ninety-eight of the original hundred shares were issued to Clapton. In 1974 he became Marshbrook company secretary. Throughout Cream, and thereafter, the device allowed Clapton to draw a salary while (wholly legitimately) protecting him from the then pernicious rates of British income tax. 'Robert', says Pete Brown, 'was *very* protective towards Eric financially. He did everything on his behalf. Lots of creative accounting.'

In February 1967 Murray 'the K' Kauffman, the disc jockey who introduced the Beatles and Rolling Stones to America, sat in an upstairs office

---

* There was also an administrative office at 67 Brook Street, Mayfair. For appearances and recordings outside Britain, Cream were signed to Stigwood's Constellation Overseas Limited.

at Radio WINS in New York. A fractious, excitable figure, all seersucker suit and straw hat, he finalized the roster for his annual Easter Show at the RKO Theatre: Simon and Garfunkel, Wilson Pickett, Smokey Robinson, Mitch Ryder and the Who. The last, included expressly at Ryder's request, themselves came with a proviso. Stigwood, in charge of bookings for both groups, insisted Cream join the Who for a combined fee of $7500, divided 70:30 in the latter's favour. The deal, effective from 23 February, required Cream to perform five times a day for ten days, frequently attended by the midgets, jugglers and freaks comprising the non-musical element of the bill. When this was reported to Clapton he was, according to Brown, 'overwhelmed', after a lifetime's speculation on the country, at finally playing in America. He had his hair specially permed and for a month adopted a form of Southern black mammy accent.

Cream arrived in New York on 22 March 1967, whereupon they transferred to the Drake Hotel on E. 56th Street. Children let loose in a toy store, they ordered copious quantities of room service and smashed the television in Clapton's room. They visited the Peppermint Lounge and the Apollo. They ran down hotel corridors and hid in laundry hampers, like members of the Monkees. On the 24th they gave a dress-rehearsal at the theatre, after which Ryder's manager, Frank Barsalona, was approached by Kauffman:

'What about this piece of shit you've stuck me with?'

'You mean Mitch? You wanted Mitch, you begged for Mitch.'

'Not Mitch. That other crap group.'

'What are you talking about?'

'You know what I mean,' snapped Kauffman. 'That piece of shit, the Cream.'

Despite this deeply unpromising beginning, Cream duly performed 'I'm So Glad' and 'I Feel Free' the stipulated fifty times, swaying, inebriate, rooted on a threadbare green rug the colour of baize or packing material. 'It was a freak show,' says Palmer, 'twelve-year-old kids in the morning, no one in the afternoon, stoned hippies at night.' From the wings Kauffman screamed 'Move! Move!' – expecting, as Clapton said, 'a James Brown thing' – as Cream went through their impassive act. There was a dispute about money. Clapton introduced an impersonation of the bewigged, wise-cracking Kauffman into the routine. He also reverted to his lifelong love of pranks, of adolescent humour, turning the dressing-room into a war zone. Eggs and flour were thrown, the shower overflowed. There was talk of exploding smoke grenades on stage until Wilson Pickett, a man previously admired by Cream, deemed this 'unprofessional'. Clapton compromised by igniting a cherry-bomb instead.

The week's real significance took place offstage in Greenwich Village. Clapton, in early morning forays to the Café Au Go-Go or Gerde's, met Al Kooper and Frank Zappa; he was greeted warmly by Dylan and without archness by Warhol. He felt, like many an Englishman in America before him, appreciated, accepted and admired on new terms – those of his own ability. Freakish on *Beat Club* or *Ready Steady Go!*, in New York Clapton merely seemed weird. 'I'd love to live here,' he announced in general. 'Everybody is so much more hip . . . My taxi driver talked to me about James Brown. Can you imagine that happening in London?'

Clapton's sense of belonging, of acceptance, was not entirely musical. In New York he was the beneficiary of a phenomenon, kick-started by the Beatles, designed to service the needs of idle, insensate and preferably English pop stars: the groupie. At the Drake Hotel girls were relayed to his room in shifts. A Brooklyn teenager named Elaine Akalovsky was standing on the corner of 58th Street and Third Avenue, adjacent to the theatre, when Clapton 'shimmied up, smiling and asking at the stage door if he might be let in'. A conversation began, as a result of which 'Eric let me know, in an oblique, British way that he was free that night at the hotel. When I showed up he looked confused what I was doing there. This is 2 a.m. and I'm wearing a white Henri Bendel number with no panties . . . Eventually he caught on.' Clapton himself later described the 'social scene' in New York as 'red hot . . . There were both ends – horrible spotty scrubbers and really nice-looking middle-class chicks', an encounter with one of whom required hurried remedial treatment at a clinic.

Then there were the drugs. The final day of Kauffman's Easter Show happened to be the day of the first Human Be-In in Central Park. The coincidence was exquisite: two musical icons of the sixties completing their debut in New York at the very moment that city symbolically launched the Summer of Love. Distantly related to the cultural revolution occurring in London, the Baby Boomer explosion took as its premise the avoidance of all dull, boring, mundane reality, for which opposition to Vietnam and experimentation with drugs were virtual specifics. In an apartment located in Sheridan Square Clapton obtained, in a spectator's words, 'a ton of grass, amyl nitrate and LSD, all of which were pushed as a pure, organic alternative to the martini-and-cigar world of straights'.

He spent the Easter weekend peacefully comatose in sundry clubs, taverns and bars, and, with Bruce's physical support, his room at the hotel.

Such was the background to arguably the outstanding record Clapton had made or has made to this day.

'The odd thing,' says Bruce, 'is that it wasn't planned. There were four days before the visas ran out. Ahmet [Ertegün, president of Atlantic Records] appeared at the hotel and offered use of the studio. It was a case of two takes and goodnight. Some musicians work best under pressure.'

Obviously Clapton himself belonged to this category. Ertegün was immediately drawn to him because of his fame. A member of Cream's road crew remembers 'Eric being singled out for special treatment, mainly because of the *Blues Breakers* album. He loved it. Jack and particularly Ginger just sat there glowering.' (Another essential for success: creative tension.) Ertegün in turn introduced Tom Dowd and Felix Pappalardi, respectively engineer and producer, both of whom advanced the finished product. As Ben Palmer says, 'For all their musicianship, Cream had a lot of outside help. A *lot*. Felix, Tom and Pete Brown really shaped that album. You could put their names on the cover.'

Disraeli Gears, released the following November, typified the mood of the year no less than had *Sergeant Pepper*. If the Beatles were about melody and harmony, Cream were their opposite. There was nothing specially melodic about Bruce, twisted notepaper in hand, spitting out Brown's lyrics in his queasy vibrato; about Baker pouring fluid on the studio console to register protest; about Clapton's increasingly distracted and drug-affected behaviour. Here were three musicians who, far from plying their trade for pleasure, did so in order not to jump out of the nearest window.

The album opened with 'Strange Brew'; then 'Sunshine Of Your Love', the song largely responsible for establishing the bottom-heavy guitar figure, or riff, as the staple of heavy rock. 'Sunshine' began life in Bruce's home in Bracknell Gardens, Hampstead, where, in Brown's memory, 'Around six in the morning and mightily pissed off, Jack grabbed his double-bass and played the famous riff. The line "It's getting near dawn" wasn't hard to come to. Eric played with it and added a chorus and the title, both of which I hated. It made it sound like a Jack Jones number.'

'Eric is fortunate,' Bruce later admitted. 'He's blessed with a realization, a vision, of what's going to be commercially acceptable . . . That's a very special touch, which I don't have. When I write songs, even "Sunshine

Of Your Love", it never crosses my mind to relate it to commercial possibilities.' In a discussion for this book he added, 'The notes for that song weren't arrived at. They just came.'

Bruce was being disingenuous. 'Sunshine's' distinctive, two-bar motif was, in Clapton's own words, 'Strictly a dedication to Jimi', who, as his reputation gained in strength, made his own ironic comment on the song by performing it on stage. Released as a single in September 1968 it was Cream's first simultaneous hit in Britain and America, contributing to the purchase cost of Clapton's country home, paying Brown's rent for life and even providing the letterhead for Bruce's stationery. Twenty-seven years after they recorded it, the PRS residual flow from 'Sunshine' is still strong. At a conservative estimate each of the song's composers have earned £200,000 in royalties.

The album's other outstanding moment was 'Tales Of Brave Ulysses', co-written by Clapton and his roommate Martin Sharp, dimly celebrating the Glands' forgotten tour of Greece. The wah-wah pedal – a rare foray into the realms of technical sophistry – was demonstrated to Clapton in Manny's, the New York guitar dealer, and used in the studio that same day. Other tracks ranged from 'SWLABR' ('She Was Like A Bearded Rainbow' – one of those moments Brown 'had fallen out of love and was scrawling moustaches on the girl's face'); 'Take It Back' ('What it says'); and 'Dance The Night Away' ('I actually did that. Good therapy'). Cream revived their *Goon Show*, pie-in-the-face persona with 'Mother's Lament', an eccentric bar-room dirge apparently included in error.

Disraeli Gears improved dramatically on the standards of *Fresh Cream*, recorded only six months before. The 'big change', in Clapton's view, was the arrival of Hendrix, the ushering in of psychedelia (actually prefixed by the Kinks' 'You Really Got Me' as early as 1964) and the concomitant use of drugs: 'We did a lot of acid, took a lot of trips . . . We did play on acid a couple of times.' The album's own legacy was the amplified, guitar-and-bass fusion – heavy metal – embodied by groups such as Led Zeppelin and Deep Purple, extended by Black Sabbath and Vanilla Fudge, and later by horrors like Motorhead and Iron Maiden. The record's Day-glo cover, designed by Sharp (during the shoot for which Clapton recalls sampling LSD for the first time), and stream-of-consciousness title (a play on derailleur gears) conceived a lasting fascination for those seeking to invest rock with a 'meaning' previously denied it. While it was true that Clapton pioneered the recording of heavily amplified, distorted electric guitar, and the album's lyrics tended to gnomic, drug-induced allusions, the record's best moments were distinguished not by unbridled rock and roll excess but by their pop-symphonic discipline and the carefully controlled ingenuity of the arrangements. Whether as an aural documentary of the times or a slab of superior blues-rock still enjoyable today, *Disraeli Gears* was a masterpiece.

Cream returned to London to give a dramatic, televised rendition of 'Strange Brew', the guitarist's clenched jaw and febrile expression suggesting a man grappling with toothache. (A distinct possibility: George Harrison later wrote the song 'Savoy Truffle' about his friend's dental problems.) Clapton spent the spring and early summer at the Pheasantry where, according to Haden-Guest, he more than once proposed to Charlotte Martin. 'The relationship between them got very tight,' confirms Brown. It was, however, insufficiently rigid to prevent Clapton bedding a blonde student named Delia Sims (who notes he 'tended to rush things sexually') at the Pembroke College Ball, Oxford, where Cream played on 27 May.

Clapton's fickle outlook on America was exacerbated by experience. The man who praised New York's 'red hot' groupies, its 'hip' taxi drivers, was back to his xenophobic self in *Melody Maker*: 'The middle-class American is such a slob – you wouldn't believe it. Life is so comfortable for them, with the car and TV, they don't want to worry and they don't even want to think. It's all very sick.' In private, both he and Bruce urged Stigwood to arrange a return to the country as soon as possible.

Clapton's attitude to the cultural revolution happening in society – to the Summer of Love whose onset he witnessed – was also ambivalent. In June he appeared with the Beatles in front of an estimated audience of 400 million, crooning 'All You Need Is Love' on the worldwide TV special *Our World*. He socialized with Bob Dylan, who gave him the lyrics to an unpublished song, 'Standing Around Shoeing A Horse' (which Clapton promptly lost). Unlike Dylan or the Beatles he remained notably quiet in advancing his views on society. Clapton's values were essentially the sound traditional values of Britain – humour, irony and a mild streak of libertarianism – with little or no effort to move the guardrails defining the limits of normal behaviour. His sympathies lay with Didion's 1967 essay *Slouching Towards Bethlehem*, in which 'adolescents drifted from city to city, children were never taught and would never learn the games that had held society together'. Even as Clapton was lined up, by association, with those seeking to burn prisons or spike the nation's water-supply, his private face remained set in self-protective apathy. 'No one's recruiting *me* to any causes,' he once told Baker. Pete Brown also had the impression of an 'essentially cautious, rather conservative' character. Even as Clapton trawled the bars of Greenwich Village or sat in his loft in Chelsea, he still spoke critically of the rootlessness and incipient violence, the paranoid rejection of authority, the contempt for family values and abandonment of self-restraint issuing on both sides of the Atlantic. There was a feeling among some in 1967 that society would atomize into non-existence and Clapton hastened to join such consensus. He may have enjoyed his new-found freedoms, his sense of being accepted and admired, but, however exotic the fringes of his life, it remained solid at the centre. Clapton, says Brown, was that 'strange phenomenon . . . the English radical who went home for tea with his grandparents'.

Now very British, Clapton boarded the return plane for California that August. Over a shirt of Oxford-blue silk he wore a football club scarf and a badge endorsing West Bromwich Albion. The driver who met him in Los Angeles found him to be '. . . a lot quieter than I'd thought. In 1967 I was just working out what life was about, and that's what I found in Clapton. He was talking to [Bruce] in that clipped, Cary Grant accent. Just a regular guy. I never met anyone less like a rock star in my life.'

In fact Clapton's arrival as a 'rock star' – if that implies global, not merely domestic status – came two nights later in San Francisco. Cream, just as they had the previous summer in Windsor, exhausted their reper-toire at the Fillmore West ahead of schedule. To Baker's frantic signal Clapton improvised a long, free-form solo, heavy on wah-wah and screeching feedback, so intense, protracted, feral, above all so loud, it physically shook a lighting bridge from its moorings. The ovation that greeted it was hardly less stirring. Next Cream played a reprise of 'Cross-roads'. This ended in a chaotic scene of delirium and applause – just as Clapton, the man who craved approval, would have wanted. Gradually, over the space of five nights, word about Cream spread. The group's arrival in San Francisco was well timed: for the generation entering col-lege, not to mention that city's native adolescent community, heavy rock became the aural equivalent, and frequent companion, of an hallucination. What Cream were providing was the musical counterpoint of a drug trip. Few of the home product, the Grateful Dead excepted, combined the same excessive volume, lighting, and lyrics – actually a potpourri of crypto-surrealist mumblings – required to convey the true spirit of psy-chedelia. When Clapton arrived in San Francisco he was amazed at the paucity of local talent. 'The [other groups] were struggling,' he later

85

informed a journalist. 'It didn't seem to me any of them had ever listened to any of the proper records ... We walked in there and cleaned up.' This re-importing of native music was, of course, the Hendrix experience in reverse.

In all this Cream were aided by a local promoter, former boxer, Korean War hero and taxi driver named Bill Graham. Graham had opened the Fillmore West, a disused skating-rink, in 1966. In a year he staged concerts by Jefferson Airplane, Grateful Dead, The Band, the Byrds, Dylan and B. B. King, before hosting Cream. In embracing both laissez-faire morals and extreme economic conservatism, Graham anticipated the yuppie, for whom 'Do your thing' tapered into his own motto, 'Just do it', by twenty years. He also surprised Clapton, if that word befits a reaction bordering on disbelief, by encouraging him to take two, five- and even fifteen-minute solos on stage, a policy born of genuine respect as well as of Graham's view that, 'As far as I was concerned, he could play all night ... I knew exactly what they wanted there and [the Fillmore] East. Noise. And I knew exactly what I was looking at with Cream. It was money.'

Gratified, in the midst of success, Clapton wrote a letter that night on Fillmore stationery. America, he now imagined, was 'where it's at' (at least his third reassessment in as many years, his attitude to the country remains ambivalent today). That Graham: quite a man. Cream, on the other hand, he believed had 'no lasting power ... The whole thing is an entertainment.' He hinted at 'creative tension' between Bruce and Baker.

It says much for Clapton's lugubrious view of life that, even at the moment of Cream's critical triumph, he was anticipating its decline. He remained strikingly cynical of the group's prospects. Heavily dependent on Pappalardi and Dowd on record, on stage the trio prospered not merely in the absence of domestic rivals, but from the voluntary seclusion of the Beatles and Rolling Stones, both of whom had given 'farewell' American concerts in 1966. Clapton knew that. He realized that Cream were, at best, a holding option, a bridge between the pop that preceded them and the rock that would follow. His letter from San Francisco is full of gloomy theorizing on the future. Recording was torturous, the tour schedule worse. Cream were 'already at each other's throats'. He predicted a career measured in months, not years.

Clapton's despondency was well founded. Cream *were* at each other's throats. In one backstage moment in San Francisco Bruce and Baker had to be physically separated. At the hotel there was an incident involving a fire extinguisher (Baker's discharge of which, says a witness, being 'the opposite of good-humoured. He was trying to ram the nozzle up Jack's ass'). Musically, too, the group suffered by comparison to their idols, one of whom performed on the same bill: whereas B. B. King's songs evolved, Cream's tended to announce their intentions and merely fulfil them. Interviewed by Russell Tyler in the Huntington Hotel, Clapton stated his 'longing' – his actual word – for solitude. He spoke disparagingly of touring, of the whole 'second-hand music scene; of the 'impossibility' of following an act like King on stage. Tyler came away impressed by how vulnerable, depressed and dispirited he was, a shy, unobtrusive character beneath a façade (sunglasses and fedora) designed to conceal it. If every adult contains his inner child, one age displayed a million ways, then Clapton's was rooted firmly in 1956, the eleven-year-old fleeing with his dog to the outside lavatory with the tin roof, hour after hour in the fetid dark while his mothers argued inside.

Cream eventually stayed two months in America. Whatever his misgivings about the group's direction, Clapton undoubtedly enjoyed the fruits this brought. There was a cheque from Stigwood; a gold watch from Graham. The trio obtained a fire-engine-red Chevrolet in which they toured Death Valley, brandishing guns in the back seat and firing aimlessly at cacti. (The car, purchased in Stigwood's name in Los Angeles, was written off – like the Princess before it – when Baker seized the wheel.) This sense of release, of the sheer possibilities of America, captivated Clapton. 'Like all of them,' says Brown, 'he had a fascination with travel. It was part of the blues tradition.' There was also, hovering below the surface, 'a manic sense of humour . . . Eric's idea of a good time was to improvise a Goons sketch while driving 90 m.p.h. across the desert in a convertible. If everything came together perfectly in Clapton's mind he was the best company in the world. If it missed, he was the worst.'

Both aspects of Clapton's character were revealed that summer and early autumn. Full of glorious improvisation one night, on another Cream were merely competing virtuosi. At the Village Theatre, New York, Clapton ('I thought, fuck that, you know') stopped playing in mid-song. He stood mute in the wings while the oblivious rhythm section completed the number. Early on he seems to have realized that Cream were admired as much for their promise as its fulfilment. 'It got to the point,' he told Steve Turner, 'where we were playing so badly and the audience were still going raving mad – they thought it was a gas. But I thought we're conning them, we're cheating them. We're taking their bread and playing them shit. I [couldn't] work on that basis.' Onstage in Boston Clapton gave a long rambling harangue against the group, only to be cheered wildly from the house.

He did, however, consent to enter Atlantic Studios with Bruce and Baker that September. At remarkable speed they recorded the raw material for the group's third album, *Wheels Of Fire* (this before *Disraeli Gears* had been released.) Again, says Brown, the contribution of Dowd and Pappalardi – in addition to producing, effectively taking the fourth musician's role offered to Winwood – was critical. Again, 'much as Eric led on stage, so Jack did in the studio ... There are musicians who, however brilliantly, interpret someone else's idea, then there are those who have the idea in the first place. Clapton was of the former, Bruce of the latter.'

On Cream's last night in America, after a drink with Pappalardi, Clapton left the studio alone. At one o'clock in the morning a bond dealer named Martin Forbes was walking up Eighth Avenue on his way to an apartment on West 71st Street. Sitting on a bench under the southern outcrop of Central Park was a man in a white shirt, coatless, smoking a cigarette, with a small briefcase or satchel in his lap. Forbes passed through a moment when he was tempted to ignore him. Something about the figure, dramatically backlit by a street-light, suggested a soul in distress. As the pedestrian passed by he saw the man was crying. Nothing about him indicated the presence of hysteria (as Forbes puts it, 'the usual sexual fall-out or drug trip'). This was a person assessing his own life and finding it wanting. This was Eric Clapton.

There comes a moment in most aliens' lives when it suddenly bears in on them that they have infiltrated the host culture. Clapton's came as he boarded the return flight to London. The scene at Kennedy Airport was riotous: security guards brawled with fans while Cream signed autographs in the mid-distance. A pony-tailed girl vaulted a barrier and ran at Clapton, removing his sunglasses and even clutching his necklace. In the space of eight weeks that summer he went from cult figure to international star, largely on the basis of his ability to translate native southern blues for a teenage audience: no small ability. After their success in San Francisco Cream took a perceptible turn for the comeatable, the compact. Songs were again returned to their original length. The release of 'Strange Brew' demonstrated their hopes of a breakthrough on FM radio. Stigwood was forever stressing the need for a more commercial approach.

In this he was supported by Clapton; somewhere between the Fillmore West and the recording of *Wheels Of Fire* he appears to have grasped the real possibility of becoming a pop star. For the first and to date only time in his career his stage act took a turn for the ornate. He experimented with the splits and the slide. He sang. He even danced. Whatever his private misgivings, his differences with Bruce and Baker, in public Clapton now leavened the intensity of his previous work with a new sense of exhibitionism. The character returning to England in October was unrecognizable from the one leaving it in August.

Such was the impression of a man waiting backstage at the Saville Theatre, London, later that autumn. Dick Heckstall-Smith, invited to the show by his ex-colleagues Bruce and Baker, was 'standing in the corridor outside the dressing-room when Jack came out with Eric. The change in both of them was stupendous. Clapton was wearing a silk kimono, beads, necklace and make-up. I put out my hand and he ignored me. Jack at least said hello.'

Preceded on stage by the Bonzo Dog Doo Dah Band (whose performance confirmed the wisdom of Cream's rejection of surrealism), the group played a seven-song set of which the highlight was Clapton's suspending his guitar on a chain from the ceiling to generate feedback. After this exertion he lay flat on his back for several moments with his eyes closed. By that stage, says Pete Brown, 'Eric was visualizing his life like a novel. He was the big rock star one minute, the moody poet the next. It kept people talking about him. He loved it.'

Also present at the Saville Theatre were George Harrison and his wife Pattie Boyd. At a party following the performance Boyd found Clapton 'terribly reticent . . . [He] didn't talk to anybody or socialize', behaviour she found intriguing: 'There was an aura around him which set him apart from the others. Definitely.'

Clapton extended his new, extrovert stage act in Britain and Europe that winter. The thrown guitars, the feedback, the pyrotechnics all suggested a man unusually influenced by Hendrix. Even in the intervals between songs Clapton seemed to relax flat out, engaging the audience in debate, pouring a drink or talking animatedly to Ben Palmer. Taken to task in a Scandinavian review for coming across 'like a version of Mick Jagger with a guitar', Clapton responded by playing an entire performance with his back to the crowd. The same article revealed the 'beautiful lie' of Cream as being the promotion of Clapton over the 'real artistic genius' of Bruce.

That was the group's glory. Cream balanced the tension between individual and collective talent without ever concealing the stress it caused. On any night a minimum of one member of the group was in dispute with the others. In part wrought by the sheer *ennui* of touring – the repetition, night after night, of identical sets, proving that even improvisation could be predictable – much also derived from personal animosity. The situation was particularly acute with Baker, an irascible character possessed of an Irish humour, always finding conditions in the real world to be incompatible with those in his head (among the latter being the notion of himself as the group's songwriter and creative leader). Bruce, a less docile figure than today, had similar misgivings. The most technically proficient of the trio, he moaned incessantly at the public's identification of Cream as 'Eric and two sidekicks'. The result was that, by late 1967, the three not merely insisted on private rooms, they stayed in separate hotels. On a visit to Denmark, Bruce left the hall after a remark in the dressing-room and caught a taxi to the airport. He was actually boarding the plane when Palmer caught up with him. On a second occasion Baker walked off stage and Cream performed as a duo. This left Clapton in the role of mediator: 'I managed to be in the middle of them and my mellowness ... probably stopped them from actually tearing one another to pieces,' he told Coleman. Ben Palmer confirms that 'Eric, basically, kept his head down. Ginger would be flicking drumsticks at Jack and Clapton stood there playing. Immediately after the show they went their separate ways. It got so that Cream only met up on stage.'

Clapton's social life was divided between the Pheasantry, the clubs – the Ad Lib, Bag O' Nails and Speakeasy – catering to the cultural élite and, from early 1968, Keith Richards's home in Chelsea. Richards's friend Tom Keylock, an intermediary in purchasing the house at 3 Cheyne Walk, remembers Clapton 'loping up the steps with his guitar and a leather satchel. Very quiet, very much in awe of Mick and Keith ... Brian [Jones] was in danger of being fired then and they had Eric lined up as a replacement. He told Mick he'd think about it.'

Clapton also returned, on at least a monthly basis, to Ripley. Villagers became inured to the sight of the native son, dressed in a ruffled shirt or Afghan smock, appearing in the Ship to buy cigarette papers or a bottle of wine. Friendly in a vague, noncommittal way, Clapton greeted old acquaintances without taking responsibility for seeking them out. He never visited his former schools. He did, however, make discreet donations – a cottage hospital, St Mary Magdalen – and became known for his marked personal generosity. Whereas, says a former associate,

'Eric always complained about money, he was incredibly lavish with gifts. I never saw a man spend a pay packet more quickly.'

Disraeli Gears, released that November, reached number five in the British charts, number four in America. By Christmas Clapton's pay packet, inclusive of record sales, royalties and concert fees, was the equivalent of £30,000 per annum – more than fifteen times that of the average white-collar worker. Of the many contradictions of his personality his attitude to money bulked among the most obvious. Frequently profligate with notes and coins, professing disinterest in the 'business' side of life, the management of his investments was entrusted to Stigwood. 'Thanks for ... the very welcome news,' a letter opened to Gail Lenox, the Marshbrook company secretary. 'R[obert] was right, as usual, all along.' Stigwood generally was. By 1968 Clapton was a rich man; he needed to be, and never felt himself wholly secure, but by the standards of most twenty-two-year-olds, even those in his own industry, he had little to complain of. He was shrewd, well managed, careful without being mean, and always received the best advice.

For a gross fee of $500,000 Cream returned to America from February to June. The tour opened, as before, in San Francisco, where Clapton, with his soupy eyes and flowing walrus moustache, framed by a pair of bristling black whiskers, was received into the Grateful Dead's home like a native. He responded with enthusiasm to aspects of local culture: LSD, marijuana and mescaline, buying amyl nitrate from the neighbourhood pharmacy. 'Addictive,' said the group's resident songwriter, Bobby Peterson. 'Clapton had an addictive personality. Whatever we did, Eric had to do two of. Here was this quiet, unassuming Englishman snapping off ammies and still taking tea every afternoon at four.' The result, in Peterson's words, was a 'weird equivocation', worth observing carefully because it pictures the state of mind of a man living half in one world and half in another, and wishing to do justice to all sides.

For their opening at the Fillmore, Cream reverted to the extended soloing and improvisational excess borne on them the previous summer. In two hours they played five numbers: one each featuring Clapton, Bruce and Baker, and two ensemble. A sixth, 'SWLABR', was briefly inserted but dropped – its complex fuzz-tone guitar and dyspeptic lyrics (misogynist in the sense a poem like 'Sunny Prestatyn' is misogynist: the man exorcizes the woman by disfiguring her) was thought too cryptic. Clapton's own moment in the sun came in 'Crossroads'. On certain nights his solo, running counter to the beat, seemed to defy the laws of volume and velocity. A high, keening sound, amplified to the edge of pain, it was delivered with apparently minimal effort; Clapton stood there looking bored. Elsewhere his playing veered from startling originality to blatant cliché – frequently in the same song or solo. Among the reviews of the tour was one in the San Francisco *Chronicle* insisting, 'Cream are either much better or much worse than their reputation ... They give out impressions faster than we can absorb them.'

The group's inconsistency only reflected events offstage. Clapton made his way through America in his fluorescent shirts and khaki jackets, with the gleaming fuzz of his hair and the psychedelic guitar he carried protectively on planes, threatening everyone with leaving. Threats were what he enjoyed. He called Stigwood in London to demand money and hint at retirement. Bruce and Baker received similar treatment. Their response was uniform: a long debate followed as to whether Clapton, whose drug habit became engrained in America, be allowed to accompany *them*. On 29 March he was arrested at a house in Topanga Canyon on a marijuana charge. Clapton spent that night in prison in Hollywood. Among others present were members of Buffalo Springfield – Jim Messina, Richie Furay and Neil Young – the last of whom suffered an epileptic seizure or fit while in custody. The four were released without trial, but not before Clapton was stripped, searched and chained at the ankle to a black militant charged with rape.

Relations between Bruce and Baker, at least, remained constant. They loathed each other. United only in their mistrust of Clapton, the two constantly argued, constantly fought, partly as a means of formalizing their aggressive intent, but chiefly out of genuine aversion to each other. In Los Angeles it was a thrown chair in the dressing-room; in Houston another dispute about cash. In Baker's memory it was in the latter city that 'Eric just said, "I've had enough" and I said, "So have I" ... That was the end.' Later, presenting this as evidence of his fickle, wandering spirit ('I didn't really ever want to be tied down to a band. The minute it started to get too routine, I wanted to get out') Clapton at first concealed the news from the press. 'All rumours are denied,' he announced in May. 'I'm happy with the group, although needless to say there has been strain ... We've been doing two and a half months of one-nighters and that is the hardest I've ever worked in my life. Financially and popularity-wise we're doing unbelievably well in America.' Chris Welch of *Melody Maker*, virtually an amanuensis for the group since 1966, was told that no decision had been taken.

Clapton's hesitation arose from the discrepancy between his senses of restlessness and concern that music had moved on, and his equally firm grasp of economic reality. Cream *were* doing unbelievably well in America. At the Back Bay Theater, Boston, the group played to ecstatic crowds who demanded three separate encores. They broke house records in Ottawa and New York. Stigwood, apprised that his star group were fragmenting, at the very moment of his heaviest investment in the Bee Gees, was appalled: 'I told [Clapton] to get back on the road and forget about it.'

He might have done so, but for two facts. Throughout the American tour Clapton had become uneasily aware that, in his words, 'the music wasn't going anywhere'; Cream's seemingly flexible, free-form approach had become its antithesis. He compared the group's single 'Anyone For Tennis' ('I hated that. Embarrassing') with The Band's astonishingly mature, simple yet elaborately played debut *Music From Big Pink*. Here, Clapton told Steve Turner, was '. . . what I want[ed] to play, not extended solos and maestro bullshit but just good funky songs'. Yet again Clapton had let his sense of curiosity, of seeking new musical styles and trends, exceed his sense of collective responsibility.

The second reason was more prosaic. On 11 May 1968 *Rolling Stone* ran a long, eulogistic interview with Clapton. He opined on his status as 'God' ('Wow! It's still going on!'), accepted the slavish if misguided acclaim of his fans ('A lot of that is for, like, what kind of shoes I'm wearing'), while studiously denying the influence of 'a Dylan or Lennon'. Anyone reading the piece would have come away thinking Clapton to be an intelligent and self-aware adult, confident of his fame, yet with an engaging sense of irony and self-deprecation.

In the same magazine, separated by the width of an advertisement, Jon Landau added the following:

Cream has been called a jazz group. They are not. They are a blues band and a rock band. Clapton is a master of the blues clichés of all the post-World War II blues guitarists, particularly B. B. King and Albert King . . . Clapton's problem is that while he has a vast creative potential, at this time he hasn't begun to fufil it. He is a virtuoso at performing other people's ideas.

When Clapton read the above he immediately rang his manager and resigned.

After the shouting had died down Stigwood offered a compromise: each of the three members would perform as a solo act while continuing to appear sporadically as a group. This bromide (close enough to Cream's outlook already), seized on by Baker, was rejected by Clapton and Bruce. The former, in Pete Brown's words, had 'had it' with life on the road; healthily aware of the rewards of touring, Clapton was affected equally by his need for roots and settling down; both Martin and Brown himself lobbied from this direction. While Stigwood, bowing to the inevitable, flew to New York to arrange a final tour, Cream returned to Atlantic Studios. In the space of a weekend they completed material for *Wheels Of Fire*. Clapton also exclusively confirmed the group's end to Chris Welch, just as he had its beginning two years before:

> Cream are breaking up. The world-famous trio are to go separate ways in the autumn.
> Said [Clapton] this week: 'I've been on the road seven years and I'm going on a big holiday . . .
> 'I went off [on] a lot of different things since the Cream formed. I went off in a lot of different directions all at once, but I find I have floated back to what I like doing as an individual, and that is playing exploratory blues . . .
> 'You get really hung up and try to write pop songs or create a pop image. I went through that stage and it was a shame because I was not being true to myself. I am and always will be a blues guitarist.'

The echo of his emotion on leaving the Yardbirds was irresistible. As then, Clapton sought out his friend Ben Palmer. As then, he returned to Ripley. He still spoke of himself as a 'scoundrel', entering nightclubs and bars with women other than Charlotte Martin. He still smoked and drank copiously. The differences were all in scale: in 1965 Clapton had been locally known but destitute. In 1968 he was well paid and famous. Trips to Michael Fish, to The Casserole and Mr Chow increased. He became familiar at the Chelsea Drug Store, a neon-lit folly nearby the Pheasantry, and at the Victorian extravagance Lord Kitchener's Valet (of which the emphasis lay on the surname's first syllable). On 2 July he met with his manager and company secretary to confirm future arrangements. (Stigwood, who knew a prospect when he saw it, signed Clapton to a new contract.) He drew funds both from Cream's second album and in expectant advance of their third.

Wheels Of Fire was released that August. Its first two sides contained among Cream's strongest material: 'White Room', an orgy of wah-wah and cryptic allusions, of which Brown says, 'It was a miracle it worked, considering it was me writing a monologue about a new flat' (the room in question was in Chiltern Street, London); 'Politician', once a poem or prototype rap, originally recorded by John McLaughlin; the blues standards 'Born Under A Bad Sign'; and Howlin' Wolf's 'Sitting On Top Of The World'. Significantly, Clapton restricted himself to rhythm guitar and occasional backing vocals. He performed as an accompanist as much as a soloist. 'White Room' excepted, he played no lead parts of any distinction; there was no self-written material. Among the reviews of the album was one describing it as 'proof positive that Bruce and Pete Brown [were] the real virtuosi of the group'.

This was refuted on sides three and four, recorded live in San Francisco the previous March. As well as 'Crossroads', Cream played a version – surely the definitive treatment – of 'Spoonful', a virtual oratorio in which the theme, at once abandoned, was gloriously retrieved after seventeen minutes. Clapton loosed notes like bolts of static. Closing the album, Bruce and Baker also performed their impromptu pieces.

Wheels Of Fire reached number one in America, number three in Britain (where reaction to Cream's breakup was typified in the headline 'We dug your sound, but you kicked us in the teeth'). It sold a million copies in the former alone. Clapton having vetoed 'White Room', 'Sunshine' was belatedly issued as a single. It too reached the Top Ten.

In the following weeks Clapton appeared on tracks for Jackie Lomax (to whom he gave his prize psychedelic guitar – an act of almost ritual sacrifice); the singer Martha Velez; sundry Rolling Stones; and, more pertinently, the Beatles' *White Album*. The session at Abbey Road's Studio Two not only featured Clapton on 'While My Guitar Gently Weeps' – a rare instance of the Beatles recruiting outside help – it cemented a friendship with Harrison and Pattie Boyd. The three, joined occasionally by Charlotte Martin, met weekly at the Pheasantry or the Harrisons' home in Esher. Gradually, over the course of the early autumn, further songs were written: 'Not Guilty'; an untitled blues; 'Badge'. The last, recorded at IBC studios, was the first and then only result of Clapton's longing for 'good funky songs'. Built on a syncopated blues riff (Bruce's) with lyrics by Harrison and Ringo Starr, 'Badge' was the reverse of the rambling chords and extended bravura solos associated with Cream. Like Clapton, Harrison shared an enthusiasm for The Band. Like Clapton, he attempted to return his own group to the simple three-minute song with meaning, to lyrical invention over inflation. Like Clapton's, the effort came too late.

Then again, the relationship between them was never wholly professional. From an early stage Clapton had eyes for Harrison's wife. Forever speaking of the 'special plain' on which musicians lived, he seemed to think his behaviour to Boyd was an artistic statement. Early in 1969 the two were walking up Oxford Street when, says Boyd, 'Eric suddenly said to me: "Do you like me, or are you seeing me because I'm famous?" I answered: "Oh, I thought you were seeing me because *I'm* famous."' The relationship, platonic at this stage, survived.

Clapton's last commitment to Cream, the American tour arranged by Stigwood, took place that autumn. In four weeks the group gave fifteen performances in nine cities. They grossed $700,000. On 2 November, 22,000 people attended their concert at Madison Square Garden, an event eclipsed in the local media only by that week's presidential election. The final performance was at the Civic Center, Baltimore, on 3 November. Cream played, in full: 'White Room', 'Politician', 'I'm So Glad', 'Sitting On Top Of The World', 'Sunshine Of Your Love', 'Crossroads', 'Traintime', 'Toad' and 'Spoonful', Clapton reverting to an (unpainted) Firebird guitar. On the final bar the trio came forward, locked hands, waved – and left. 'They were the past,' gushed the Los Angeles *Times*. 'They were the present. They may even be the future', a truism highlighted by the fact that Cream's support group in America was Deep Purple.

That left the London performances. The two concerts at the Albert Hall on 26 November 1968 amply demonstrated the group's strengths while not disguising their weaknesses. After an extended version of 'Steppin' Out' – first recorded in an era of archaic remoteness with Mayall – Clapton raised an arm (omitting this time to link it with Bruce's and Baker's), his strange, pumping gesture suggesting intense emotion, smiled, and walked off. He was in a 'foul temper', according to a witness, at the party that night at Stigwood's mansion in Stanmore.

Cream's demise had left him in unusually volatile mood. Dozens of letters a day arrived daily at New Cavendish Street, most of them hostile, some viciously so, bemoaning the group's breakup. The majority were intercepted by Stigwood but Clapton saw some and was aghast: flattered

1 The Green, Ripley,
Clapton's birthplace
and home from
1945–65 *(N. Chelberg)*

Previous page: 'It
turned out he
wasn't happy right
from the start'
(Rex)

One reaction to
Clapton's deification
(Roger Perry)

In the frame with
the Yardbirds:
Keith Relf, Jim
McCarty, Clapton,
Chris Dreja, Paul
Samwell-Smith
(Redferns)

The joke requiring
an Englishman, an
Irishman and a
Scotsman might
have been
expressly created
for Cream
(Redferns)

A relatively rare face-to-face meeting with Jimi Hendrix in London (*Rex*)

The Rainbow concert, 13 January 1973. As a comeback, the event was
at least a year too early (*Rex*)

Clapton's cameo in *Tommy*
(Syndication International)

The man posing as 'Eric
Cleptomaniac' on tour of
America, summer 1974
(Redferns)

Clapton's ever-vigilant managers Robert Stigwood (*Syndication International*) and Roger Forrester (*D. Rees*)

On stage, 1977. The relaxed, low-key approach Clapton's longtime fans found so puzzling was in fact an alcoholic haze *(Rex)*

Above left: With Pattie Boyd (*Press Association*) *Above right:* The Carl Perkins Tribute reunited Clapton and the other 'Graduate of Boyd University', George Harrison *(Rex) Below:* Hurtwood Edge

Leaving Heathrow for the last time as a single man, March 1979. Clapton told reporters, 'I got fed up with being turned down by birds in the pub. It's time for the Big Drop' *(Syndication International)*

and fawned on for years, to be execrated was a new experience. His reaction was indifferent in public, but exorbitantly clear in private. The zeal with which Clapton took to Harrison and his adoption of 'good funky songs' both suggest that, even before Cream's final performance, another sea-change, illustrated by Clapton's appearing at the Albert Hall with straight hair and jeans, was under way. Immediately after the second concert he approached Brown with the admission, 'God knows what I'll do now.' Short of 'going on a big holiday', an ambition Stigwood himself deterred, there were no immediate plans. Clapton may even have had second thoughts about prolonging the relationship with Bruce and Baker – or so one of them believes. As usual, says Brown, 'Eric's attitude was a mixture: keen to be shot of the routine and hassle, he was terrified of the alternative. Having decided to leave the band, he didn't necessarily want it to happen.'

He continued to reap the considerable benefits of Cream's success. The group's last two singles, 'White Room' (issued over Clapton's objections) and 'Badge' were released in January and April 1969 respectively. The *Goodbye* LP appeared in March. Half a documentary of Cream's farewell concert in Los Angeles, half recorded in the studio in London, the album topped the charts on both sides of the Atlantic. Critics were particularly drawn to 'Badge' (an inexplicable flop as a single) and the reprised 'Sitting On Top Of The World', a jazz-blues excursion in which Clapton's solo was both soulful and sincere, not always synonymous. There followed a plethora of reissues, doodlings and studio outtakes – *Heavy Cream, Cream, Portrait of Cream, Best of Cream, Live Cream* – some good, some not so admirable. Bootlegs also appeared: *Hello Again, Royal Albert Hall* and *Steppin' Out*. Throughout the seventies and eighties Clapton's attitude to the group hovered between extremes of joy and horror; there were periodic outbursts, tempered by more public expressions of goodwill or nostalgia, a strange amalgam of affection and regret. A former associate of Stigwood's was present when the group met briefly in 1975: 'It was more of an ego trip for Eric than the others. Cream fed his security. After that band Clapton had an exotic appeal to women. Suddenly he was dating models like Jean Shrimpton. It was that moody-but-magnificent gunslinger thing he cultivated. Chicks loved it. They didn't give a fuck about him in the Bluesbreakers.'

Clapton's next appearance was among the strangest of a not uneventful year. From 10 to 12 December 1968 he joined the Rolling Stones, the

97

Who, Lennon and Yoko Ono, as well as the thimble-riggers, midgets and freaks comprising the Christmas folly known as the Rock and Roll Circus. Given responsibility for organizing the event, Tom Keylock remembers Clapton 'there in his cardigan, white socks and sneakers, chain-smoking, keeping himself aloof and scowling like a man with conflicting worries ... The whole thing was a drag, from the problems with filming to the hassles with managers. A nightmare.' Clapton did, however, leaven the morbid tone of the proceedings by appropriating a clown's outsize red crêpe bow-tie and exercising his 'exotic appeal to women' with at least one fan backstage. He also consented to join Lennon, Jagger, Richards and Mitch Mitchell in a pickup group to play 'Peggy Sue', 'Yer Blues' and the woeful 'Yoko Ono Jam', all unreleased to this day. Plans to issue the Circus commercially were vetoed by Jagger, partly on creative grounds, partly legal. 'Before discussing Eric Clapton's availability for your LP,' read a note from Stigwood, 'I would like somebody to discuss with me the question of the contract for his appearance in the TV show ... I await your reply.' Clapton himself left with an apologetic grin: happy, as he would be throughout his career, to appear on outside projects, he deferred to Stigwood on all matters of protocol or payment (a typical arrangement of its time, in which the mania for random exchange between artists was matched only by the lively interplay among their managers).

There was a second, more substantial result of Clapton's appearance. It advanced the rumour, first heard in July 1968, of his joining the Rolling Stones. Originally proposed as a replacement for Brian Jones – then facing drugs charges and likely imprisonment – by Christmas more wholesale changes in the group were envisaged: the idea was that Bill Wyman, too, would quit, leaving Clapton and Richards on guitar and a second recruit on bass. The moment passed, but not before Jagger, in a characteristically oblique approach, had sounded Clapton's intentions. 'There was a ton of bullshit about "Suppose this ..." and "Let's pretend that ...",' says Keylock, 'which was typical of Mick. Everything was vague, just in case you refused him. Eric did that.'

As to the matter of a more intimate friendship, Keylock believes, 'A lot of camp behaviour went on, mainly involving musicians putting on makeup and batting their eyes at each other. It appealed to Mick's vanity to come on to someone like Clapton. That's all it was – a tease. Not that it helped get Eric into the Stones.'

Clapton could have been excused his moment of obstinacy. Cream had left him in no great hurry to join a group, however exalted, of equally fixed public image. He continued to speak disparagingly of being in a group at all. It was at least five years – arguably longer – before he came to terms with Bruce and Baker. In semi-retirement in 1973–4, Clapton made a number of unflattering remarks about his former colleagues. A year later there was a chance meeting at Stigwood's office, of which Clapton's version reveals both the misgivings and excessive sense of pride he harboured about the group. 'The three of us . . . tore the place apart and came back to my house flying – really flying – on cloud nine. Took acid and just started talking. It was a summer's day, people were arriving and we were out there, sitting on the terrace, in chairs, facing the same way, the three of us, almost as if we were expecting people to come. And people were arriving and sort of walking round the corner, down round the side of the house, walking round there and stopping, as if they were approaching a *court.*'

A less agreeable reunion took place at the same house in May 1979. As part of Clapton's wedding celebration an impromptu group formed consisting of himself, Jagger, Richards, Wyman, three ex-Beatles, Jeff Beck – and Bruce. Ben Palmer was also present. 'Everyone was jamming in the marquee on Eric's lawn . . . At some stage it was decided that Jack was taking things too seriously. A conscious effort began, encouraged by Clapton, to isolate him. Jack ended up playing by himself on a corner of the stage . . . Eric was standing there laughing . . . When he came off Jack broke down and cried, literally sobbing with rage. It was the end of ten years' hassle, as he saw it, by Eric.'

Eight years passed before Clapton and Bruce's next significant meeting. In February 1987 Clapton guested on two tracks on the latter's album *Willpower*; there was a joint appearance at the Bottom Line Club, New York; even a spontaneous performance for *The South Bank Show* (proving, if nothing else, that Bruce had forgotten the chords of 'White Room'). If little about the above suggested the presence of intimacy, Clapton tending to withdraw at moments of possible conciliation, at least the previous air of mutual suspicion was replaced by one of wary respect.

Relations with Baker were equally strained. After a misguided and, to Bruce, insulting attempt to play together after Cream, Clapton and his drummer descended to a level of bare civility for twenty years. In February 1990 Baker joined Bruce on tour of the US to promote the latter's album *A Question Of Time* ('the way Ginger stumbles over the drums,' noted

Village Voice, '[being] like watching Grandpa prove he can still decap beer bottles with his eye socket'). *You* magazine found both musicians eager to discuss their former colleague.

[Baker]
 'The majority of the world is convinced that Cream was Eric Clapton's band and he enjoys it. Cream was *my* band. I formed it. I did most of the hard work. And I got the least out of it . . . I hate that stuff Clapton does now.'

[Bruce]
 'I was interested in the music but [Clapton] was always very ambitious, very intent on becoming a big star . . . He and Robert Stigwood joined together to push him as the star of Cream. They had a problem because I was the lead singer and wrote most of the songs. They went ahead and did it anyway.'

There, things should have ended. Bruce returned to his homes in Colchester and Stuttgart, enjoying both 'the opportunities that Cream brought' to play with the likes of Miles Davis, and 'the absence, unlike Eric, of any record company bullshit'. Baker, after a long period of exile in Nigeria, primarily to avoid payment of an outstanding tax bill, settled first in California and then Colorado. Periodically restating his 'hard work' and lack of return from Cream, his other interests included: the British class system, the marijuana laws, the CIA, FBI and IRS – and polo, to all of which, excepting the last, Baker remained opposed. Asked in 1990 about the chances of a reunion with Clapton and Bruce he replied, 'None.'

By then the supporting framework of the group had collapsed. Felix Pappalardi was shot dead by his wife after a brawl. Ben Palmer retired to Wales and Martin Sharp to Australia. Pete Brown returned to poetry and occasional writings for the groups Battered Ornaments and Piblokto. Alienated from Bruce, he saw Clapton in 1985 after an interval of sixteen years: 'He was perfectly friendly though, as usual, in a remote, hazy way.' Brown's subsequent offer to submit lyrics for a new album was declined by Clapton's management. Stigwood himself, after a period of ill health, reverted to his theatrical career, producing a revival of *Grease* on the London stage in 1993.

The first stirrings of a Cream reunion were heard in 1991 when a compilation film, *Strange Brew*, briefly topped the British video charts. It was followed by a second release, *Fresh Live Cream*, two years later.

By then Clapton, whatever his private views on Bruce and Baker, retained at least three songs associated with the group in his stage-act. He spoke approvingly of the 'positive electricity' between the three and, to *Rolling Stone*, of the prospects for a full reunion:

It's still [possible], as long as we're all alive. But it hinges on how much people change, and how much they don't change. If we got back together, how far back would it go into the misery of what we experienced? Would that come back with it? It scares the living daylights out of me, because there was a lot of hostility, a lot of aggression and a lot of unpleasant personality clashes . . . We'd have to do it for love and out of the desire to have a good time. Not for money.

In fact the predominant motive behind Cream's coming together after twenty-five years was neither love nor money, but nostalgia. On 12 January 1993 Clapton appeared, cropped-haired, in glasses, with Bruce (suit) and Baker (shirt and tie) at the Rock and Roll Hall of Fame in Los Angeles. After a photo-call estimated by Bruce at 'ten seconds, maximum' they played 'Sunshine Of Your Love', 'Politician' and, as a tribute to the late Albert King, 'Born Under A Bad Sign'. If lacking the verve of the originals, the songs were seized on by the two thousand guests, each paying upwards of a thousand dollars, as evidence, said *The Times*, 'of a peculiar renaissance . . . three men with a combined age of 150 indulging in a last-ditch stand . . . a nostalgic rerun of past glories'.

'It was wonderful,' says Bruce. 'An unmitigated delight . . . Terrific . . . A triumph.' Others, less sanguine, noted the compelling link between other set-piece events in Clapton's career (Live Aid, the Grammys) and the subsequent boosting of his record sales. If, all sides agreed, the pleasure of each other's company was reason enough to re-form – and the Hall of Fame has a notable track record in reconciling warring parties – then the presence of other factors seems not to have hurt: as well as money, there was the question of Clapton's solo career, established but creatively exhausted until the one-off success of *Unplugged* in 1992. In public all three members of Cream spoke warmly of the prospects of an additional special or one-off appearance, most notably to celebrate the fiftieth anniversary of Atlantic Records in 1997. In private Bruce adds only that 'relations between the four of us – the group and Eric's manager

– are very, *very* delicate. Things change on a daily basis. Don't count on anything. Don't count anything out.'

'With Cream,' says Clapton, 'we had our ups and downs. We had good gigs and bad gigs. We had gigs when you could have mistaken us for Hendrix, it was that good, and other times we were like the worst band in the world.' Critical judgement is likely to fall between the two. Their American success places the group on a plane only slightly less exalted than the Beatles and the Rolling Stones. Like the latter, they had a powerful stage-act and, in Bruce, the most technically gifted member of the three groups.

What Cream lacked was either interest or instinct for 'putting themselves across'; for re-examining cultural values and mores; for harnessing the raucous, liberating aspects of rock to showbusiness convention. Unlike a Jagger or McCartney, Clapton had no talent for selling his group's message. Such efforts as he made were confused and contradictory, failings applying equally to Clapton himself. He was a recluse who loved nightclubs and parties; a blues purist who indulged in flower-power and psychedelia; an Englishman whose attitude to America bordered on schizophrenia. He complained of the need to dress and act flamboyantly, yet eagerly did so. On stage Clapton's performances tended to be brilliant without being solid, his impatience to solo extending and sometimes distorting songs past recognition.

With their constant feuding, their insistence on separate dressing-rooms and eventually hotels, their bombast and their risible comments to the press, Cream took the send-up of pop music to new heights. With their grasp of both blues and jazz, their obvious love of their craft and the technical genius of their best work, they remain in the pantheon of British rock.

5

God Is Dead

Changeable, easily led, susceptible to ideas, Clapton's next major influence was George Harrison. For a period from late 1968 their social, musical and eventually romantic minglings meant that, in the public's eye, they became associated as a single unit: a thin, milk-pale Englishman of retiring outlook whose few public utterances concealed a complicated emotional life.

In 1968 Clapton, like Harrison, had grown tired of the demands of a full-time group; like Harrison he yearned for the chance to perform his own songs without abandoning the lifestyle his previous career had brought; like Harrison, his first act on declaring independence was to buy a house in the country.

On consecutive weekends in October and November Clapton set out in Harrison's Indian-painted Mini, armed with *Country Life* and sheaves of estate agents' orders-to-view. His needs were simple: quiet surroundings, a large garden, room to rehearse and play in, within striking distance of both London and Ripley. After six or seven false starts he found the home he remains in to this day.

Hurtwood Edge, Ewhurst, on the southern fringe of Winterfold Forest, was approached down a gravel driveway (eventually adorned by a totem pole), conveniently separated from the main road by a pub. The house itself was Italianate: an adobe façade, the interior tiled, white-walled, the curtains and rugs of oriental design. The circular stairs led past the master bedroom to a turret at the top of which a room was set aside for music – arched red-framed windows, bare floor and walls, a fire smouldering in the old-fashioned grate. The garden was reached by the living-room, a verandah letting on to the terraced steps overlooking the sixteen acres of box hedges and sequoia trees, the swimming pool and ponds. When Clapton moved in in early spring he brought with him a pet donkey, his

Labrador (and eventually a macaw named Screaming Maurice); other touches – a one-armed bandit and jukebox, Clapton's presentational records and awards – followed. The surrounding area, largely undeveloped for a century, had profound associations for him, for it was here that Rose and Jack Clapp had once driven with their grandson at weekends.

Built in 1910, Hurtwood Edge retained the qualities of an Edwardian mansion – the grounds, the vaulted interior, the constant smell, as one guest puts it, of 'Labradors drying on the rug', the sense, only partially offset by the arrival of guitars and other material from Chelsea, of belonging to another era. The estate, which Clapton bought for £40,000, was the single major investment of his life. He spent the first weeks of 1969 briefing the designer David Mlinaric, entertaining appreciative friends and arranging for Jack and Rose to visit from Ripley. They cried when they first saw the house.

There were other luxuries: a Ferrari, a Mercedes, a vintage motorcycle; the extensive wine collection in the cellar. Charlotte Martin, debating whether or not to leave Chelsea, was relieved of the choice by a message from Clapton: he hoped they would 'allways [sic] be friends' but that 'pressing NEW arrangements' had come into effect. These included liaisons with the model Cathy James and Pattie Boyd's sister Paula before Clapton fell in with Mlinaric's friend Alice Ormsby-Gore. Barely seventeen, she moved into Hurtwood Edge in April 1969; left it in May; returned in early 1970 and, not without protest and prevarication, remained with Clapton for four years. Despite her belief that 'I was in love with him, and vice versa', there was a sense that Clapton used Ormsby-Gore as a contrast gainer: 'Although we had some good times,' he told Coleman, 'I'd never describe it as head-over-heels in love. All the time I was with Alice, I was mentally with Pattie.' Paula Boyd was 'a surrogate Pattie in my mind'.

The affair with Ormsby-Gore, embracing alcoholism, heroin addiction and reported violence, eventually brought the intervention of her father Lord Harlech. There were letters ('I love you both so much that I cannot bear to see what you are doing to yourselves . . . Please let me help'), in which the view of addiction as a fault of the individual, not of society, was angrily rebutted by Clapton. Harlech tried other tactics. At a party for Mick Jagger, another rock star he patronized, Tom Keylock heard the former ambassador 'go ape' at the latest report of his daughter's and Clapton's behaviour. According to Keylock, 'The exact quote was "If they won't sort it out, I'll have it done for them. By the law."' A dinner companion of Harlech's in February 1974 – by which time Clapton and Ormsby-Gore were undergoing heroin withdrawal – adds, 'It was the hardest job of David's life. And the worst. Negotiating with Kennedy was simple by comparison.'

Clapton's attitude to his emotional life as a whole was complex. Constantly stressing his love of the 'female persuasion', his behaviour to its members veered between reverence and contempt. Throughout his time in Ripley, Clapton had been snubbed by girls, confused by his feelings for his mother, disappointed with himself. The nervous hostility he had shown towards women as a boy increased steadily as a man. In the Yardbirds, Bluesbreakers and Cream he became an avid procurer, or patron, of groupies ('I think I've laid a thousand by now,' he told Steve Turner), retained a rigidly traditionalist approach ('going berserk', his future wife said, 'if I couldn't find his shirt') and, above all, conducting affairs on his, and only his, terms. A woman, now married and living in California, romantically linked with Clapton in 1970 remembers him as 'just bristling with hostility . . . He hated giving in to a woman. Hated anything with a feminine touch. Feathering the nest – no way. Weak and shallow, intense but tender – that was Eric.' She might have added 'insecure'. Clapton's attitude to sex, like so many of his attitudes, stemmed from his sense of disillusion and being put upon, primarily by his mother. Early in his career Clapton asserted he was traumatized as a child. In later years he frequently returned to the theme. Clapton's relationship with Pat inflated both his ego and his insecurity. He loved her but never trusted her. As with his mother, so with Ormsby-Gore: Clapton may have avoided being 'head-over-heels in love' simply out of self-defence. He may have abused her only to protect himself. If a charge of aggressive intent were lodged against Clapton he might have answered it with a plea of self-defence. 'On top of everything else,' says Ben Palmer, 'he was fucked up, himself. Chronically.'

Clapton's next move was a purely random one – as so many would be – when, in March 1969, he accepted an invitation to appear in the television special *Supershow*. This project, an extension of the Rock and Roll Circus, was supervised and co-produced by Tom Keylock. By the simple expedient of approaching the musicians direct and offering them £100 to play the material of their choice, Keylock assembled a cast including Stephen Stills, Roland Kirk, Jack Bruce, Buddy Guy, Buddy Miles and Led Zeppelin. Clapton, contacted at the Scotch of St James, agreed with the proviso that 'no one tell Robert [Stigwood]; a condition which Keylock, with memories of their previous encounter, was only too anxious to meet. When the day came the producer found Clapton to be polite, quiet and almost morbidly shy. There was, nonetheless, a sense of 'definite expectancy' at the guitarist's arrival. Clapton appeared at the side door of the disused factory hired for the event, late, lit a cigarette (of what Keylock calls 'questionable quality') and walked on. In two largely improvised numbers he traded solos with Guy, glared at Stills – appearing not so much threatening as gravely concerned – and nodded affably at Bruce. Dick Heckstall-Smith was also present: 'Clapton was on his best behaviour, asking everyone if he was too loud, if we minded his amplifier. He obviously loved that type of gig more than the big set-pieces. If Eric could have played in clubs and still earned the money, he would have been a happy man.'

The presence of Keylock served to underline the continuing bond between Clapton and the Rolling Stones. Early that spring he guested on the group's *Let It Bleed* at Olympic studios; Clapton played on 'Love In Vain' and 'I'm Going Down', the latter of which never appeared on the album. According to the late Ian Stewart, the decision to fire Brian Jones, by now irrevocable, was preceded 'by hours of to-ing and fro-ing about inviting Eric . . . Mick was in awe of him, whereas Keith didn't give a fuck. One thought him too good, the other not good enough.' While no formal approach was ever made, it is certain that, had he wanted it, Clapton could have had the job. (Jones's replacement was Clapton's successor-but-one in the Bluesbreakers, Mick Taylor.) Keylock was also present in Cheyne Walk when 'Mick, in his usual roundabout way, skirting the issue, again asked if Eric had any plans . . . Clapton said he was forming a group.'

In fact preliminary moves to do so had begun as early as January. Resuming a long, irregular relationship with Steve Winwood, Clapton had spent a weekend at the latter's home, where they discovered a mutual love of the 'funky songs' foretold by *Music From Big Pink*. According to Winwood, Clapton described Cream as 'too self-indulgent', wanting 'to play *songs* rather than leave each player undisciplined'. That left the question of timing. In 1966 Winwood had turned Clapton down on the basis of his commitment to another group. In 1969 he was unemployed. As to a name: 'Eric called it Blind Faith because that's exactly what we had in the project.'

Not long afterwards a Leicester-based quintet named Family were surprised by an incident as they walked on stage in New York. 'We were literally standing there,' says the group's drummer, Rob Townsend, 'when Rick [Grech] announced, "I'm leaving. This is the last gig."' Grech, whom Townsend describes as a 'kamikaze guy', later revealed that, in response to a call from Clapton, whom he knew from impromptu sessions in the Speakeasy, he was joining Blind Faith on bass.

Finally, acting on a promise to 'see [the drummer] right', on leaving Cream, Clapton accepted an application from Baker. If ever there was a case of blind, or unseemly faith, this was it: Clapton later admitted that from that moment the group, hailed immediately as a substitute Cream, was doomed. A member of Stigwood's office present at rehearsals that spring says it was 'obvious . . . Eric was unhappy from the start. He was more or less forced into hiring Ginger by Winwood and, of course, Robert himself . . . Immediately Stigwood coined the phrase "supergroup". He definitely saw it as Cream Mach 2, whereas Eric just wanted to play blues and soul. Clapton was incredibly easily led and, because he never said "no", ended up reversing himself months afterwards. He regretted that group as soon as it started.'

Stigwood, immune to such doubts, urged Clapton both to record and tour. The group, minus Grech, entered Morgan Studios as early as mid-February (an instrumental single was released by Island Records as a limited edition); later transferring to Olympic, where Clapton resumed his association with the Rolling Stones, present in the same building. (A recording exists of his negotiating with Mick Jagger; Clapton's voice is not merely small in comparison, but close to inaudible.) Moving rapidly in his floral shirt and sunglasses, Stigwood next arranged for Blind Faith to perform in America. A one-off appearance in London's Hyde Park was announced for 7 June.

Then and only then was the inevitable exclusive supplied to Chris Welch:

It's sounding good, the Eric Clapton, Stevie Winwood, Ginger Baker Band. Forget about Cream. This is a new group with a new sound . . .

Times have changed considerably for the guitar star who was hailed as 'God' by fans of the burgeoning British blues scene and went on to achieve riches and fame in America with Cream . . . Today he lives in a £40,000 multi-roomed mansion, deep in the Surrey stockbroker belt.

'I feel as if I've achieved nothing,' [said Clapton]. 'I've got miles and miles to go ... I don't know if my playing keeps up with the image. I do my best.'

Hyde Park perfectly illustrated the different roles Blind Faith would play: Baker, stage-centre, guffawing and slugging his beer; Grech mute; Winwood and Clapton himself smiling and muttering distractedly, like men uncertain of their bearings. Incredibly, a number of critics, used to the guitarist's previous persona, failed to recognize the lank-haired man in the wings – so much of Clapton's life was spent in obscuring his image that imposture and disguise blanketed even his looks. At Hyde Park he wore a teenager's T-shirt and jeans, reverting for the first time since 1965 to a Fender Telecaster. Reviewers were divided as to whether his playing was inept or merely lazy: technically weak or exercising a wilful negative energy. (Clapton's egotism could be gratified by appearing laid-back in comparison to others.) His motivation was unknown. What was known was that Blind Faith played a nine-song set largely distinguished by Winwood, and that Clapton, in his own words 'shaking like a leaf', determined there and then that the group was finished.*

For a month Clapton commuted between Hurtwood Edge and London; between courting the Boyds and recording; between Ormsby-Gore and Stigwood. According to his manager's assistant, 'Eric almost lost it when Robert gave him the American itinerary.' Blind Faith's tour was touted as a triumph not of musical enterprise, but of scale and revenue, the presentation more extravagant than anything Clapton had done before, as if grandeur and overkill had replaced the last vestige of meaning in the performance. Stigwood's own motivation was revealed immediately: 'They are going to make a lot of money in appearance and on records and [Hyde Park] was the best possible beginning ... I am going to make a great deal of money out of [it] all over the world.'

Blind Faith appeared in New York on 12 July 1969. The concerts there, in California and Phoenix, confirmed Clapton's worst fears for the group: the seventy-minute set, woefully under-rehearsed, was attended by near-anarchy from the floor. At the Forum in Los Angeles the performance was stopped twice as police hauled fans from the auditorium. Less than a year after admitting having 'had it' on the road, Clapton found himself playing to delirious, rioting crowds who threw cherry-bombs and

---

* 'He was convinced it would be another circus,' according to Grech, who saw 'Eric crying his eyes out' following the performance.

called for 'Crossroads'. His sole comment – 'The kids come to a show now with one idea: violence and to heckle the cops' – if anything downplayed the changes since 1968. The first voicing of student unrest, bolstered by escalation in Vietnam and the election of Richard Nixon as president, had grown to a chorus. By May 1969 daily scorecards were being published listing the campuses 'on strike', the administration buildings 'occupied' – hundreds were involved. In a speech on 3 June, Nixon spoke of the 'self-righteous arrogance', abetted by 'permissive' faculties, at the core of which lay male college students threatened with military conscription. Incongruous as it seems to connect these things with music, connected they were. In 1967 Cream had provided the aural counterpoint of an hallucination; in 1969 a concert by Blind Faith (or the Who, or Led Zeppelin, or the Rolling Stones) was a surrogate protest rally, a confrontation between concertgoers and police played out to the amplified beat from the stage. While men like Clapton continued to insist on the pre-eminence of 'having a good time', their groups were being seized on as the marching bands of the revolution.

There were other problems, musical and personal. Whereas Clapton and Winwood, financially secure, asked merely to develop their own material, Baker and Grech insisted on a more commercial presentation. 'Sunshine' was revived, as was Baker's drum solo from 'Toad'. ('Ginger took the reins because Steve and I were both so laid back,' Clapton said. 'We were in no hurry to get anywhere, whereas Ginger could see . . . zoom, the bucks.') A member of Free, supporting Blind Faith in America, speaks of 'old grievances' being aired and of a 'dead atmosphere' in the group as the tour progressed. In Denver Clapton played one solo in the course of a sixty-minute performance, then responded angrily to a reporter who asked if that were sufficient illustration of his role. In Seattle he was said by the critic Janine Gressel to have 'brought the house down, while not standing out much', recurrent proof of the fact that, as Winwood puts it, 'We could have gone on, farted, and got a response.'

In all this Clapton was influenced by the group's second support act, Delaney and Bonnie Bramlett, an engaging mix of country, gospel, rock and blue-eyed soul, who echoed the 'good funky songs' of The Band. While other groups were experimenting with Moogs, mellotrons and wah-wah pedals, the Bramletts retreated through the swing doors of a western saloon-bar with their saxes, trumpets and upright pianos. Clapton was enchanted. His patronage of Delaney Bramlett, in particular, was intense. Clapton took to the older man as he once had to Mayall and

Bruce (and eventually fell out with him, as he had with them).* In New York they publicly consumed, in Bramlett's words, 'Marine-corps strength LSD', after which – in Clapton's – 'Delaney looked straight into my eyes and told me I had a gift to sing, and that if I didn't God would take it away.' It was rather to Bramlett's credit that he was able to repeat the argument the next day.

On 15 August, as Blind Faith played to orgiastic scenes in Los Angeles, their debut LP was released. The album marked the first scaling-down of the heights Clapton routinely achieved in Cream, the switch from Gibson to Fender reducing the guitar to just one element in an overall sound dominated by Winwood. Only the coda on 'Had To Cry Today' revived memories of *Disraeli Gears*. Elsewhere there were covers of Buddy Holly; a Latinized solo on 'Do What You Like'; the acoustic 'Can't Find My Way Home'. Clapton's first self-written lyric, 'Presence Of The Lord' ('I have finally found a way to live/Just like I never could before') was fastened on as evidence of a new, reconstructed personality, the disc jockey Scott Ross going so far as to announce on air that 'Eric [had] found Jesus.' Ross, not unusually, missed the point. By 1969 it had become almost required of rock stars to comment disparagingly on the barrenness of being, the levity of lives distinguished only by the twin totems of drugs and money. Clapton, like the Beatles, like members of the Rolling Stones, like Pete Townshend and Bob Dylan, may have longed for the dignity of belief. Like them, he eschewed the idea of conventional dogma – with its threat of effort and self-denial – in favour of the intoxicating idea of mysticism. Clapton might have found religion, but it rarely saw expression in more than the lighting of joss sticks and vague protestations of communal goodwill. He accepted the privileges of faith without accepting the responsibilities.

There was another, more practical context for 'Presence Of The Lord'. In 1967 a London policeman named Norman Pilcher, attached to the Chelsea Drug Squad, had made a career of raiding local rock stars: Lennon and Hendrix were arrested, Jagger drawn aside in the street. According to Anthony Haden-Guest, Pilcher twice visited the Pheasantry. As Clapton later told Steve Turner, 'He wanted me because he was a groupie cop . . . I was on the run from flat to flat and when I finally got

---

* Even then Clapton retained his sense of ego. 'I knew that I had the drawing power,' he later said. 'I could make the public aware of [Bramlett] just by putting my name on the bill.'

out of town the pressure was off. It was such a relief, and it was just such a beautiful place that I sat down and wrote the song.' ('Superimposing your religious experience on to the actual situation of being on the run?' asked Turner. 'Exactly,' said Clapton.)

Blind Faith, which generated more than a million orders before release, topped the charts on both sides of the Atlantic. (There was a brief hiatus when the original cover, showing a naked eleven-year-old girl, was withdrawn in America.) Clapton continued to receive guarantees, his first significant songwriting royalties, as well as a share of Blind Faith's $20,000 a night performance fee negotiated by Stigwood. Materially wealthy, he was notoriously short of ready funds. Clapton, like most rock stars, lived essentially on pocket money. He could be impulsively generous, but admitted to anxieties, relieved by a burst of hectic phone calls to Stigwood, about the absence of 'serious cash'. Clapton complained continually of being 'skint' as he was chauffeured from his hotel suite to the group's chartered jet. He insisted that loans be promptly repaid, yet forgot to reimburse Hendrix's bass player Noel Redding until twice reminded to do so. For the raw necessities of life, for clothes, for food, for transport and accommodation, Clapton continued to rely almost entirely on his manager. Their personal contract was renewed that autumn, while the others made separate arrangements. In September Grech wrote a letter to his ex-colleague indicating 'Blind Faith is no "family"' – Townsend was meant to feel the ironic edge of this – and bemoaning the lack of 'team spirit'. In private Grech also complained that the songwriting duties had been 'stitched up' to his prejudice.

Grech's remarks were rendered vertebrate by the recording of two songs, on which Clapton guested, for the bassist's solo album, a record which, after discussion between Stigwood and Chris Blackwell, took five years to release. Clapton next appeared on Lennon's 'Cold Turkey', a partnership extended by their appearance at the Rock 'n' Roll Revival Festival on 13 September. Alerted by a phone call in mid-morning Clapton was *en route* to Toronto by early afternoon, the group – Lennon, Klaus Voorman, Alan White, himself – famously rehearsing in the first-class cabin of the jet. At midnight the Plastic Ono Band took the stage. They played, in total: 'Blue Suede Shoes', 'Money', 'Dizzy Miss Lizzie', 'Yer Blues', 'Cold Turkey' and 'Give Peace A Chance', at which point Yoko Ono, previously secure in a white bag, emerged to perform 'Don't Worry Kyoko' and 'John John'. According to Allen Klein, Lennon was moved to announce the dissolution of the Beatles there and then in favour of a working arrangement with Clapton. (The idea was quietly dropped when it was pointed out that Lennon would forgo a million-dollar advance.) Clapton's own feelings were ambivalent. He admitted to the 'excellence' of the Toronto concert, while maintaining in private that Lennon and Ono had hijacked the event for their own benefit. (Among Clapton's complaints was Lennon's imperial treatment at Toronto airport – immediately whisked into a Cadillac limousine flanked by Hell's Angels while he, Clapton, stood waiting in the rain.) He did, however, attend a reunion of the Plastic Ono Band at the London Lyceum that Christmas.

Dick Taylor, guitarist with the Pretty Things, also played with Clapton at the Speakeasy one night that autumn. Whereas in Cream, 'Eric had seemed, to put it mildly, on the edge', now all was 'friendliness, charm and a certain reserve of manner'. Taylor's suspicion that Clapton had 'had it with being a Christ figure' was borne out by the facts. Deification had taken its toll. Mobs followed him about, and Clapton, who as late as the Bluesbreakers had been known to share a drink at the saloon-bar with fans, learned to hurry out of the stage doors of stadia and hockey arenas and make his way to safety through side streets and roped-off alleyways. A reaction set in, not only in the way he dressed and acted, but in the music. All the evidence suggests that, on *Blind Faith*, on sessions for Grech and Doris Troy – even with Lennon and Ono – Clapton was already cultivating a more subdued, minimalist style. In doing so he anticipated the market generally, the harnessing of the more subversive aspects of rock to its commercial potential. Raucous, liberating guitar needs the context of raucous, liberating material; by 1970 the trend had shifted from the individual to the elaborately packaged group, to form over substance, to rock as Muzak, entertainment and eventually soundtrack. Clapton realized and accepted this. According to Taylor, he was already extolling the virtues of the Seekers and Scott Walker, insisting – the old man inside the young – that 'music should be fun'. That winter Clapton played host at Hurtwood Edge to Marc Bolan.

His own sense of humour was extended to Delaney and Bonnie Bramlett. In early November, at Clapton's expense, the couple flew to England. The plan, originally made in New York that summer, was to translate their mutual love of blues and soul into an album and tour. After a poorly received performance by the Bramletts in Germany, Ray Connolly was summoned to Clapton's house to interview the putative group – the idea was to sell tickets for British and Scandinavian dates that December. Connolly arrived at 6 p.m. to find 'ghostly figures stumbling about . . .

dazed with sleep'. Clapton himself appeared, yawning, smoking a fat cigarette, and lay on his back in front of the fire. The whole experience, says Connolly, was 'unnerving ... People kept drifting down to the living-room, lighting up, barely awake.' The house itself was vampire-dark, littered with exotic instruments and, in certain visible places, none too hygienic. The huge Indian rug had been extensively soiled by dogs.

The resulting tour opened at the Albert Hall on 1 December. Connolly, reversing his role as the group's mouthpiece, turned in a review ('Delaney and Bonnie ... currently the most fashionable fad of the rock sophisti-cates') at least hinting at what he now calls 'Eric's gullible side', his shiftlessness, and 'refusal to be identified' with a single cause. At the Albert Hall Clapton stood in the wings in his jeans and waistcoat, agitating a Les Paul while Dave Mason played such audible guitar as there was. Clapton's muted performance was affected as much by outside factors as his stated preference to be 'one of the band'. A recreational user of marijuana and LSD since 1967, in 1969 he had graduated to cocaine and later heroin. He continued to drink voraciously. Clapton's habits masked a complicated private life. By year's end he was rotationally bedding James, Ormsby-Gore and Paula Boyd while still lobbying the last's sister. To aggravate matters, Clapton, long prone to excess, now had both time and resources to indulge himself. Given the constant proximity of drugs and his manager's inability to restrict them, the outcome was predictable: by then, says a Stigwood employee, 'you could tell Eric's condition just by looking at him. His eyes were like marbles.'

Immense effort went into concealing Clapton's emotions. George Harrison was unaware of his friend's ambitions. Harrison even joined the Delaney and Bonnie tour at the Empire, Liverpool (where he cheerfully sang 'Everybody's Trying To Steal My Baby'); the concert and the one that followed were recorded for the traditional live album. At the party backstage Clapton commented on his lifelong interest in girls who, for one reason or another, were unavailable. This ironic light was now obliged to be cast on his feelings for Pattie Boyd. To Keylock he also remarked on his 'near escape' from joining the Rolling Stones, then giving the singular concert of their lives at Altamont, California.

Blind Faith, meanwhile, not so much died as expired. There were meetings with Stigwood and Chris Blackwell; a rehearsal at Hurtwood Edge; a reunion with Winwood at Trident Studios in November. Despite protests from Baker and Grech, Clapton – clinging to Delaney Bramlett as the stock father-figure in his life – declined to record a second album.

The derelict members of Blind Faith briefly re-formed in Airforce. It was a number of years before Clapton and Baker spoke again. Grech, after a year with Mike Bloomfield and a failed effort to record a country album, returned to Leicester, indulging his 'kamikaze' instincts, where he died in 1990. He retained mixed feelings about members of the group, particularly Clapton, whom Grech described to Rob Townsend as 'personally ambitious under the skin'. The same conclusion was drawn by Winwood. 'Looking back,' he told Ray Coleman, 'it's obvious that Blind Faith, just like the Yardbirds and John Mayall, was a stepping stone for Eric . . . Eventually he could not remain a member of any band. He'd have to go solo.'

Going solo was Clapton's next move. At intervals between January and June 1970 he recorded the basic material for an eponymous album, released in August. An amiable mix of blues and gospel, with obvious overtones of Delaney and Bonnie, the LP saw the first flourishing of Clapton's songwriting, with lyrics, he insisted, that were 'personal . . . what [was] happening in my heart' – none of the detached edge of a Davies or Townshend. 'Slunky', the opening track, was a Stax pastiche worthy of King Curtis; it, 'Blues Power', 'Bottle Of Red Wine' and 'Let It Rain' were the album's enduring moments. All four, like the record as a whole, bobbed and wove engagingly without ever quite achieving forward momentum. There was an accompanying version of J. J. Cale's 'After Midnight', largely ignored at the time, later a matrix for Clapton's whole career: it virtually invented the inoffensive, bland-yet-addictive sound of modern legend. The British reviews of *Eric Clapton* were mixed; phrases like 'anaemic', 'vapid' and 'self-effacing' confused Clapton the guitarist with the singer-songwriter he now became. His vocals, previously restrained, proved to be adequate and even inspired. Among the American notices was one rightly describing the album as 'Clapton in chrysalis . . . from risking chaos and sometimes succumbing to it . . . to the more laid-back posture of a team player, deliberately avoiding the high-energy ambience of his work with Cream.' If ever there was a statement of future intent, *Eric Clapton* was it.

The thousands that winter who filled the Fillmore West, scene of Cream's apotheosis, were confronted with a rail-thin, bearded character (strangely resembling George Harrison) equally at home with love songs, soul and gospel. Clapton *did* assume the posture of a team player. Seasoned critics wondered at the evanescent figure in the shadows with the battered Fender guitar. Their surprise derived from how thin his own instrument sounded and how raucous the others. Clapton was so retiring he seemed almost not to be present; as at Hyde Park, hardened fans were left wondering aloud if this were 'really Eric Clapton'. He retained his ability to mimic and even alter his appearance: now into Harrison, the next night Bramlett or Leon Russell. 'He *becomes* different people,' his publicist told the *Sunday Times*. 'When he was with [Harrison] he bought a big house like George's and a big Mercedes . . . When he was with Stevie Winwood and Blind Faith, he went back to jeans and wanting to live in the country. When he met Delaney and Bonnie he gave up travelling first class and just climbed into their bus.'

His need for acceptance, for association and for approval led Clapton to an almost promiscuous involvement with other groups: between January and July 1970 he recorded with Ashton Gardner and Dyke, with Stephen Stills and Jonathan Kelly, with Ringo Starr, Howlin' Wolf and Jesse Ed Davis, with Billy Preston and the Crickets. By early April Clapton's relationship with the Bramletts had cooled. Even during the recording of *Eric Clapton* there were disputes about living expenses and money – what Connolly calls 'the air of tension beneath the shared bonhomie'. In extending their relaxed, laissez-faire lifestyle to their personal spending habits, the Bramletts perhaps made a defect of their merits. A member of Stigwood's staff remembers 'Bonnie – the original steel magnolia' appearing at Clapton's hotel, 'yelling, literally howling at him for bread . . . They were all on a tight leash.' So much so that when the Bramletts' backing musicians raised the question of their own expenses – repeatedly and in public – all three were fired. Bobby Whitlock, Jim Gordon and Carl Radle arrived in England that spring. They stayed, as before, at Hurtwood Edge. As before, Ray Connolly found an atmosphere of 'middling chaos' at Clapton's house: musicians in cowboy boots lolled by the fire as precious blues albums warped on the mantel. In May the quartet played on Harrison's *All Things Must Pass* at Abbey Road. Observers found Clapton to be nervous and distracted. It was now that he first entered into a standing arrangement with his supplier: a gramme of heroin to go with a gramme of cocaine. ('I thought, what's it like, this naughty drug? So I tried it.')

This sense of chance, of events merely unfolding, was Clapton's trademark; all his life he spoke of things 'happening' without conscious effort. He accepted heroin as the logical adjunct to cocaine, itself the successor of LSD and marijuana. His habit did not sweeten his temperament. If Clapton had been under the impression that drugs were beneficial to his playing, Whitlock soon disabused him: 'I told Eric in Abbey Road he was playing off-key. Not too quiet or loud – out of *tune*. He almost decked me.' Clapton did, however, consent to rehearse with Whitlock, Radle and Gordon at Hurtwood Edge (his gnomic comment to the first was that the band should have 'no horns or chicks') and to be talked by Stigwood into performing. A tinge of what psychologists call moral masochism – allied to a healthy appetite for money – yet again persuaded Clapton to join a group against his own wishes. As the quartet – announced as Eric Clapton and Friends – took the stage at the Lyceum, Tony Ashton, a man who shared Clapton's minimalist sense of humour, suggested the name Del, or Derek, and the Dominos. A group now synonymous with the expression of unrequited love began life as a *Goon Show* caricature.

The tour that followed advanced Clapton's reputation as an eccentric – an original stylist whose sheer inability to pace a song made some wonder how he could ever have been taken seriously, a shrinking violet who let off stink-bombs and was barred from clubs. The Dominos interlude was the final span in the bridge between Clapton as fully fledged slave of the blues and the more unobtrusive quality of his later work. The audiences at Dagenham, Dunstable and Norwich received a nine-song set, of which the highlight was the single 'Tell The Truth', moving through radical shifts in mood, pitch and tempo. Radle later imagined that this, as much as Blind Faith, was 'the moment Clapton rediscovered himself'. Whitlock also notes that 'Eric's playing began to come more from the heart than the wrist.' The use of the Fender Stratocaster, six of which he bought from the dealer Ted Newman Jones that summer, was an aesthetic judgement by Clapton, a deliberate step back from the world of power chords and histrionic soloing. Whereas with Cream the guitar was the whole point, in Derek and the Dominos it was only one part of the total effect. Clapton's consequently diminished role was reflected in the correspondence pages ('Unless Eric Clapton finds his feet again as a good, fast and tasteful guitar player, the critics will find another' . . . 'If Clapton wants to lose his crown to another young guitarist, he only has to carry on what he's doing' . . . 'After seeing Clapton looking like a de-greased Elvis Presley and playing poorly disguised rock and roll, I came away feeling sick') then, as now, a useful sample of what ordinary fans, as opposed to the writers in magazines, thought. There was a torpid quality to the Dominos' music that may in part be explained by their backstage habits: marijuana for Whitlock, LSD for Radle, heroin and

Scotch for Gordon. Never one to pass up the chance to send an obscure signal, Clapton himself appeared on stage wearing a cocaine spoon dangling from a necklace.

He continued to see Pattie Boyd. Late that summer there was a party at Stigwood's house in Stanmore following the London première of *Oh Calcutta!* Harrison arrived alone from the studio where he was finishing *All Things Must Pass*. As he parked he was surprised to see his wife and Clapton walk past him arm-in-arm down the lane. Although laughed off at the time, this was the moment, as Harrison later admitted, that he knew 'Eric had done it with Pattie.' At home that night Clapton spent an hour on the phone to his lover. Considering the later explosion of their affair it burnt with an inordinately long fuse. It may be that Clapton trusted in the irresistible outcome of a marriage in which the husband seems to have barely acknowledged the existence of the wife. According to John Lennon, Harrison was 'an intelligent man, who was thinking all the time; and all the time he was thinking his best friend was sleeping with his missus'. (Or, as Clapton himself put it: 'Pattie was just trying to get George's attention, get him jealous, and so she used me . . . All she wanted was for him to say "I love you" and all he was doing was meditating.') While Boyd retreated with Harrison to Henley, Clapton returned to her younger sister.

The Dominos arrived in Miami in late August to record with Tom Dowd, the man who virtually invented stereo, at Criteria Studios. Each day Clapton arose at his beachfront hotel at noon. He gave himself a perfunctory shave, drank Ripple and Gallo, took pills, strummed his guitar and drove to the stucco building at Northeast 149th Street. Slowly, over the course of a month, the basic material rehearsed in Hurtwood Edge and London was refined into a double album. Clapton also entered into a relationship with Duane Allman after attending (and falling asleep at) a concert by the Allman Brothers in Miami. Duane arrived in the studio on 28 August in time to play on the reconstituted 'Tell The Truth'. The perennial male influence in Clapton's life for six months, he both extended and engrained his friend's drug use. Dowd and Ahmet Ertegün both lectured Clapton in the studio: the latter says he 'laid it out what would happen if Eric kept using. I told him he would die.' Even Leon Russell, a man who enjoyed a drink himself, was horrified at Clapton's dual addiction to alcohol and heroin. The disc jockey Scott Ross also remembers haranguing Clapton about the 'medical consequences' and being given some impractical physical advice in return.

In the midst of this, fourteen basic songs were recorded and mixed, including, on 9 September, a set of lyrics written by Clapton, set to music by Gordon and Allman, in turn influenced by Albert King's 'As The Years Go Passing By'. When, at Hurtwood Edge, Paula Boyd first heard 'Layla', she packed her bags and left.

The Dominos toured America in October and November; again Clapton's playing was loose to the point of detached; again there was talk of 'failing to lay the ghost' (of Cream), of audiences 'walking out during the performances . . . and those that stayed seeming bent upon calling out Clapton's name during the solos'. Whitlock confirms that there was a general misapprehension that 'the group was Eric and three backing musicians' and that much of the apathy of the performance came from 'sheer fatigue, downright exhaustion and too many drugs'. As often the case, Clapton's attitude to his critics was reflected in his humour, much of it directed at the pressure on him from 'my fellow slaves' to return to the blues. At the nadir of the American tour Clapton grumbled to Radle backstage, 'If I didn't love this music, I'd hate it.' In other moments of exasperation, he noted that 'Anyone who has been persecuted for two hundred years probably deserves it.'

Clapton felt, with good cause, that his adherence to the black rural tradition – to the blues – was a vulnerability when it came to a mass audience. Forever stressing his 'purity' of intent, he was equally swayed by Stigwood's demands for a more commercial sound. *Layla*, the album and the song, accelerated the process begun in Blind Faith and continued in Delaney and Bonnie. What Clapton was doing was ad-libbing in the manner of a sportsman extemporizing over a basically sound technique; having developed the blues to the limit the market and his own ability would permit, he improvised in other areas. To the native tradition of Jimmy Reed and Blind Willie Johnson were added touches of rockabilly, country and soul, even of prototype rap and disco (both of which rely on the mood and tempo swings characteristic of 'Layla'). What Clapton became was not so much a musician as a musicologist.

Evidence of his more profuse side is provided by the late Ian Stewart, the sometime Rolling Stones pianist. Stewart was present when Clapton, Jagger and Bill Wyman, along with Harrison and Al Kooper, hosted a birthday party for Keith Richards on 18 December. 'About ten of them plugged in and played "Brown Sugar". It was unrecognizable. But brilliant . . . I happened to be talking to Clapton's roadie, who told me Eric was having money problems. He was down to £50 while Stigwood sorted out some deal. The roadie and I talked, then Eric came over and asked how I was. "Broke," I said, "in mind, body and pocket." Clapton immediately laughed. "Do you want any bread? I can give you fifty quid."'

Layla was released that Christmas. It extended, or formalized, Clapton's affection for The Band: the first three tracks could all have been performed by Robbie Robertson (the fourth, 'Nobody Knows You (When You're Down and Out)' once was). Elsewhere there were references to Hendrix ('Little Wing'), Delaney and Bonnie ('Anyday') and even to Harrison ('I Am Yours' – inoffensive but trite). Clapton brought genuine pathos to the dirges of 'Bell Bottom Blues' and 'It's Too Late'. If the predominant theme of *Layla* was unrequited love, its expression was the title track, a song now virtually synonymous with the state. 'Layla' was, of course, a paean to Pattie Boyd. Clapton's lyrics, including the line 'I tried to give you consolation/When your old man had let you down' were a direct observation on his predicament; no greater analysis is needed than that. Despite the song's having been accelerated and greatly enhanced by Allman; despite its celebrated coda having been written by Gordon and the uncredited Rita Coolidge; despite mutterings over the years concerning the originality of the central theme, 'Layla' was among Clapton's definitive moments – exquisite pain translated as exquisite music. It may have been the one Dominos song whose writing was improved by drugs. According to Whitlock, 'Eric had the middle, the title, and some lyrics . . . Duane wrote the intro and [Gordon and Coolidge] the piano part. We were all into the song. And we were all into getting stoned.'

Layla failed to make the LP charts on either side of the Atlantic. The single, finally released in July 1972, reached number 7 in Britain; eventually, like 'Yesterday' and 'Satisfaction', it attracted a second and third generation of fans, surviving its transfer into football stadia, windswept, echoing among the drink cans and old programmes while someone posing under the name 'Eric Clapton' preened in an Italian suit in the mid-distance. Long before Live Aid and *Unplugged*, 'Layla' had lost meaning except as a palliative against ageing. Listeners experienced a conjuncture between temporary euphoria and nostalgia. Vague memories were stirred of the first time the song's early chords were heard. Because of its subject matter – love not merely of a woman, but of a woman identified by Clapton – 'Layla's melodramatic aspect was seized on by the press. The song's sub-text sustained it after its novelty had faded.

If Clapton had died in 1971 he would now be widely regarded as the most emotive, if not technically gifted guitarist who ever lived. It was, above all, his vulnerability; the sense that Clapton, unlike a Page, Richards or Townshend, played *de profundis*. A cause of widespread female interest, it was immediately and inherently attractive. First and foremost, Clapton played music for purists. As his reputation grew, he attracted a second wave of fans who wanted, plainly put, to mother him. Clapton's career to then had helped set the seal on the sixties – the *Blues Breakers* LP, Cream, Hyde Park – no less than the Beatles or Stones. Like them he invited equal interest in his offstage activities; he inspired imitators and exhibitionists (there was a period when every rhythm and blues group had its Clapton figure, playing long wailing solos with varying degrees of success); his withdrawn, apparently morbid personality attracted curiosity and respect. All these factors collided in 'Layla'. Clapton was applauded for the huge achievements of his past, admired for his present, pitied for the future. 'Whatever he does, and it's unpredictable, he obviously has a problem,' noted a critic. 'Chronic introspection,' suggested another.

The Dominos, after briefly regrouping in London, disbanded the following May. As always with Clapton, the end was dramatic: after a failed effort to record a song entitled 'Till I See You Again' there was a physical confrontation at the studio. Clapton's own version – 'I said something about the rhythm being wrong and [Gordon] said, "Well, the Dixie Flyers are in town. You can get their drummer" . . . I put my guitar down and walked out' – if anything underestimates the event; according to Whitlock, 'they were both yelling, howling at each other across the floor. Eric unstrapped his guitar and swung it at Jim. If he'd hit he would have killed him.' The Dominos returned to obscurity, Whitlock in Memphis, Radle to Tulsa. Duane Allman was killed in a motorcycle accident in October 1971. Gordon himself, telling police he 'heard voices' and 'saw things', was sentenced to sixteen years' imprisonment in 1984 for the murder of his mother. Despite a 'supportive message' relayed through an intermediary, Clapton neither visited nor wrote. Gordon watched the Grammy ceremonies in February 1993 on television at Atascadero State Hospital, California. When 'Layla' won he uttered a sound described by one inmate as 'like an animal howling at the moon'. Then Gordon went on the rampage: the steel door with its sliding panel, the walls, chairs, table and windows were all beaten and spat on. While Clapton stood in his dinner jacket smiling and waving, Gordon was sedated and returned to his room.

*   *   *

By spring 1971 Clapton had passed through seven professional groups in eight years. Even in an industry notorious for the brevity of its relationships, it was a notable track record. A liaison with Clapton, as a succession of ex-friends and colleagues could testify, was no guarantee of long-term involvement. Even as he remained essentially a private person, one who concealed his soul from others, he engaged in a series of intense casual relationships. He was reclusive but not shy; self-effacing but not modest; egotistical but not secure. At the core of Clapton's personality was his self-absorption, his relentless analysis of his own character. Until 1971 he had little or no life away from music. Such relaxation as he allowed himself came in the form of schoolboy pranks. Perhaps it was the adolescent instincts Clapton had never indulged while growing up; perhaps because he had always been fascinated with the exotic, weird and unusual. Whatever the cause, Clapton in private became a proficient slapstick comic while, in public, still restricting himself to gloomy prognostications or Delphic utterances on the future. Like many comics, the violence of his self-hate was expressed as violence towards others. 'He could yell at people until they burst into tears,' says Chris Dreja. 'Eric saw relationships as violent. A lot of girlfriends in those days were reduced to hysterics.' Clapton's dealings with women also included touches of maudlin self-pity. After playing 'Layla' to Pattie Boyd he resorted to emotional blackmail: 'I told her that either she came with me, or I hit the deck. I actually presented her with a packet of heroin and said, "If you don't come with me, I'm taking this for the next couple of years."' Boyd's refusal merely precipitated the eventual outcome. The deaths in autumn 1970 of both Hendrix and Jack Clapp may have also contributed. A simpler explanation for Clapton's addiction, borne out by the facts, is that he sampled heroin from insecurity; he emulated Gordon, Radle and Whitlock for the same reason anyone emulates anybody else – to be liked and win approval. Naturally thin-skinned, Clapton felt particularly hurt by taunts of being 'scared' of the drug. His response was a typical overcompensation, a period in which, in his own words, it became 'a snort of coke in one nostril, a snort of smack in the other, a pint of cheap wine in one ear, a bottle of Scotch in the other'. Clapton's three-year layoff with the flu had begun.

First, on his twenty-sixth birthday, Clapton attended the Rolling Stones' farewell party, following their decision to emigrate, at Skindles Hotel, Maidenhead. His was among the voices raised loudest when Jagger, registering protest at the closure of the hotel bar, ejected a table through a plate-glass window. At the party's continuation in Cheyne Walk Clapton fought with Ormsby-Gore (restored in the Boyds' absence). 'He treated her like a servant,' said Ian Stewart. This was Ormsby-Gore's lot. During the week she was normally at Hurtwood Edge, looking after the house and grounds while Clapton stayed in London; at weekends she fed him and waited on him. In return, all she asked was that Clapton stayed reasonably faithful, accepted her advice on which drugs to take and continued to play music. Even this was too much. He snapped at her or lapsed into moody silences; to avoid talking to her he played his stereo at top volume; at other times he shut himself away in his tower and painted toy models.

Clapton did consent to appear at Harrison's all-star Concert for Bangladesh in New York. His playing at the two events was uneven; his appearance ragged; Ormsby-Gore fed him methadone linctus, a heroin substitute, from a scaffolding tower beside the stage. At the inevitable party Clapton, in his blue denim jacket and boots, was distant, self-absorbed, quiet, unassuming. He spoke, if at all, in epigrams – 'my romance with wealth is over' – complaining of the relative failure of *Layla* and other commercial projects. Later in the month, when John Lennon proposed that he, Clapton, Yoko Ono and Ormsby-Gore invest in a yacht, sleeping *au naturel*, late and with whomever they chose, berthing in Tahiti, the guitarist's reply was immediate: 'Who pays?' When Lennon declined to underwrite the project it was quietly shelved.

Relations with Harrison were equally enigmatic. By 1971 he, Clapton, Pattie Boyd and Ormsby-Gore had entered into a conspiracy (both men wanting the other's partner) something akin to a domestic comedy. Clapton made the comparison himself: 'It really was like one of those movies where you see wife swapping – *Bob and Carol and Ted and Alice* . . . Those were the times.' A better analogy might be the conditions that produced *Frankenstein*. The quartet met frequently at the Harrisons' gothic mansion, candlelit, where the antique portico offered percussive effects when the wind blew. Parlour games were organized, including a more elaborate version of Sardines, allowing Clapton and Boyd to hide in the bedroom closet. There 'really were nights', according to one of the women, 'when lightning flashed and the four of us chased around like something out of Shelley. It was wild.' The meetings are described as if no one else was present in the house. In fact both the Harrisons and Clapton employed gardeners, cooks, chauffeurs, maids; when, from time to time, Clapton appeared in the tiled kitchen at Hurtwood Edge it was to search for the chocolate bars and pastry on which he existed for three years. 'He just ate, ate, ate,' says a man employed to cook for him. 'You can imagine the effect.' According to Albhy Galutin, a Miami session pianist involved with the Dominos, 'I was at the [Bangladesh] concert and hadn't seen Clapton since *Layla*. It almost broke my heart.'

His Hollyfield schoolfriend Richard Drew, pursuing a career as an artist (responsible for the cover of *Led Zeppelin III*), arrived at Hurtwood Edge that summer. He was greeted by a 'friendly but subdued' Clapton, his hand clasped on the banister, looking 'very English'. According to Drew: 'It was a scene of widespread but mild chaos. Eric sat upstairs in the tower, mumbling, hunched over a guitar. Always strumming. Alice would appear at the door with cigarettes, tea or the news that their concert tickets were missing. Next it was the cook with a plate of chocolate biscuits . . . Here was this slumped form, receiving employees like the Sun King. You got the impression he probably didn't even put the toothpaste on his own brush. He was genial but he was in a different world.' When Drew left, having failed to obtain a commission, Clapton, 'like a monarch dispensing alms', presented him with an enamel ring.

As with so much else in Clapton's life, drug addiction was a purely random development. He took cocaine; his supplier gave him heroin; he took heroin. Looking back, Clapton stressed this point above all others ('[It was] a rotten trick because I would have never started if it hadn't have been lying around'), his own helplessness in the teeth of the giant forces that overwhelmed him. Nobody who starts taking drugs thinks they will become addicted. It just happens. Clapton consistently and resolutely, as at other times in his life, failed to grasp the consequences of his actions.

Four immediate causes have been advanced for the subsequent outcome. There was the commercial disappointment of *Layla*; the deaths of Hendrix and Jack Clapp; the unavailability of Pattie Boyd. (A fifth, Duane Allman's death, occurred nearly a year after the devils had caught at Clapton's heels.)

Layla did disappoint. Previously Clapton had been a success, now he was a failure. Certain fans, unaware of his new persona, failed even to connect Clapton's name with the album. (*Layla* revived when a 'Derek is Eric' campaign was launched by Polydor.) Given the view of Dowd, one fully shared by Clapton – 'When I finished doing *Layla* I walked out and said, "That's the best goddamn record I've made in ten years"' – it was natural to feel let down. There was also the question of the income

Layla failed to generate. When previously Clapton thought that his gifts had been recognized ('I am God'), he felt justified in seeking to perfect the work rather than the life. Now, because he believed the critics when they praised him, he was forced to believe them when they criticized. Clapton faced a disturbing and even demoralizing crisis.

His grandfather's death, Clapton admitted, was 'traumatic, mainly because of what it did to Rose'. On the other hand, Clapton's connection with Ripley since the day he moved out in 1965 had been, at best, sporadic. He still appeared at the Ship, parking his Ferrari in the gravel surround; he still remembered Rose's and Jack's birthdays; but in private he would endorse the view that it was 'a nice place to come from . . . and a lousy one to go back to'. It was 1987 before Clapton, prompted by a television interviewer, admitted even to considering the link between his grandfather's death and his addiction.

The relationship between Clapton and Hendrix has also been exaggerated. There was an artistic association. There may well have been respect. Clapton could sense a romantic figure in many ways more capricious than himself. The two were not, however, intimate. With the exception of the period immediately following Hendrix's arrival in England, they rarely socialized or attended each other's concerts. There was only the most cursory professional relationship – a singsong in Greenwich Village, a brief duet in the Ad Lib Club in London – between them. When the American died, Clapton (between European dates with the Dominos), citing his fear of a 'showbiz event', declined to attend the funeral. In so far as he admitted to feelings for Hendrix, they were directed inward: 'Nobody could be blamed [for his death], but I felt incredible fury. I just had this terrible, lonely feeling.' Pete Brown is more blunt: 'He felt let down that Jimi had died and left Eric, as he saw it, to carry on on his own.'

The situation with Boyd was more complex. But there were compensations: Clapton and his best friend's wife enjoyed a number of encounters in 1970–71. Then there was the question of Ormsby-Gore, an intelligent if unassuming woman to whom, as she says, Clapton was 'very open' about his intentions. Throughout the period 1969–74 Clapton continued to enjoy the undivided attention of one woman while intermittently seeing another. Many have borne greater hardship with equanimity.

Another reason advanced was the romantic or artistic association of drugs. There was a sense of identification (as Pete Townshend put it, 'wanting to be like his heroes – deadbeats living out of empty baked bean cans') with the original bluesmen. Clapton spoke particularly admiringly of Huddie Ledbetter, quoting his seminal lines:

> Well a nickel is a nickel an' a dime is a dime
> I snort cocaine any old time,
> Hey hey baby have a whiff on me,
> Whatever happened to the friends I know,
> Who needs friends when you can have snow . . .

Clapton, of course, knew as much of conditions in rural Texas – those that spawned Ledbetter – as he knew about the Antarctic. He was always careful to measure the distance between his heroes' makeshift, ad-libbed lifestyle and his own more measured one. The ambiguity that can be seen in his attitude to the blues came naturally and honestly to Eric Clapton. He studied the culture like a curator. His adoption of surface elements of the blues – the Delta transposed to stockbroker-belt Surrey – bore all the conviction of a man self-consciously slumming, or, as Brown says, 'of a showman juggling knives': knives sufficiently blunt never to cut him.

There was also a literary, or sub-literary pretext. Clapton quoted Coleridge approvingly and Blake without complaint. The latter's aphorism about 'The road of excess [leading] to the palace of wisdom' made a particular impression. Clapton spoke of 'wanting to take a long dark journey . . . and come out the other side', of being vulnerable to drugs through living 'on a very intense plane of emotional necessity'. What Clapton meant was that drugs provided a daily substitute for the immortality of being on stage. When, in 1971, he ceased to perform altogether, as much from sheer lack of opportunity as any other motive, the drugged state took over. Clapton took heroin, in part, to obscure the truth that, outside music, his life had no distinguishing meaning. His addiction was a form of madness through which he intended to preserve his sanity.

For years Clapton had admitted and even protested to an obsessive personality. Early on he shocked Rose and Jack by his accounts of debauchery backstage and in hotel rooms with the Yardbirds. He horrified people when he spoke of drug orgies in Cream. Everything he said was true, but Clapton increased the volume to the point where his voice began to distort. His declarations of excess bore the ring of affectation. He constantly stressed the waywardness of his life not only to project himself, but to offend those who were easily shocked. 'A large part of it', says Ben Palmer, 'was Eric talking himself into a lifestyle. Because he thought the only way for musicians to live was on the edge, that they needed to be "nursed", he ended up believing it . . . He quoted me those lines by Blake and I said, "Bullshit. It's not about wisdom, it's about buying a myth. It's a cop-out."'

Finally, Clapton's retirement was a recognition that his first, most creative period was over. Like the other originals of British pop – the Beatles, the Stones, the Kinks – his motivating force was exhausted within seven years. Clapton had achieved his starting ambitions. In this period he poured out ten albums and hundreds of concerts, while active in outside projects and collaborations. His name was redolent of titanic plans and achievements, self-loathing, paranoia and redeeming talent – almost an allegory of the sixties themselves. From 1971 (like the Stones, the Kinks and members of the Beatles) Clapton would no longer be seen merely as a musician or performer. He would be a synonym for nostalgia. Pete Brown believes that 'Eric's retirement was a deliberate career move. The only way you could take two years off in those days was to quit altogether . . . It's that simple. Clapton wanted to think about life while pop went through its cyclical fit with Sweet, Slade and Gary Glitter.'

Clapton's seclusion in Hurtwood Edge had two distinct phases. There was the period where, accompanied by Ormsby-Gore, he saw his family and friends, visited Ripley and London and wrote at least two songs, 'Give Me Strength' and 'Let It Grow', among the most enduring of his career. For six months he retained a notably more polished image than the raddled hophead of later legend. 'Mentally,' he told Ray Coleman, 'I was totally aware of what was going on, what I was doing to myself . . . not lying in bed all day long taking H.' There was a subdued, dispassionate aspect to Clapton's addiction: he knew he was being talked about, encouraged it, and enjoyed the significant prestige of the hermit.

The other, less agreeable side was the man who pawned his guitars to finance his habit, who fought hysterically – and violently – with Ormsby-Gore and slammed his front door in the face of old friends. Ben Palmer was among those who visited Hurtwood Edge in 1972. 'I actually turned up twice,' he says. 'The first time there was no reply, although I knew he was in. On the second occasion I was greeted by Eric telling me, in so many words, to get lost.' Clapton's mother, among others, had the same experience.

Another friend who saw Clapton in London was appalled that the 'quiet, self-effacing' man of previous acquaintance had become a scrounger and boor. 'Because both Eric and [Ormsby-Gore] were junkies, there were incredible scenes about who was keeping the best stash back for themselves . . . I wasn't prepared for the violence. What really shakes you isn't the foul things foul people do – you get used to that. It's the foul things people like Eric do. He cared about a tenth as much for what happened to others as for what happened to him.'

Speculation was rife about Clapton. Both his mother and grandmother ('I tried to talk to him once . . . he just laughed') were aware of his condition. Ormsby-Gore's father, whose worst fears in 1969 must now have been realized, both wrote and visited. Of fellow musicians only Pete Townshend – regularly summoned by 'hysterical' phone calls, grasped the situation. Beyond a general conviction, expressed by John Lennon, that 'Eric will be back', there was little conscious interest by his peers. In so far as the press expressed a view it was that Clapton had been overwhelmed by fame, an assumption made by *Sounds* in a full-page profile:

> [Clapton's] fate has been not unlike other musicians who have grown to the stature of virtuoso stars. The strain seems to be particularly wearying for great guitarists, probably because of the major role of the instrument within contemporary rock . . .
>
> The proof of this is contained in [Clapton's] contribution to rock in the last year. It has dwindled from a few things in the studio and on stage to nothing . . .
>
> Almost inevitably Derek and the Dominos were destined not to survive. There had been an attempt to integrate Clapton into a group rather than forcing him into the role as frontman and leader. But there was no escaping the limelight, even though it was stipulated that his name was not to appear in the billings. The people still came primarily to see Clapton as they had for several years; and it reminded you of the fairground freak sideshows.

In truth Clapton continued to appear on albums at an almost profligate rate. He never intended to stop playing altogether, merely to distance himself from the insults of the critics. This was a period, says Mick Jagger, when 'every musician and his dog turned to Eric', a man apparently unable to pass by a creative vacuum without a pathological urge to fill it. Between 1971 and 1973 Clapton, ostensibly retired, played on sessions for Leon Russell, Buddy Guy, Bobby Whitlock, Bobby Keys, Stevie

Wonder – and John Mayall (recording tracks at IBC, one of the Blues-breakers' original studios). He performed with Harrison in New York and Russell in London. He continued to record in the sub-sitting-room/ studio at Hurtwood Edge. He still visited old colleagues and friends (and Stigwood for money) in London. He still frequented restaurants and clubs: Clapton attended a reception for Harrison on 25 February 1972; he hosted a birthday party for his girlfriend, apparently believing it to be her twenty-first (Ormsby-Gore was born on 11 April 1952); and he accompanied Keith Richards to his villa in the South of France, roughly equivalent, in addicts' terms, to a phoenix chasing an arsonist.

Clapton retained the impulse to travel, to move, to put a distance between himself and his troubles. The teenager who had cycled for hours up the Portsmouth Road had become an adult whose pulse quickened when he sat in his Tour de France Ferrari or walked into the lobby of a foreign hotel. Few other archetypally English musicians have left England as often. Travel had provided inspiration for Clapton's music and the freedom of life on the move. It was also a means by which to escape obligations, to enjoy varied but fleeting experiences. Throughout his semi-retirement, Clapton continued to appear in London, Paris and New York. His excursions were always undertaken in style. After the success of 'Layla' in July 1972 he enjoyed a generous allowance from Stigwood; Ormsby-Gore's father also contributed to expenses.

Clapton's ordeal, in a word, did not always cut very deep. Aspects of his working life survived during his retirement. Clapton retained his long-standing interest in display and dressing up. He was among the first rock stars to switch from what Connolly calls 'Maoist uniformity' to *haute couture*. He became an habitué of Tommy Nutter and Mr Fish; he thought nothing of buying a dozen suits on Marshbrook credit, or making gifts to those to whom he took a liking. Even at Hurtwood Edge Clapton dressed fastidiously, sitting alone, dripping with makeup, at his polished refectory table. If, at times, he suggested a scene from *Sunset Boulevard*, Clapton was firm in his insistence that elements of 'normal life' be preserved. According to Ben Palmer, 'even at his nadir, Eric was still together – beautifully tailored, poised, and cracking jokes about his condition. When he threw you out he did it with style.' The overall impression, Palmer believes, was of a man struggling to find himself interesting.

Clapton's spiritual life, his apparent 'born again' status were the subject of interminable debate. What *were* the beliefs of the man called God?

Like most of his generation, Clapton was brought up to respect organized religion: both his grandparents were practising Anglicans; Clapton himself attended St Mary Magdalen; the parish register records his baptism and confirmation. 'Eric was there every Sunday,' recalls Matthew Wood, 'always neat, always tidy and always punctual.' Years later, in London, he began to question the basis of his faith more rationally. He met people who had their own spiritual beliefs, for whom God, in Dylan's phrase, was apparent in a daisy. He concluded that faith was largely a matter of environment and conditioning. This discovery, along with his dabbling in the occult, revealed the lack of intellectual depth to Clapton's religion. In practice, as has been seen, it was rarely much more than mysticism. Heavily impressed by the paranormal and bizarre, Clapton developed his more orthodox side when, on tour with the Dominos:

> Two guys came to my dressing-room . . . Christians . . . We knelt down and prayed and it was really like the blinding light and I said, 'What's happening? I feel much better!' And then I said to them, 'Let me show you this poster I've got of Jimi Hendrix.' I pulled it out and there was a portrait of Christ inside which I hadn't bought, had never seen in my life before. And it just knocked the three of us sideways. From then on I became a devout Christian.

Following within a year of the declarative 'Presence Of The Lord', the incident, much publicized in America, afforded Clapton cult status among the born-again fraternity. He responded with the zeal of a convert. For long periods, sometimes up to a month, he swore off drink and drugs. He bought a large King James Bible, which he set ostentatiously on a lectern in Hurtwood Edge. His physical appearance – bearded, gaunt, often adorned by a flowing tunic and sandals – added to the impression that this was a man cognizant of matters spiritual. In the end, like Clapton's other incarnations, his Christian affiliation proved ephemeral. By 1972, on the ingenious grounds that Harrison, a 'deep thinking man', had been incapable of restraining his wife from sexual adventuring, Clapton had broken with 'fucking religion'. Begging letters from Christian groups went unanswered. The Bible was removed from Hurtwood Edge. Clapton reversed himself on the question of faith apparently without hesitation, while at the same time retaining an interest in the value of ritual. 'I can't say I believe in the Bible any more than I do in a television set,' he announced in 1974. (He did, however, insist that Anglican blessing be conferred at later moments in his life – his wedding, the birth of his son – and that his concerts be closed with the trite but pleasing 'God bless you'.)

There followed Clapton's familiar rejection of that previously held sacrosanct. At various times in the 1970s the disc jockey Scott Ross, George Patterson (husband of the doctor who weaned Clapton from heroin) and his own bass player Dave Markee were violently resisted when trying to reconvert him. The last, a member of Clapton's group for three years, was constantly 'laughed at, abused and hassled by Eric and his manager. There was an unpleasant, childish side to it, like Clapton's gang versus my gang. On his own, he was a different proposition.' Markee's conclusion that Clapton remained interested in the 'externals of religion' found expression in an increasing reliance on ritual. Clapton was known to cross himself, flamboyantly and in public, in the dressing-room. He repeated the same mumbled imprecation each night before going on stage. He developed a fixation with the number 30, with black cats and ladders. Once, at Hurtwood Edge, he violently ejected a pair of shoes left under a table, then brooded for hours on the 'bad karma' of the event. If Clapton rejected formal religion, he quickly replaced it by superstition.

In rock music, like other performing arts, professional status tends to be a function of mystique rather than technical ability. The fans will tolerate almost any lapse except a failure of image. Clapton understood this and, even in seclusion, played on it intuitively. Throughout the period 1971–3 he collaborated with Stigwood to ensure a steady flow of repackagings and compilations (*Heavy Cream, Live Cream Vol. 2, The Dominos Live In Concert*), leavened by suitable profiles in the musical press, intended to prepare Clapton's audience for a comeback. There was never any reference to permanent retirement. The official line, peddled by Stigwood and his energetic broker Roger Forrester, was that Clapton was both 'resting' and 'writing', recuperating from his unending efforts on his fans' behalf while composing new material for their benefit. Immense effort went into keeping Clapton's name before the public. Stigwood and Forrester realized that 'creative reflection', the phrase vigorously pushed in the press, would be both understood and applauded by Clapton's buyers; it suggested intense and even heroic soul-searching on their behalf. They also realized that, in order to benefit from the strategy, Clapton would sooner or later have to appear in public.

Here Forrester's considerable talents were stretched to the full. By late

1972 Clapton's main activities were restricted to assembling toy cars, badminton, and sitting alone listening to short-wave radio. Always prone to dramatic changes in weight, he put on twenty pounds in a month. He ceased to travel more than a few miles at a time, anxious to 'take enough [heroin] for a day and then get back by nightfall to score some more'. The extent to which Clapton relied on drugs was revealed by his account of what he described to Bruce as a 'quiet get-together' with his colleagues from Cream:

> The three of us . . . tore the place apart and came back to my house flying – really flying – on cloud nine. [We] took acid and just started talking.

Clapton's fans were a various body, and not all were strangers themselves to LSD; even so, in view of the fact that the reunion with Bruce and Baker also included a quantity of cocaine snorted, bottles of brandy drunk and an assortment of other drugs swallowed, few would have described it as a 'quiet get-together'. When Forrester and others visited Hurtwood Edge they encountered a pudgy and ponderous figure, dressed in an ill-fitting white suit, more anxious to discuss Airfix models than music. Clapton, for all his and his manager's intentions, was in danger of vanishing altogether. In late summer 1972 a picture appeared of Elton John and Rod Stewart in a London nightclub. In an indication of the way the pop zeitgeist was moving, Clapton, who had been sitting with them, was cropped from the photograph.

The story might have ended there but for the role of Bob Pridden, equipment manager of the Who. Pridden, who lived near Hurtwood Edge, became friendly with Ormsby-Gore; between them they suggested that Pete Townshend invite Clapton to a concert by the group in Paris. The reunion led to additional meetings. As well as mediating the 'hysterical' scenes between Clapton and his girlfriend, Townshend was invited to hear the tapes of his friend's previous two years' work: a fragment of Derek and the Dominos, an acoustic blues, the rough drafts of 'Give Me Strength' and 'Let It Grow'. Simultaneously, David Harlech, whose initial response to his daughter's condition had dwindled to one of mute resignation, was attempting to organize a concert, loosely designated the Fanfare For Youth, to celebrate Britain's entry into the Common Market. Slowly, over the period of the late autumn and winter, he, Townshend and Ormsby-Gore persuaded Clapton to appear. The event, seized on by Stigwood and remodelled 'Eric Clapton's Rainbow Concert' – the idea of European unity, not for the last time, making a false start – was announced for 13 January 1973. Clapton, his manager now insisted, was back.

The musical community responded in force. In the first days of the new year a group including Townshend, Winwood, Grech, the percussionists Jimmy Karstein and Jim Capaldi, and the guitarist Ronnie Wood, hastily named the Palpitations, assembled at Wood's home in Richmond. In 1973 Clapton, the man who still feared rejection, was treated as a celebrity by his own peers. The rehearsals at Wood's house were witnessed by a recording engineer also involved in Clapton's later career: 'I used to dread Eric showing up in the afternoon – two or three o'clock and immediately touchy, aggressive and domineering ... He was a pain. Everybody thought he was brilliant and wonderful and a great guitarist and all that. An artist. But he just made life hell for anyone involved in the show. He and Townshend hauled off at Steve Winwood one day for not turning up. Screamed at him on the telephone.'

In preparing for his comeback Clapton may have been tense, anxious, concerned, in his manager's words, 'under no circumstances, to screw up' at the Rainbow. His behaviour at Wood's house certainly suggests a man under pressure. Clapton might have agreed with Stigwood and Forrester that his retirement was purely temporary; having said that, he didn't necessarily want it to end. The two-year period from 9 September 1970 (the day he recorded 'Layla') to 9 September 1972 (the reunion with Townshend in Paris) was a critical phase in Clapton's life, the addiction to drugs accompanied by a reliance, no less addictive, on his own company. Given the implications, it was hardly surprising that his behaviour at rehearsal was tetchy, or the performance itself uneven. In fact the two shows (the first at 6.30 p.m., the second, scheduled for 8.30, beginning two hours late) were in sharp contrast. Clapton, who appeared at the theatre minutes before curtain-up, was merely tentative in the opening 'Layla', 'Badge' and 'Blues Power', such tension as there was provided by the interplay between Townshend and Winwood. In the second set the songs were given more intelligent construction. Dressed in his white suit, almost theatrically pale, haggard, Clapton invested 'Presence Of The Lord', in particular, with the intensity of the original, bowing and opening his arms like a vision of Piaf or Judy Garland. Backstage, a musician was foolish enough to accuse Clapton of having 'slowed up'. He responded by playing the opening chords of 'Crossroads' at top speed, perfectly, and left-handed. Clapton then handed his Stratocaster to an assistant, commented on the 'showbiz' element of the night – and left.

The event (released as *Eric Clapton's Rainbow Concert* in September 1973) together with the award of a Grammy for his performance, nearly two years before, on *Bangladesh*, convinced critics that the man dubbed Eric Claptout was back. There were signs – his involvement in the Dominos' live album, a session with Keith Emerson and Mitch Mitchell issued as *Music From Free Creek* – that Clapton, however tentatively, intended the comeback to be permanent. Certain fans still hold his real career to have begun at the Rainbow, his retirement a necessary hiatus between the fanatic he was and the entertainer he became. Yet others believe that Clapton never fully recovered from going off his head in 1971–3.

Full critical judgement was, at first, suspended. For a year no permanent advantage accrued from Harlech and Townshend's initiative. Clapton returned to Hurtwood Edge, where his habit both continued and worsened. It was the period after his theoretical decision to kick heroin that the drug's effect was most virulent. Not only did Clapton, now existing exclusively on a diet of chocolate, deteriorate physically (spreading beyond the narrow confines of his Charles II chair, says one guest, like a ripe cheese), he became a threat to both Ormsby-Gore and himself. Clapton set about his girlfriend frenziedly when arguing about drugs. Both parties were known to burn themselves with cigarettes to mask the more insidious pain of withdrawal. In order to prevent him leaving the house Ormsby-Gore more than once removed the rotor-arm from Clapton's car; the motorbike was also disabled. Merely obtaining drugs – the top-speed drive to London or the arrival of Clapton's dealer at Hurtwood Edge – became the highlight and focus of the couple's life. The weekly 10-gramme packet of heroin was seized on like famine relief. When Clapton once inadvertently spilt the contents on the floor he said nothing, merely dropped to the ground and began snorting the rug.

All this, the drugs, the violence, the physical decline and ruin, was effectively shielded from the press, elements of which loyally praised the Rainbow event while scouring the horizon for evidence of more substantial activity. Among the saner headlines were 'WELCOME BACK, ERIC', 'CREAM CRACKER' and more imaginatively, 'GOD TALKS'. Clapton himself, meanwhile, spent a year dazed beyond speech at Hurtwood Edge.

Help came to hand in the form of David Harlech. Among Harlech's numerous achievements – his mediation between Macmillan and

Kennedy, his role in the Cuban Missile Crisis and the subsequent commissioning of Polaris, his presidency of the Board of Film Censors and other public office – not the least was his weaning of his daughter and Clapton from heroin. Harlech arranged an appointment at the London clinic of Meg Patterson, later physician-by-appointment to the music industry, then an obscure homeopath practising neutro-electric therapy, a form of mild acupuncture in which a current is passed through electrodes attached to the ears. The idea was that the charge generated would affect the natural opiates of the brain – endorphins – allowing rapid if not always painless withdrawal.

In the event Clapton and Ormsby-Gore were cured of the physical dependence on heroin within a week. They suffered only a day of the dreaded symptoms. More long-term therapy followed at Hurtwood Edge and Patterson's home in Harley Street. The doctor and her husband George formed a number of conclusions about Clapton: he 'wasn't interested in life at all', 'had lost all confidence in his creativity', yet spent hours 'playing toy soldiers . . . talking and listening to records' with the Pattersons' two sons (an identical scene to that witnessed by Pamela Mayall nine years before). Clapton himself was unduly childlike, lying for hours drawing and colouring, 'terrified', he said, of 'simple everyday procedures'. According to Patterson, she once asked, ' "Eric, could you make coffee for yourself this morning because I'm so busy?" He said: "Meg, I don't know how to make coffee." He wasn't fibbing.'

George Patterson, meanwhile, reached the following diagnosis:

> His illegitimacy had an impact on him and he felt embarrassed that other kids might get to know about it, or even that he felt they did know. So he withdrew more and more. In fact, he concentrated more and more on learning and he learned music by listening to it. Basically, this was the big thing in his life that had produced various reactions. There were three: one was that he hated his mother; the second was that he wanted to be the best blues player in the world; the third was that he wanted to lay as many women as possible – he wanted to lay a thousand women.

While the Pattersons offered sympathy, support and the family environment he craved, Clapton, not without protest and delay, returned to music. (Among the few letters he opened at the time was one from Carl Radle, suggesting the two play together. 'Maintain loose posture –

stay in touch,' read Clapton's reply.) During the course of a month he resumed playing the guitar, 'just strumming,' says Patterson, 'never [finishing] a song'. Equally gradually Clapton replaced his addiction to drugs with a craving for alcohol – raiding the Pattersons' kitchen, collapsing in their bathroom – which was to prove particularly acute in the years ahead. (Ormsby-Gore, denied the consolatory release of art, quickly became an alcoholic. By 1974 Harlech's attention had shifted to his daughter's consumption of two bottles of vodka a day.)

The last, critical phase of Clapton's recovery was supervised by Ormsby-Gore's brother, Frank, on his farm near Oswestry. For two weeks Clapton rose at dawn, milking cows and baling straw, cutting logs and taking long solitary walks whose inevitable destination was the pub. What he thought about as he trudged through the tangled black gum and dripping leaves, his whistle echoing off the flint and dry-stone walls, is unknown. What is known is that Clapton told an unusually perceptive questioner, Tom Lloyd-Roberts, that 'Being a junkie is like being part of a club. All my heroes were addicts ... The problem is, half of me wants to go out young like they did. The other half wants to settle down, play the guitar and make money.' Lloyd-Roberts (with whom Clapton downed five or six doubles in an hour) was left with the impression of a 'self-centred but kindly' individual, whose very awareness of his options suggested which one would prevail.

There was an immediate, tangible reason for Clapton returning to work. After the relative success of 'Layla' in July 1972 his annual royalty cheques had dwindled; even his residuals from Cream, for which Clapton wrote only a handful of songs, barely covered expenses. Among these, of course, had been the cost of his supply of drugs. 'It wasn't a significant sum,' Clapton later insisted. 'It wasn't a question of selling things.' Nor, however, was it an insignificant sum, £1500 a week consistently for three years. (Clapton may not have 'sold things', but a number of expensive guitars were offered in part-exchange for heroin.) By the time he left Oswestry in March 1974 Clapton's financial state was parlous. Not only was Stigwood insistent on the need to record and tour, he pointed to the vacuum created by Clapton's absence. ('He said ... I hadn't really appeared, I was therefore much more saleable and my market had gone up.') A review of Marshbrook's books also confirmed the need for revenue. In the end the most persuasive voice in Clapton's ear may have been his accountant's.

Whatever the cause, the effect was that Clapton appeared at the China

Garden, Soho, on 10 April 1974 to formally relaunch his career. Townshend was present; Elton John, Rick Grech and Ronnie Wood; the Pattersons, Stigwood and Roger Forrester. Clapton himself sat smiling in his Shetland sweater, his hair cropped to Bluesbreakers length, anxious, says a guest at the restaurant, 'that we all knew how well he was doing . . . I still remember Eric showing off his new white Roller. Of course it was borrowed.'

6

No Alibis

Muttered asides – Clapton's ejection from a nightclub, his plunging through a plate-glass window – provided the noises-off in rehearsal for his latest performance: that of (his own phrase) a 'common-or-garden British lunatic'. The process began when he was approached by Townshend to appear in the film version of *Tommy*. For three days Clapton wandered, dressed as a prelate (an image perpetuated by burning itself into Ken Russell's eye), around a marine barracks in Portsmouth. The first indication that the quiet, reclusive demigod had taken human form came when he, Townshend and Keith Moon were evicted from a pub. A local teenager named Jenny Pocock witnessed the scene: 'He was totally gone . . . I never saw anyone consume as much brandy . . . I was an extra on *Tommy* and I'll never forget this as long as I live, Clapton, Townshend and Moon picking a fight with an entire ship's company of sailors. It was wild, the police came. He was driven away shouting, "Let me at them! Let me at them!"'

Next Clapton addressed his private life. After his interlude in Wales there was a reunion with Ormsby-Gore. It was short-lived. Assured by the Pattersons that both parties would benefit from a separation, Clapton broke with his long-suffering girlfriend. (Ormsby-Gore was given to understand that the move was 'temporary and physically essential' while she underwent detoxification.) Cathy James briefly returned as chatelaine of Hurtwood Edge. The real focus of Clapton's attention, meanwhile, reverted to Boyd; at a party at Stigwood's house following the China Garden reception, he said to Harrison, confessing his great secret, 'I'm in love with your wife. What are you going to do about it?' Harrison's reply was memorable: 'Whatever you like, man. It doesn't worry me.' This sense of resignation, of indifference to events beyond his control, did much to settle the eventual outcome. In Clapton's own words, 'Suddenly

[Boyd] was in limbo and I think it was at that point that she became disillusioned with George.' He later quoted Harrison's remark as proof of his not having 'stolen' his best friend's wife, 'because I did tell him straight away'.

The actual transfer was achieved that month. After a session for *Tommy* at Ramport Studios, London, Clapton and Townshend drove to the Harrisons' mansion. While Townshend and his host talked music, Clapton disappeared into the recesses of Friar Park with Boyd. There, the domestic comedy compared to *Bob and Carol and Ted and Alice* declined into stage farce. When Harrison briefly left the room a hissed aside sounded from the shadows.

'I need another hour.'

'What?' said Townshend.

'I need another hour before you go.'

Whatever Clapton said in the allotted time, it was enough to persuade Boyd to leave Harrison for ever. She moved into Hurtwood Edge that summer. The triangle thus formed became a proverb for an industry whose morals were already largely proverbial. In an interview with *Rolling Stone* on 28 May, published in July, Clapton referred to 'Layla' as 'a woman I felt really deeply about and who turned me down', whose husband '[had] been writing great songs for years about her and she still left him', the whole experience a 'wife-of-my-best-friend scene'. Full disclosure followed when Clapton travelled to America. He and Boyd were seen backstage; at the airport; entering and leaving hotels. A second interview confirmed the identity of the 'mystery blonde' briefly called on stage in New York. Narcissistic, Clapton was at the same time not narrowly egotistical. He was interested in everything around him, even though everything eventually led back to himself: the affair with Boyd, constantly reiterated in the press, was always related to its theatrical or soap-opera context. (Clapton asked one questioner if he couldn't appreciate the drama of 'digging' his best friend's wife, and seemed genuinely surprised that he couldn't.)

Remarkably, the relationship with Harrison survived and even prospered: despite admitting it 'got quite hostile' and to having 'be[en] thrown out of each other's houses', Clapton insists today, 'I think the world of the man . . . He managed to laugh it all off when I thought it was getting really hairy. I thought it was tense, he thought it was funny.' A woman close to Pattie Boyd confirms that she and Clapton were 'terrified of George's reaction . . . waiting for him to show up with a gun'.

Instead Harrison gave a single comment to the American press – 'There comes a time when splitting is for the best. It's no big deal' – before returning to Friar Park. Within a year he met a secretary, Olivia Arias, whom he would marry.

That settled, Clapton flew to Miami. At Criteria studios, home of *Layla*, he was reunited with Tom Dowd and a group comprising Radle, George Terry (guitar), Jamie Oldaker (drums), Dick Sims (keyboards) and the singer Yvonne Elliman. The last, an exotic Japanese-Hawaiian, scion of the Hellmann's mayonnaise family, had been discovered by Tim Rice and Andrew Lloyd-Webber singing at the Pheasantry Club, Chelsea. After an audition at Lloyd-Webber's flat Elliman was hired for the part of Mary Magdalene in *Jesus Christ Superstar*. Through that she met Stigwood. Through Stigwood she met Clapton. When Rice appeared that summer at the Warwick Hotel, New York, he was confronted with his protégée and '. . . a highly emotional Eric, whose attention drifted between a bottle of brandy and Yvonne'. Clapton's attention to Elliman overlooked that she was married to Bill Oakes, president of Stigwood's record company.

*461 Ocean Boulevard** was recorded in two weeks – ten usable tracks and accompanying outtakes, of which there were many. The album, released in August, was the first on which Clapton showed true pop star potential. Whatever his previous reputation with the guitar, it was obvious from the opening number that his solo career would be equally based on his fragile but effective voice. Ideologically, Clapton travelled notably light. Among the reviews of *461* was one describing it as 'ephemeral . . . rarely bringing off the feat of "singing the blues" without spoiling the effect . . . an all-things-to-all-people effort that is neither compelling nor satisfying'.

Despite its eclectic content (rock, soul, gospel, country and reggae vying with traditional blues) and egalitarian structure (Clapton wanting to 'just sit down [with the group] and find the lowest common denominator we could groove with') there was much to commend in *461*. If neither compelling nor satisfying, Clapton tending to play hide-and-seek with his talent, the frankness of the lyrics held its own pleasures. 'Let It Grow' and 'Give Me Strength' both dated from Clapton's period of

---

* The address of the house in North Miami Beach where Clapton spent his time, still standing today although stripped of the palm tree seen on the album cover. It died immediately after Clapton moved out.

seclusion, while, coincidentally or not, the album opened with a song called 'Motherless Children'.

461 Ocean Boulevard continued the process, started in Blind Faith, of deicide, of consciously dismantling Clapton's mystique. Like Bob Dylan, perhaps the only other solo artist to match the breadth of his vision and his impact, Clapton set an early standard that led followers to await each new project with fanatical expectation. Like Dylan (whose own comeback, *Planet Waves*, dashed such hopes with questionable choices) Clapton orchestrated his return on his own terms – creating music, as he put it, 'to satisfy the people I was playing with'. There was nothing unknown or especially original about *461 Ocean Boulevard*. At the same time it *was* a new LP by Eric Clapton. As much on promise as fulfilment it reached number three in Britain, number one in America. Agreeably laid-back as the record was, there was a way in which public reaction to the record was also muted. Its most appealing aspect was not that it was as good as it was, but that it was ever recorded at all. Those who bought *461* as an act of reflex loyalty were never again so impulsive. Clapton's next album, arguably a more refined one, was a commercial and critical flop.

461 also contained a single, 'I Shot The Sheriff', characteristic of the overall mix: adequate rhythm and guitar, underpinned by an anaemic organ tone at the centre. 'Sheriff', written by Bob Marley, earned Clapton reproof from some quarters for exploiting native music and praise from others for his willingness to experiment. (It also involved a phone call to Marley which, according to a musician who heard it, 'read like a Harold Pinter script . . . he couldn't understand a word Bob said. Eric may have been a big fan of the Rastas, but coming from Guildford he wasn't exactly on their frequency.')

Clapton returned to England in mid-May. He was seen at the Who's pioneering concert at Charlton, looking, said *New Musical Express*, 'fit if not flushed, earthily dressed compared with the average backstage chic in denims and trench-coat . . . [Clapton] was loquacious about everything except music, referring any suggestion of an interview to Robert Stigwood and spending most of his time with Pete Townshend'. Townshend, having delivered Clapton from one addiction, now became his co-conspirator in another. Relishing their roles as what Clapton called 'working-class lad[s]' for whom 'things like tennis and skiing were definitely not on' the two spent most evenings in the saloon bar of the nearest pub. Frequently waiting at the door when it was opened at six, Clapton would start drinking immediately (wine and champagne, followed by brandy), one treble after another until he became bellicose. Towards closing time the inevitable debate occurred with the landlord: would he comply with the arcane and archaic licensing law, or would he allow Clapton one more drink? (The then manager of the Green Man in Berwick Street remembers the look of 'flinty aggression' which accompanied the question.) The ensuing fracas would be settled by the intervention of Alphi O'Leary, the bodyguard assigned to Clapton by Forrester, escorting his charge outside to the Ferrari.

Clapton's drinking persisted when, in June, he was reunited with his group in the West Indies. Ostensibly a rehearsal for the American tour arranged by Stigwood, the two-week stay rapidly assumed the characteristics of a carnival: not only did Clapton retain his fondness for Elliman, he allowed himself other distractions. There was an interlude with a local beauty queen; an incident at the hotel; another episode requiring O'Leary's intervention in a bar. 'Eric', says George Terry, 'was just finding what life was like without dope, and, not much liking it, substituted with booze. It was wild.' Clapton himself remembered 'ending a (rehearsal) number by falling flat on my face . . . and crushing some parts of my guitar underneath me'. According to Forrester, 'The only certainty was that Eric would be in a permanent alcoholic haze.' When two musicians appeared at the rehearsal-room door, asking politely if they might come in, they were treated to a harangue of choice expletives. Because he was drunk, and attempting to entertain his cronies, such outbursts were not entirely characteristic. They were a sort of misplaced lark. Yet in one crucial sense they were not larks at all. In a public bar or restaurant Clapton was prepared to dissemble his feelings about the natives, some of whom could be persistent in their requests for autographs and other favours. In private he was rarely able to restrain his more churlish side, engaging in the kind of populist language common at the time he grew up. Despite his undoubted feeling for the blues, he had surprisingly little contact with its leading practitioners. None had played with him on a regular basis. His few meetings with original bluesmen – Sonny Boy Williamson, Howlin' Wolf, Buddy Guy and Junior Wells, not an inordinate number over a decade – had been unconvincing, while a more contemporary performer, Stevie Wonder, refused to talk to both Clapton and Townshend on the grounds of having been 'snubbed' by *Tommy*.

Eric Clapton and His Band made their debut at a fairground in Stockholm on 20 June 1974. Reed-thin, bearded and wheezing, looking uneasily like the actor Bill Oddie, Clapton vied for attention with the plate-spinners, jugglers and clowns, some of whose acts his also resembled. The first suggestion that the man who returned to the stage in 1974 might not be the one who left it in 1971 was supplied by Steve Clarke, in a report filed after the next night's concert in Copenhagen:

> 'Where's the slash-ouse around 'ere?' asks Eric Clapton, sitting beside a champagne bucket into which he's recently salivated. We're at the Plaza Hotel, a plush little number complete with first editions of Dickens in the library and antiques in the loo.
>
> Clapton looks a little jaded. His velvet jacket, green with red trim, is split at the shoulder; a scarf hangs down from his neck and instead of a carnation peering elegantly from his button-hole, Clapton has a cluster of plastic tulips.

The circus transferred to America, opening at the Yale Bowl on 28 June. Nightly for six weeks the lights went down in Chicago, Memphis and Long Beach on the sight of 'Legs' Larry Smith (formerly drummer with the Bonzo Dog Band) agitating a loud and frequently atonal ukulele. After the shock had worn off Clapton himself performed Charlie Chaplin's 1935 ditty – a homage to Puccini – 'Smile'. That set the tone. 'Presence Of The Lord', 'Little Wing' and 'Badge', as well as generous selections from *461*, all followed in kind. Even 'Layla' was played strictly for laughs.

Clapton, the man previously so remote he seemed in a different dimension, who played entire concerts with his back to the audience (to improve sound quality, he always insisted), now appeared in public in dungarees or a plastic mac, goosing Elliman and accompanying himself with a duck-whistle. Once content to stand on stage without speaking he became one of rock's great face-pullers and shouters. At the climax of 'Crossroads' his voice rose almost to parrot register. Unsurprisingly, the set itself was uneven, such cohesion as there was supplied by Radle and George Terry. The latter notes factually that 'while Eric was working on his voice, and the larger problem of being a leader', it was he, Terry, who played most of the guitar. In his rapacity to entertain, to incorporate varied styles and trends – more the function of a musicologist than a musician – Clapton risked depriving his songs of their own central characteristics: diversity was one thing, setting 'Layla' to a reggae beat was another.

The nadir was reached in Buffalo. Not only was Clapton near-blind, having caught conjunctivitis, he was also blind drunk. Before the perform-ance at the War Memorial Stadium he engaged in a protracted drinking spree with members of The Band; even as Clapton's name was announced he emerged at a run, panting, skidding at top speed into a potted palm as he tried to pull up alongside a first-aid worker backstage.

'Got an aspirin about you?' he asked.

The zenith came in New York. By then Eric Cleptomaniac and the Diddcoys, as he christened them, had blended into a group. While part of this was due to growing confidence on Clapton's part, there was also a material cause: Terry notes that the amplifiers and equipment 'were of better quality at the end than the beginning' and that 'Stigwood's purse-strings loosened' as the success of the tour became known. There was extended applause for, in particular, 'Blues Power' and 'Let It Grow'. The audience grew ecstatic at a version of 'Have You Ever Loved A Woman' (in which the singer sniggered after the line, 'She belongs to your very best friend'). Clapton could have been excused his moment of triumph when he played 'Layla' that night. Boyd herself waited backstage, enduring Clapton's public flirtations with Elliman, after joining him from Los Angeles. It was a rare exception to the no-women-on-the-road rule later imposed on Boyd, as it had been on Martin and Ormsby-Gore. 'That *was* disturbing,' she says. 'I saw nothing after [1974] when he travelled the world. I felt cut off.'

The tour ended on 4 August, the same week *461 Ocean Boulevard* was released. If Clapton emerged with his reputation intact, there was also a feeling of having attempted too much, too soon. Terry believes it was 'pathetic, in the truest sense, seeing Eric floundering in public'; a member of the road crew, who prefers anonymity, also says it was 'half comic and half tragic, like seeing Elvis in Las Vegas'. For years Clapton had been persuaded by managers and promoters to play unsuitable venues: first in the confusion surrounding the original direction of Cream; then Blind Faith; finally in the identity crisis of Derek and the Dominos. If it was possible to sympathize with Clapton, who continued to state his prefer-ence for 'intimate gigs', it was equally possible to see that he deferred too often to his manager, the authority-figure to whom he clung like a son. Ben Palmer agrees that there was something 'childishly weak' in his friend's character, while Keith Richards's comment that 'Eric needs someone to kick him up the arse' also comes to mind. (In the event, sending Clapton to America was probably the last decision Stigwood made on his behalf. Roger Forrester, who bitterly opposed the tour,

would henceforth take greater responsibility for his day-to-day management.)

Clapton himself has 'great, great memories' of the tour. According to
him, professional standards were maintained whilst drunk – 'Only the
people very close to me had any inkling of how bad it was' – a view
disputed by at least one concertgoer in the correspondence pages of
Rolling Stone:

> Eric Clapton stunk when he came to Buffalo. First he walked out
> on stage so drunk he couldn't sing worth shit. He was constantly
> cursing the crowd. Many of the fans left before the show was over
> only to miss members of The Band lift Clapton up and carry his
> drunken corpse off-stage.

This was Clapton's lot. Whatever his efforts to rationalize his condition
– and they were ingenious – the truth was that he was an addictive
personality. Clapton drank for the same reason he once took heroin or
bought thirty shirts in a day. In so far as his mental and spiritual growth
stopped dead in adolescence, Clapton remained half child, half genius:
like every child he was prone to excess, like many a genius he could be
waspish in his relationships. John Mayall agrees that Clapton's character
was 'unformed and fluid', capable of the childlike virtues of enthusiasm,
curiosity and frankness, as well as the less admirable traits of moodiness
and self-indulgence. 'When I knew him he brooded a lot,' says George
Terry, 'and when he brooded he drank.' What Clapton needed was some
strong, humanly sympathetic figure to curb his extravagance without
confining his enthusiasm. Nothing suggests that by 1974 he had found
such a man.

In one sense Stigwood's and Forrester's influence was positive: as a
result of the tour and the success of *461*, Clapton's finances had revived.
(There was also a renewal of interest in his back-catalogue, both *Disraeli
Gears* and *Layla* returning to the chart.) The momentum established in
April was maintained in August; days after the final concert in Palm
Beach, Clapton was at work on a new album in Jamaica (smoking, he
said, 'trumpet joints' with Peter Tosh). After that the tour continued to
Canada, Japan, Europe – and Britain, though the last was restricted to two
Christmas shows at Hammersmith Odeon. Neither was an unqualified
success. What was affectingly British in Denver or Memphis seemed
merely affected in London. Clapton's Cockney interjections, the source

of much humour in America, were rounded on by the home audience. According to *Melody Maker*:

'You old bankrupt!' was one less than charitable remark hurled from somewhere in the circle, and 'Get on with it, you old ----.' Even Eric was moved to respond: 'What a rowdy bunch of idiots.' Perhaps not the wisest rejoinder, but when Clapton mimicked the cry of 'Layla' you got the impression he was genuinely peeved.*

Clapton ended 1974 in greatly better condition than he began it. With *461* he retrieved his ambition, seemingly lost after the Bluesbreakers, of achieving recognition over adulation. With some exceptions, audiences were prepared to accept him as a singer-songwriter as they once had as a virtuoso guitarist. Not only had Clapton's finances revived, he took greater personal interest in them. Despite a justified reputation for spending small sums extravagantly he exercised rigid control over the annual balance sheet. On 10 September 1974 Clapton became company secretary of Marshbrook. Such was his desire to capitalize on his comeback that he agreed with Forrester on the need to spend a year out of England. The decision to migrate to the Bahamas was conveyed to Clapton's mother and grandmother, with both of whom relations also improved. When, in August, his half-brother Brian died in Canada, Clapton flew to join Pat at the funeral. Later in the year he threw a party for Rose at which he assured her, 'I won't ever do that [drugs] again.'

The corollary was that Clapton did something equally harmful, becoming first a drunk and then – in so far as the distinction can be made – an alcoholic. By late 1974 his intake was two bottles of cognac a day. Just as he had drugs, Clapton took to drink with the conviction that he could 'handle' it. Just as with drugs, his confidence was misplaced. There was a point, like that reached in Buffalo, where Clapton's judgement was seriously impaired. He risked alienating his audience entirely. Whereas Clapton's guitar technique had long been debated in the press it would have been unthinkable, a year or two earlier, for a letter to have begun: 'Eric Clapton was "God" once, but I think Clapton today is a cunt.'

* There was a footnote: at the traditional party at Stigwood's that night, Mick Jagger, having heard that his second guitarist was leaving the Rolling Stones, approached a number of candidates to replace him. Clapton, as he had in 1968–9, declined on the grounds of 'having my own album to do'. Ron Wood, despite having released a record with just that title, had no such inhibitions.

His embrace of world music was pursued with corrosive zeal. Already Clapton's presence in Jamaica had brought criticism, as well as a rebuke from the *Daily Gleaner*, wary of 'hired guns' exploiting native talent. Clapton cordially returned the paper's suspicion. The editor was 'obviously loopy', he reported. While Stigwood and Forrester defended Clapton from the prevailing (but not yet proven) charge of racism, even they failed to prevent the occasional imbroglio. In January 1975 Clapton worked with the Jamaican guitarist Arthur Louis on a number of songs, including Dylan's 'Knockin' On Heaven's Door'; the single was released under Louis's name on 29 July. Exactly ten days later a version, similar in point of style and arrangement, was issued by Clapton. 'You can imagine Arthur's reaction,' says a musician present at the session. 'If it wasn't Eric's own doing, there was a lot of talk to that effect.'

Clapton spent the early weeks of the new year at Hurtwood Edge. Boyd, conscious that 'Alice had left her stamp on it', set about making her own mark on the house. The tower room, scene of rehearsals with Blind Faith and the Dominos, as well as more exotic recreation, was an early priority. Boyd also found, and redeemed, 'lots of brown envelopes containing about £5000' in uncashed cheques. It is doubtful that the couple were ever closer than during this period. The relationship, never as idyllic as thought by the more credulous of Clapton's fans, on the whole justified the faith of those who felt the anguish of 'Layla' and his subsequent addiction had not been in vain. That Clapton was wary of anyone, not excluding his lover, needs no restatement. His aloofness and his short temper were proverbial. Ben Palmer, Clapton's long-suffering friend, believes there was 'almost a sense in which Eric hurt people to defend himself' (Palmer would have known). None the less visitors to Hurtwood Edge over the period 1974–5 came away with the impression, in Terry's words, of 'a completely happy couple'. Even Harrison, so far from showing up with a gun, was reconciled with his wife and best friend. The scene was more absurd than alarming. 'George, Pattie and I actually sat in the hall of my house' (Clapton told Coleman) 'and I remember him saying: "Well, I suppose I'd better divorce her." And I said: "Well, if you divorce her, that means I've got to marry her!" In black and white, it sounds and looks horrible. But it was like a Woody Allen situation.'

On 30 March 1975 Clapton turned thirty. The inevitable party was thrown at Stigwood's: Rod and Britt, Elton, Ringo, Ronnie Wood, and Pat McDonald 'wandering around utterly thrilled, saying, "Hello, I'm

Eric's mum. Who are you?"' The feud, as he once deemed it, between Clapton and his mother was over. But the reconciliation went skin deep. A part of Clapton never forgave her for abandoning him, and that part spoke when – long after 1975 – he continued to complain of the pain of his early life. On the other hand he grew fonder of Pat as he grew closer to her in experience. It was because Clapton valued his mother's common sense and advice so highly that he was so resentful of her having withheld it. He was overheard by a guest at Stigwood's promising to 'do better by her in future'.

Clapton's immediate attention was concentrated on his emigrating to Nassau. In early April he and Boyd settled in the Bahamas while O'Leary remained to caretake Hurtwood Edge. It says much for Clapton's improved financial status that the man reduced to pawning guitars in 1974 was forced into tax exile in 1975. Then, for £1500 a week, he bought the cocaine and heroin that served as a substitute for work. Now, for $2000 a month, he rented the home where rehearsals took place for a tour of New Zealand and Australia. (The house itself was owned by a lawyer by the striking name of Sam Clapp.) Of the ten concerts given, George Terry remembers only an incident in Sydney, 'where somebody had spiked Eric's brandy with acid. After two numbers he threw up on stage', leaving Terry himself to take over. Returning from the final concert on 22 April for a week at Hurtwood Edge, Clapton's Ferrari was in a high-speed collision with a lorry. While his own memory is of 'sitting there with blood pouring down my face . . . smiling', the policeman who cut Clapton free recalls 'A very shaken young man, deathly white and crying. If he was smiling, I didn't see it.' Following as it did an incident involving a motorcycle in the Bahamas, it was obvious that Clapton – with his penchant for fast cars and alcohol – tended to the accident-prone. Equally obviously, he emerged from his encounters with notable luck. The same police officer believes that 'in nine cases out of ten, the driver of [Clapton's] car would have been dead. When I got to him he was upside down, crushed against the steering-wheel and bleeding. But he walked away. Incredible.'

Loudly and often luridly recounting the tale in the saloon bar, Clapton acquired a reputation for toughness he did not entirely deserve. While provoking the occasional brawl in the Speakeasy or Tramp he also went out of his way to avoid the physical consequences of his actions. An irate husband, incensed by Clapton's attentiveness to his wife, would be invited to take up the matter with O'Leary. Such incidents were common:

although Clapton frequently complained that women occupied the time he might otherwise have spent writing songs, he welcomed them as a way of passing the time in which songs showed no signs of coming. Lurching randomly from one table to another in a nightclub or bar, relishing his status not only as a rock star but an accident victim, it was inevitable that Clapton's behaviour would repel as much as attract.

The second album in Clapton's comeback, *There's One In Every Crowd*, was released in April. It failed commercially and critically. Despite Clapton's flirting with the Gibson associated with his work in the Blues-breakers and Cream, the record retrod the ground examined in *461*. There were moments of mild experimentation – the reggae treatments of 'Swing Low Sweet Chariot' and the sequel to 'I Shot The Sheriff', 'Don't Blame Me' – but elsewhere Clapton clung to second principles: gospel, soul, and blandly played pop. Again Clapton's voice dominated his guitar. Again there was minimal soloing: the lead on 'Better Make It Through Today' alone recalled the elegant but unobtrusive work of J. J. Cale. If *Crowd* continued the process, begun in Blind Faith, of reducing Clapton to an ensemble player, it also ran the risk of exposing him as a singer-songwriter of merely limited ability. Of the self-penned numbers only 'Better Make It Through Today' and the contrived but effective 'Pretty Blue Eyes' bore scrutiny. A representative review was the one opening, 'It's got something, but it's hard to say what', a critique with which Clapton himself agreed: 'I'm not sure which direction the [fans] want me to go in, and it puts me in a bind because I'm not sure which direction *I* want to go in.'

This sense of confusion, of hovering between worlds, was borne of Clapton's self-confessed laziness, his weakness as a judge of taste and style, and his lack of an authority figure to dominate his music in the way Stigwood and Forrester dominated his career. He had no sense of the narrative or topical power of rock (an admittedly common failing in the mid-seventies), a weakness he admitted in an interview with Steve Turner:

Q The relaxed sound you've got going now still reflects the culture around it, doesn't it?
A How do you mean? What kind of culture?

The tour of America that followed confirmed the hold exerted by Clapton's management in terms of personal control if not artistic direction. Every aspect of the itinerary, from the choice of Clapton's meals and clothes to the decision to exclude Boyd was taken by a committee to whom earlier industry figures – Brian Epstein, Andrew Oldham – seemed dilettante by comparison. When Clapton arrived in New York in June he was kept under lock and key by O'Leary and a second body-guard named Mick Turner. The faintly risible sight of a man approaching, in professional terms, late middle age being 'grounded' by his staff was admitted by Clapton himself in an aside at the Warwick Hotel: 'It's a drag because I am thirty years of age, and I believe I have the right to make my own decisions ... It's not going to change because [Stigwood and Forrester] still don't trust me. There's not much I can do about it. It's very difficult. I sneak off whenever I can, but there's always somebody watching me.'

A notably different approach was taken by the Rolling Stones, then simultaneously touring America. For the second time in six years Clapton was able to compare his lot with that of the group he turned down: in 1969 he made a satisfying if self-effacing debut with Delaney and Bonnie at the very moment Hell's Angels committed murder under Mick Jagger's gaze in California; now, in 1975, Clapton paced the floor of his hotel suite while Jagger enjoyed unfettered liberty in New York. When, on 25 June, Jagger persuaded Clapton to join him in the studio (producing the gloriously unstructured 'Carnival To Rio') the guitarist responded with the zeal of a child. A man then closely associated with the Stones remem-bers, 'a degree of coke snorted and brandy drunk. Then there were the girls ... a big brunette for Mick and a blonde for Eric, both dressed in these come-on, trashy skirts. Hooker clothes. When Clapton came out he was laughing how the chick had wanted butter smeared all over her. "Well," he said, "it beats a Mars bar."'

The tour itself was a composite carnival-circus, distinguished by Clap-ton's onstage antics, artfully contrived pop and the occasional blues stan-dard. Since 1974 Clapton had forsaken much of his newer material for songs like 'Tell The Truth' and 'Little Wing', become fascinated by Latin rhythms (adding Santana as a support act) and exchanged most of his surface levity for irony. Instead of coming on the deranged rock star, he expressed the conceits of deranged rock stars (whilst, of course, indulging those conceits all the more). In the 1970s a number of artists had begun to pronounce on the self-revelatory nature of live performance, on the mixture of fear and exhilaration with which they laid themselves open to an audience. Clapton wasted no time on metaphysical asides.

149

When he walked on, dressed in working overalls and a beret, he announced his one and only obligation: to entertain. The crowds at Cleveland, Detroit and Tucson received a two-hour package of loosely choreographed songs, jokes and monologues, Clapton ensuring that each moment of real force – 'Layla', or an extended 'Bell Bottom Blues' – was followed by an equal moment of facetiousness or irony. He retained his essentially light-hearted approach to his work. While winning plaudits from elements of the press, now dominated by those who had grown up with Clapton in the 1960s, it also earned rebuke from others, like Keith Richards, who accused Clapton of a 'condescending' attitude to rock and roll.

Standing centre stage, immediately behind or next to Clapton, George Terry shouldered more than his fair share of the load. His view of the group at work is illuminating:

> Eric was on cruise-control a lot of the time. He'd tell you that. When he came back, at least for the first couple of years, he played almost no lead guitar to speak of. Singing and being one of the guys was what he was into . . . There were nights when Eric was barely awake, and other nights when we'd be ambling along, playing a blues, and Eric would let rip with some incredible, unrehearsed solo, two or three minutes long and totally spontaneous. When he was good he was that great.

A sense of Clapton's internal view of himself, his feelings about the past, came in Seattle. The writer was present when he appeared, pale despite the seasonal weather, in the foyer of the Moore Theatre, a crumbling structure of no great distinction on Second Avenue. Clapton, present to rehearse for a concert at the Seattle Coliseum, was not entirely uninterested. Under the façade he was neither facetious nor light-hearted at all. He spoke darkly of the 'drag' of nightly performance, complaining of 'the same faces gaping up' from the stalls, contrasting his lot to that of a journalist – 'getting paid to sit on your arse all day in Seattle' (a town, incidentally, of which Clapton became fond). As to his past, specifically the point of a Cream reunion, then as ever a rumour, Clapton shrugged, touching the tip of his soiled blue beret, 'I can't even *remember* it, let alone dig it', an amnesiac claim he retrieved at convenient moments for another twenty years. ('He remembers all right when it comes to royalty cheques,' snapped a member of Clapton's entourage.) The overall impression was of a fractious, uneasy personality, anxious to stress the misery of his life ('It's like a fucking circus ... How would *you* like it?') whilst projecting the compensatory virtue of humour. The man who stood at four o'clock complaining of *angst* and alienation stood at eight among the plastic palms, clouds and other stage props (suggestive of a farce treating boisterously of life on the ocean waves), smiling and laughing, accepting a bottle of rum to illustrate the effect. Whatever the tedium of touring, the 'circus' of existence, Clapton retained the ability to speak ironically of himself in public, displaying, as one critic put it, 'a remarkable faculty for sleight of mouth'.

In private he continued to grumble at the restrictions imposed by O'Leary and Turner, at the excessive management style of Stigwood and Forrester. When 'Swing Low Sweet Chariot' was released as a single (earning Clapton critical derision) he complained of 'not even know[ing] it'd been put out until someone told me ... I actually didn't think there was the need for it. I still don't.' There was an incident when Clapton, wanting to socialize with members of the group, was physically barred from doing so. On another occasion he overcame opposition to join Bob Dylan in the studio, one of a troupe who recorded tracks eventually released as *Desire*.

Long inured to Clapton's preference for sudden, passing attachments, Forrester can only have shrugged when his client revealed his latest enthusiasm. At Christmas 1975 he bought Boyd a racehorse. It was followed by a filly named Via Delta, trained by Toby Balding, eventually winner of the Fortnum & Mason trophy at Ascot. When Clapton tired of the animal it was replaced by the two-year-old Nello (his nickname for Boyd) and finally the Ripleyite, who won races at both Goodwood and Brighton. If it were true, as Balding says, that 'Eric absorbed the language and the thinking behind racing and his enthusiasm [was] enormous' it was equally true that his fondness for the sport allowed Clapton to adopt yet another role: that of the tweed-suited grandee, quaffing champagne in the winner's enclosure at Ascot. There was a suspicion, as with all Clapton's changes – if that word suggests a process bordering on reincarnation – of parody, pastiche and, above all, impermanence. Later in the decade, when his trainer wrote advising Clapton to purchase two additional horses he was answered, 'Bugger all this long-term investment nonsense. The football season starts in a couple of months.'

Closely linked to Clapton's fondness for the turf was his discovery, also in 1975, of Ireland. That September he appeared (alongside Jagger, Sean Connery, Shirley MacLaine and Burgess Meredith) at a benefit for the Central Remedial Clinic and Variety Club outside Dublin. After a number of visits there in the mid-seventies Clapton bought the Barberstown Castle Hotel in County Kildare, an eleventh-century ruin described in its prospectus as 'atmospheric'. Again, while it was true that Clapton enjoyed a number of liquor-logged weekends at Barberstown, it was also true that he enjoyed the extra income it generated. In the last year he owned it the hotel contributed a gross profit of £120,751 to his accounts.

The live album taken from the previous year's tour, *E. C. Was Here*, was released on 14 September. Spearheaded by 'Ramblin' On My Mind', *E. C.* generously featured the collective talents of Terry, Oldaker, Radle and Sims. Clapton was reduced to a role as ringmaster, calling the key changes and adding the aside 'Did I mention any names?' (as, in America, he was known to snigger) at the crucial moment in 'Have You Ever Loved A Woman?' Much as he complained of the 'soap-opera' aspects of his life with Boyd, he still hastened to amplify them in public.

Clapton ended 1975, as he had 1974, by touring Japan. When he arrived in October, the country was in a combustible state: the temperature was unseasonably high and the political heat, following a recent bribery scandal, was overpowering. In Kyoto Clapton had to elbow his way through a mob protesting at 'foreign invaders' to enter the Kaikan Hall. Once inside, his reception was polite if restrained, housewives sitting alongside unsmiling Salary Men, igniting their cigarette lighters and calling for 'Rayra'. After initial reservations, Clapton added Japan to his stated list – also including Ireland, Ewhurst, Miami and Seattle – of 'loves', comparing it, though neither category could ever be taken for granted, to the 'hates' of the American midwest, France, Poland and the Middle East.

Prone to such classifications wherever he went, Clapton now found the 'finest studio' of his life, Shangri-La outside Los Angeles. Originally drawn there by The Band, Clapton soon discovered other attractions to the building hurriedly converted from a brothel. Instead of the normal perspex booths and utility furniture, Shangri-La included a maze of corridors, a panelled dining-room, water beds and french windows opening on to the beach. In the two months Clapton was there, the building, at times reverting to its original use, assumed all the qualities of a kibbutz: at various moments Dylan, Townshend, Wood, Van Morrison and members of The Band were all in residence. Unsurprisingly, the resulting

152

sessions were more notable for the social life generated than the quality of the music produced.

'Eric was close to Bob [Dylan] and he was close to Ron [Wood],' says a source, present at Shangri-La, named Ted for the purpose of the story. 'He was friends with all the musicians and their families . . . Clapton was so impressed with Dylan. He would kind of scamper after him.' Ted it was who discovered Dylan and Clapton in a bedroom at Shangri-La, 'Bob lying on his back under a teenage chick . . . sucking at her teats as if she were an animal, holding her in place with his hands and mouth. She was moaning. Clapton was sitting in a chair off by himself, watching. It was like a scene from Marat-Sade. Weird.'

Then there was the occasion Clapton arrived at the studio with two oriental girls in tow, smiling widely and assuring Ted they were anatomically sound; a second night on which the guitarist's water bed ruptured violently; yet another on which Clapton was discovered with a Negress and a length of silk in a striking combination. If all this was no more than traditional musicians' licence it also confirmed that Clapton's involvement with Boyd proceeded along traditional musician's lines. He was faithful to her in his fashion. His commitment to his partner and his vaunted aloofness notwithstanding, Clapton was rarely indifferent to the undoubted temptations his status brought. Nor did he hesitate when encountering his colleagues' girlfriends or wives socially (the manner, after all, in which he first met Boyd). Later that spring, when Clapton was introduced to Levon Helm's lover Libby Titus, his response was simple: 'I'll take her off your hands.' He did.

The Shangri-La interlude occupied seven weeks from February to April. It was followed by more impromptu sessions for Stephen Bishop, Rick Danko and Joe Cocker (for the last of which Clapton was briefly reunited with Bonnie Bramlett); in May, his year in tax exile over, he returned to Hurtwood Edge. Clapton was at home when, on the 14th, the Yardbirds' singer Keith Relf was killed in an accident. Clapton, though unavailable to attend the funeral, was on stage the following night with the Rolling Stones in Leicester. After an elaborate if ragged version of 'Brown Sugar' he returned to the dressing-room where he was seen, 'inert', by the pianist Ian Stewart. (It would be redundant to note the debilitating effect of life with the Stones, or to add the words of Nick Kent, present on the tour: 'By that time the heroin abuse had got so bad even the roadies would come in and score . . . it was heroin city.')

Clapton himself had last undertaken a British tour in 1970. Now, capitalizing on the release of the Shangri-La album, *No Reason To Cry*, he announced dates in July and August. In yet another reversal (a bewildering one, had any Clapton fan been resurfacing after six years) this was to be 'Eric's Summer Paddle', an eccentric odyssey embracing such venues as the Spa Pavilion, Bridlington, and Hayling Island's Holiday Camp.

Evidence of Clapton's new persona – the aspirant cockney who used racecourse slang and swore at the audience – came on the first night. After opening the performance with two acoustic songs and failing to close it with 'Layla', Clapton came forward in his jeans and patched shirt: 'I hope you've had a good time. Personally, I'm boring myself silly.' In a long review of the man and the concert, the *Daily Express* quoted Clapton as insisting, 'I want to create good music and get on stage and play it. It's exciting', a statement the paper found inconsistent with his departing the stage at Hemel Hempstead – 'It was as if he had suddenly decided to end a game of darts at the local.'

The same reviewer came away from Clapton's performance at Crystal Palace genuinely shocked: 'You get the feeling Eric is impatient with audiences . . . and with the entire business.' So far from improving with time, he got worse. Neither could it be concluded, from Clapton's soloing at Crystal Palace, that he was even the second best guitarist present – both Terry and the guest Larry Coryell upstaged him. There was a sense, grasped by the audience no less than the critics, that Clapton's playing depended almost entirely for its effect on his flirtation with musical fads (notably reggae), whereas a true original's technique – Hendrix's, for example – was timeless because it encapsulated truths still recognizable years later. The feeling that Clapton might be an ephemeral figure was lent ironic weight by *Melody Maker*'s placing its review of Crystal Palace next to a glowing profile of the Sex Pistols, irritably demanding an end to 'dinosaur rock'.

Nothing prepared the audience for the events that followed on 5 August. It was perhaps tactless of Clapton to utter an aside on 'suntans' as he stepped on stage at the Birmingham Odeon; more so to ask after the first number, 'Do we have any foreigners in the audience tonight? If so, please put up your hands . . . I think we should vote for Enoch Powell.' To continual boos from the crowd Clapton went on to give an extended diatribe on race, ending with a plea for Britain to 'stop [from] becoming a colony'. He then delivered a set described by the *Evening Mail* as 'lacklustre' before exiting to catcalls from the house.

Reporters at the Albany Hotel next day found Clapton at his most mischievous. Unworried by his remarks, which he dismissed as impractical if not already forgotten, he concentrated on selecting bets for that afternoon's race-card (winning 'several hundred quid', according to the hotel's barman). Pressed by his accomplice Ray Coleman for an explanation, Clapton described Powell, sacked for his 1968 speech attacking the Race Relations Bill from an adjacent Birmingham stage, as 'a prophet'.

In a statement notably obtuse even for one of his calling, Clapton went on:

> I don't think Enoch Powell is a racist. I don't think he cares about colour of any kind. His whole idea is for us to stop being unfair to immigrants because it's getting out of order. A husband comes over, lives off the dole to try to save enough to bring his wife and kids over. It's splitting up families ... Racist aggravation starts when white guys see immigrants getting jobs and they're not. Yeah, I'm getting a lot of stick for what I said, but so did Enoch. He was the only bloke telling the truth for the good of the country. I believe he is a very religious man and you can't be religious and racist at the same time. The two things are incompatible.

Leaving aside the wider implications of the last sentence, it was possible to see that, in adopting the sound working-man's values over rock-star hedonism, Clapton took for granted that the sound values included those of bluntness and intolerance. In choosing to articulate his (famously equivocal) views on race in, of all places, Birmingham – where the National Front had recently obtained 16 per cent of the total vote – Clapton revealed more of the protean side of his character than he might have wished. Having started out a lover of all things black, that being the road to success, it was now clear he had no such convictions. Clapton, a weak and indecisive man, covered his irresolution by persistent obstinacy on small points and a love of pretence and play-acting. Being weak he followed the lead of strong characters close to him. He assumed what he thought to be the identities of other people, whereas in fact he rarely grasped more than the surface characteristics. In the early 1960s it had been Robert Johnson and the Kings; a decade later Charlie Parker and Lenny Bruce. Now, in 1976, Clapton had a new role-model: Alf Garnett. With his preference for pints of beer and football (a sport he now patronized), his plainness ('Eric's Summer Paddle') and plain-spokenness –

above all in his views on race and immigration – Clapton echoed the celebrated screen bigot. He might even have thought his speech at Birmingham to be populist.

It was not. Among the reactions was that of *Melody Maker*:

> Eric Clapton opened his Birmingham concert last week with a confused harangue on race, which seemed singularly out of place.
>
> Bewildered Brummies heard Clapton, who after all copped half the licks in his repertoire from our darker-skinned brethren, urging them to vote for Enoch Powell to stop Britain from becoming a colony.

Of readers' letters, not untypical was the comment of Peter Bruno of London:

> When I read about Eric Clapton's Birmingham concert where he urged support for Enoch Powell, I nearly puked.
>
> What's going on, Eric? You've got a touch of brain damage. You're going to stand for MP, and you think we are being colonized by black people.
>
> Own up. Half your music is black. You are rock music's biggest colonist.

At this stage Clapton himself, having at first laughed off the incident, put pen to paper in a letter to the media:

> Dear everybody . . .
>
> i openly apologise to all the foriegners in Brum . . . its just that (as usual) i'd had a few before i went on, and one foreigner had pinched my missus' bum and i proceeded to lose my bottle, well, you know the rest, anyway i'm off up the pub, and i don't live in america, and i think i think that enoch is the only politician mad enough to run this country . . . yours eccentricly,
> e.c.

This was rich stuff; evidence not merely of Clapton's half-formed intellect, his affectations, his holding of drunkenness responsible for distortion whereas the opposite effect was more likely, it also strongly suggested the presence of Stigwood and Forrester. The interval of more than a month between Clapton's speech and his letter can only have been used to gauge reaction. When this became clear – critical response varying from 'hot-making and intemperate' to Bruno's imputation of 'brain damage' – crisis management came into force. While Clapton affected to be indifferent, even amused at the incident, he was deeply hurt. Having sedulously courted a new audience since 1974 he was in no great hurry to abandon it. At a meeting with Forrester on the tour's closing night, 17 August, Clapton was heard to fret that his concerts would no longer attract, as if by divine right, 'the cats'. The job of translating such loss into financial terms was left to his manager. The handwriting of Clapton's letter may have been his own, but the impetus behind it and its contents were Forrester's.*

Clapton's outburst, following as it did rumours of a generally ambivalent attitude to race, attained wide currency. Certain fans, observers and fellow musicians never forgave him. The critic Ray Connolly describes the incident as 'regrettable'; the writer and polemicist C. L. R. James as an example of 'pure, unalloyed evil'. Later in the 1970s, when Clapton appeared at London's Island Studios he found it 'Terrible . . . lots of Rasta men about, just hanging around, playing pool, [one of whom] came up to me and said, "Is it true you really don't like black people?"' At the same time the pressure group Rock Against Racism was formed by Bruno and other supporters, a rare case of music provoking a cause it might normally be expected to support and a source of embarrassment to Clapton in later years.

From the ridiculous, or offensive, to the sublime: the same week Clapton penned his apology he also wrote a song not far behind 'Layla' in its expressiveness. Waiting for Boyd to join him downstairs at Hurtwood Edge – piqued at their lateness for a party he wanted to attend – Clapton again experienced the consolatory side of art. Where other men would have fumed or tapped their watches Clapton began to hum. Within a minute he was in the downstairs studio; within five recording the basic track for what became 'Wonderful Tonight'. When it was released the following year few of the song's fans (and there were many, including Barbara Cartland and members of the Royal Family) could have known

---

* The specific incident referred to occurred in the Churchill Hotel, London, where, in Clapton's hearing, a Jordanian tourist commented on Boyd's 'child-bearing hips' – a tactless remark, given that she was infertile.

that the celebrated opening stanza ('It's late in the evening/She's wondering what clothes to wear') was an expression of impatience, or that the final verse, 'It's time to go home now/And I've got an aching head . . .' understated a condition later described by Clapton as 'drunk and incapable again'.

By the time he wrote 'Wonderful Tonight' on 7 September Clapton had finally released the album recorded at Shangri-La, *No Reason To Cry*. There were pleasing collaborations (a duet with Dylan on 'Sign Language'), the usual Band impersonations – competently performed by The Band – and familiar moments of reggae and calypso, dabblings increasingly at odds with Clapton's early music, which had a much broader appeal and was actually steeped in the most conservative of traditions. He seemed, as Lester Bangs said, 'not to stand for anything'. Among the many criticisms of *No Reason* was one accusing Clapton of cronying; almost every available rock star guested on the album, giving it a loose, disjointed feel not helped by the poor mix. If there was a predominant influence it was the country-folkish tones of Don Williams, latest in a series of laconic, unprepossessing singer-songwriters to catch Clapton's ear. If the results were occasionally uplifting – 'Hello Old Friend', the Layla-esque 'Black Summer Rain' – there was also a surfeit of the kind of family favourites best left to Elton John. By now, three years into his comeback, Clapton seemed to have no doubts about his legend. He wanted to demolish it. *No Reason To Cry* was his most anonymous outing since Delaney and Bonnie, such soloing as there was supplied by Terry and Robbie Robertson. Clapton's edgy, under-enunciated leads came out in warbled bursts. It may be that, as he says, 'some of the best stuff didn't get on the album'.

Returning to London, Clapton willingly escorted Boyd to the haunts – the Speakeasy, the Marquee and Tramp – of his bachelorhood, as well as to a Don Williams concert in Hammersmith. His willingness did not, however, extend to allowing Boyd to join him on tour. Clapton left for America in early November, an uneventful month highlighted by his appearance at The Band's farewell concert in San Francisco. Clapton arrived at the Miyako Hotel on the 24th. On the 26th he celebrated Thanksgiving as only he could: a banquet of turkey and salmon washed down by bottles of brandy and lemonade. After that Clapton picked up his Stratocaster and played effortless solos for an audience of Dylan, Ringo Starr and members of The Band (as well as one naked woman supine on the bed), a more polished performance than the one he gave at the official concert that night. After ad-libbing his way through 'All Our Pastimes', Clapton gained speed in 'Further On Up The Road' when – in front of a crowd of 5,000 and a later film audience of millions – he dropped his guitar. The most celebrated instrumentalist of his day was reduced to garage-band level, fumbling, buckled at the knees, while Robertson filled in. The incident, trivial in itself though fascinating to the director Martin Scorsese, symbolically conveyed the popular view of Clapton: an amiable buffoon, admired less for his talent than for his mythical status, a purveyor of pop hooks that might, but for their excessive blandness, have found themselves whistled up window-cleaners' ladders, and prone to comic and often bewildering antics on stage. When *The Last Waltz* was released in 1978 Clapton's contribution was described by one critic as 'hollow . . . sounding as though [he were] playing through a partially blown amp . . . and mugging, for all the world, like one of The Archies'.

The new year brought yet another reversal. On 14 February 1977 Clapton played an unpublicized concert at Cranleigh village hall, near Hurtwood Edge. His speed of acceptance ('That dance of yours. I'll do it') of an at best whimsical invitation and the concert itself – Boyd dancing a can-can while her lover jeered and hollered – suggested that the curtain had gone up on yet another performance: Clapton as community celebrity, happy to help local causes and not above appearing on request in a pub or shop to stimulate trade. Nineteen seventy-seven was the year he took a more visible part in village life. It became common to see Clapton, alone or with a friend, strolling down Cranleigh high street or regaling the locals at the Ship. He donated money to the Round Table and St Mary Magdalen. He was even complimentary about his old school. If it was possible to see evidence of Clapton's restless and protean side, it was also possible to see a craving for domesticity and roots. It was to this craving that his new outlook was a response. When a local woman named Linda Chandler was out with her two daughters she was surprised to see 'Eric . . . walking along with a shopping bag, whistling to himself [and] looking exactly like one of us'.

This informality spread in time to Clapton's music. Late in 1976 he reacquainted himself with Gary Brooker, once leader of Procul Harum, now landlord of the Parrot Inn adjacent to Clapton's house. Brooker declines to be interviewed on the relationship, but, given the physical proximity and the presence of a fully stocked pub, it can be thought to have been a close one. (Brooker was to become a member of Clapton's group in 1980.) Not only did the two discover a mutual love of fishing – a long-standing enthusiasm of Clapton's, existing between football and horse-racing and, later, video games and cricket – they collaborated in frequent knees-up, piano-and-banjo singalongs of the sort associated with Chas and Dave (an act Clapton admired). Something of this approach now communicated itself in the studio. In spring 1977 Clapton guested with Townshend and Ronnie Lane on their album *Rough Mix*. According to Dave Markee, the bass player on the session, 'it was a case of Eric loping along, usually on dobro, in an effortless but aimless way ... All of us knew he wanted to play what he called "traditional English music". What he really wanted was to have a traditional English lifestyle.'

Clapton's 'roots' persona, unveiled in 1976, was extended in 1977. The British tour that began on 20 April was characterized by the same primal, back-to-basics approach; eschewing the waiting Mercedes, the group travelled by coach or train, the atmosphere akin to a works outing, Clapton carousing and providing off-key harmonies on 'Maybe It's Because I'm A Londoner' and 'Bubbles'. He played his full part in the celebrations surrounding the Queen's Silver Jubilee, insisting on taking breakfast (Remy Martin and lemonade) from a coronation mug and marking the day itself in, of all places, Dublin by appearing in a Union Jack vest. The month, whose highlight was a London performance in which Clapton's grandmother appeared on stage, was described by *Sounds* as 'like a sixties package tour – the passing of Clapton-the-purist into the pop craftsman equally at home with love songs, reggae covers and the inert country-rock twang' of Williams.

The relaxed, low-key approach that Clapton's long-time fans found so puzzling – revealed not in 1977 but three years before – was in fact an alcoholic haze. For every moment of chaotic inspiration there was a matching moment of mere chaos. In the course of four weeks it became apparent to anyone not previously recognizing it that Clapton's working-class, cockney affectations concealed a failure of his own creative nerve. For years his playing had been the glue that held the sound together, an intuitive balance of rhythm and lead guitar underpinned by Clapton's sense of what would and would not work on stage. In 1977 this sense seemed to have left him. According to George Terry, 'Eric had always been good at grasping not just the basic song, but its sub-text.' Now Clapton was in danger of losing the plot altogether: his contribution limited to what Terry calls 'incredible, unrehearsed' bravura rather than more substantial achievement. When fans cheered the opening chords of 'Crossroads' or 'Badge' they applauded not the – frequently inept – treatment of the songs themselves, but the memories they stirred. In 1969 Clapton had enjoyed the prestige of near-heroic status. In 1977 he was a nostalgia-night exotic, associated with glamour and style, yet whose glories lay exclusively in the past. Sensing this, he might have drunk from embarrassment if for no other reason. Drink in turn exacerbated the process. Towards the end of a concert at the Rainbow on 29 April, a performance in which he struggled to co-ordinate himself, Clapton began to feel ill. 'It got worse and worse,' he said later. 'I walked off stage . . . and Townshend comes in, comes up to me and says, "You call this *showbusiness?*"' The irony of Townshend, not averse to a drink himself, lecturing Clapton on professionalism was seized on by the press. 'Once he was loose,' says Don Short. 'Now he was disjointed.'

The same theme recurred in Europe that summer and in Japan, as usual, in October. Clapton, to his credit, continued to tour voraciously without the material need to do so. Compromised he may have been by personal weakness, but he still kept to a schedule. Like a number of sixties survivors he sacrificed the novelty of his original message – and the blues, after all, was an adult sort of music – for a more bland but enduring perspective. He admitted as much in the press: 'Some people have short, frantic careers during which they reach incredible heights and do amazing things. But I don't want that. I want to be a rock and roll marathon runner, not a sprinter.'

In this and other ways Clapton leant heavily on his manager. Nineteen seventy-seven was the year Roger Forrester fully took over. Forrester – gruff, hard-headed and defensive where Stigwood was bluff and entrepreneurial – not only assumed responsibility for concert tours and albums; he personally formed an advance guard to inspect dressing-rooms, scrutinize stages and supervise studios; so hands-on, according to George Terry, 'he even sat down with us abroad and explained the customs regulations of what we could and couldn't take home'. His influence extended to the running of Clapton's company (of which Forrester had become a director on 1 February 1977); the management of his client's finances, expenses, habits, hobbies (they attended football matches together) and the protective – some said over-protective – control of his every utterance to the press. In the whole history of such relationships few have been as symbiotic.

Clapton was sometimes painfully susceptible to male influence. At various times in his career, members of his groups – and others, like Stigwood, Townshend and Harrison – had served as the stock father-figure, Clapton absorbing their characteristics and appearance (even, in Harrison's case, his lifestyle) to the point where his personality seemed an extension of their own. Now, as he moved into middle age, Clapton began to hanker for a relationship that would meet his immediate needs while offering something like permanence. Forrester, who understood this side of him perfectly, became a confidant and friend. He remained the lodestar of Clapton's life, offering career advice, counselling, public relations, personal security and touches of marriage guidance. 'Eric', says Jack Bruce, 'wouldn't sneeze without Roger's say-so.'

It was Forrester who arranged the European tour (an extension of the British leg, the group travelling by private train); who accompanied Clapton to Scandinavia, intervening between his client and the media when, on 9 June, Boyd's divorce from Harrison became known; who supervised recording sessions at Olympic, sending in 'sick-notes' when Clapton failed to appear. 'Whatever you think of Roger', says George Terry, 'he was incredibly protective of Eric. Everything, down to picking up the phone directory, was done for him.' Freed of any obligation other than to play guitar, Clapton produced his best work since *Layla*.

There were still moments of disparagement. Not only was Clapton confused by his own identity, he seemed baffled by his talent: throughout the seventies he swung from wild extremes of arrogance and self-effacement, from being the 'greatest guitarist in the world' to 'an unskilled labourer-musician who finds it difficult to get in tune'. Some of this confusion was apparent in *Slowhand*. While the cockney intonations and Clapton's desire to lose himself in the band remained, so did the pre-comeback flashes of brilliance. *Slowhand*, if not, as claimed by Don Short, 'the best album of Eric's career', may be the most representative; it tends to be either very good or very bad. The note-by-note shuffles are matched by inspired moments like 'Cocaine'.

The album most famously included the song written for Boyd the previous autumn. 'Wonderful Tonight' is not so much good or bad as a matrix of all Clapton now had: an instinctive sense of rhythm and melody too often spoilt by bathos, the lyrics absurdly diluting the message. 'Wonderful Tonight', on the other hand, became a standard, even a model of its kind, bracketed with 'The Lady In Red', 'I Just Called To Say I Love You' and other devotional love-songs whose classification as rock would at best be provisional. (In later years it became known that the Queen herself admired the number, an endorsement unlikely to have been afforded Clapton's early work.)

Slowhand also contained 'Cocaine', written by J. J. Cale in the style of 'Sunshine Of Your Love', and 'Lay Down Sally', a lightweight frolic with vaguely derivative country-rock phrasing. They, 'The Core' – a welcome return to late-sixties form – and 'Wonderful Tonight' (occasionally joined by its clone, 'Peaches And Diesel') became onstage standards. Others from the album fared less well.

If *Slowhand* suffered from Clapton's attempts, never fully resolved, to purge his earlier reputation, it gained from the more cohesive production style of Glyn Johns. Johns, if nothing else, had a clear idea of how guitar-based albums should sound. The result was a characteristically conservative yet touching display of midlife musical values. Johns followed his usual habit of emphasizing the vocals and guitar hooks – not, as per current fashion, the rhythm section – and *Slowhand* would be understood as wholly Clapton's even without his name on the cover. It was a substantial hit on both sides of the Atlantic.

Clapton began 1978 by guesting on the compilation album *White Mansions*, a negligible work except in so far as it reunited him with Dave Markee and Henry Spinetti. The bass player and drummer, previously involved in *Rough Mix* as well as projects for Leo Sayer and Joan Armatrading, would, within eighteen months, replace Radle and Oldaker in Clapton's band. More pertinently, as practising Christians, they again brought to the surface all their employer's conflicts about religion. While Clapton (baptized an Anglican) was heard to comment admiringly on the Church of Rome as 'the last bastion against Commies', his attitude to spiritual matters remained fluid. It was the most fickle side of a personality known for its fickleness. When, later in the seventies, Markee presented Clapton with a Bible he was impressed by 'Eric's obvious sincerity' in accepting it. Clapton, he decided, was 'confused', 'hurt' and 'soft at heart' under a veneer designed – and polished by Forrester – to convey the reverse. His conclusion that 'Clapton was one person alone and another with Roger' found expression on tour in America: in a single day Clapton knelt praying in Markee's hotel room, then jeered his friend as a 'God squadder' when meeting him in a crowded restaurant later.

On 1 February 1978 Clapton began a world tour that lasted until Christmas. In deference to his new liking for country in general and Don Williams in particular, he appeared on stage in a stetson and boots, while Williams himself played in support. He tirelessly promoted 'Lay Down

Sally', briefly a hit in the country and western charts (vying, equally implausibly, with the Rolling Stones). Clapton relished the chance to act, as he put it, the 'native Yank' no less than the common-or-garden British lunatic. The truth was that, by now, Clapton's music, both the instrumental backing and his own voice, had assumed a kind of mid-Atlantic tinge; introducing 'Layla' he made a speech starting 'This here's a toon' and ending, '. . . I hope very much you enjoy it.' His restlessness and inability to settle on one perspective was the despair of his manager. Forrester was constantly called on – returning a £50,000 speedboat, rebuffing stray musicians promised 'a gig with Eric' – on his client's behalf.

A member of the crew responsible for the tour remembers that, hardly surprisingly, Clapton was spoilt. No one could have been fawned on and indulged as he was without coming to expect special treatment. He 'sweet-talked his way out of being arrested' after a rowdy encounter with Brian Wilson in Las Vegas (where, Terry says, the group gave the concert of their lives). Feeling tired after a performance in St Louis, Clapton cried off a party arranged in his honour at a minute's notice – forgivable, but inconsiderate given the trouble to which the host had gone. Clapton's treatment of chauffeurs, bodyguards and other staff could be high-handed. He screamed at O'Leary when kept waiting for a drink. Clapton went 'simply out of his head' according to Truman Capote, when, at a reception at Studio 54, 'the waiter was a tad slow in appearing'. On the other hand, though he took his privileges for granted, Clapton never seemed to assume that he himself was anything special. There was, said Andy Warhol (also, inevitably, present at the party), a sort of 'ingrained conceit' about him. It was a case of a 'weak and often submissive character' compensating by outbursts of rudeness.

In 1968 Clapton had spoken darkly of the *ennui* of travel, the tedium of touring; his criticism in *Rolling Stone* had found him in unusually febrile mood. Now, a decade later, he happily bounded on to the same stages once slouched on with Cream. The difference lay not only in Clapton's perspective; there was a sense in which he reacted to brandy as, before, he reacted to drugs. Whereas he responded to one by becoming morose, the drink's effect was the reverse. Then he was an eremite, now he was an extrovert. Clapton considered alcohol a more benign influence than LSD or cocaine. Life as a drunk was unpredictable, but a life of sobriety was impossible. Brandy, wine and beer had become his constant companions, his most dependable friends. Sometimes, late at night, he would take his bottles and flasks out of his bag, count them and fondle them as, at Hurtwood Edge, he was known to count and fondle his guitars. Having beaten heroin, Clapton saw nothing ironic in exchanging one addiction for another. Both as a boy and a young musician, drink had been with him as a part of growing up. Clapton felt guilty about taking drugs; alcohol, on the other hand, was merely fulfilling a family tradition. He admitted as much to Steve Turner ('I've been drinking hard since I was fifteen . . . Vicious? No, it's quite nice') and to others alarmed at his condition. In 1978 Clapton was happy to drink and, with some exceptions, a happy drunk. Part of O'Leary's job was to ensure that his employer reached the stage at precisely the right level of inebriated bonhomie. Usually he succeeded. The long-term consequences might go uncounted, but in the meantime Clapton gave ninety concerts in a year.

The effect on Boyd was less positive. While Clapton travelled America his lover stayed home in Surrey. The constant proximity of other women (though Clapton was more discriminating in the way he filled out time between concerts than some, and Elliman had by now left the group) might only have exacerbated a relationship that was, at best, turbulent. Not only were there differences about careers and children – Clapton insisting on one and demanding the other – but Boyd, too, took comfort in the bottle. By 1978 her consumption was not far behind her partner's. While some of this may have been the shock of the new ('After the spiritual life with George, I seemed to be surrounded with mayhem,' she told Coleman; '. . . he'd even bring back tramps from the pub'), it was a measure of her despair that Boyd drank for support. Like Ormsby-Gore before her she felt isolated by Clapton's absences and threatened by his behaviour. There were days when, rising in mid-afternoon, he barely acknowledged his companion before locking himself away with his brandy and toy cars. Like others of his profession Clapton attracted an entourage, and Boyd became used to the arrival at Hurtwood Edge of strangers demanding lunch or other favours. Once it was a female singer who suggested that Clapton and Boyd join her in bed. (They refused.) Already prey to anxiety and depression, Boyd took solace in drink, in her ex-husband and in members of her family.

Among the last was Boyd's sister, once linked to Clapton, now involved with a man named Nigel Carroll. A friendship developed with Clapton to the point where Carroll was placed on the Marshbrook payroll, rising in time to the job of personal assistant. (O'Leary remained present on tour.) Carroll's first assignment was to escort Clapton to football matches, primarily at West Bromwich Albion, the team supported by Jack Clapp in the 1950s. That spring the two appeared for the side's fixture against Nottingham Forest. The same month that Clapton sat drinking champagne with Capote and Warhol he slouched on the West Bromwich terrace, swinging a rattle and urging his team to put the boot in. His love of football extended beyond the two-year horizon of his previous obsessions. For a time Clapton, Forrester and Carroll became regular Saturday attenders of the team's matches, the last, then a teetotaller, driving the Mercedes. In time Clapton adopted the alias 'W. B. Albion' when on tour. He insisted on having news of the club's results passed to him in America. The sleeve of the album Clapton released in 1978 included a picture of a West Bromwich scarf. Predictably, his enthusiasm for the working-man's sport, as for the working-man's music, cooled. John Evans, the club's secretary, says today that 'I know of no interest on his behalf over the four years I have been here.' The main purpose of Clapton's involvement seems to have been as an outlet for his 'blokish' personality, amusement (menacing a rival supporter with a convincing toy gun) and an opportunity to drink. Inevitably, it also increased the distance between himself and Boyd.

On 19 April Clapton was present at the fiftieth birthday celebration for Alexis Korner at Pinewood Studios. At some point in a chaotic evening a group including Korner, Zoot Money, Mel Collins, Chris Farlowe and Dick Heckstall-Smith took the stage; the last thought Clapton, joining in on 'Hey Pretty Mama', to be 'subdued' and 'in no very good mood'. When Paul Jones, last encountered in the *What's Shakin'* session in 1966, also arrived, he was treated to an 'icy' sidelong glance from Clapton. After a version of 'Stormy Monday Blues' the guitarist, whose sunken, unshaven appearance contrasted with Jones's youthfulness, called the singer aside. 'His exact words were "Go back to school,"' says Jones. 'It could have been amusing or it could have been a put-down. He wasn't smiling when he said it.'

The world tour launched in February continued in June. On the 23rd Clapton appeared as support for Bob Dylan in Rotterdam and again at the Zeppelin Field, Nuremberg, where the group performed in the lee of Hitler's podium. Despite limiting his description of the event to 'brilliant', Clapton was taken to book by one critic for the 'richness' of appearing 'in the very spring of fascism . . . particularly when seeming to endorse the f-word in a recent outburst in Birmingham'. The same reviewer found Clapton's 'confused' personality at work on the music: whereas once, whatever the paucity of his records, he seemed able to give a facsimile of himself on stage, by 1978 there was evidence that Clapton's lifestyle had caught up with him. Being a 'rock and roll marathon runner' could involve setting a sluggish pace. By the time he appeared, staggeringly drunk, in front of 250,000 fans at Blackbushe on 15 July, even Ray Coleman was reporting:

> If the Trade Descriptions Act applied to rock concerts, Eric Clapton would be hauled in front of the appropriate committee and asked to explain his lacklustre performance . . .
> I doubt if even the most loyal Clapton fan will deny a deep-down disappointment. Sure, he played quite well, but it was all so blandly unobtrusive that you had to pinch yourself occasionally as a reminder that here, live on stage, was a living legend.

Blackbushe included a scene witnessed by the same source present at Shangri-La two years before: 'Backstage Eric and [Dylan] took fire extinguishers and blasted each other with them, which made the bands hysterical. Then [a member of Dylan's group] . . . went into the bathroom and came out and opened up his hand. He had all different kinds of pills. Eric poured a brandy, put them in his hand and walked off with them. There must have been a dozen capsules. Different colours.' Later still Clapton and Dylan (in whose company he invariably thrived) were seen boarding a helicopter – the very use of which, says Terry, 'thrilled Eric' – together with a girl known on the tour as 'No Knickers . . . that particular item and her were strangers'.

There were two other results of the concert: Dylan and his backing singer Helena Springs presented Clapton with two numbers, 'If I Don't Be There By Morning' and 'Walk Out In The Rain' inserted in the sessions already booked at Olympic; both Marcy Levy (Clapton's own vocalist alongside Elliman) and George Terry resigned. The one departure – proof that it is possible to value someone and still exploit them – meant that Clapton was deprived of his remaining female foil. The other meant that, for the first time since his comeback, he was forced to play the guitar.

7

Drifting Blues

The amended group, Clapton, Radle, Sims and Oldaker, returned to the stage in November. In five weeks they gave thirty concerts in seven countries, among the highlights Clapton's fanatical rapport with the audience at West Bromwich and a performance in Glasgow where, according to Ian Stewart, who guested on the number, 'Eric let fly in "Key To The Highway", playing with that woebegone look on his face ... He was so intense it was frightening. God knows what [the fans] thought he was about.'

Most fans thought that what Clapton was about was emotion and nostalgia, fuelled by an overpowering sense of melodrama, investing the songs with a gravity strikingly at odds with his behaviour offstage. An illuminating picture of Clapton on tour was provided by the film-maker Rex Pyke. Pyke was given access not only to concert stages and studios, but to hotel suites, dressing-rooms and the private train in which Clapton again travelled Europe. The resulting documentary, *Eric Clapton's Rolling Hotel*, produced two moments of genuine pathos. The first came in Paris with Stigwood, then in the throes of losing his remaining management stake in Marshbrook to Forrester. In an apparent reference to Stigwood's accountancy methods with Cream, Clapton buttonholed his former mentor backstage: 'Right ... now's the time for some questions ... There are a lot I haven't dared ask and here they all are.'

'This isn't the right time.'

Signalling for Pyke to continue filming, Clapton delivered a parting salvo at the man he once described as 'father'.

'If it wasn't for me and Ginger and Jack you wouldn't have been able to bring the Bee Gees over. Would you?'

'True.'

'There you go, then.'

The second feature of *Rolling Hotel* came when Ben Palmer, accompanying Clapton in Europe, suggested that the support act, Muddy Waters, another man Clapton admired, be allowed to travel on the train rather than the musicians' bus. He was refused. Palmer still retains a sense of anger at the incident: 'Here was Muddy, sixty-three and in bad health, stuck in the back of the coach with the roadies. There was something odd about the white musicians sitting like King Tut in the dining car while the blacks got boxed lunches.'

For these and other reasons *Rolling Hotel* was never commercially aired. There was a private viewing at the National Film Theatre; segments survived to be included in later videos; but Palmer, among others, found the end-product unwatchable –'not only because of Muddy, but for other incidents as well'. 'Eric was just *gone* in those days,' says George Terry. 'Being his friend required a very strong stomach.'*

Backless, the album recorded at Olympic that summer, was released in November. '[There was] a general sort of apathy involved,' says Clapton, a truism which comes across on the record: while 'Tulsa Time' and 'Golden Ring', sardonic but fairly witless, emerged as foot-stamping stage favourites, most of the rest avoided heavy-riffing guitar histrionics for less demanding brands of mood music. The country pastiche 'Promises' brought Clapton a wide AOR radio audience. At a time when the charts were dominated by the soundtracks for *Grease* and *Saturday Night Fever* (both released by Stigwood), by Boney M, Blondie and Abba, the 'ditties and pleasant melodies', as Clapton called them, of *Backless* seemed hopelessly self-effacing by comparison. This was the year of which he admitted later, 'I was really unsure of what I was here for.' The albums and the singles still came out on time – Forrester saw to that – but there was a growing feeling that Clapton was irrelevant, an ex-party balloon now reduced to a ragged triangle of limp red rubber. The revival foretold by *Slowhand* had proved illusory. *Backless* was invertebrate.

Relations with Stigwood (which would improve) touched bottom in 1978. Not only did Clapton consider himself ill-advised by his ex-manager, he blamed Stigwood, repeatedly and in public, for not making him more money. Pete Brown, who knew both men well, believes that 'while Eric earned incredible sums from Robert, he needed them to

* It would be unsurprising to note that Pyke found his subject 'terrific' at comic imitations and able to quote at length from *The Caretaker*. Clapton's suggestion of the title 'Bernard Jenkins' shows he was familiar with the play as early as 1965.

support his lifestyle. He spent money like a sailor on shore leave.' Clapton retained a keen attention to finance, as opposed to notes and coins, throughout his career. On the straitened canvas of his interests, the management of his investments loomed among the most conspicuous. His stints in the Yardbirds, Bluesbreakers and Cream were all punctuated by disputes about money, Clapton insisting that, as the star of those groups, he was entitled to more than mere sidemen. Although he was a rich man, maintaining Hurtwood Edge even during his retirement, Clapton realized that he could always be richer.

This sense of ambition was both understood and seized on by his new manager. Forrester appeared in his designer blazer and jeans, a thin, balding man with the look of a prematurely hatched bird, whose Adam's apple danced up and down his narrow neck, cracking jokes about Stigwood's shortcomings and promising to make Clapton fabulously wealthy. He succeeded. Less convincing was Forrester's promise to the media to be 'totally candid' regarding Clapton and himself. A journalist who encountered him in 1978 came away with the impression that 'Roger was thirty-three, a Londoner, and would rather have died than speak a lie.'

Forrester was in fact born in the Municipal Maternity Home, Grimsby, on 15 August 1940. His legal name is Roger France Wright. Forrester's father, George, was a Grimsby police constable, his mother, Keturah, of continental descent. Gravitating to London in the 1960s, Forrester worked as a booking agent for British rock and roll acts like Tommy Steele and Marty Wilde before joining the Stigwood Organization, arranging tours and negotiating energetically with local promoters. (Bill Graham retained fond memories of this process until the day he died.) Living a few miles from Clapton at Frimley Green, Forrester developed a close personal rapport with his client, escorting him to pubs and football matches (in time introducing him to cricket) and emerging as the perennial father-figure in Clapton's life.

Jack Bruce, for years also involved with Forrester, is among those who believe 'Roger [to be] fantastic with money, less so with artistic direction'. Pete Brown describes him as 'a particularly astute hustler, among whose assets is having seen how Stigwood handled Eric, and improving on it'. It has been said to Forrester's credit that he was prepared to oversee aspects of Clapton's life which Stigwood tended to avoid; it can also be said that he overlooked a creative decline more acute than another manager might have had the *sang-froid* to ignore. Both Bruce and Brown share respect for Forrester's financial acumen while voicing doubts about the drift allowed to enter Clapton's career.

Control was tightened in other areas. After Clapton's 'confessional' interview to *Rolling Stone* in 1974, strict supervision was enforced of his every appearance in the media. Collaborative projects, once freely entered into, were subject to the same scrutiny. *Ad-hoc* activities were discouraged. When Tom McGuinness, Clapton's friend from the Roosters, approached Forrester for help in compiling a documentary tribute to Hendrix, he was 'turned down flat . . . Next day I went direct to Eric, who was happy to appear.' Pete Brown speaks of 'incredible conditions' imposed by Forrester on a Cream retrospective video, 'primarily to ensure that Eric's interests, as he sees them, were protected'. Forrester, on the other hand, took a noticeably more bullish approach towards projects of his own devising. In 1989 Chris Dreja was surprised to receive word from PolyGram acknowledging his 'clearance' for a Yardbirds segment to be included in the video *The Cream of Eric Clapton*. 'What they meant,' he says, 'is that they had Forrester's clearance. No one asked me about it.'

Clapton's capacity for money-management, the first object of Forrester's attention, was among his most erratic. As early as the Roosters, and at later times in his career, he liked to claim he had 'no interest' in finance, as a result of which he was 'permanently broke'. Certainly Clapton thought nothing of buying a dozen suits, a rack of shirts, even a new car or motor-boat, on impulse. He retained a markedly more conservative attitude to giving money away. Throughout the seventies Clapton frequently omitted to pay his bill at the Speakeasy or Tramp; the word 'slowhand' was given ironic meaning to those who sat with him in restaurants; there was genuine surprise when Clapton produced his wallet in a pub. Despite giving Coleman the impression he was 'a stickler for "playing the game" . . . hating debts or promises that betting money, however small, will be paid later', he took a cavalier approach to his own obligations: both Noel Redding and in later years Forrester himself failed to collect on money owed. A neighbour present during Clapton's residence in 1975 notes that 'the only thing Eric spent in the Bahamas in a year of partying was twelve months'. Later in the decade the songwriter Stephen Bishop was startled to be approached by an unsmiling Clapton demanding '£200 in pound notes' for a recording session. (Bishop, a long-time friend under the impression that his involvement was gratis, paid up.) Clapton was a firm believer in self-help. 'I've made it – so can they,' he once told Dave Markee. Because of the way he was brought up, he felt no liberal guilt.

Clapton, however, was often liberal, whether it was donating guitars and clothes or offering Ian Stewart his last fifty pounds. Just as he was egotistical without being secure, he was lavish without being generous. A man like Jim McCarty, 'waiting for hours' to be bought a drink might be rewarded months later by an expensive gift. Clapton's changeable attitude to money included a large measure of naïveté. He was well into his thirties before realizing the need to bank, as well as receive, incoming cheques. A member of Clapton's group in the 1980s was unnerved to be told, when asking the cost of a new jacket, 'I didn't buy it. It was nothing. I got it on a credit card.'

All this suggested a man with a confused and confusing outlook on money, a spendthrift who avoided unnecessary debts, who scrutinized balance-sheets and questioned expenditure, yet with all the credulousness of an Elvis Presley. Forrester was quite right to manage him as he did. While Clapton was once as likely to tip excessively as tip at all, in later years he became noticeably more cautious. Terry remembers him 'being the first to buy duty-free' from the first-class cabin of the jet. Markee thought that, in small things, he showed 'signs of stinginess' and that 'what really stung Eric was the thought of having been burnt by Stig-wood'. As well as instituting domestic economies Clapton took personal interest in the running of Marshbrook, a company whose turnover rose fifty-fold in a decade, and combined with Forrester to form his own record label and music publishing business in the early 1980s. 'I'll give one thing to Roger,' says Markee. 'He put Eric on a footing for life. He could stop working now and not miss it.'

Except, of course, Clapton would miss it. For all the money, the hobbies and distractions he had no appreciable life outside music. In a message to a fellow guitarist that winter Clapton confessed that 'high-minded Eric', 'a pro', was tailoring his work to please the market. The idea of being a professional (the very word he used to McGuinness) was impor-tant to Clapton: it meant making a living by selling music; constant productivity; a willingness to compromise and even to perform below par in order to support the overall 'career'. (The amateur or part-timer could afford to play only when he felt; the professional had a schedule to keep.) Throughout the decade Clapton continued to press Forrester for more tours and concerts, the nightly equivalent of what he deemed his 'fix'. Another musician might have been more wary of the responsibility. The addict could not afford to be fastidious.

Nineteen seventy-eight ended in a display of family unity: Clapton performed at Guildford Civic Hall while his mother, grandmother and girlfriend clapped from the balcony. (Harrison and Elton John also appeared.) Despite the back-to-roots, affable tone of the evening, serious differences remained between Clapton and Boyd. Left alone at Hurtwood Edge for much of the year, increasingly reliant on alcohol and Valium, the woman extolled as Layla was on her way to becoming, as she put it, 'a deadbeat and bore'. The couple separated that Christmas.

Compounding the situation was Clapton's relationship with George Harrison. The two self-styled 'graduates of Boyd University' were entering one of their cyclical bouts of intimacy. Harrison played at the Guildford concert on 7 December. Clapton repaid the favour by performing on Harrison's solo album being recorded at Friar Park. Next the two appeared together at the Henley cinema, sharing an outsize box of popcorn and informing the startled manager that they were there to protest against plans to close the building. All this led one observer to comment on the irony of 'Pattie ... apparently distraught at the breakdown of another relationship ... while her ex-husband and estranged lover whooped it up'. Among Boyd's complaints about Clapton was the simple charge that, in point of human feeling, he was 'cold'.

The couple reconciled in February. Clapton, bleakly admitting in private to being nervous and bitter, yet again displayed his deep-seated reluctance to deal with his partner.

Despite giving a neighbour the impression that the couple had reunited, however precariously, Clapton's eye roamed once more. In March Boyd invited a colleague from her modelling days, Jenny McLean, to Hurtwood Edge. Entering the living-room she found her friend and her lover 'sitting very closely together on the sofa'. Philandering, for Clapton, seems to have been partly a means of satisfying his need for support and reassurance, but also a revenge for the childhood traumas he associated with women. Martin, James and Ormsby-Gore had all felt the sharp edge of Clapton's tongue. Now, when Boyd started a conversation Clapton interrupted her with the words, 'Can't you see I'm in *love* with this girl?' The silence that followed this admission was deafening. Boyd retreated upstairs, where she reached in her handbag for a bottle of Valium. She took one. Four or five pills had already been swallowed before she telephoned her sister to collect her. Crying and stumbling in the dark and rain, Boyd moved out that night.

In saying that he failed to understand women, Clapton concealed the extent to which he chose his ignorance. Such efforts as he had made with Boyd were patchy: a love song or other dramatic gesture rather than the humdrum process of compromise and consent. Nor would Boyd have taken pleasure from the relatively few days on which Clapton was neither recording nor on tour; those were spent drinking with Forrester and Carroll. While Boyd fretted and waited at Hurtwood Edge Clapton went to the football. His 'lunchtime half' frequently extended to dinner. He forgot birthdays and anniversaries. In translating the values of fifties Ripley into his own life in the 1970s Clapton was perhaps guilty of more than chauvinism. His attitude to women was partly resentful, partly nervous.

Also disappointed. Pat was only the first in a long line of mother-figures by whom Clapton felt let down. The sense of absent or withdrawn affection was one he never lost. In December 1969 he commented on his 'lifelong interest' in girls who, for one reason or another, were unobtainable. To dramatize his disappointment Clapton cast himself as an outsider, someone never able to be 'a success' in love. (If love was restricted to numerical chances, Clapton was notably successful.) At certain moments in his life a sense of alienation or abandonment was deliberately contrived – 'the [girls] loved it,' says Chris Dreja, 'that moody James Dean look'. At other times Clapton felt genuinely put on. The overall effect was a man who craved love and feared commitment, who spoke disparagingly of his absent, 'unreciprocating' mother and who, for all his promotion of women as equals, might have imagined himself more equal than others.

While Boyd flew to California in tears, Clapton began an Irish tour accompanied by McLean. On 17 March, after a St Patrick's Day concert in Dublin, the couple spent the night together at Barberstown. On the 18th Clapton assured a local reporter, Hugh O'Neill, that the affair was 'for keeps'. On the 19th it was all over. (McLean refuses to discuss it, but confirmed at the time that it was 'Eric's doing'.) At this stage Forrester intervened. Over a game of pool at Frimley Green he bet his client £10,000 that he could ensure his name's appearance in the national press. 'Done,' said Clapton. 'ROCK STAR WILL MARRY IN ARIZONA NEXT WEEK' ran the morning's headline in the *Daily Mail*.

Whatever his motives, there is surely poignancy to be discovered in the notion of Forrester extending his control of Clapton's life to include his marriage. It is uncertain whether he wanted Clapton to moderate his behaviour; to settle down; or, less plausibly, to 'be happy'. What is certain is that Clapton, after physically attacking Forrester in his office, calmed down sufficiently to agree, 'I want to be with Pattie.' (That and the fact that he never paid his manager the money.)

While a message was relayed to Boyd in Malibu ('Marry me or get on your bike'), Clapton, Forrester and the usual entourage flew to Tucson where a tour was scheduled to open on 28 March. Once arrived O'Leary block-booked six local churches while Clapton, likening marriage to the 'big drop', purchased a white suit with velvet collar, black shirt and white string tie for the occasion, neither party referring to the fact that the bride's availability was by no means certain. Despite considering the circumstances of Forrester's bet 'cheap' – and retaining doubts about Clapton's involvement with McLean – Boyd duly agreed to appear: the couple were married by a Mexican pastor (shortly to leave the ministry) at Tucson's Apostolic Assembly of Faith in Christ Jesus on 27 March 1979. The bride was given away, aptly enough, by Forrester. The record producer Rob Fraboni was best man. If the local press experienced qualms about their invasion of Clapton's 'strictly family affair', they would have felt better to know that Forrester had stage-managed the event for optimum publicity. He claimed to detest any sort of public scrutiny, yet made it his practice to scatter misleading clues in the media. Booking two-thirds of Tucson's available churches in a day was not the act of a man seeking anonymity. As a result Clapton achieved more feature-length attention than would have resulted from a purely private ceremony. Anyone was able to interview Reverend Sanchez or, for a $12 fee, to obtain copies of the wedding certificate. As the party – Clapton, Boyd, Forrester, the Frabonis, O'Leary and Carroll – made their way down the wooden steps of the chapel the local press arrived in force: fans bayed and reporters brawled behind barriers as the registrar politely noted that the licence fee remained due. Clapton's friends paid on his behalf.

Boyd knew very quickly that her job as Clapton's wife would be no better than her career as his mistress. For days all went well; there was a reception that night at the hotel, ending in the mandatory cake-fight; on the 28th Clapton called Boyd on stage at the Community Center and sang 'Wonderful Tonight'; they travelled together to Texas and New Mexico. The blow fell in Oklahoma. Less than a week after marrying, Boyd was told she was not wanted on tour. While Clapton returned to the stage his wife flew to Los Angeles and thence to England. 'I was upset,' she told Coleman. 'He obviously wanted me to become the little housewife.' A friend of Boyd's, currently living in London, describes even this as an understatement: 'She was totally annihilated by Eric and his manager. It was like dealing with the Mafia ... [Clapton] was permanently sorry for himself and would get sorrier as the day wore on. He made a sort of virtue out of self-pity. That and his vicious streak were what got to Pattie.'

In the last week of April a firmament of rock musicians, their wives, partners and families received invitations to a party for 'me and the old lady' and asking them to contact Hurtwood Edge to confirm. Among those ringing Ewhurst 888 were: Harrison, McCartney and Ringo Starr; Townshend, Elton John and Rod Stewart; Mick Jagger, Keith Richards and Charlie Watts; Jeff Beck and Jack Bruce. Ripley was also represented: Clapton's mother and grandmother, Guy Pullen and others (who were told, 'You don't have to bring a present if you don't want to.') The reception was memorable for the galaxy of stars occupying the stage erected in Clapton's garden; the ritual humiliation of Jack Bruce by his host; and that Jerry Hall, overwhelmed by the event, fell asleep on the newlyweds' bed. ('I felt so terrible later,' she says. 'They'd spent their honeymoon night making love on the floor of the bedroom closet.') The next afternoon Clapton appeared in the Windmill Inn at the gates of Hurtwood Edge, drinking brandy with members of the Rolling Stones and Who and striking one villager as 'rather morose, under the circumstances'.

Clapton's reception was on 20 May. On the 22nd he flew to America, where the fifty-night tour resumed in Augusta. Earlier in the year, Forrester had pointed out what a growing number of fans had since realized: production-type songs like 'Layla' and 'Badge' required a fuller guitar sound than Clapton could muster. His ability to play both rhythm and lead – Clapton's intuitive sense of pacing – had left him. The all-embracing quality of his work with Cream was lost. The experiment of paring the group to a quartet had proved a failure.

Albert Lee, a guitarist previously involved with Chris Farlowe and Emmylou Harris, joined the tour in America. His presence gave the band a richer, more structured sound. Certain numbers, notably the intricate work of Clapton's early career, were now faithfully reproduced. Recognizing that such memories are sacrosanct, Clapton diligently created perfect facsimiles of the originals, duplicating the exact harmony vocals (mostly supplied by Lee) and emulating every nuance of Baker's double-bass drumming (expertly done by Oldaker). Yet problems remained: there was a feeling that the facsimiles, for all their finesse, were just that. Among the reviews of the tour was one stating the performance to be 'formulaic and stale, with too few departures from previous sets ... Something was missing – the true spirit of abandon that Clapton once routinely summoned in his playing.'

Clapton's support act, in every meaning of the phrase, was Muddy Waters. Sensing 'pain' and 'spiritual strife' in his protégé, Waters pleaded with Clapton for a return to the basics: 'He kept hammering it home to me that there was nothing wrong with being a blues musician. He said a guitarist didn't have to be *appealing*, to play the biggest halls and sell the most records ... I can never thank Muddy enough for spelling it out to me.' Waters's support was the more poignant in light of his treatment on Clapton's tour the previous year. Nor was his eminently sensible advice acted on immediately; Clapton continued his excursions into reggae, gospel and country, while even his stage sound-mix was eccentric, the vocals layered lavishly on top, guitars and keyboards somewhere behind and bass and drums relatively faint in the distance – the sort of sixties pop sound favoured by Cliff Richard. (Richard now 'respect[ed] Clapton's music enormously'.) Clapton had sacrificed in emotion what he made up for in experience. By mid-1979 some form of reinvention appeared necessary, if not essential. Clapton's last five tours of America had, like Russian dolls, become diminishing versions of an identical idea. The same flirtations with musical fads, the on-stage patter, the playing of identical tunes, note for note, as though plugged into a piano roll device – all these suggested, to those who knew Clapton best, that a change was coming.

The result was that in August, Radle, Sims and Oldaker, the three musicians consistently involved with Clapton since 1974, each received a telegram firing them from the group.

Within a year Radle, the man whose letter had helped sustain Clapton through heroin withdrawal, was dead. He was thirty-four. According to a later interview Clapton gave *Rolling Stone*: 'I broke up that band because we were all fucked up, we were killing one another, fighting ... And it was all drug-related.' He limited his comment on Radle's death from kidney poisoning to 'sad'. Ron Wood, who knew both men well, was more blunt: 'Carl was a lovely guy. He had nothing left after the [Clapton] thing.'

While some supported Clapton's action, others felt that he behaved badly to Radle, making him the scapegoat for his own inadequacies as a bandleader. If the group were 'fucked up and killing one another', it reflected as much on Clapton as the group. Drugs would never have been an issue without his at least tacit acceptance of them. As at other times in his career, Clapton expressed the violence of his self-loathing by violence towards others. Radle, an increasingly bitter and reclusive figure in the winter of 1979–80, always believed he was a victim of 'Eric's ability to leave you behind'. (Another theory, endorsed by the man who replaced him, was that 'Carl . . . had asked for more money on tour of America, and Clapton turned him down.')

By the time Radle died in May 1980 he was relieved to have put Clapton behind him. Even speaking of him was too painful a reminder of the old days when everything lay in the future. After July 1979 the two never met again, although years later Clapton referred to him in print as 'a brother'. A member of Radle's family believes he 'may' have sent a letter in his final weeks – knowing full well that he would never receive an answer, for Clapton was no correspondent. When, in July 1980, he was asked by Dave Markee how he felt about Radle's death, Clapton 'looked down, shrugged . . . and told me to pray'.

Markee and Henry Spinetti, the rhythm section involved on *Rough Mix* and *White Mansions*, were contacted by Forrester that summer. According to Markee, 'a number of signals were sent out . . . including one from Clapton saying, "I'm going up a tree. Stay in touch"' (an unconscious echo of his reply to Radle five years before). Slowly but deliberately – the process by which all such decisions were reached – a formal invitation was made to Markee, Spinetti, the keyboardist Chris Stainton and (six months later) Gary Brooker to join the group. The new all-British quintet made its debut at Cranleigh village hall on 7 September, a pleasing venue given Clapton's status as a virtual cottage industry in the community. According to Linda Chandler, 'It was quite common to see Eric in Ewhurst or Shere, alone or walking with Pattie . . . He always took the time to talk.' Locals at the Windmill Inn became inured to the sight of Clapton drinking brandy in the saloon bar or sitting in one of the rattan chairs overlooking the downs and his own property. A member of Cranleigh Round Table adds that, 'Whatever he did elsewhere, Eric was the most generous, down-to-earth person in the community you could ask for.' At the core of Clapton's restlessness it was still possible to see a longing for roots and domesticity. His behaviour to local residents, his periodic assertions of his 'blokish' personality, even his decision to live a few miles from his childhood home, were all part of what Markee calls an 'unsatisfied longing to be loved'. In this there was something appealing about Clapton – something honest and natural – which made his feelings of frustration and disappointment, expressed on innocents like Radle, still more poignant. Clapton's character was almost a case of arrested development – the childlike virtues of enthusiasm, innocence and spontaneity marred by the childish vices of self-indulgence, weakness and deceit.

There were physical constraints. Clapton's temper was, says Markee, radically affected by 'the booze and all it did to him'. By late 1979, having increased his habit to two and a half bottles of brandy a day, Clapton had developed a matching addiction to painkillers. He contracted 'crippling' twenty-four-hour double vision. Such interest as he had in food was satisfied by a takeaway meal in the studio, after which Clapton would belch or otherwise accompany the music. Looking back from a perspective of fifteen years, Markee remembers

A desperately unhappy man. Eric seemed only to have two emotions: a sort of ecstasy and black despair. He was at his best between two and three in the afternoon – after the first double brandy. *That*'s when he was lovable. His charm was that he was the same with everybody, no matter who they were. The studio cleaner was as big a friend as his manager. He was prone to statements like, 'This is the best band I've ever had' – and he meant it. You couldn't resist him. The other side of Eric was the man who was bitter, uptight and self-pitying, who thought himself hard done by in life. 'Why me?' he'd always say. He seemed incapable of understanding that, compared to most people, he lived in the lap of luxury. There was a deeply morose streak that came out as he drank. *That*'s when it became Clapton-the-superstar and us the hired hands. Eric could be charming one minute and treat you as if he'd never seen you in his life the next. Always the two extremes: delirium and despair. Never contentment.

A second member of Clapton's group remembers that 'Even at gigs like Cranleigh, there was a sense of distance . . . He was always touting us as his "brothers", but really it was Eric Clapton and his band. There was a conscious effort to drive him and the group apart. Forrester and Carroll saw to that.'

Clapton's playing on tour that autumn was a curious mix of the self-abasing and pretentious, his treatment of standards like 'Cocaine' and

'Blues Power' ('Layla' was dropped) suggesting a man both obsessed and bored with himself. The depths were reached in Poland. After a relatively peaceful performance in Warsaw, the group arrived in Katowice on 17 October. If it was possible to applaud Clapton's motives for the event ('I like to do unusual places') and his obvious distress at the outcome (riot police beating back fans with clubs) it was equally possible to see that this was an occasion when his policy of 'leaving it to Roger' backfired. Katowice was an incredibly ill-conceived concert. Markee confirms that 'All of us, Eric included, were aware of it only a few days before. In retrospect, someone should have gone ahead, sat down with the police and *handled* it. It wasn't as though it was unforeseeable.' (The Rolling Stones had encountered almost identical problems in Poland twelve years before.) Instead of 'handling' the matter Clapton was forced to adopt crisis tactics – fleeing the country in tears while the authorities threatened Forrester with arrest and impounded his currency.

From there the group flew to Tel Aviv and Jerusalem (Clapton refusing to leave his hotel room, throwing his bedside Bible at Markee) and finally the Philippines and Japan. The live album recorded in Tokyo, *Just One Night* – released the following May – perfectly illustrates the contradiction Clapton had become. *Just One Night* was, in fact, heavily edited, mainly, as Spinetti says, 'because Eric was so pissed he played at least one chorus out of tune'. While the record achieved a sort of bluesy languor there was also a danger that, in constantly belittling his ability, Clapton was flirting with the possibility of merely voicing what the audience thought. A man needs to possess a sizeable ego to have to subdue it so totally. It was notable that while Clapton restricted his playing on *Just One Night* (as on every album since his comeback) he was still willing to perform blistering solos for an audience of six in a hotel or dressing-room. His opinion of his own talent veered from excessive pride to inordinate gloom. Just as Clapton was ecstatic or desperate, so his playing tended to either extreme. Given the adoring Japanese audience (and the noted acoustics of the hall), standards like 'Tulsa Time' and 'Cocaine' could hardly fail; others, like 'Blues Power', were recharged and improved on. If *Just One Night* failed to emulate the live event, it did enough to suggest that Clapton retained his ability at least to interpret the blues. The best moments tended to be his – the worst ones a collective failure. The group enjoyed a drink themselves and it would be churlish to blame the unevenness of the product on Clapton alone.

A telling review of Clapton's life in the seventies came a few days before the New Year, as he boarded the return flight to London. 'Eric was *gone*,' says Markee. 'When the plane was called he was slumped there. Plastered. Vomit on his chin. Stinking to high heaven. Like most drunks, he tended not to overdo it with baths. I walked over and – I'll never forget this – Clapton caught my eye. The tears came out of him like a bursting dam. "Help me," he said. I walked him to the plane while the others stood and laughed.'

It had been a harrowing decade for Clapton, but even he must have been appalled at how it ended: staggering drunk through a foreign airport, vomiting, in tears, receiving the jeers, howls and catcalls of the mob.

The new year began with a return to the 'anonymity-obscurity' (as Terry calls it: 'playing Eric Clapton without being him') of session work. In two months he guested on albums for Brooker, Ronnie Lane and Stephen Bishop, the last of whom paid Clapton £200 for the privilege. He saw the release of the Alexis Korner album recorded in 1978. There was a rush of activity in the first weeks of the decade, the group living from day to day, hand to mouth ('like an army,' says Markee) awaiting their call. In March they assembled in the studio.

The resulting sessions were a low point even by Clapton's variable standards. Of the thirteen songs hummed, improvised, rehearsed and recorded only five were ever released – and even then in radically altered form. Typical of the whole was 'Freedom', a negligible reggae pastiche eventually grafted on to the soundtrack of the film *Water*. Others ranged from the maudlin ('Help Me Lord') to the merely mundane ('Something Special'). Much of the problem stemmed from the competing claims of the three would-be songwriters present. 'It was a case of Gary with his band, Albert with his or even me with mine,' says Markee. 'Because Eric was in one of his passive it's-nothing-to-do-with-me moods, we just indulged ourselves . . . There were some good songs, but they didn't add up to an album.' When RSO heard the tapes of the session they were appalled. 'It would have been different,' says an executive then associated with the label, 'if it had been a group title. There was some decent material. Unfortunately none of it had to do with Eric Clapton. We'd never have put it out under his name.' In 1967 Clapton had gone to Companies House to prove for tax purposes that he no longer existed. From then on his earnings would be paid into Marshbrook. Had he the courage of his own lack of conviction he might have also considered removing his name from his album covers. There was a case to be made, on the basis of his current form, for seeking a purely anonymous berth in a group. The 'decent material' recorded that spring might have been successfully marketed by RSO. In the meantime, their reaction was: 'Eric Clapton didn't care. Why should we?'

The inevitable tour – less a habit with Clapton than an addiction – opened in May. The playing was surprisingly fluid, though, again, a leading role was taken by Albert Lee. The audiences in Oxford, Edinburgh and London endured a two-hour set in which the revived 'Layla' fell among 'After Midnight', 'Cocaine' and 'Wonderful Tonight'. There was even a version of Brooker's current single, 'Leave The Candle'. If, as he later said, Clapton was 'doing the gigs, but just pushing the buttons', he could still deliver competent replicas of old standards. His best nights were among the best nights anywhere. After six years it remained O'Leary's job to ensure Clapton's brandy infusion was strictly timed to allow him to perform onstage. His acting ability (a quality remarked on by Stigwood) was such that Clapton could be 'stoned out of my brain but would [seem] to outsiders to be fairly *compos mentis* ... I had the ability to let my drunkenness out of the bag only when it was in an appropriate setting.' Markee also comments on his employer's 'unnerving knack' of appearing sober in public. It is rather to Clapton's credit that, during the long years of his inebriation to 1981, there was not a single cancellation.

When Jeff Beck joined Clapton on stage at the Guildford Civic Hall – their first public outing together since 1966 – the critics were agreed: though both had fallen from several of the thrones they once occupied, elements of the old verve remained. Nor could it be decided, in the battle of Golden Guitar Greats, who was the winner. 'While [Beck] ... was full of thrilling noises,' wrote *Melody Maker*, 'Eric remains the more *instinctive* player.' There was praise in the same review for Clapton's musicians. Markee remembers 'coming off stage in Guildford and Eric *beaming* with pride. He was chuffed because we, an all-British band, were better than the Americans.' In a break with tradition, Clapton now intended to keep his group together. Throughout the spring tour he repeatedly stressed his love of his fellow travellers. Among their virtues were their 'all-British' values, their humour and native understanding of Clapton's roots. The man who changed his opinion of America half a dozen times before setting foot there was back to his xenophobic self. Clapton insisted (rather ostentatiously) on consuming beer and fish and chips backstage. He ejected a more exotic dish through a window as deficient in 'sauce'. Far from the urbane globetrotter of legend, Clapton still mistrusted foreign culture and continued to quote loyalist politicians. Markee remembers him commenting favourably on Margaret Thatcher. Remarks disparaging to the mother country, however light-hearted, were violently rebutted. Everything Clapton said and did was characterized by a sense of extreme personal patriotism. He even hired Chas and Dave as his support act.

Just One Night was released that May. It drew respectful if not glowing reviews, among them the *New York Times*:

> Like most of Mr Clapton's recent recordings, his [album] is dominated by commercial soft rock and evidences little of his celebrated mid-sixties fire. He is a singer and songwriter who now just happens to play guitar.

Such was the man who summoned his group in July to Nassau. Not only did Clapton find the Englishness of the venue convivial, it reunited him for the first time since 1974 with Tom Dowd. The result was Clapton's most satisfying record since *Slowhand*. Less agreeably, the album also highlighted the problems of collaborating with a man whose status as a star was constantly reiterated. Gary Brooker contributed two songs to the session, 'Thunder And Lightning' and 'Home Lovin'', deleted from the eventual album on the grounds of being 'insufficiently Clapton-like'. (It was a brave man at RSO who decided what Clapton was like.) Markee also notes that 'contributions from the group, which Eric solicited, were never acknowledged financially . . . I wrote at least half the song "Rita Mae" [eventually released as a single] without a credit. That was typical.'

What Brooker and Markee were witnessing was the relentless promotion of a man – apparently indifferent to the process himself – by his management. Every afternoon Clapton arrived at Compass Point accompanied by O'Leary or his guitar technician Lee Dickson, strumming his trademark black Stratocaster, lighting a cigarette and humming one of the 'ditties and pleasant melodies' he cheerfully admitted his work to be. While Markee, Brooker or Lee advanced the idea into the finished concept, their contribution (with the exception of the track 'Catch Me If You Can') was never recognized. It was his manager, not members of his group, to whom Clapton deferred. Forrester gave him something that he had never had before and which he now realized he needed desperately. All his adult life Clapton had been surrounded by obsequious advisers and fawning employees. Stigwood was an honourable man, ready to tell him when he felt he was doing wrong, but he did so with exaggerated respect, respect for Clapton's status if not always for the man. Forrester respected neither status nor man. He did, however, have a shrewd intuitive grasp of his client's personality and his value as a star. While Clapton insisted on being 'one of the boys', a team player who lavishly praised his colleagues in the studio, Forrester resisted all efforts to promote the group to a wider audience. 'Without Roger,' says Markee, 'it could have been another Derek and the Dominos, a gang of equals with one guy out front. Instead it was always "Eric Clapton and his Band". We felt that.'

Clapton himself was in abject condition. Addicted for years to spicy foods, curries and 'thousand on a raft', he now rarely ate at all. Such calories as he digested were supplied by the brandy. To counter the effect of a bad back he increased his consumption of painkillers to fifty a day. There was an incident, not witnessed by members of the group but much discussed afterwards, when Clapton swallowed an entire bottle of Valium. 'He really did try to kill himself,' says a woman close to Boyd. 'As usual with Eric, he somehow survived.' ('It was a bottle of pills washed down by a bottle of brandy,' says another source, 'from which Clapton woke up stone sober and angry.') As well as double-vision Clapton developed a purple body rash, extending down to his fingers, a reaction to six years' chronic liver abuse. Amazingly, even in this wretched state he continued to function adequately in public. When a committee of Clapton's family and friends attempted to warn him about his health they were irritably rebuffed. So long as he still performed and the records still appeared – and they did, thanks to massive assistance from the group – he considered things 'under control'. Forrester's intervention in Clapton's life did not extend to pointing out the prospect of his death.

'Eric was always on a slippery slope,' says Bobby Whitlock. 'When I knew him he was still re-living his childhood, fighting the battles that were as much a part of him as an arm or a leg. He really did "drink to forget", although of course it had the opposite effect. Eric became harder and harder to get through to.' While Brooker had the impression that 'part of the problem was that [the group] revered him, and didn't mix, whereas he'd enjoy coming round to my hotel room for a chat,' a different explanation is provided by Markee: 'I respected Eric rather than revered him. As for not mixing . . . Clapton on his own was one thing. Clapton after a few drinks, egged on by Forrester and Carroll, was something else. You *couldn't* get close to him. Roger was acutely paranoid of Spinetti and me trying to "convert" Eric, whereas the main thing was just to sit down and talk to him. I did that a few times and found a warm but very hurt guy who knew he was being used. Eric alone in his room would ask your opinion or admit he was scared. Eric with his gang would heap abuse on you and slam the door in your face.'

The group left Nassau in August and, after a brief Scandinavian tour, retired for the year. In four months Clapton, a known socializer, left Hurtwood Edge a half-dozen times. What did he do? All the evidence suggests that outside the confines of the studio and the concert stage his life had no central meaning. Unlike a Dylan or Lennon, Clapton (after 1976) was notably reticent in political sayings. Unlike a Jagger he never yearned to be a serious cultural figure. When Clapton read a book it was likely to be a potboiler. His idea of a night out was *The Mousetrap*. Clapton was, moreover, a home-lover of unusual devotion. Although he lacked depth, he had great breadth. He began to develop the normal domestic hobbies. He learnt something about house maintenance. He liked to amble about his garden – of which he was 'inordinately proud,' says Markee – filling in the time between opening hours. A regular at the Windmill Inn confirms that Clapton was apt to appear 'bleary-eyed, at lunchtime, and stay until gently persuaded to leave'. Since he spent much of his time in the pub sitting alone gazing out of the window it was possible to form the impression of an 'apparently lonely man, in no hurry to get back to whatever haunted him'. To the various causes advanced for Clapton's alcoholism, Markee plausibly adds another: boredom.

To sit at home with Boyd did not satisfy Clapton for long. Encouraged by Brooker he developed a passion for fishing, taking to the sport with all the enthusiasm with which, once, he had taken to football and racing. This particular pastime was something of a tradition: as a boy Clapton had spent hours on the river Wey at Ripley: the Clapp family crest was a pike swimming. Intrigued, Clapton appeared at the local sports shop owned by Peter Cockwill, who remembers, 'Eric overnight becoming an expert, buying himself a place on the river . . . While [Brooker] taught him to fly-fish he still had a longing for what he called his "roots" – coarse fishing. The fastest I ever saw Clapton move was when he caught a ten-pound pike.'

Harmless enough in itself, the hobby inevitably extended the distance between Clapton and his wife. For days he, Brooker and Cockwill disappeared into the country. Boyd's emotions – the celebrated model reduced to gutting trout and serving them to Clapton and his friends – can only be guessed at. 'It became anti-social,' he admitted. 'It definitely contributed to a division between Pattie and me.' When Clapton was not on the river he continued to support West Bromwich Albion – for whom his last devotional act was to play a benefit concert in 1981 – or sit in the local pub (where Boyd herself appeared one evening, alone and in obvious distress). The substantial sum that Clapton made from his music was needed to support his wife, his house, his cars and his hobbies, but it may have added to his prevailing sense of inertia. He earned just enough money to indulge himself. In 1980 Clapton's emolument from Marshbrook was £145,000 – modest by rock star standards, but quite enough to keep him in rods, reels and brandy.

At this stage Clapton's career, already apparently at its darkest, turned black. He met Phil Collins. Clapton's recent work had been marginally less trite than Collins's oeuvre turned out to be, but, as the most popular exponents of the easy-listening style which both thrilled and dismayed their fans, the two had much in common. For a time from 1980, when Clapton guested on *Face Value* and Collins returned the favour by helping construct a studio at Hurtwood Edge, their careers became synonymous: there were two collaborative albums and a host of appearances at each other's concerts.* In the public's eye they, and later Mark Knopfler, became associated as a unit – 'a big mistake,' says Pete Brown, 'in that it turned Eric into just another entertainer. Those albums [with Collins] sounded obsolete as soon as he made them.' For at least ten years before he met Collins, Clapton was continuously under the spell of one professional influence or another: The Band, the Bramletts, Harrison, Townshend, Carl Radle, Dylan and Don Williams all served in the role of musical *Obergruppenführer*. It would be churlish to say that Collins with his two-song repertoire – the fast one with horns and the slow one on piano – accelerated a decline that may already have been terminal. There was, however, an awful sameness about his work with Clapton: so much so that at least one record guide refers to it as 'a seemingly endless

---

* There was a falling-out in 1994 when Clapton, reading an interview in which Collins asked, 'How can he stand up there in a £5,000 suit and play the blues?' told *Q* magazine: 'The point is, *Phil*, that the blues is a state of mind, it's got nothing to do with acquisition. [Collins] should understand this.'

soundtrack . . . under-played, over-produced [and] beyond the pale'. Forgiving critics still billed Clapton's music as revolutionary in its grittiness, but only inches from its surface realism flowed the teenager's undercurrent of frivolity: 'Drinking wine, pulling women [and] making gigs' were the three activities he sang of on 'Help Me Lord'. The falling-off of standards since *Layla* was all the more startling set against Clapton's fanatical allegiance to purity in the 1960s. It may be that, as Chris Dreja says, 'there was always a side of him willing to change course, even on a point of principle. The irony is that in the early days Eric was too idealistic, and later on not idealistic enough. While we were still playing the blues, he went in for elevator music with Phil Collins.'

Nineteen eighty-one began with a tour of Ireland, the highlight of which was reached offstage: Clapton appeared at the Barberstown Hotel where, in the words of one employee, 'he propped up the bar from three in the afternoon until eight the next morning. All efforts to close for the night were met with the words, "Fuck you. I *own* the place."' He also played a single concert at the Rainbow – from which he donated the profits to a trust fund administered by Meg Patterson – scene of his putative comeback eight years before, where Clapton referred to his new album as the 'best thing released by *anybody* since 1973'.

It proved not to be. *Another Ticket*, issued that February, was undeniably an improvement on the likes of *Backless*. Even so, Clapton's tongue must have been firmly in his ample cheek to compare it to *Station To Station*, *Time Loves A Hero* or *Some Girls*, not to mention the likes of the Sex Pistols. If not conspicuously improved as a guitarist or songwriter, Clapton had at least progressed as a singer. By 1981 his voice – fuelled by a forty-a-day cigarette habit – had matured into a mellow, smoky and full-toned instrument: his work on 'Floating Bridge' and 'Rita Mae' (which strongly recalled 'After Midnight') was outstanding. Elsewhere there was a faithful rendition of Muddy Waters's 'Blow Wind Blow', the mawkish title track, and an inoffensive collaboration with Brooker, 'Catch Me If You Can'. Appropriately enough, given Clapton's physical condition, 'I Can't Stand It' was released as a single.

An idea of Clapton's internal sense of himself came in his one major interview to promote the album, given to the *Daily Mirror*. The tone was aggressively populist. Clapton, he assured the paper, 'went down the pub in Ripley on Fridays' (though not caring for the 'toffs and tourists' he met there); his greatest love was for betting; he admitted to being a chauvinist and boor. The interview was ended by the arrival of Collins at the wrought-iron gates of Hurtwood Edge: '"My son, my son,"' [said Clapton]. '"Have a drink . . ."'

The impression was of a no-nonsense egalitarian, studiously down to earth, a man who eschewed pretension and stressed his impeccable working-class credentials. Unmentioned were Clapton's Mercedes and Ferraris, his wardrobe of designer suits, his physical decline and hair-trigger temper. He may not have been able to help his inverted snobbery – it was a kind of addiction – but Clapton went too far in claiming to survive on his weekly £150 wage packet. In 1981 he earned £140,000 from Marshbrook; he also formed his own production company (initially named Pattisongs) and E.C. Music, incorporated on 19 November 1981 'to . . . carry on the business of publishers and printers of sheet and other music, scores, lyrics, pamphlets, books and magazines of all kinds'; Clapton and his manager served as directors. The following year the two took over a clothing company named Quickhawk, incorporating it on 6 January as Duck Records – one of the aliases used by Clapton's groups was the Duck Brothers – 'to acquire and dispose of copyrights, rights of representation, licences and any other rights or interest in any . . . song, composition, picture, drawing, work of art or photograph and to print or publish anything of which the Company has a copyright'. Again Clapton and Forrester were directors; Forrester's assistant Diana Puplett was company secretary. The principal activity of Duck was the management of Clapton's own record label; *Another Ticket* would be the last album nominally released by Stigwood. While there was no breath of anything underhand in Clapton's business affairs, his close attention to financial detail, his 98 per cent ownership of Marshbrook and his periodic residence in Eire for purposes of tax avoidance all suggest a man far from the grinning *ingénu* depicted in the *Mirror*.

An American tour in support of *Another Ticket* opened in Oregon on 2 March. From there Clapton flew by chartered Viscount to Seattle, where initial rehearsals for the tour had taken place at a local theatre. In 1975 Clapton had admitted to fondness for the city. Now, with Seattle's additional attraction for the angler, it became a passion. On 5 March Clapton, dressed fastidiously in white jeans and black leather jacket, arrived in the bar of a hotel on Elliott Bay. Seemingly anxious to please – bowing ironically when applauded – he appeared cheerful but distracted; when given a drink he handed back the glass, after inspection, in objection to the presence on the rim of a crack or chip 'in which germs might accumulate'. Markee's point about 'not getting close to Eric' was rendered vertebrate by the ensuing tableau. Clapton sat in a booth surrounded by O'Leary, Carroll, two other employees and a blonde woman other than his wife. Fans and autograph seekers were discouraged. The irony of the scene was notable: Clapton-the-common-man sitting in a crowded lounge surrounded by his bodyguards and handlers. By loudly insisting fellow drinkers 'respect Eric's privacy' Carroll and O'Leary achieved more public scrutiny than would have resulted from unimpeded access to their master. Throughout it Clapton sat hunched over an unusually exotic-looking drink, arguing constantly with the blonde, pausing only to cough explosively when lighting his fourth or fifth cigarette of the hour.

The three concerts that followed at the Paramount Theatre were typical: after an extended delay the curtain rose on Clapton's band performing Albert Lee's 'Country Boy', seguing into a Procul Harum medley sung by Brooker. Then, and only then, did Clapton lope unannounced on to the stage. The concert proper opened with 'Tulsa Time', maintained its jaunty momentum with 'Lay Down Sally' and 'Blues Power', slumped into 'Wonderful Tonight', climaxing with 'Further On Up The Road' and 'Layla'. Given Clapton's evident confusion between numbers (at one stage forgetting his own whereabouts) he came startlingly alive the moment he strapped on a guitar. The concert gave proof of his professionalism. It also proved that, with few friends of his own, Clapton needed an audience more than most. He was happiest in front of a sea of undifferentiated faces. According to Markee: 'He had an emptiness in him. The most fun Eric ever had was playing to a crowd . . . Uncritical love was what he wanted.' Whatever the cause, it was hard to deny that Clapton, even on auto-pilot, retained vestiges of his old self, or that the headline in the morning paper, 'Seattle Fans Get Their Money's Worth', was broadly accurate.

The eighth concert of a projected forty-five concert tour was at Madison, Wisconsin. 'Eric was lost,' says Markee. 'As we were changing he looked dreadful, ashen-faced, tired and sick. "Pray for me," he said. "I can feel the skin coming off my bones." ' After a barely animate performance Clapton was floundering – playing the wrong notes – in the climax to 'Layla'. 'I looked over,' Markee says, 'and there was Forrester on stage, frantically drawing his finger across his throat. I'd never seen that before in real life. He literally pulled Eric off and got him to the airport. It was desperate.'

On the midnight flight to St Paul Clapton sat hunched, silent and not drinking. At the airport Forrester, sensing for the first time a genuine emergency, directed the limousine to hospital. Clapton was examined, X-rayed and driven to his suite at the Radisson Plaza Hotel. By the time he arrived the doctor was on the line: 'Get him back here immediately. He's got an ulcer that's about to explode. We want him back in.'

'I saw Clapton in Minneapolis in 1979,' says Adam Hilditch, then an intern at United Hospitals. 'He looked great – a guy in a silk suit whose tan gleamed from five rows back. I couldn't believe it was the same man strapped to a gurney in the ER. It sounds bad, but my first thought was, "Jesus – what a waste." He was just lying there, out of it. His manager was screaming at someone on the phone.'

Estimates vary as to how long Clapton, if untreated, would have lived. According to Coleman, 'one [report] said he had forty-five minutes'. Hilditch himself believes 'he could have gone at any time . . . I personally thought he wouldn't make it.' Clapton had not one but five separate ulcers, the largest of which was described as the size of an orange. His four-week stay in hospital (and Forrester's cancellation of the remaining thirty-seven concerts) made headline news in America. Boyd was photographed arriving from London. Townshend and Don Williams also visited. Clapton received messages from his family, from Bruce and Baker, from members of the Rolling Stones and Dylan, as well as from ordinary well-wishers and fans. By the end of his third week in hospital it was noted that 'almost single-handed, Eric Clapton has triggered a boom in the greeting-card industry . . . [One manufacturer] compares it to the sort of volume normally associated with a presidential event.'*

The most perceptive comment came from Robert Palmer in the *New York Times*. Echoing, but not quoting, Thomas Wolfe's dictum that people in the same profession tend to be the same everywhere, Palmer compared Clapton's fate with that of Mike Bloomfield, formerly guitarist with Dylan and Paul Butterfield, found dead of a drug overdose on 15 February:

---

* The reporter was being disingenuous. He forgot to mention the 500,000-odd cards sent that week to Ronald Reagan, shot in an assassination attempt on 30 March.

Mr Clapton's illness and Mr Bloomfield's death are unrelated incidents, but they are both indications that time has not been kind to rock's original guitar elite . . . By the beginning of the 70s, guitarists like [Clapton and Bloomfield] had begun to feel that long solos and flashy playing were more a means of ego gratification than a legitimate musical style. They were growing older, and as they matured they began to value musical teamwork more highly. Some white guitarists felt guilty because the black bluesmen who had originally inspired them were still struggling, still relatively unknown, while white imitators reaped unheard-of rewards.

. . . Viewed from this historical perspective, Mr Clapton's decision at the beginning of the 70s to de-emphasize instrumental bravura and develop his singing and songwriting was both intelligent and inevitable, whatever one may think of the music that has resulted. One hopes he will be well and touring again before long. In concert, he is still capable of an urgency that *Another Ticket* and most of his other recent albums conspicuously lack.

Among the family and fans, the columnists and the colleagues, two other groups took special interest in Clapton's welfare. The extensive file maintained by the FBI over a period of fourteen years refers with notable emphasis to 'the . . . coincidence of subject falling ill, *to say the least*, in same month as wounds sustained by [the President]'. The file also alludes to the 'inflammatory' remarks made by Clapton in 1976, coinciding with America's 'first and only Nazi resurgence since the 1930s'. If lacking the scale and comic depth of the Bureau's reports on Jagger or John Lennon, Clapton's file reveals him to have been under at least passive scrutiny since 1967. While much of this merely involved stockpiling press cuttings it also says volumes for the leadership style of J. Edgar Hoover, a man, according to Gordon Liddy, who 'hated pop stars. All of them.'

The second party especially concerned with Clapton's health was his group. Early on, Markee appeared at the hospital with a poster bearing the legend, 'Here's Another Mess', and a new Bible. Clapton, he says, 'was actually in tears when I arrived. He thought he'd let us down. I sat there for an hour, reading the Bible, until Nigel [Carroll] threw me out. After that it was impossible to see Eric.'

Eventually the crisis passed. The group returned to England while Clapton, on weekend leave from hospital, went fishing in Seattle. Even this proved traumatic. At dinner in the Westin Hotel a row broke out with Carroll (Clapton wanting to order brandy, his assistant vetoing it); a window was smashed; on its way to the airport Clapton's car, driven by a twenty-year-old woman named Gail Allison Coe, was in collision with a taxi. The man returning to St Paul had added bruised ribs and pleurisy to his ailments. Prescribed damp air as treatment, Clapton made the reasonable observation that 'I can get it by sitting in my garden.' He flew to London overnight.

'I'd like to congratulate Eric Clapton on his good sense,' says Adam Hilditch. 'Unfortunately, I can't. Even in hospital he was pushing it – "Will three drinks be all right? Will *four*?" – sneaking in booze from outside. Either he just didn't know how ill he was, or he didn't care.' Clapton himself admits, 'Within a couple of months of being out I was back on a bottle or two bottles a day. And I didn't give a damn about my health.' Markee confirms that his employer was in 'dire shape' at a group meeting that summer. And another musician notes that 'by then, Eric was back on spicy foods, late nights and bottles of Scotch' (his substitute for brandy). He would have 'needed a heart of stone,' says Markee, not to have listened to Boyd. 'She begged him to stop drinking.' Unable to grasp the seriousness of his condition, Clapton did, however, show concern for others. When Gary Glitter was hospitalized that year with alcohol-related problems the first person he heard from was 'Eric ... saying he was there if I needed him.'

The other side of Clapton was the man who fought and screamed at Boyd (whose own alcoholism continued to develop apace); who disappeared for days at a time fishing; who constantly made dates with his group which he failed to keep; who was incoherent by mid-afternoon; who slept with other women and flouted his wife. Everything about Clapton was changeable, including his repertoire of put-on accents and personae. Pete Brown remembers that 'he could affect at least twenty different voices' from his capacious internal wardrobe. On the rare occasions when he was not being someone else, he spoke in an unexpectedly soft Home Counties accent with the odd cockney overlay. On the occasions, still rarer, when he was not alone in his studio/bar he socialized exclusively with other musicians. In 1981 this meant Phil Collins and, to a lesser extent, Brooker, Spinetti and Markee. 'He only really loosened up with a guitar in his hand,' says the last. 'Because everyone has a different idea of who or what Clapton is, he's confused himself. Even with us, he tended to act out roles.' Uncertainty as to 'who or what'

Clapton was led to some curious events: rumours of a Cream reunion in August 1981 were scotched only when the man claiming to be 'Eric's manager' was revealed as a fake while, in a separate incident, an impersonator ran up mountainous bills in Clapton's name and wrote to the Fender company asking for 'my guitars'.

Clapton himself emerged on 9 September, when he appeared in the first of three concerts for Amnesty International. Encouraged by Forrester and Phil Collins (who provided backing vocals) he duetted with Jeff Beck on ''Cause We Ended As Lovers' and 'Further On Up The Road', performed a strikingly reworked 'Crossroads' and closed with the ensemble 'I Shall Be Released'. Onstage all was pandemic goodwill, speaker after speaker expressing, in Sting's words, the 'global vibes' of the occasion. The real action came in the dressing-room, in a scene witnessed by *Rolling Stone*:

> And was Eric – out of sight since ulcer problems forced him to cut short a US tour last spring – his usual delightful self backstage? 'We had a few arguments,' chuckled [the promoter] Martin Lewis. 'On the last night he kept asking me, "I've never been so fucking badly treated in my life. Where's the wine? Where's the booze?" So I told him, "I'm tired of arse-licking rock stars like you. I'm bloody watching the show."'

In October Clapton and the group toured Scandinavia, an instantly familiar return to the life abandoned in March. 'It was booze, booze, booze,' says Markee. 'If Eric had learnt anything in hospital, he didn't show it.' Clapton's playing was loose to the point of detached; his behaviour as manic as in the same cities in 1974. Rock bottom came in Randers, where Clapton attempted to play saxophone on 'Further On Up The Road' before announcing his decision to 'kick ass' in a local nightclub. Dawn was coming at the window before he returned to the hotel. In late November the group began the usual pre-festive tour of Japan.

This seemingly straightforward event, a ten-day excursion allowing the band to be home before Christmas, was a turning-point in Clapton's life. For nine months Markee, Spinetti and, to varying degrees, Lee, Stainton and Brooker had pleaded with their employer to stop drinking. As late as December 1981 there seemed no hope of such an outbreak of sanity. Clapton continued to swallow painkillers mingled with brandy and Scotch and – almost lost in the mix – a dwindling number of tablets to control his ulcers. When Markee or Stainton suggested he 'for God's sake, cool it' they failed to grasp the depths of his addictive–obsessive personality. One of Clapton's most notable qualities, as with many an addict, was his insularity: his apparent belief that the world started and stopped as he woke and slept. Like a child, he was convinced that if he closed his eyes he was invisible, and that nothing could possibly be happening in a room before he opened the door and went inside. While this meant that Clapton continued, up to a point, to perform adequately in public – as long as he stood upright for ninety minutes he failed to see the problem – it also meant that he was shielded from the full consequences of his actions. He never heard the muttered conferences between his family and manager or read the reports of his erratic public behaviour. He was like the declining Elvis: screened by a clique of fiercely protective but uncritical advisers who assured him, time after time, that he was 'wonderful tonight' onstage. So long as the conspiracy endured, so would Clapton's drinking.

The bubble was pricked when, on 9 December, Clapton himself approached Forrester in Tokyo. 'For the very first time ever,' his manager told Coleman, 'Eric said he didn't want to appear on stage. I couldn't believe it.' As well as a recurrence of the purple rash covering his entire body, Clapton had begun to shake so violently he could scarcely hold his guitar. 'We barely got through that gig,' says Markee. 'Luckily, it was enough for the Japanese for Eric just to *be* there. As we came off Roger called him into a private room, where we could hear them shouting . . . Eric was in tears.' Now, seven and a half years after it first became apparent, his manager informed Clapton he had a problem. The intervention itself was dramatic: according to Forrester his words were, 'I don't *think* you drink to *excess*, Eric. I don't think *anything*. I *know* that you're an *alcoholic*.' Markee confirms that, on the return flight to London, 'Roger was grimly determined that *something* had to be done.'

After Christmas at Hurtwood Edge (part of which he spent asleep among a pile of logs in the cellar) Clapton was driven to the airport on 7 January 1982, strapped on to a flight to Minneapolis and taken under protest to the Hazelden Foundation, an austere concrete building north of the city. It was among the bleakest of a growing number of rehabilitation centres known for their bleakness. While Forrester returned to the Radisson Plaza, Clapton was shown to a billet, dosed with Librium and told he could anticipate a rigorous and uncompromising four-week programme of detoxification.

Among the features of the Minnesota Method was an emphasis on practical discipline. For the first time in his life Clapton made his own bed. He learned to set and clear a table. As he had in Oswestry eight years before, Clapton discovered the therapeutic value of exercise. Within a week of arriving at Hazelden he was taking long walks in the grounds, eating, not drinking, and, above all, attending the twice-daily prayer meetings. (Clapton would later tell Markee that this was the 'most profound' part of his treatment.) At the same time, as he later admitted, 'there was still this rebellious thing coming out', the famous rock star playing games with the nurses and orderlies. All that changed when in early February Boyd arrived at the clinic. This crisis, arguably the pivot on which Clapton's whole life turned, was prefaced by the sending of a questionnaire to Hurtwood Edge. Had her husband raped her, Boyd was asked. Was he violent? What was he like when he was drunk? The exact answers to this, the confrontational part of Clapton's therapy, may never be known. What is known is that, when he was shown the completed document, he broke down and wept. 'When I read out to some of the other inmates what Pattie had said,' Clapton admitted, 'how I had treated her without realizing it – that broke my heart. I was made to understand that I'd behaved like an animal.'

Clinics tend to be idle killers. They rouse themselves to truthfulness only when they sense that a patient is demoralized and they can give the *coup de grâce*. When Clapton first arrived at Hazelden, carrying a secreted bottle of whisky, he remained what he always had been: a problem wrapped in a riddle inside a mystery. Nothing about him was certain. He recognized this and played on it – played up to it – enjoying the significant status of the enigma, someone beyond the lure of the pigeonhole. Up until 1982 Clapton's chief failing was an incurable fixation with his image, primarily as a loner, in the eyes of the outside world. Like David Bowie, he seemed incapable of walking down rock's hall of mirrors and averting his eyes from the endlessly distorting reflection. There may be no more embarrassing position than that of protesting one's own importance, of being the person in the crowd to say, 'I'm not as you are.' Yet Clapton had said something like that all his life. Now, overnight, he was reduced to the level of a normal human being, self-admittedly 'frightened of the outside world'. A deeply chastened man, sober for the first time in eight years, he returned with his wife to Hurtwood Edge.

It had changed in his absence. Boyd, shrewdly sensing that the pendulum had swung in the other direction, removed all traces of hard liquor from the house. Certain friends, long used to an open invitation, now found their way barred at the gate. The house, in the words of one woman who did enter, 'began to look less like a war zone' than before. Clapton himself joined Alcoholics Anonymous, attending meetings in England and eventually America (where he believed there was less 'shame and guilt' attached to his condition).* Despite giving Boyd and others the impression that he had sworn off drink for life, within two years Clapton was enjoying beer, wine and occasional spirits. By mid-1985 he described himself as 'drinking in moderation'; two years later he recorded a song for an American beer commercial, earning reproof from, of all quarters, Keith Richards. If, in 1982, nothing suggested that his endorsement of the adage 'One is too many and a thousand isn't enough' was less than total (for the first twelve months it was Boyd who secretly partook) then, equally, nothing suggested that Clapton's resolve would outlast his other numerous forgotten promises. The consequences of 'stopping drinking' lasted long after he eventually returned to drink.

For instance, the way Clapton looked and dressed: the man 'stinking to high heaven' in 1979 was described by Boyd in 1982 as 'crisp and smart . . . *severely* clean'. Always interested in clothes – even when alone he insisted on dressing up – Clapton now discovered designer wardrobes. Overnight he adopted the Versace label (baggy trousers, shirt buttoned up, no tie) then, just as quickly, discarded it. The company found out what a hundred deserted friends already knew: that a pledge of allegiance by Clapton was no sort of lifetime guarantee. In the late eighties he abandoned Versace for Armani. The event may have seemed like a stylistic footnote, but Versace reacted waspishly by saying Clapton now 'looked like an accountant'. Armani replied that this was the very image their client had been keen to relinquish. It was a traumatic time for Clapton, but even he might have been struck by the irony of the scene: two of Europe's wealthiest and most resourceful companies unable to agree on the cut of his suits.

From March to June 1982 Clapton read, wrote, fished, and constantly agitated for a return to live work. He continued to depend on his manager

* It was unfair of Truman Capote, shortly before he died, to speak of rock and Alcoholics Anonymous having 'sprung up from the same seed'. Coincidentally, though, the first-ever AA meeting in Britain took place on the day Clapton was born.

practically, psychologically, and also financially. Forrester in turn kept Clapton's diary, arranged his appearances, dealt with promoters and musicians and increasingly supervised the running of his company. (In 1982 Marshbrook had a turnover of £191,223, of which £160,469 went on administrative expenses.) But these activities were merely the scaffolding: his major role was to be the person who thought about his client's needs and organized his life more than anyone outside his family. Shortly after leaving Hazelden, when Clapton – in a typical outburst – demanded that Forrester arrange a tour, it was promptly done. Markee remembers being 'phoned at home by Roger, saying Eric was going up the wall with boredom and wanted to play. I thought it was too early, and said so.'

Markee's objection, overruled by Forrester, was well founded. In 1974 Clapton had returned to live work only weeks after completing his cure, a decision even his manager thought mistaken. Now, eight years later, history was repeated. Clapton, Brooker, Lee, Stainton, Markee and Spinetti met for rehearsals in May; by early June they were on a sixteen-city tour of America. Among the first stops was Minneapolis, where Clapton not only paid a courtesy call at Hazelden but attended a much-publicized Alcoholics Anonymous meeting. (So anonymous that T-shirts bearing the legend 'I'm Eric. I'm an alcoholic' were widely on sale in the city.) 'Not surprisingly,' says Markee, 'Eric was totally lost in America . . . quiet, uptight, and struggling to come to terms with life. He should never have been allowed back so soon.' 'It was a rash decision,' Clapton admits.

The tour ended on 30 June in Florida. Spinetti remembers Clapton 'running up the stairs to the stage to show that he, as a non-drinker, was fitter than us'. The playing, even in a single night, veered from the startlingly original to the banal; on some numbers Clapton held back his head and, clenching his hand, seemed physically to wrench notes from his guitar, his playing of which was faster than anyone else's yet wholly unhurried; on others he shuffled asymmetrically around the stage, winking at Brooker, goosing the ever-pliant Lee and sounding, in one critic's words, 'as if only semi-familiar with the chosen repertoire'. The effect was a manic-depressive atmosphere in the crowd, as one song hoisted them up, and another let them down, by turns. After a barely recognizable 'I Shot The Sheriff' – Clapton adding mere descant to Lee's lead – the group segued into 'Blow Wind Blow' from *Another Ticket*. On cue Muddy Waters himself walked on, a small, squirrel-cheeked man with an oriental moustache who, in Markee's words, 'wiped the floor with us'. A mark of

Clapton's respect for his mentor was the removal of the cigarette he otherwise kept in his mouth when not actually singing.

'Just then I looked over,' says Markee, 'and saw an absolutely *stricken* look on Eric's face. He was staring at Muddy with his "I can't believe it" expression – the same one he had when hell broke loose in Poland – the look of someone paralysed by his own sense of inadequacy. That's when I knew we'd all be fired.'

8

The Sane Englishman with His Guitar

It was an important part of Clapton's self-projection that he never wanted to be confused in the public mind with Surrey Man, with whom he shared an address but not a desire to lead a settled, orderly life. No sooner had he returned from Hazelden and the American tour – a logical moment to concentrate on his marriage – than he left Boyd again. That summer he was seen at a series of clubs, restaurants and concerts, sometimes alone, sometimes with other women, before settling – of all places – in north Wales. Just as he had in 1974 Clapton rose early (though not on this occasion labouring on a farm), taking solitary walks and surprising one local hotel owner, David Evans, by 'appearing in a dazzling red suit and ordering tinned salmon with vinegar'. According to one witness, Clapton used demotic language to cast aspersions on the quality of the food and, in particular, of the gazpacho served as a first course. ('It's fucking *cold*' is Evans's exact memory of the words.) When Clapton left in his Ferrari there was a minor incident involving a stone urn in the courtyard.

What Clapton was doing, or attempting to do, in Wales was writing songs. In order to launch the record label of which they became directors that December, Forrester and his client agreed on the need for a commercially viable album. Furthermore, the record, capitalizing on the music publishing business founded in 1981, was to be self-written. The idea was for Clapton to arrive at Compass Point in August with a dozen original titles. In the event he appeared in September with less than half that number.

There was a 'terrible atmosphere', according to Clapton's bassist and drummer, at the studio in Nassau. Evidence that their employer had adopted yet another persona came when he summoned his personal guitar technician, Lee Dickson. Dickson was ordered to spray Clapton's signature black Stratocaster a violent green. He refused. Next there was a row concerning financial provisions for the group. When at last recording began Markee found Clapton to be 'short-tempered, gruff and hostile', complaining about the re-release of 'Layla' as a single and angrily bringing one session to a close by slamming his guitar (not the Stratocaster) into a brick wall.

The suspicion was that Clapton, as Markee puts it, 'struggling to come to terms with life' post-Hazelden, frustrated by his inability to write, took out his resentment on his colleagues. The clinic always advised its out-patients to expect a full year of irrational behaviour, and it proved not to have been lying. So long as Clapton had struggled with the madness outside his life it was relatively easy to postpone casting out the devils within. When, at least temporarily, the bottle was beaten he came to realize that some form of internal exorcism was overdue. Another musician present in Nassau confirms that 'you could see Eric looking for a new problem to grapple with. He wasn't someone who could leave well enough alone.'

Within a week of arriving at Compass Point Clapton had withdrawn from the rest of the group. They saw him, if at all, as he crossed hurriedly through the studio complex before locking himself in a private room with Forrester. Factions formed, the other five rehearsing under Dowd's direction while their leader brooded or listened impassively to playbacks. It might be wondered why, when Clapton made his disapproval so obvious, his group persisted in their efforts to win him round. 'Loyalty' is the word used by Spinetti; Markee adds that 'everyone was concerned about Eric and wanted to do their best by him'. Though the atmosphere in the studio remained 'poisonous', there was a conscious effort by the musicians to help Clapton through what he himself recognized as a transition.

On his eighth day in Nassau Clapton sent Brooker, Stainton, Markee and Spinetti (Lee was excused) a note, asking each to report to him individually in his chalet. When Markee arrived he was greeted by 'Eric, sitting alone behind a desk, looking very businesslike. In about thirty seconds he told me that the band was being fired, though we might be needed, he thought, for a tour. I asked him why and he said we just weren't right for him.'

It is not impossible to feel sympathy for the decision. Neither of the albums the group had made for Clapton was especially distinguished, though no worse than most of his recent output. There was truth to

Clapton's claim that 'they were a great band for touring and going on stage with, but [in the studio] not up to the standard required'. His verdict that 'I'm a blues guitarist, and that just wasn't a good blues band' won at least tacit support from Stainton, who subsequently wrote Clapton a conciliatory letter and was promptly rehired as a result.

On the other hand, it seemed strange, not least to Markee and Spinetti, that Clapton had taken three years to form an assessment of their abilities. Brooker, too, was intensely hurt by the decision. As the group who had supported Clapton through his twilight years, frequently covering for his shortcomings on stage, they felt deserving of more than, as Markee puts it, 'confirmation from the Head that we were being expelled'. Nor did Clapton's comment to one of the four that 'You spend too much time playing tennis' actively endear him to the musicians.

A more plausible objection to the group was that they reminded Clapton of a period he preferred to forget. When rewriting the past, a first priority is always to impugn that previously held sacrosanct: Clapton's order to deface his guitar, the abandonment of his house and the replacement of his musicians were all part of this process of reappraisal. Another factor was the advice given by Hazelden that 'if something bugged me, I should be assertive about it'. To use a word not then in vogue, Clapton felt empowered by firing his friends. The firmness with which he did so may have surprised even himself: 'It was a terrible thing to do, and it was probably over the top,' he told Coleman. 'They must have thought that I was flipping out' – a notion that had, in fact, occurred to at least one of them. Whatever the cause of Clapton's action, its result was to alienate the very people – fellow musicians – whose approval he so desperately wanted. Albert Lee left the group by mutual agreement in 1984; Stainton and to a lesser extent Spinetti were reconciled to the decision; Brooker was incensed; Markee never saw Clapton again.

In their place Dowd, through his long association with the label, summoned a group of Atlantic house musicians: Donald 'Duck' Dunn, formerly involved with Otis Redding and Wilson Pickett (and recently reincarnated in *The Blues Brothers*) and the drummer Roger Hawkins, known to Clapton since an Aretha Franklin session in 1968. Ry Cooder was persuaded to guest on guitar. They, Clapton, Lee and Stainton – restored to the group after a month – continued to rehearse and record for the remainder of the year. When *Money And Cigarettes* was released in February 1983 it earned generally favourable reviews, though critics were divided as to whether it marked the 'restart' Clapton himself insisted.

His new-found assertiveness was further illustrated in a run-in that winter with Pete Townshend. In the course of a long peroration on drugs in *Rolling Stone*, the Who guitarist offered the thought that 'Eric lost two and a half years and no one will ever know what might have happened had [he] not done that'. This seemingly anodyne comment – one that the speaker was uniquely qualified to make – enraged Clapton. He wrote to Townshend insisting that any future remarks be delivered 'face to face, instead of blabbing to the papers'. Though the relationship was patched up – in 1993 the two did a stand-up routine at an awards ceremony in London – a member of the Who, also close to Clapton, confirms that for years 'they both thought the other had gone mad'.

Clapton ended 1982 by playing with Chas and Dave on their Christmas television special. Given his cockney proclivities and rudderless musical direction, concern was expressed, by a member of Cream, among others, that 'Eric would make a bloody fool of himself'. Nor was the stage-set, a makeshift East End pub, immediately encouraging. In the event Clapton restricted himself to a country-rock version of 'Goodnight Irene' and a preview of 'Slow Down Linda', one of the tracks recorded in Nassau. Although he did nothing to harm his reputation neither did he do anything conspicuously to help it. It would be difficult to argue with the verdict of one reviewer that 'The aim was classlessness, but the result was a lack of class.'

A single, the ludicrous 'I've Got A Rock n' Roll Heart', was released in January. It prefaced the album recorded at Compass Point, *Money And Cigarettes*. Clapton's fixation with The Band in general and Robbie Robertson in particular found expression in 'Everybody Oughta Make A Change' (axiomatic, in Clapton's case) and 'Ain't Going Down', the latter not wholly diminished by being a carbon of 'All Along The Watchtower'. There were three songs directly aimed at Boyd: 'Man In Love', 'Pretty Girl' (allowing Clapton to rhyme 'everything' with 'ring') and the instructive 'The Shape You're In', also released as a single, in which his wife's drinking was addressed in terms of Clapton's own experience:

> I'm just telling you, baby
> 'Cause I've been there myself . . .

Elsewhere there were covers of Albert King's 'Crosscut Saw'; the barnyard-blues pastiche 'Crazy Country Hop' and a third single, 'Slow Down

Linda', a jaunty if fragile rocker existing in a bracket with 'Tulsa Time' and 'Lay Down Sally'. *Money And Cigarettes*, the first release on Duck, distributed by Warner Brothers, confirmed Clapton's role as a team player; harnessed to other notable stylists like Lee and Cooder he went out of his way to avoid the hoped-for guitar heroics. Compared to his early career the album was a modest – by Clapton's standards, blushingly modest – success. There were agreeable moments: Cooder's slide playing on 'Man Overboard'; the robust drumming on 'Crosscut Saw'; Clapton's gruffly mature vocals. But they *were* moments. *Money And Cigarettes* was Clapton pleasing himself, not the crowd. Its real value may have been therapeutic.

Of the two commodities cited in the title: first Clapton liked cigarettes. Early in the new year it was announced that his winter tour of America would be sponsored by Camel. This seemingly logical arrangement, a progression from the Rolling Stones' epoch-making endorsement of a men's perfume, caused Clapton inordinate trouble. Among the objectors to the contract was the American Lung Association, deeming it 'inconceivable' that Clapton should 'neglect . . . his social responsibilities as a famous person'. The controversy simmered through January and early February, when Nat Walker, a spokesman for the cigarette firm, issued a statement: 'We felt that the music of a guy like Eric Clapton fits the interest profile of a Camel smoker. Music is important to the brand.' (Walker failed to mention that since the early 1960s Clapton had smoked Rothman's.)

Clapton also enjoyed spending money. In theory, as a result of his various companies, his fortune should have substantially increased. In practice, however, Clapton's expenditure frequently exceeded his income, and he was notoriously susceptible to luxury purchases. Records show that in 1983 Marshbrook's turnover fell to £133,589 (a 30 per cent drop on the previous year), leaving a profit after tax of £23,957. The figures for Duck Records in the same period were £6,000 and £106 respectively. More surprisingly, turnover for E.C. Music, Clapton's publishing company, for the year to 30 September 1983 was a mere £7,626, which, after administrative expenses of £8,897, converted into a loss of £1,271. While Clapton continued to enjoy the best advice on his investments, and Hurtwood Edge had increased tenfold in value since he bought it, the fact remains that, in a full year, the combined profit of his three principal companies was just £22,792. It may be that the arrangement with Camel was less whimsical than at first thought.

* * *

On a night in January Clapton rang Markee and Spinetti to confirm that their presence would, in future, be more sparingly required. Even then he managed to give the impression that there 'might, one day' be collaborative projects (Spinetti did play briefly with Clapton in 1986); the man who felt himself 'strategized against as a kid' found it distressingly hard to say no as an adult. By contrast Forrester, on whom the burden of such statements usually fell, had no such inhibition. He shielded his client from all but his most personal obligations. His versatility was notable: unlike some managers, who concentrated on arranging tours and left private matters alone, Forrester took a detailed interest in everything. (A musician who knew Clapton in the 1970s compares the relationship to a 'kind of up-market nursemaid service'.) It was rather to Clapton's credit that, both in the matter of firing his group and subsequently confirming the decision, he alone spoke to the parties involved.

Lee, Stainton, Hawkins and Dunn were retained for the tour which opened on 1 February in Seattle.* The audiences there, in Los Angeles, Austin, St Louis and Pittsburgh were awarded a nineteen-song set, heavily weighted to Clapton's later career, of which the inevitable highlight was 'Layla'. Reviews, as always, were mixed: the group's exacting style of attack wasted few notes and at times the faster songs declined into head-banging. 'Worried Life Blues' was genuinely affecting, a title that Clapton might have been born to play. From there, though, the programme deteriorated, the middle section merely duplicating the running order on *Money And Cigarettes*. (By the time the tour reached Europe in April much of the newer material had been dropped.) Neither did the anticipated duetting with Cooder occur, with the exception of a single night in Philadelphia. There was nothing wrong with the concerts – after twenty years, Clapton knew better than most how to engage an audience – but neither was there the spirit of release associated with his early work.

On certain nights Clapton was greeted by banners in the crowd protesting his involvement with a cigarette company; on others the audience seemed only to reflect the placid, even sluggish atmosphere on stage (where Dunn stood smoking a pipe). Hawkins, the barometer of the group's high spirits, looked especially subdued – after a performance in Dallas he was replaced with Oldaker (who, along with Stainton, proved there *was* a way back into Clapton's favour). Clapton himself had begun to show signs of restlessness as early as the first week. His dissatisfaction

---

* Cooder became the support act.

with his private life and the struggles to avoid drink led to some fractious moments offstage, notably in Texas, where a second member of the group had to be dissuaded from joining Hawkins on the homeward plane.

Clapton was in Switzerland when Muddy Waters, his hero and sometime mentor, died in Chicago that April. Whether for geographical or personal reasons, he did not attend the funeral. For all his adult life Clapton had been morbidly shy of relationships and for nearly forty years had attempted to control and impose a pattern on his feelings – if he felt pain at the loss of Hendrix, Allman, Relf, Radle and Waters he successfully kept it to himself. Public grief, because it threatened to overwhelm reason and expose Clapton's emotions, was feared and internal mourning preferred. Unqualified friendship, because it exposed Clapton to hurt, was kept in check by a vigilant self-discipline, and if a relationship failed or a person died the suffering was concealed beneath a veneer of cynical resignation. Or it became grist to the mill, material for the blues. There is nothing to suggest that Clapton's friendship with Waters and the rest was other than real, or his commitment to them less than all he was capable of. There were, however, limits. From an early age Clapton had taught himself that humans were essentially unreliable, human relations not to be banked on. Above all, no one, not excluding his wife, was allowed a privileged position in Clapton's life such as they might one day abuse. Only under the most harrowing circumstances in later years did the sharply disciplined mind collapse, revealing hidden emotions and destroying his carefully crafted façade.

He remained happiest in front of a sea of identical faces: adoring, uncritical and, above all, undemanding of Clapton's affection. He gave eighty-one concerts in 1983, of which the peaks were a hometown appearance in Guildford (Collins, Jimmy Page and the inevitable Chas and Dave all guesting) and a benefit for Save the Children in London. Boyd attended both events. Clapton and his wife reconciled that summer, though without acutely visible pleasure on either side. Not only was Boyd kept at the emotional distance Clapton imposed on all his partners, there was a sense in which her status had been diminished, not the reverse, by his cure. Having come to the conclusion that 'one of us should be sober some of the time', Boyd increasingly forfeited the role to her husband. As Clapton's drinking decreased so hers accelerated. Where once he relied on her to supervise his home, prepare his food, pour his drinks and act as a Maginôt Line against unwelcome visitors, Clapton now assumed these duties himself. There was still a relationship, but after thirteen years, four of them as man and wife, it was an emotionally spent one.

His disinclination to stay at home can be gauged by the amount of work Clapton took on in 1983. As well as tours of Britain, Germany, Holland, France, Italy, Switzerland and two separate visits to America, he appeared on sessions for a plethora of other artists, including Ringo Starr, Christine McVie and, more crucially, Roger Waters. The recording of *The Pros And Cons Of Hitch-Hiking* that August was significant in that it introduced Clapton to at least two musicians prominent in his later career – and that it brought him to the edge of a professional crisis with Forrester.

When, early in 1984, Waters proposed a world tour in support of his album, Clapton's was the first name solicited. His immediate acceptance can be put down to a number of facts: loyalty on Clapton's part; the welcome boost to his income the tour provided; a genuine love of playing; anxiety at the prospect of a year for which concerts in Europe, the Middle East, Australia and Hong Kong and the recording of a new album were the only fixed points. Another reason Clapton accepted Waters's invitation may have been that it removed him from Hurtwood Edge. Although Clapton may have overstated Boyd's faults, there were serious fundamental flaws in the marriage aside from the major impediments caused by her alcoholism and inability to have children. Boyd was an essentially happy, uncomplicated woman whose husband's mood swings constantly amazed her. Then, too, his long-established work schedule and apparent addiction to touring made it difficult to coexist for more than a few weeks at a time. Finally, despite ascribing his plan of 'laying a thousand groupies' to youthful ambition, Clapton continued to be seen, frequently and in public, with other women.

Those were the causes. The effect was that Clapton accepted Waters's offer, precipitating a major dispute with his manager. Understandably anxious to place Clapton at the centre of any stage he stepped on, Forrester was aghast that he would consider a mere sideman's role in a troupe of no less than nine musicians. (Clapton's tendency to seek anonymous parts in travelling revues – Brian Casser, the Glands, Delaney and Bonnie – preceded Forrester's tenure.) According to a then associate of Harvey Goldsmith, who promoted the British leg of the tour, 'Clapton made no bones that he and Forrester had fallen out about it . . . It was a clash of wills. Part of the reason Eric did it was to show who was boss.'

Clapton may have spoken for himself when it came to music, but in all other ways Forrester was paramount. In the early 1980s a number of rock stars – Townshend, Warren Zevon, even Keith Richards – were paraded in support of a new, reconstructed lifestyle, exemplars of the 'just say no' era then dawning in America. Clapton hastened to join such consensus. The man who by his own admission spent most of the 1970s in a narcotic fog was insisting by 1985: 'I don't believe in any kind of excesses any more. I don't want to do it because I don't like the after-effects. Drinking and taking dope . . . I've done all that and I'm lucky to be alive. I regret those years because they were wasted and I can never get them back.'

It was not always thus. Unmentioned in later interviews was Clapton's treatment of women, notably Ormsby-Gore, whilst stupefied; his periodic violence, both to himself and others; his cavalier attitude to friends like Ben Palmer; his lying; cheating; and more recently his short-changing of fans confronted, on certain nights, not by Clapton but a drunken impersonator. It was much to his credit that he eventually overcame his addictions to drugs and drink; less so that he then adopted a self-righteous tone in the few interviews Forrester allowed him. Genuine as his conversion was, there was something unsettling about Clapton's rushing to join Townshend and the others in the confessional.

Late in 1983 Clapton played a total of eleven concerts in support of ARMS (Action Research into Multiple Sclerosis) in both London and America. Even this initiative – prompted by Ronnie Lane, recently diagnosed with the disease – was marred by events backstage: immediately after the Albert Hall concert on 20 September, Clapton, still grinning with delight at the performance, caught sight of his old Yardbirds adversary Paul Samwell-Smith. It was their first meeting in eighteen years. 'Right away,' says Jim McCarty, also present backstage, 'Eric started hassling Paul,' still complaining about the memo issued by Gomelsky in 1965. McCarty was not alone in finding something unnerving in the way Clapton went from 'beaming goodwill' to 'snarling rage' in the course of a split second.

Tension also surrounded the ARMS concerts scheduled in America. Clapton violently objected to the presence of Rod Stewart on the grounds of Stewart's alleged indifference to Lane's welfare. Kenny Jones, a friend of all three parties, and a neighbour of Clapton in Ewhurst, smiles broadly when questioned on the subject. Others were less oblique: according to Harry Shapiro, '[Clapton] was so disgusted at Stewart's previous lack of support that he threatened to walk off if Stewart walked on.' After discussion with the promoter Bill Graham, Joe Cocker and Paul Rodgers were added to the line-up in America, where concerts took place in Dallas, San Francisco, Los Angeles and New York. Clapton's playing on standards like 'Layla' and 'Wonderful Tonight' was unexpectedly ragged, though nothing prepared the audience for the chaos of the polyphonic 'Stairway To Heaven' (Andy Fairweather-Low, an ephemeral pop figure of the sixties who would become Clapton's lieutenant, supplying the rhythm). 'Musically, it was a mess,' says Anthony Haden-Guest. 'But that wasn't the point. The point was seeing Clapton, Beck and Page on stage together.'

Haden-Guest, last encountered living with Clapton in Chelsea, was present at the party on the tour's final night in New York. 'What was interesting,' he says, 'was seeing Eric and Joe Cocker, two of rock's biggest topers, standing demurely in the corner sipping orange juice.' Others also commented on the strikingly rejuvenated appearance Clapton (bereft of beard) now cut. Certain critics treated his survival as if it was a kind of listless fluke. Yet the fact that Clapton could remain a viable figure after twenty years in the industry – only Jagger and McCartney rivalled his longevity – owed much to his own resilience and that of his untiring manager, constantly seeking ways to extend a career built on adolescent *angst* into adulthood.

One obvious opportunity was provided by film. In January 1984 Clapton recorded the theme music for *The Hit*, an otherwise forgettable vehicle for his friend John Hurt. Later in the eighties he took on a number of such projects: *Edge of Darkness*, *The Color of Money*, *Buster*, *Homeboy*, *Peace In Our Time*, *Licence To Kill*, *Communion* and the successive *Lethal Weapon*s. As the decade progressed Clapton and Forrester gradually added a second brand to the guitarist's portfolio while carefully maintaining the flagship label. By 1986 (the year of *Color of Money* and *Lethal Weapon*) there were parallel paths in Clapton's career: his own albums and concerts vying with the singularly lucrative option of soundtracks and scores. The quality of much of the work did not prevent the press from making the most of Clapton's apparent change of direction. Mere mention of the word Hollywood was enough to fuel the customary accusation that Clapton, in keeping with a number of sixties contemporaries, had sold out. The *Lethal Weapon* project, in particular, added to the steadily accumulating belief that the surviving rock archetypes had become caricatures. Clapton himself was aware of the charge. Once the decision to become a family entertainer had been taken, a great deal of time was spent in denying it. At the height of the debate in the mid-eighties – 'Eric Claptout' being revived in the tabloids – he told Ray Coleman: 'I'm used to such a buzz, playing on stage in front of an audience. You can't get that from writing film scores ... This is my destiny.'

Immediately after completing *The Hit* Clapton convened Lee, Stainton, Oldaker and Dunn for a European tour. The crowds in Zurich, Milan, Belgrade – and later Cairo and Jerusalem – were treated to no fewer than twenty-two songs, to which 'Bottle Of Red Wine', 'Key To The Highway' and 'Motherless Children' were added from Clapton's spacious back repertoire. They were also among the first to hear a new offering, recorded that spring, among the highlights of Clapton's entire career. 'Same Old Blues' – the very title was ironic – was a startling return to the genre, mining the territory of love gone awry, supposedly stemming from Clapton's anger with his producer (though the root cause of the song was surely marital). It was among the material written at the now traditional Welsh retreat. Clapton arrived in Montserrat that March clear-eyed, two years into his alcoholic recovery, at breaking point with his manager, and separated from his wife. Now he was ready to record an album.

Clapton's 'loneliness at the top' had led him to some strange associations, not least his choice of the unremarkable Phil Collins as a producer. Collins himself felt 'Eric's last couple of albums [had been] a little bland' and flew at the chance to 'shake up his music and make it stand again'. The group who assembled at Air Studios – Clapton's touring band, shorn of Lee but enhanced by the percussionist Ray Cooper and Marcy Levy on vocals – were instructed to lend a contemporary ear to the sessions. The idea was somehow to endear Clapton to a younger club audience. Anything smacking of the 'old sixties scene', Collins announced, was out. What was needed was a new scene altogether. To illustrate the point Clapton himself appeared at the studio with a guitar synthesizer.

The resulting album, *Behind The Sun*, issued the following March, was notable for its surfeit of evanescent pop songs and lightweight lyrics. 'From a writing and production standpoint,' says Pete Brown, 'it was a mess. Both the albums Eric made with Collins are disposable, whereas his best work still sounds fresh thirty years later.' When Lenny Waronker, president of Warners, first heard *Behind The Sun* he was appalled. 'There was nothing happening,' he told an associate in Los Angeles, 'just aimless ditties sung by Eric.' Others suggest that there were insufficient potential singles for Waronker's taste. Clapton was ordered back into the studio to record four additional songs – a salutary reminder of the need for saleable 'product' as demanded by Warners.

While in Montserrat Clapton met a twenty-eight-year-old Anglo-Iraqi woman, then living on the island with her English husband. Within a week of being introduced to Yvonne Kelly an affair had begun. Its intensity encapsulated Clapton's approach, both physically and emotionally, towards the opposite sex. He was a ladies' man. 'I just love the company of beautiful women. I have a weakness in that department,' he informed *Rolling Stone*. It does not need repeating that the relationships, conducted entirely on Clapton's terms, were predominantly short-lived. His liaison with Kelly might otherwise have been a mere milestone down the road to divorcing Boyd but for the birth of a daughter, Ruth, early the following year.

After Kelly parted from her husband Malcolm in 1992 she and the child returned to the family home in Carr House Road, Doncaster. They attended Clapton's season of concerts at the Albert Hall in the new year. A spokesman was quoted in the press as saying, 'He is looking forward to seeing a lot more [of Ruth]. They are getting to know each other properly again.' Clapton's affection for his family was real enough – though, again, that he showed his concern by presents and elaborate meals at San Lorenzo rather than a daily interest in their welfare comes as no shock. According to the same source, Clapton and Kelly remain 'the best of friends ... determined Ruth will be happy. [He] has paid maintenance for her since she was born.'

At the heart of Clapton's affair with Kelly, as with other women, was an unfulfilled longing for fatherhood. As early as 1965 Pamela Mayall had the impression 'he loved kids and pined for one of his own'. Although Clapton had loved Boyd on her own merits, the relationship quickly showed signs of nervous strain, not least from her inability to have children. It was doubtless this condition which caused him to explode with rage at the reference to his wife's 'child-bearing hips' in 1976. Added to the other stresses in the marriage it was a miracle, Markee believes, that 'neither had jumped ship before'. Another chance to do so was now thrown into Clapton's lap. Although his relationship with her mother cooled quickly, it was significant that Clapton doted on Ruth Kelly and boasted to a friend in 1985 of being 'truly happy' for the first time in his life.

*   *   *

The tour with Roger Waters went ahead, over Forrester's strong objection, in June and July 1984. For six weeks Clapton stood, stage left, playing what his manager called 'second fiddle' to the Pink Floyd *éminence gris*. According to Coleman, 'Eric quickly tired of what he regarded as a pretentious atmosphere.' Neither could Waters's brand of *angst*-ridden techno-rock have endeared itself to Clapton, a man who still professed love for the 'purity' of blues. The tour was, none the less, distinguished by at least one song, 'Sexual Revolution', played with unequalled ferocity. It also introduced Clapton to the guitarist who would replace Albert Lee in his group.

There were many reasons for Clapton's decline, his reduction to a designer accessory for a lesser musician. Among them was the relative indifference of his work since 1974; his over-exposure on the concert stage; and the fact that, as a performer, he seemed not to stand for anything. By 1984 a number of critics had commented on the redundancy of a personality who, for many, had sustained and nourished a love of the blues. In deserting Clapton, his fans were registering protest at the unevenness of his output over a decade, not necessarily criticizing the man himself. The unpopularity of his work overcame the affection in which Clapton was still held. Whatever the cause of the slump, the consequences were severe. In 1984 Marshbrook turned over £151,582 against expenses of £191,090, a recorded loss of £39,508. During the same period E.C. Music and Duck showed profits of just £5,742 and £394 respectively. For all his immense reputation, it was hard to disagree that Clapton's best days, professionally speaking, were behind him. It was symptomatic that two of 1984's best-selling albums were the retrospective *Backtrackin'* and the Yardbirds compilation *Shapes Of Things*, both celebrating the guitarist's past rather than his present.

In June, between London appearances with Waters, Clapton discovered yet another enthusiasm. He met the England cricketer Ian Botham. His new consuming interest began when, after a day in the Lord's pavilion, Clapton was heard to comment on the 'Englishness' and 'vibes' of the sport he had played as a boy but largely ignored since then. By the end of the summer Clapton and Botham were fast friends. The former player Len Hutton was present when the two of them 'came bounding up the stairs, sounding like children in the playground'. In time cricket came to replace fishing in Clapton's life. At this stage it was merely a hobby, a way to socialize with those he admired and who uncritically admired him. Later in the decade, for a year or two, it became an obsession.

Clapton's other professional appearance of the summer was at Wembley, to play with Dylan alongside Van Morrison, Chrissie Hynde and Santana. The concert was notable for the impromptu, unrehearsed nature of the material (Dylan showing Clapton the chords of 'Tombstone Blues' as it progressed). There was an incident when Hynde and Clapton physically collided onstage. The guitarist later expressed surprise that a fellow professional should be ignorant of 'the first rule of playing live', failing to grasp the relative position of the other performers. He also admitted to 'not know[ing] who [Hynde] was' – further evidence that, in musical terms, Clapton inhabited an earlier, already vanishing world.

His commitment to Waters ended, Clapton returned to Hurtwood Edge in August. Within days his wife – who by this stage knew of the affair with Kelly – had moved out. According to a present friend of Boyd's, 'Eric was upset that she would have mentioned it. His meaning, as Pattie took it, was that the real fault was hers for having spoken.' It was evident that there were other flaws in the Claptons' marriage. Relatively few women could have borne the drunkenness, the long absences from home – their husband's self-admitted 'inability to find [himself] in a relationship without wanting to get away' – without complaint. It would be churlish to place the blame for the crisis squarely at Clapton's door. Yet there was surely poignancy to be found in Boyd's claim to have 'felt more earthed at Eric's home than at George's' in 1974; exactly a decade later Boyd told the same friend in London, 'It was either leave [Hurtwood Edge] or die.'

When Clapton attended Phil Collins's wedding on 4 August he did so alone. By the time he returned from an Australian tour that autumn, Boyd was gone. During the winter they spoke frequently by phone, Boyd apparently confirming that she was 'still in love' with her husband but needed to 'assert [her] individuality'. Visitors to Hurtwood Edge found Clapton deeply depressed by the separation. His biographer was told that 'I will never love another woman as much as I love Pattie', the stringer from *Rolling Stone* that 'She's the only one I've ever really loved.' Coincidentally or not, Clapton began drinking again for the first time since leaving Hazelden. Despite repeated requests to return, Boyd spent Christmas 1984 apart from her husband. Clapton, after re-recording material for *Behind The Sun* in Los Angeles, played host at Hurtwood Edge to his mother and grandmother.

As Clapton's drinking grew, so did his gloom. Pete Brown saw his old friend that winter for the first time in sixteen years. 'Eric was deeply hurt, but in a low-key, subdued way,' he says. 'He was even thankful things were no worse.' Clapton's hopes for a reconciliation with Boyd were not wholly groundless. On 2 January 1985 the couple appeared together at Ron Wood's wedding in Denham. Despite surprising at least one tabloid photographer by arriving side by side, even this reunion proved temporary. Wood's own description of the event ends with the words, 'Clapton was fighting outside the church with Pattie. They never made it inside.' Nine days later, on 11 January, Yvonne Kelly gave birth to a daughter in Doncaster Maternity Hospital.

Early in February Clapton and Boyd spent two weeks together in Israel. On the 17th they were seen arm in arm at the opening of the film *Brazil*. By the end of the month Boyd had returned to Hurtwood Edge. The exact nature of the compromise reached may never be known, but both parties repeatedly stressed it was a case of being 'impossible to live without [the other]'. Along with Clapton's lifelong tendency to 'want to get away' came infusions of love for Hurtwood Edge, his family, for Ruth Kelly and for Boyd, now, for the first time in her life, 'overwhelmed' by her husband inviting her on tour. The couple travelled together on the British and Scandinavian dates arranged for the early weeks of 1985.

It was at this point that, after years of self-effacement, Clapton chose to extend the distance between himself and his musicians. Instead of loping unannounced on stage or affecting the look, as *The Times* put it, 'of a man startled by the raising of the curtain', Clapton waited for his colleagues to take up their places before making his own entrance. On certain nights his name, as though not already familiar to the audience, would be spelt out in neon lights. On a video released that February he stood conspicuously on a podium while his group posed in matching uniforms at his feet. George Terry, who played one concert with his old employer that spring, confirms, 'The camaraderie was missing.' Gone was the spirit of egalitarianism and ensemble playing associated with earlier tours: when Clapton stepped forward now, spotlit and over-amplified, the eye moved to him as it had in the Yardbirds and Bluesbreak-ers. In London the arms waving aloft stretched back twenty rows from the stage, though sagging noticeably during the songs Clapton introduced with the dreaded words, 'This is a track off the new album.' Even so, sufficient material remained to satisfy even the blues diehards present, and, by restricting his playing to a series of bravura solos (Tim Renwick, of Waters's group, providing rhythm), Clapton avoided the risk of over-extending himself.

Behind The Sun was released that March. Its opening track, 'She's Waiting', set a standard sadly not matched by the remaining ten songs. The album fell somewhere between a radical reinvention of Clapton and the next step on a continuum from the easy-listening sound unveiled in 1974. If, as he said, the intention was to create 'a true portrayal of what I could do in all the areas', that included some notably thin material. While 'Waiting', 'Forever Man' and 'Tangled In Love' all emerged as concert favourites in the 'Blues Power' mould, most of the rest gave evidence of an uneasy alliance between Clapton, Collins and the Warners quality-control department. 'Same Old Blues' was a particularly ambitious move on Clapton's part, an uncompromising dirge with the makings of a thrilling solo. Musically, the song tapped into most of the varied themes incorporated through the years. Lyrically, its source material was Clapton's marriage – also the influence behind 'Never Make You Cry'. *Behind The Sun* should have ended with 'Just Like A Prisoner'. Instead, Clapton, as if to touch one last base, eked out the title track alone with Collins. The impression, as for the album generally, was of striving for effect through simplicity, something Clapton achieved radiantly on *Blues Breakers*, and emerging merely as simple.

Clapton turned forty on 30 March 1985. The event coincided with, and may have crystallized, a process of coming to terms with the past. (Celebrating the fact, Alice Ormsby-Gore, whose father's memorial service Clapton also attended, was invited to the party at Hurtwood Edge.) In private, to his family and to the growing number of interviewers sanctioned by Forrester, Clapton stressed his contentment at reaching middle age. His gaze was fixed firmly on the future. Having been 'serious' and 'the straightest person that lived' in his twenties and hell-bent on destruction in his thirties, Clapton admitted to being 'more relaxed' and 'happier' than before. There was also the bonus, not having 'cavorted around the stage like Mick Jagger', of enjoying a career untrammelled by age. As if to demonstrate that destiny had summoned him to greater things, Clapton announced the longest single itinerary of his life, a forty-five-concert tour of America extended over fifteen weeks.

Lest this be taken as evidence of more permanent stability, Clapton now began to drink again. Ian Stewart encountered a 'distinctly festive Eric' early that year; Pete Brown believed him to have 'apparently overdone the Bacchic rites'; to Boyd's friend he appeared merely 'pissed'. Among the self-revelatory statements Clapton made to the media was one admitting 'part of my character is made up of an obsession to push something to the limit. It can be of great use if ... channelled into constructive thought or creativity, but it can also be mentally or physically or spiritually destructive.' Anyone would have forgiven Clapton his lapses from the austere standards set at Hazelden. But it grated to hear him speak of 'establishing a balance', brandishing his cure as if it were an Oscar. Most rehabilitation clinics, Hazelden included, paid at least lip-service to the idea of giving up drinking. Clapton felt no such obligation. He continued to speak fulsomely of his recovery while enjoying wine and beer, falling into the embarrassment of not practising what he preached. Of course it was possible for Clapton to have intensely happy moments of insight as a result of his experience. They could have been hinted at, for instance, in his lyrics. But protesting his 'cleanness' while continuing to drink privately was Clapton, yet again, accepting privilege without responsibility. There was a sense of making virtue out of vice.

The ease with which Clapton stepped into the role of the modest but self-confident adult, anxious to dismiss past excesses, was revealed in an interview with Robert Palmer to promote the American tour. Palmer, an intelligent man, formed the impression that 'Clapton still found the idea of an interview about as appealing as a trip to the dentist'. After a number of false starts the meeting finally took place in Forrester's office. The tone was one of genial frankness: Derek and the Dominos 'copped a lot of dope'; for two and a half years Clapton and Ormsby-Gore 'got very strung out'; in the seventies 'There were many occasions when I had to be led offstage and given some black coffee or some oxygen ... I was really on the edge of collapse.' Palmer came away impressed at how alert, how urbane and how sensitive Clapton was. He neglected to mention the qualities of pretence and play-acting. Just as earlier interviews had given Clapton a reputation for varnishing the truth about himself, largely because his actions always seemed to contradict his words, so C. L. R. James, reading of Palmer's claim to 'have trouble picturing [Clapton] as a racist', replied simply: 'I haven't.'

The summer tour opened on 9 April at the Convention Center, Dallas. Expectations were high. Where once rock stars had made a habit of appearing late, under-rehearsed or insensate on stage, the mid-eighties brought a return to the virtues of competence, punctuality and, above all, professionalism. Clapton understood this and played on it astutely. The core-values movement would have been substantially weaker without his influence. Exactly on time the house-lights dimmed and Clapton, resplendent in his Versace suit, bounded on stage. The set that followed neatly divided into three: an opening burst of crowd-pleasers like 'Tulsa Time' and 'I Shot The Sheriff', a generous helping from *Behind The Sun*, and the closing salvo of 'Cocaine', 'Layla' and 'Further On Up The Road'. Though Clapton left to applause less rapturous than that which greeted him, reviews were generally respectful. Relatively few of the crowd had, after all, come to listen. It was enough that Clapton appeared.

The truth of this was apparent from the moment he played his first solo. The palpable delight that greeted the familiar (bearded) figure in the spotlight proved that Clapton's was an unusually devoted audience. Nor did the wild reaction to his – as it turned out, merely competent – treatment of 'Tulsa Time' indicate less than consummate joy at being in the presence of a legend. Clapton responded with a performance of winning amiability. Where once he stood completely impassive (or, on other occasions, lay totally inert) now he illustrated each solo by a gentle swaying motion half-way between a dance-step and a shrug. He laughed more than previously. And, whatever its real function, there was surely irony in the sight of Clapton, a man whose career was built on legedermain and 'sleight of mouth', appearing on stage with a magician's table.

On 8 May Clapton guested on *The David Letterman Show*. The appearance was notable for the reintroduction of 'White Room' into the guitarist's repertoire. The song, last performed in 1968, was added to the set with which Clapton launched the second leg of the tour in Canada. His playing on these occasions was variable, straying from startling embellishments on the originals to abject banality – Clapton not only avoiding the limelight, but avoiding playing altogether – sometimes in the same song or solo. Well aware of the unevenness of his output he none the less retained the ability to hold a crowd by sheer presence or, at worst, by improvisation, a fact Clapton acknowledged in the press: 'I don't dry up. Not completely. I can usually fool an audience . . . I can play an adequate solo any time, but what I try to do is put myself into a state of mind where I empty myself of all ideas and let something develop. It's like rolling the dice.'

Part of Clapton's appeal lay, of course, in his longevity. As has been seen, audiences appreciated him not merely for the present but for his ties with the past. He was like a monument, not necessarily attractive in himself, but widely admired for having survived so long. Clapton's huge record collection leant heavily towards work by his friends Freddie King, John Lee Hooker and Muddy Waters. The most celebrated bluesmen of the last twenty years were each a significant beneficiary of his patronage.

When Clapton took to the stage in 1985 it was as a popular mainstream musician, instantly recognizable, yet straddling the enclosed worlds of contrasting styles and times. Imagine if Chuck Berry had composed an opera, and then written a Broadway musical; imagine if Robert Johnson were still alive, casually collaborating with the Rolling Stones; or if *The Sun Years*, *Rubber Soul* and *Brothers In Arms* were all the work of a single artist. The analogies are preposterous, but apt – although the Johnson comparison is probably over-generous to Clapton. While he had out-standing albums to his credit, his real strength lay in interpretation rather than innovation. For this reason Clapton was never in danger of running out of material. Musicians who draw all their songs from their own experience tend to go round in ever-decreasing circles as gradually they have only the act of writing itself to write about. (Frank Zappa reached this point in 1967 by recording *We're Only In It For The Money*.) So long as Clapton charted a course as a musicologist, incorporating blues, rock and pop with touches of calypso, country and soul, his work succeeded where a concert of themed material might have failed. Both on record and stage, the Clapton camp left nothing to chance: 'I Shot The Sheriff' wooed the black or reggae-loving vote, for instance, while 'Layla' and 'Cocaine' could be relied on to raise interest in stadium rock-lovers. Added to the residual affection that so many had for Clapton himself, it was easy to see why his concerts invariably sold out. Finally, there was always the chance that Clapton would surpass himself. It hardly needs saying that he played best when hurt, under strain or emotionally upset, occasions which, if less frequent than before, still accounted for a percentage of the total. The commemorative video of the American tour, *Live '85*, rarely touches the heights Clapton once routinely scaled; it does, however, prove that in his professionalism, his choice of material and his merging of diverse styles, he was a musician for all seasons.

Clapton never met his natural father, Edward Fryer. It was ironic, then, that he was in Toronto, preparing for a concert at the Kingswood Music Theater, when Fryer died outside that city on 15 May. While it would be tempting to conjecture on Clapton's inner thoughts, suggesting that, like many men, he grew curious about his father as he grew older, the period seems to have been one of sustained self-sufficiency. By 1985 Clapton appeared neither inquisitive nor resentful about his upbringing. He made no effort to seek out Fryer and was absent from the funeral. If, self-evidently, Clapton preferred to keep the matter of his parentage quiet, it was also true that he echoed Fryer in much that he did and admired. To the latter's dying day he retained a love of music, art and books, at least two of which were inherited by his son. In spite of their mutual wariness and lifelong separation, these two now seem to have had much in common, not least in their singular attitude to personal relationships. Above all, both looked on marriage as an unrelenting, and on the whole unprofitable game of wits.

At the same time as Clapton lost his father he was left by his wife. Following their reconciliation in February, Boyd had travelled with her husband in Scandinavia and America. The relationship, Clapton assured the press, was still viable. As late as the Philadelphia concert on 13 July the couple were seen smiling and carousing together. After the tour there was a 'second honeymoon', the fourth or fifth so designated, in Antigua. Surprisingly, given the pressures on the marriage, Boyd seems to have forgiven her husband's affair with Kelly.

Less easily excused was Clapton's 'intimidating' behaviour since 1982. After leaving Hazelden, Boyd told Ray Coleman, her husband 'said he didn't want anyone to get close to him'. The following two years saw an acceleration of her own addiction. While Clapton returned to the concert stage and the studio his wife remained alone at Hurtwood Edge. His hobbies – cricket, playing pool or fishing – tended to be all-male pursuits or, by their nature, solitary. Boyd, having had at least a protective role when Clapton was drunk, found herself without one when he was sober. Then there was her husband's attitude to her own alcoholism:

I was very dogmatic about that. You see, she likes to drink and I became very strict about that and I started to put her down. I was very intolerant. Then I would go out on the road and not take her with me; and so we began to drift apart. And after about a year of that you come to the realization that you've got very little in common any more.

The fabric of compromise between husband and wife had been torn apart, and there was no way to stitch it together again.

There was a final, material cause for the divorce. Clapton, he later announced, 'tried and tried to have a baby with Pattie, but it never happened. It became such a pressure ... Our marriage suffered as a result.' The pressure may have been greater in view not only of Ruth Kelly, but of a second love-child born to Clapton in 1986. When he bedded the Italian dancer-model-photographer Loredana Del Santo (moving her to a house in Eaton Mews South, Belgravia) Clapton, in her own words, 'persuaded me to keep my child. [He] told me he would kill himself if I had an abortion.' The effect on an already demoralized Boyd can be imagined. She left Hurtwood Edge that winter, ceding her place first to Del Santo, then to a series of lovers, none of whom appeared to gratify Clapton as she once had. The couple divorced in 1988. Both parties insist they remain friends (certainly Boyd speaks more warmly of Clapton than friends do on her behalf); there are occasional sightings together in London; Clapton still dedicates songs to his ex-wife on stage. Friends at the Riverside Club in Chiswick were told by Boyd that 'Eric gives me his hand-downs to auction for charity.' The image is trivial, but it is remembered and quoted: Richard Drew's earlier comparison of Clapton to 'a monarch dispensing alms' is immediately recalled.

The highlight of the tour – the relaunch of Clapton's whole career – came at the Live Aid concert in Philadelphia. In the frenetic weeks leading to 13 July, when Bob Geldof's office began to resemble 'something between a travel agency and an executive nanny service', he found negotiations with Clapton and Forrester 'remarkably calm ... Since Pete [Townshend] had already passed the word to Eric, the only question was whether he could get there in time from Dullsville, USA.' Clapton and his group appeared the day beforehand from Denver. Immediately on arrival there was evidence of tension: while speaker after speaker praised the vastness and global quality of the occasion, Clapton waited in a make-shift dressing-room also containing the Beach Boys and Madonna, with neither of whom he was on speaking terms. Denied time to rehearse he sat watching a television monitor, becoming, in his own words, 'a hundred times more psyched up than for a regular gig'. The temperature in the waiting area was 110 degrees. When, finally, he was called to the stage Clapton encountered security obtrusive even by American stadium standards; pet dogs had been issued with identity badges. A disturbance ensued when Donald Dunn, a heavyset man smoking a briar pipe, was informed that relations of the group – the word 'uncle' was mentioned – would be welcome in the guests' enclosure. Finally in place, Clapton watched as his guitar technician, Lee Dickson, debated stage etiquette with the resident crew, and ended up rolling around under the piano, discussing the matter.

Next, as Clapton stepped forward to sing 'White Room', he was knocked sideways by an electric shock. Few of the 90,000 crowd, or the 1.5 billion watching on television, could have known that his first priority from then onwards was avoiding further contact with the microphone. Somehow he got through the song, and another from *Behind The Sun*. Until then the audience had been merely euphoric. As Clapton trailed into 'Layla' they became ecstatic. The fists clenched aloft reached to the far corners of the arena. Clapton stood there, a small bearded man in white shirtsleeves, the sane Englishman with his guitar. As Oldaker and Phil Collins played the final beat Clapton shouted, 'God bless you', raised an arm, and left.

It would be hard to overestimate the boost given to Clapton's career by Live Aid. Since 1974, while commanding respect, he had failed to excite new audiences. More or less the same people attended Clapton's concerts every year (70 per cent of those filling in a questionnaire in 1983 describing themselves as 'repeat customers'.) All that changed in 1985. In the week following the concert two of the top three American albums were Clapton's.* Sales of *Behind The Sun* increased. Coming as it did in the same year, the compact disc revolution and its ally, the back-catalogue reissue, both profited a number of artists thought, creatively speaking, to be on the way down rather than the way up. No one benefited from this phenomenon more than Clapton. Within the space of five years *Time Pieces* (volumes 1 and 2), *The Cream Of Eric Clapton*, *The Early Clapton Collection* and *Crossroads*, each compiled from the archives, would reach the Top Twenty. Eighteen months after Live Aid, Clapton played the first of his annual seasons at the Albert Hall, an arrangement difficult to imagine in 1983 or 1984. In 1985 Marshbrook turned over a total of £179,995; in 1986 the figure was £397,562. E.C. Music more than doubled from £64,678 to £143,799 in the same period. While there were mumblings about the true intent of Live Aid – Jonathan King complaining of 'cynical self-interest' by certain stars – such grumbles were either too obscurely positioned or appeared too late to impede Clapton's success. His stock in 1985 was higher than at any time since Cream.

The charge of opportunism levelled against Clapton is undoubtedly wide of the mark. From the early 1970s he had worked tirelessly on behalf of a variety of charities in Europe, Asia and America. All the same, it was a remarkable revival for a career apparently nearing conclusion, if not semi-death in Las Vegas (where Clapton had cancelled a concert to

* The records were *Layla* and the re-released *Fresh Cream*.

appear in Philadelphia). In the mid-seventies no self-respecting record collection had been complete without *Blues Breakers* and *Layla*; *everyone* had *Disraeli Gears*. A decade later, dog-eared copies of those albums might still make furtive appearances at dinner parties, but Clapton had rarely been seen in the charts for fifteen years. He may have viewed Live Aid as a chance to put his long experience, ceaseless globe-trotting and undoubted professionalism to good use in promoting a cause which raised not only money but his own profile. An impression remained that he and Forrester had appreciated the promotional aspects of Geldof's offer. Clapton is still the only rock star to have appeared on behalf of every major cause, from Bangladesh to Nelson Mandela, over a period of twenty years (and, for that matter, to have a cause, Rock Against Racism, formed against him). The fact remains that the repercussions gave Clapton's own career a definite lift: in 1984 he was reduced to playing sideman for a musician still dabbling in student art-rock while Clapton recorded *Blues Breakers*. In 1986 he released the best-selling album of his life.

An idea of what form Clapton's renaissance might take was provided by his next project. At Pete Townshend's studio he recorded the soundtrack for the BBC serial *Edge of Darkness*, a job Clapton described significantly as 'like falling off a log'. Theme music, scores and television and film work of every kind came to occupy an increasing amount of Clapton's time. His accompaniment for *Edge of Darkness*, widely praised by the critics (and certainly in keeping with the story's joyless scenario), earned Clapton a British Academy Award.

Plans were also made to record a second album with Phil Collins. The collaboration between the two men – guesting on each other's records, appearing at least annually on the same stage – was extended in 1985. Anthony Phillips, a predecessor of Collins in Genesis, was present at a house party that summer at which 'a long, bony hand emerged from a deck-chair to retrieve a stray cricket ball'. It was Clapton. According to Phillips, 'Eric was having the time of his life, primarily with Collins and Mike Rutherford. The chief thing I remember is the awe with which he was treated. You felt that, even in a garden full of rock stars.'

Collins was present when Clapton gave his usual home-town concert, following the equally familiar tour of Japan, that October. It preceded dates in Switzerland and Italy. While in the last Clapton took the opportunity to expand his collection of Versace suits; he appeared (and briefly played) at a Sting concert in Milan; he was seen with Lori Del Santo there and on his return to England. Despite the obvious seriousness of the affair – by November Del Santo was pregnant with their first child – it was jealously concealed in public. When the couple appeared in London on 3 December punches were thrown and insults exchanged with photographers. Clapton, questioned by a reporter, would only admit they were, indeed, good friends. Technically, the marriage to Boyd went on.

It would be wrong to imply that the razor-suited executive and budding family man returning home that Christmas was any less real than the person who left it that February. Bob Geldof might have been right: Clapton *was* remarkably calm. By rock-star standards, he was almost shockingly normal. Even so, it would be equally wrong to associate Clapton's commercial renaissance with more widespread personal stability. The ending of his marriage, his siring of love children by different women, his bursts of temper and aversion to strangers all suggested a man whose emotional development lagged behind that of his career. A number of habits from Clapton's untutored youth remained. Despite being 'dogmatic' about Boyd's drunkenness, there is evidence that he himself reverted to drink after leaving Hazelden. Though never approaching the consumption of his twilight years, he continued to enjoy a glass of wine or beer. As is well known, the principal function of alcohol – at least alcoholism – is to create the chaos which only alcohol can address. The purpose of addictive drugs is to make life impossible without them. It would be an error of logic, of course, to suppose that life with them must be easy. Without them, it is impossible; with them, it is difficult. Clapton might have given up heroin, and all but recreational drugs in 1974; he might have given up alcohol, and all but the occasional drink eight years later. Neither of those achievements, however admirable, meant that he became easier to deal with. A songwriter who saw Clapton frequently in 1985 says: 'There was an unknowable quality about him, a standoffishness. His whole body said, "Fuck you."'

Clapton ended 1985 by accepting an invitation from Harrison to appear in a tribute to Carl Perkins. The event at Limehouse Studios, later released on video, was notable for a version of 'Matchbox', previously performed by the Dominos in 1970, and a second song, 'Mean Woman Blues', in which Clapton played a solo by which even Perkins was impressed. In the same week he attended the funeral of the Rolling Stones pianist Ian Stewart. According to Ron Wood, 'He gave us a lot of support when [Stewart] died ... afterwards we went to Clapton's home to vent ourselves by having a low-key jam session.' The photographer Gered

Mankowitz, who knew Stewart well, confirms that 'Eric really helped out the Stones, to the extent that there was talk about him joining . . . Wood wasn't exactly flavour of the month at that point.' Jeff Griffin, a BBC producer and neighbour of Stewart, also believes 'Clapton's affection for the Stones in general, and Stew in particular, was real. In some ways Ian was the kind of guy – low-key, down to earth, unpretentious – Clapton yearned to be.'

A year that had begun with a wedding ended with a funeral. Clapton's career was relaunched; he lost his father and his wife; his first child was born and his second was due. In theme music and soundtracks Clapton had discovered a lucrative new opportunity. His bank balance had improved significantly. His name was again linked with the Rolling Stones.

Nineteen eighty-five also saw a gradual acceleration of the process by which Clapton moved from blues purist to popular musician. His hostility to commercial rock softened, and one or two of its exponents broke through his reserve. He declared himself impressed by Sting and Lionel Richie. He played live with Dire Straits. Clapton gained practice at making the speeches and awarding the prizes it was the lot of the senior statesman to make and award. On 25 February 1986 he presented the Stones with a 'Lifetime Achievement' Grammy at the Kensington Roof Gardens. The event was significant not only for the continuation of a relationship with the group whose career seems, at times, to have shadowed his own; it also throws ironic light on Clapton's domestic arrangements.

In the imbroglio surrounding Boyd's departure, Clapton had spent the early weeks of 1986 in a rented flat in London. After the Grammy ceremony Keith Richards, in Wood's words, decided to 'go over [there] and tear the fucking place apart'. According to the same source, Clapton's entire furnishings consisted of 'a bed, a sofa, an exercise bike, and about five cases of Jack Daniel's'. The Rolling Stones left at seven the next morning after one of the most bibulous nights with which even they were ever associated.

Even that scene paled by comparison to the occasion, also in 1986, when Clapton appeared at a reception in London ('hugely impressive,' says the PR woman who organized it; 'he did all that "show me where the troops are", meet the people stuff'), where a guest's complaint at his robustness of phrase was met with the bizarre protest, 'You can't arrest me. I'm Eric Clapton. Call Maggie Thatcher!'

As the moment of possible relapse loomed Forrester and Clapton seemed to come together, in self-protective alliance, to ensure the momentum of Live Aid continued. In April Clapton appeared at Sunset Sound Studios, Los Angeles, to record a new album. Collins was producer. Dunn, Stainton and Oldaker were missing. When Clapton had gone to Los Angeles in December 1984 to re-record tracks for *Behind The Sun* he was introduced to Nathan East and Greg Phillinganes, respectively bassist and keyboard player at Lion Share Studios. They, Collins and the saxophonist Michael Brecker formed the nucleus of the new group; Katie Kissoon, a backing singer on the Roger Waters tour, was also present. Over six weeks fourteen basic tracks were recorded, the most intriguing of which was 'Lady Of Verona', dealing as it did with Del Santo. A hint of the speed at which the relationship progressed was given by the song's tempo; whereas Clapton's paeans to Boyd tended to be stately or occasionally sluggish, 'Verona' would have suited an early Little Richard album. The sense of a man in the grip of a Layla-like obsession was irresistible. It must have been galling to Clapton to have the song omitted from the finished album.

The disc jockey Andy Peebles met Clapton when he returned to London that summer. Not unused to the daily arrival of celebrities, there was 'palpable excitement' among the staff at Broadcasting House when the guitarist appeared, accompanied by his girlfriend. 'The entire office was there, the typists put on make-up. Eric arrived and consented to be interviewed . . . He was friendly enough, in a distant kind of way.' Peebles, a known admirer of Clapton, remembers being 'unimpressed' at the body of records his guest chose to play in the allotted hour. A sense of his wider cultural tastes was supplied by Clapton's parting words to Peebles: 'I'm off to see *The Mousetrap*', a play then continuously in production for thirty-three years. (In private Clapton also admitted that 'vast areas' of his early career had been erased through drug abuse.)

Clapton agreeing to appear on so prosaic a programme as *My Top Ten* was further evidence of a shift in the way he was being packaged. Until at least 1981 the bulk of Stigwood's and Forrester's promotion had been product-led – in other words, based around the singles and albums. After Live Aid it became a campaign in which the most valuable asset was Clapton himself. From the self-professed 'one man and his guitar versus the world' to the middle-aged cricket-lover and pop veteran, it would be easy to see Clapton's progress as that of a brooding loner into an all-round entertainer. Entertainment being what sold, it did not take a genius to predict Clapton's next pose: that of a genial elder statesman, eager to

Clapton, Conor and
Lori del Santo (*Rex*)

Previous page: Ruth Kelly
(born 11 January 1985)
with her parents (*Rex*)

With Mick Jagger, the man
whose offer Clapton turned
down (*Syndication
International*)

'I just like the company of beautiful women ... I have a weakness in that department'.
Clockwise from top left: Clapton with Marie Helvin (*Rex*), Jilly Johnson (*Syndication International*), Yelitza Negrete (*Rex*) and Susannah Constantine (*Rex*)

28 March 1991 (*Rex*)

Clapton's first public outing after Conor's death, with Tatum O'Neal (*Rex*)

With Phil Collins, responsible for two of Clapton's more successful, and less distinguished, albums (*Rex*)

Orchestral nights (*Rex*)

A ritual exchange of guitar and cricket bat took place with Ian Botham (*Rex*)

Clapton with the Princess of Wales at the premiere of *Rush* (*Press Association*)

The sane Englishman
with his guitar
(*Rex*)

Following page: The Duchess
of York with Clapton dressed
as the Invisible Man – an
unconscious irony, some
thought – for the start of the
London–Monte Carlo Rally
(*Press Association*)

With Dylan at Madison Square
Garden. According to Pete
Brown, the two operative
words to describe Clapton
were 'intelligent' and
'dignified' (*Rex*)

please and willing, at all times, to align himself with causes. In the coming year he appeared or played at functions for Alcoholics Anonymous, the Prince's Trust, Comedy Aid and the cricketers David Gower and Clive Radley, while contributing to charities in and around Guildford and Cranleigh. Clapton's transformation into the 'showbusiness type' he once despised was embodied in a long hagiography on *The South Bank Show* in 1987, the same year he launched his season of concerts at the Albert Hall. Promotional videos, once angrily resisted, were released to accompany his occasional singles. And Clapton returned to the screen on *Top of the Pops*, vigorously miming in front of a smattering of teenagers, his first appearance on the programme in twenty years.

It is tempting to assume that Clapton recognized his creative *volte-face* as easily as he achieved it. It is slightly harder to believe that it was unconnected to a wider strategy orchestrated by Forrester. By 1985 it was clear that, while still commanding residual respect, Clapton was a static figure, uncertain of his bearings and alienating a substantial number of old fans while not attracting sufficient new ones. Both as a songwriter and guitar virtuoso his best days were behind him. It was Forrester's genius to dramatically alter Clapton's image so that he became a stalwart, appreciated for merely having survived, someone who not only did good works but was himself endorsed by the great and good. In 1986 it became known that the Duke and Duchess of York, considered by some the epitome of youthful chic, admired Clapton's work. The Royal Warrant was extended when, on 20 June, he appeared at the Prince's Trust concert at Wembley alongside Collins, Jagger, Bowie, George Michael and Tina Turner.* It took a master of the dark arts of spin-control successfully to alter Clapton's image so that the heroin addict of 1974 became the showbusiness trouper of 1986. With an alchemist's touch, Forrester turned creative decline into commercial triumph. Early in his career Clapton had spoken gloomily of his prospects as a blues guitarist, believing he would 'never get over to the public'. His major success lay not in his ability to communicate his goals but in his abandonment of them. For all his occasional talk of 'beauty' and 'purity' of expression, both his albums and concerts and, above all, his public works signalled that by 1986 Clapton had already significantly changed tack.

---

* The event saw the first appearance of the 'Eric Clapton Signature' Stratocaster. Shortly after Live Aid, Dan Smith, head of the Fender company, had approached Clapton with the idea of his endorsing a custom-built guitar.

It paid dividends to do so. As has been seen, Clapton's income rose substantially in the twelve months following Live Aid. His company accounts for 1986, signed by Clapton himself, show total assets less liabilities of £119,567. The sense that Marshbrook and its principal might be on a firmer footing was lent symbolic weight by the company's moving to Rolls House, in the centre of London's financial district. Forrester himself took premises in Harley House, a Victorian mansion block whose very appearance – dark, with gothic, weather-stained arches – suggested steadiness, security and a sense of permanence.

Clapton toured Europe and Scandinavia in July 1986. The concerts were notable for the debut of a new group – Phillinganes, East and, on drums, Collins – and Clapton's introduction to a future collaborator, Robert Cray. As further proof of his desire to attract as wide a support-base as possible, the set was extensively overhauled. Where once Clapton had succumbed to amnesiac loathing of his early work, the tone now was unashamedly nostalgic. No fewer than four Cream songs – 'Crossroads', 'White Room', 'Badge' and 'Sunshine Of Your Love' – were included, while, as a further attraction, Collins sang his hit 'In The Air Tonight'. The concert at the NEC, Birmingham, on 15 July was later successfully released as a video.

In choosing to spotlight generous amounts of his past career, Clapton risked inevitable comparisons with his early technique. There were signs (as he had recognized himself in 1979) that his ability to play innovative noises, to play a *lot* of guitar without sounding fussy, had left him. Unlike a Hendrix, or, closer to home, a Jeff Beck, he never seemed to be struggling with something volatile and difficult to handle, risking the possibility that he might fail or, more likely, gloriously succeed on stage. There was a sameness about his note-by-note reproductions of original hits. The rough edges once routinely heard in the Bluesbreakers or Cream had been removed. Even Page's or Townshend's histrionic ability and speedy chord negotiations were missing. At the same time, twenty-three years as a professional had left Clapton with an understanding of stage-craft and an encyclopaedic grasp of detail which greatly enhanced the performance. He was never going to go seriously wrong playing the raw material of his youth. In replacing the air of unpredictable charm once surrounding his concerts Clapton may have been doing no more than showing his age. In an interview that summer he admitted, 'When you're in your mid-twenties you've got something that you lose . . . If I was a sportsman, I would have retired by now.' There were times in Europe when he seemed to be gasping rather than singing, and Phillinganes confirms that 'the tour took it out of all of us'.

The sense that Clapton might be diminished – at least different – from his youth was reinforced by the birth of his second child, Conor Loren, in St Mary's Hospital, Paddington, on 21 August 1986. All parties agree he was a doting father. A member of the Groucho Club, where Clapton had dinner on the 21st, remembers him 'bubbling with pride' and 'insisting it was the best day of his life'. Henry Spinetti, recalled to play with Clapton and Dylan, and on a film project that month, also had the impression of a man 'devoted to family'. (Clapton's devotion did not, however, extend to living full-time with Del Santo and Conor; mother and son remained based at Eaton Mews South.) Another musician present at Townhouse Studios remembers 'the change [as] stupendous . . . Eric was handing out baby photos in the control-room.'

The film project was *The Color of Money*. Clapton's contribution, 'It's In The Way That You Use It', was also featured on his album *August* (for Conor's birth), perversely released that November. Other highlights included 'Tearing Us Apart', a jaunty duet with Tina Turner; 'Bad Influence', whose synthesizer and thumping bass-line instantly evoked Phil Collins; 'Hold On', a slab of rousing if conventional funk-rock; and both 'Miss You' and 'Behind The Mask', whose lavishness of style also strongly recalled their producer. Rock bottom was touched with 'Take A Chance', occupying the same ludicrous niche as 'I've Got A Rock n' Roll Heart' and 'Holy Mother', another of Clapton's excursions into maudlin self-pity (and obscurely dedicated to The Band pianist Richard Manuel, who committed suicide in March 1986).

August has its redeeming features. 'Holy Mother' apart, the producer's chirpy and non-cerebral qualities come through: there are R&B undertones, punchy horn breaks and familiar examples of Collins's ability to fashion a memorable pop hook. Because Clapton was reaching beyond his own experience on the album, his lacklustre playing can almost be excused. Between them Collins and the Warners marketing department – constantly agitating for 'another "Layla"' – produced a sound at odds with Clapton's angst-ridden lyrics. The distance between the songs' subject-matter and their performance makes the tunes seem oddly disconnected – another feature of Collins's work.

On the debit side, *August* continued and greatly accelerated the process of reducing Clapton to just another middleweight pop star. As Pete Brown says, 'It sounded obsolete as soon as he made it.' There were a number of songs apparently significant only to Clapton, Collins and their immediate clique. Even Dire Straits and Madonna sounded contemporary and rootsy by comparison. *August* may have been a successful album in 1986 – it sold a million copies in Britain alone – but it sounds curiously dated in 1999, more so than Clapton's work from the sixties. There was a feeling that the guest appearances, the expense, the lavish production, the cover photograph by Terry O'Neill were no more than substitutes for what Clapton once had: raw, unadorned emotion. The comment of one reviewer that 'the whole album sounds like the soundtrack of a bad Eddie Murphy movie' may be unfair. Even so, it was hard to be forgiving to a musician who now admitted, 'I sold myself a long time ago. I made some kind of deal with myself to get along, to please people, just to make life easy. It disturbs me a little to hear myself say that, but I have to admit it. Who am I kidding?'

Finally, whatever its strengths or defects as an album, *August* was the vehicle that defined Clapton's future direction. In showing just how he proposed to extend a career built in the mid-sixties into the early nineties, the record was astonishingly unspecific. There were relatively few moments of even mild experimentation. Neither did it pay much respect to Clapton's first principles. On the other hand, in laying out a smörgasbord of pop-rock styles, Clapton rightly calculated that the album would appeal to a broad adult market – those for whom CDs furnished a room – while not antagonizing members of his old audience. In this respect *August* worked brilliantly. As an album it may have been weak, unconvincing and, above all, chronically confused. As a strategy it was perfect.

When, alone in his Ripley bedroom, Clapton had listened to *Uncle Mac's Hour*, among the first guitarists he heard was Chuck Berry. That was in 1956. Clapton was a self-conscious eleven-year-old, confused by his parentage, already answering to the nickname 'Loony'. Berry had just released his seminal 'Wee Wee Hours', a song which introduced many a teenager to the blues. Thirty years later, the shy suburban boy, now an international celebrity, was invited to play at Berry's sixtieth birthday concerts. What's more, 'Wee Wee Hours' was in the repertoire.

The event, a relatively rare meeting between Clapton and a childhood hero, took place in St Louis. It was a striking example of the disparity between the blues disciple and his role models. The first hint of trouble came when Berry, in Clapton's words, 'sat down next to me on a couch and said, "Hi, I'm Chuck Berry, you're Eric Clapton. Nice to meet you."

Then he said, "Hang on a second," and shouted, "Bring the camera in" ... He then started to interview me about him.' Next Clapton showed his host a rare – and valuable – Gibson ES-350T (the guitar with which Berry had his original hits), a gesture that, according to Keith Richards, 'rubbed Chuck the wrong way'. Finally, as so often in Berry's long career, there was a dispute about money.

The two concerts that followed, released as *Hail! Hail! Rock 'n' Roll*, were relatively uneventful. (Some detected irony in Berry's introduction of his guest as 'Man of the Blues'.) Clapton's performance, he later admitted, owed much to being 'frustrated' by the time he was called, after two hours in a waiting area stocked only by food, drink and a television showing continuous pornographic videos (lesbian lust being Berry's preferred subject matter). It must have been a relief to return to the anodyne world of soundtracks. Clapton recorded the score for *Lethal Weapon* at Townhouse Studios between 8 and 16 December 1986. He also played a series of successful club dates in America to mark the launch of *August*. Keith Richards joined Clapton on stage in New York, proving, if nothing else, that he was unfamiliar with the chord structure of 'Layla'.

As a result of his early difficulty in reconciling with either his family or childhood friends, Clapton had become more reclusive and aloof, thus setting up a vicious circle of solitude. The depths were reached when, in 1972, both Pat and Ben Palmer were turned away from his door. At the same time, Clapton still had a longing for roots and domesticity. He was one of the few British rock stars not (yet) to own a property abroad. He continued to live a few miles from his childhood home. Of all the changes taking place in Clapton's life from 1985, the most conspicuous was in his attitude to the community. There was nothing new, of course, about his helping deserving causes. As early as 1977 he had played an unpublicized Valentine's Day dance at Cranleigh Village Hall. (Even then, Clapton was criticized by some for cheapening his image. 'Why does he do it?' asked Chris Dreja. 'Has he become a caricature?') The difference was that, from the late eighties, there was a boom both in Clapton's charitable works and the way they were promoted. Becoming a constituency celebrity may have been the final plank in Clapton's post-Live Aid platform. It may have been in what one musician calls 'abject self-interest'. Certainly it did nothing to harm Clapton's social life to make himself accessible to his local fans. There was a woman in Shere, for instance, who briefly enjoyed the fame of having 'slept with Eric'; on one occasion a local at the Windmill Inn was surprised, though not shocked, to see Clapton drive by, leaning across a strikingly attractive blonde to 'give a quick, cheery wave' and simultaneously tooting the Ferrari's horn (what was surprising was that the girl was topless); a set of well-known local twins were seen walking down the drive to Hurtwood Edge. Improving his community relations may, therefore, have been a fillip for Clapton's private life. Equally, he might have felt that he owed it to himself to translate his fame into good deeds.

Whatever the reason, the result was that he became increasingly popular as an opener of fêtes, kisser of babies and sponsor of causes. When Linda Chandler attended Clapton's charity concert at Dunsfold Village Hall that Christmas, she came away impressed by 'the nicest man in the world'.

9

'I Tend Towards Delusions of Grandeur'

If Live Aid had relaunched Clapton's career and *August* defined it, the Albert Hall embodied it. Negotiations to have him host an annual season of concerts – a sort of alternative proms – had begun after the Prince's Trust party in 1986. Despite imaginative treatment by one journalist, no evidence ever emerged that either Clapton or his manager had any financial stake in the venue. None of Forrester's nine directorships linked him to Royal Albert Hall Developments or its principal Donald McNicol. As he grew older, and the physical strain of touring the world greater, it made sense to have Clapton's fans travel to him, rather than vice-versa. The choice of the arena already patronized by, among others, Hendrix, Led Zeppelin, the Who, Deep Purple and Black Sabbath may not have been as startling as some thought. The residual affection Clapton felt for the hall where Cream gave their farewell concerts helped settle the matter. It appealed, he admitted, to his delusions of grandeur. That the Albert Hall responded as it did, with a standing invitation, speaks volumes for Clapton's acceptance as a corporate entertainer, a man whose older fans now ringed 'EC – RAH' alongside their engagements at Ascot and Henley.

Clapton's first season at the Albert Hall began on 6 January 1987. That year he played a total of six concerts, backed by Phillinganes, East and Mark Knopfler on guitar. The drums were played alternately by Collins or Steve Ferrone, previously involved with the Average White Band. 'They worked their collective magic,' the *Express* allowed – and the events were indeed, says Phillinganes, magical – echoing the generally favourable, and at all times respectful opinion of the national press. *The Times*, *Telegraph* and *Guardian* all sent their arts correspondents. In reacting to his new image, the only criticism came from a source once four-square in Clapton's corner – the trade and music titles. As so often the case with rock, the reviews reflected the writers' own perspective on society (the *Express*'s 'collective magic' being *Raw*'s 'Thatcherite cop-out') rather than anything the musician said or did. In fact, plans to issue the six concerts as a live album were halted only by the simultaneous release of two greatest-hits collections. A third record, it was thought, would glut even Clapton's rapacious fans.

Clapton's European tour that winter was his first of any importance since 1978. Then he had been considered a casualty; now he let it be known – through the title of a new book – that he was a survivor. The occasion was marked by a wave of profiles and interviews in the press, almost all of them generous. The generosity in part, no doubt, reflected Clapton's status as an elder statesman; but it also signified a major shift in perception since Live Aid. In summer 1984, when Clapton had appeared at the Ahoy Halle, Rotterdam, as part of the Roger Waters revue, he was greeted by *Vrij Nederland* as 'just another obsolete character, trading in on old glory'. Two and a half years later, the paper reviewed Clapton's concert at the same venue as 'stunning . . . terrific . . . breathtaking in its ability to recapture the past'. Six of the fourteen songs played, it was noted, dated from the sixties.

The sense that Clapton had ascended the same throne occupied by Collins, McCartney and other approved entertainers was confirmed that February. At a televised ceremony described by *The Times* as 'gushingly effusive' he received a British Phonographic Institute award for services to music. As a metaphor for social assimilation – the ex-addict and alcoholic waving to an audience of Conservative politicians, churchmen and elderly actors – the scene was memorable. The governing image was, again, one of survival. Clapton was praised for having 'lasted', 'endured' and 'straddled the shifting public taste' (as though a fickle public was just something an entertainer had to put up with). His appeal was not, however, merely nostalgic. Clapton also made every reasonable effort to attract a younger audience. It would be easy to mock, as some writers did, this pandering to the market: appearing on *Top of the Pops*, after all, was one thing; singing 'Love Like A Rocket' on *Saturday Superstore* was an act of almost surreal inanity. His rehabilitation had been remarkable to behold, a return to critical and public favour that even he might have been surprised to witness, but Clapton went too far in trying to be all things to all people. It should not have escaped Forrester's attention, during his long apprenticeship to Robert Stigwood, that enthusiasm comes more naturally from the consumer, not the provider. Successful

PR has to be pitched a fraction below delivery. There was a suspicion, as at other times in his career, of both parody and play-acting in Clapton's efforts to appeal to seven- and eight-year-old children.

Still, the figure 'warmly greeting' Jack Bruce in 1987 was radically altered from the one insulting his old colleague in 1979. When Bruce arrived in the studio to record his album *Willpower*, he found Clapton 'totally supportive', 'charming' and 'a pleasure to be with'. Dick Heckstall-Smith, once a colleague of Bruce's in the Graham Bond Organization, was also present. 'Eric was a changed man,' he says. 'Instead of the moody, reclusive guy I remembered, here was a normal adult who smiled a lot and bragged about his son.' (Conor Clapton was baptized at St Mary Magdalen, as his father had been, that year.) His new amiability even extended to attending a fortieth birthday party for Elton John, a man with whom Clapton had previously exchanged Fortnum & Mason Christmas hampers but very little in the way of intimacy. It may have been perfectly natural for two superstars of British rock, both enjoying a professional Indian summer, to seek out each other's company. (There were, of course, other parallels, not least in the impressive control of their managers.) None the less, there was poignancy to be seen in Clapton's friendship with a figure practically embodying the showbusiness tradition he once avoided. According to an unnamed guest present at the party in Windsor, the two men were 'thick as thieves', 'chatting and laughing' and jointly smoking 'what was probably a cigarette'.

On 11 April 1987, after a charity performance at Cranleigh Golf Club, Clapton began his nineteenth American tour. The support act was Robert Cray; Collins returned on drums. The generally retrospective tone remained – Clapton's mere announcement of 'Crossroads' or 'Layla' was enough to bring shouts of 'God' from the house. (The previously sacred gap between songs, once used to tune guitars or, at best, harangue the audience from behind a brandy, was now polished into a sort of comedy routine. Americans like something to share, and Clapton's catch-phrases and jokes, seized on as much as the songs, were widely repeated in the days after the concerts.) On 15 April Clapton appeared alongside Collins, Albert King, Paul Butterfield and Stevie Ray Vaughan at a benefit for B. B. King. His playing on 'The Thrill Is Gone', later released on video, was a tidy example of his breadth of musical references. One was reminded of the days, apparently forgotten, when his canon of note mastery and improvisational flair was matched by an equal command of rhythm. King himself denied that either Clapton's technique, or his devotion to the blues had been dulled by age. 'He ain't finished,' the sixty-one-year-old informed *Rolling Stone*. 'He may only be getting started.'

King was right in saying that, as a physically static performer whose craft lay in the infinite acquiring of experience, Clapton could expect a career measured in decades rather than years. He was, as he always put it, 'no Mick Jagger'. As to whether he remained devoted to the blues, there were differing opinions. Among the reviews of the American tour was one describing it as 'disjointed and spotty . . . the enduring trademark guitar spoilt by messy full-band arrangements'. Clapton himself admitted to Roger Gibbons, 'I think I just apply myself to what I know is contemporary . . . I try to bend with the wind.' Yet another journalist had the impression of a man 'desperately trying to find something to believe in'.

At the heart of Clapton's youthful passion for the blues had, of course, been a sense of his own pain and suffering. While much of this may have been imaginary, it undoubtedly made for some stirring music. No one would have begrudged Clapton his apparent middle-aged contentment. Even so, his aimless, let-it-all-hang out strategy could have done with stiffening by the stoic reminder that music was *not*, as he now claimed, always about 'having a good time'. By losing track of his earliest experiences he risked also abandoning his first principles.

Like many who have set great store in clinging to their beliefs, Clapton was all too practised at the art of compromise. He had long believed – and in conversations at Nassau had often told Markee – that 'events overwhelm us, and the improbable becomes inevitable'. For years Clapton had tried hard, sometimes too hard, to stay close to his roots. When money and success made this impossible, he simply became rootless. He lost creative and professional momentum and all but abandoned a style that only needed amending. In short, he over-compensated. It hardly needs adding that the vacuum was filled, as always, by the designated best friend in Clapton's life – in this case Collins – a process he described as '. . . depending on the influence of [the person involved]. It's as if, like a sponge, I absorb the general vibe and the change slowly starts to take place, new patterns of thought, new forms of language, new musical directions . . . then suddenly it's all over and we have to say goodbye until the next time.'

In the sixties and seventies Clapton had shied from appearing even to support the Royal Family. Now, when the annual Prince's Trust concerts came to be organized, his was the first name inked in. The two events on

5–6 June 1987 were notable for the appearance of not only the ubiquitous Collins but of both Harrison and Ringo Starr; they and Clapton combined on 'While My Guitar Gently Weeps'. The second of the concerts was later released as an album. The Prince's Trust both endorsed and accelerated Clapton's assimilation, and that of rock generally, into the British Establishment. It was the first major fault in the battle-lines drawn up in the 1950s, the first hint for many believers that their role-models were no more 'rebellious' than they should be. A few months later, when performers like Elton John appeared virtually under Royal Warrant, the crack deepened, threatening the whole premise on which rock had been founded. But Clapton's fall came first.

The broadening of his support-base, his continual tours and one-off performances and the plethora of reissued albums and CDs did Clapton no harm financially. Marshbrook turned over a total of £498,649 in 1987, a rise of nearly 30 per cent over 1986. The company remunerated its highest-paid director £231,945. E. C. Music showed a similar increase, from £143,799 to £166,429. (Curiously, Duck continued to post an annual turnover of just £2000, the same as for the previous three years.) It was in the mid and late 1980s, post-Live Aid, that Clapton became seriously wealthy. It was then that he developed the vague hauteur, the glassy stare, the obtrusive entourage that would, if not protect him, at least insulate him from the media. Interviewing Clapton in the 1970s had all too often been an exercise in surrealism, an opportunity for him to hold forth on a stream of subjects – race, religion, football, horse-racing, fishing – currently obsessing him. A decade later, according to a man who would know, 'you didn't *get* an interview with Clapton. What you had was an audience.'

It was rather to Clapton's praise that, at a time when his career assumed regal dimensions, he continued to be regarded as a model constituency celebrity. According to Linda Chandler, 'Eric was always at his nicest on his own, talking to people as if they were no better, and no worse, than himself.' When a local man named Duncan Caine formed a rock group and dropped an 'appallingly rough' tape in the Hurtwood Edge postbox, he was surprised to be rung by an 'incredibly friendly, supportive' Clapton inviting him to visit the house. (When Caine did so after the pub had closed one evening he was turned away on the reasonable grounds of it being too late at night.) St Mary Magdalen church was among the many beneficiaries of Clapton's charity. Anyone could write to Hurtwood Edge and receive, if not an individual reply, at least a signed album or photograph supplied by Warner Brothers. On a personal level, Clapton continued to play host to his eighty-year-old grandmother, as well as to Adrian Clapton and his wife Sylvia. (The last, an ex-telephonist, became particularly adept at fielding the 'two or three calls a week supposedly from Eric's friends . . . I can tell by someone's voice if they're fibbing.') One of Clapton's major limitations as a musician was his incapacity for detachment – not from himself, but from the suburban values of the world in which he lived. That same failing fuelled his craving for roots and domesticity. He even reconciled fully with his mother, living a few miles from the town where the locals had been so harsh to her in 1945.

By the late 1980s, Clapton's aura and reputation were undiminished, but his hopes of achieving anything significant were fading. As he entered his mid-forties, his life settled into a routine of guest appearances, charity events and long uninterrupted stretches at Hurtwood Edge, a semi-retirement in the area he had known all his life. His official tours remained tightly scheduled, hour by hour, night by night, months in advance. He still relied on Forrester to strike the right balance between musical activity, media stardom and 'quality time' at home in Ewhurst. As has been seen, at the heart of Clapton's restlessness it was possible to glimpse a longing for home and family. While some of this was undoubtedly nostalgia – as Matthew Wood says, 'enjoying the fifties a lot more than he had at the time' – there was also something genuinely sentimental in Clapton's character, a need for approval from the very people he felt had rejected him as a boy. In living at Hurtwood Edge, he continued to be obsessed with converting his enemies, the unknown villagers who had once scrawled graffiti on his wall. He was drawn to the local community by a mixture of insecurity and arrogance. Clapton might enjoy a quiet walk or a drink in the Windmill Inn, but even then his superstar status would be asserted. To one villager, who prefers not to be named, there was 'something patronizing' about the way Clapton appeared from time to time, 'asking if there were anything he could do, without taking responsibility for actually acting on the answer'. According to Matthew Wood, 'he wanted to be seen as an accessible, down-to-earth guy. But not *too* accessible. There was always the Ferrari.'

Closely linked to Clapton's craving for roots and tradition was his discovery of cricket. In August 1987 he played in a charity match in Finchley and later performed for two hours in a marquee on the boundary. A month later he appeared at the county ground in Worcester where, according to Tim Rice, 'his eyes lit up at the prospect of donning whites'. Andy Peebles, present for the day, remembers 'Eric, absolutely in his element, staying in a pub with Ian Botham, having the time of their lives'. (When Peebles asked him to dedicate a track from *August*, Clapton chose 'Tearing Us Apart' – 'a bit racy,' the disc jockey notes, 'for Radio 2 listeners'.) Godfrey Evans, the former England wicket-keeper, also met Clapton at Worcester. He was 'down to earth', 'mild' and 'charming', constantly sipping a drink 'which may or may not have been lemonade'.

The contents of Clapton's glass continued to be a subject of speculation in 1987. The same month he met Evans at Worcester, Clapton re-recorded 'After Midnight' at the Power Station, New York, specifically to promote Michelob beer. It was a curious decision for a recovering alcoholic. By the time the commercial aired that December Clapton was again in treatment in Hazelden. Later he would recall the embarrassment of watching the advertisement on television with his fellow inmates.

Nothing suggests that Clapton's struggles to stop drinking in 1982 had been less than genuine. For a year or two, at least, he seems to have been completely abstinent. At the same time, it irritated some, a former friend among them, that he appeared to take a 'morbidly self-righteous' attitude to a problem that remained, at best, half solved. There was a sense in which Clapton the abuser had become Clapton the abused, a tragic victim of his own dysfunctional desires. Nobody accused Clapton of reverting to the sort of alcoholic haze characterizing his life in the 1970s. Nor is it certain whether he expected the wholly negative reaction his commercial produced. What is certain is that even Keith Richards found Clapton's Michelob endorsement bizarre. The man who charmed local villagers and came alive the moment he stepped on to a cricket pitch was still capable of some strangely perverse career moves. It was possible to see the logic which Clapton and Forrester applied in agreeing to the brewery's offer. Both men had long been fascinated by showbusiness and may have felt that a wider audience – sixty million people saw Clapton playing 'After Midnight' while a voice-over crooned, 'The night belongs to Michelob' – was only the just reward for a career approaching its fourth decade. If so, they miscalculated the sort of public scrutiny Clapton could expect as he advanced from stardom into celebrity. Yet it would be a mistake to suppose that logic had broken down in both manager and client. What made it possible for Clapton and Forrester to operate in the seemingly contrary worlds of rock and commerce with such unstinted gusto was that they had the most plausible reasons to believe that what they were doing would work to a final good. The returns filed by Marshbrook in 1988 proved the efficacy of the policy. Financially, Clapton was vindicated. Morally, in endorsing even as mild a drink as Michelob he was yet again guilty of accepting privilege without responsibility.

The ruthless efficiency with which Forrester more typically packaged his client found expression in the *South Bank Show* profile aired that December. For the Yardbirds, Clapton informed Melvyn Bragg, 'it was all a joke . . . I was a fanatic'. He none the less 'never accepted the fact that I was the best guitar player in the world'. Cream, after the initial honeymoon, 'were all going in completely different directions'. As a result, Clapton had 'tried to lay back and be as economic as possible . . . and got severely criticized for it'. The starting point for the blues he described as 'having some kind of emotional trauma, some kind of upset in life'. As to his susceptibility to alcohol and drugs, Clapton cited the mixture of energy and emotion with which he laid himself bare before an audience: 'When you open up your heart and soul, you're left with a void . . . you need nursing . . . you need something to calm the pain.'

The impression was of a lucid, even articulate figure, unafraid to criticize his employers – 'Warner Brothers wanted [*August*] to be a commercial album' – yet keen to draw the fruits of the liaison to his interviewer's attention (' "Holy Mother" ', Bragg duly intoned, 'is Clapton's Christmas single.') With all the virtues of the blues purist – even Rose Clapp was heard to insist that 'he never really commercialized' – Clapton also showed an unusual willingness to admit his faults, and, as before, stressed his vulnerability and need to be 'nursed' above all other qualities. Just as Clapton was drawn to the community with a cross between conceit and insecurity, so his attitude to his role-models remained ambivalent. Into the mix went fear, mistrust, envy and a sort of compensatory arrogance not ruling out the possibility of respect. The irony of Clapton's position lay, of course, in his commanding an audience larger than that dreamed of by the most successful original bluesman. 'You couldn't help but smile,' says Hughie Flint, 'when someone like Buddy Guy begged to play with Eric. In my day it was the other way around.' Guy himself appeared on the *South Bank Show*, duetting with Clapton on a number in which only one guitar was audible.

Clapton may have achieved more in material terms than he ever thought possible. The house in the country, the Ferraris, the designer suits were all witness to his ability successfully to interpret the blues to a mass audience. In addition, however, as increasingly bitter criticism mounted of his squandering of gifts, his rudderless direction and that, as Lester Bangs put it, 'he seemed not to stand for anything', he became correspondingly more insecure, self-conscious and self-protective. Instead of improving, his relations with other musicians, and particularly with blues musicians, became more strained and awkward. At the core of Clapton's insecurity, of course, lay a longing to be accepted and admired by his contemporaries. A session like the one with Guy was significant not only for itself but for the impression Guy might form of him. Clapton's compulsion to be noticed by his peers was motivated partly by vanity. But, like much of his vanity, it had a basis in reality. Both he and Forrester believed, with some justification, that Clapton's celebrity status had to be constantly protected. That meant his appearances with other musicians, however exalted, were carefully arranged in order to show Clapton to maximum advantage. In short, he became the star of any show. Like anyone confronted with his less hallowed, but no less talented heroes, Clapton could consequently feel guilty, an emotion that he tended to translate into anger. As early as 1963 members of the Yardbirds had found him 'uptight' at appearing with Sonny Boy Williamson, largely because, in Jim McCarty's words, 'he was embarrassed at even being on the same stage . . . Playing with real bluesmen always brought out Eric's paranoia.'

Clapton ended 1987 by undertaking an Australian and Japanese tour and, as he had in 1986, a charity night at Dunsfold village hall. The events were richly symbolic of his career as a whole: the lucrative arena performances paid Clapton's bills and allowed him the luxury of playing to a few hundred villagers who, perhaps alone of his fans, continued to insist that his status as 'God' was inviolate. According to Duncan Caine, 'He got even better as he got older.' A more critical note was struck by those present at Clapton's Birmingham concerts in the new year. It was widely felt that, with no new album in over a year, the events were merely a repeat performance of 1987, inflation ('Same Old Blues' was extended to twenty-five minutes) tending to replace invention. The charge of sameness against Clapton's concerts at the Albert Hall was levelled by Adam Sweeting in the *Guardian*:

> Whatever the shortcomings of his recent recordings, Clapton still pulls in a crowd who bark and bay for more as he ploughs through a set judiciously weighted with Golden Greats . . . There are several

hoops through which he feels obliged to jump, like the ghastly Wonderful Tonight and the whining Holy Mother. Layla now presents the same sort of problem as Bruce Springsteen's Rosalita – everybody wants to hear it, but it needs a break.

It comes as no surprise that Clapton increasingly occupied himself with film work – scores for *Buster*, *Homeboy* and *Peace In Our Time* were all recorded in the first half of 1988 – and that his primary appeal continued to be nostalgic. *The Cream Of Eric Clapton*, released the previous September, enjoyed an unbroken run of seventy-nine weeks in the charts. Meanwhile Polydor issued the six-record *Crossroads*, a retrospective collection extending from the Yardbirds to *August*. Despite the inclusion of at least one track, 'For Your Love', of dubious appeal to Clapton and another, the re-recorded 'After Midnight', of questionable taste to the public, *Crossroads* was a compilation of rare distinction. Particularly praiseworthy was the executive producer's sniffing-out of five unreleased tracks intended for the Dominos' follow-up to *Layla*. One of these, 'Evil', stands as a hint of what that group might have achieved had they buried their differences, although, without the differences, they might never have achieved *Layla*. *Crossroads* earned fawning reviews and sold a million copies worldwide.

For the third year running, Clapton appeared at the Prince's Trust concerts in London, where he joined Collins, Elton John, the Bee Gees and Joe Cocker in the distinctly ragged finale, 'With A Little Help From My Friends'. There was some carping at the Prince's presentation to Clapton of a model silver Stratocaster to mark his twenty-fifth year in the industry. One musician backstage considered this 'a bit rich . . . Charles, presumably on his wife's advice, honouring a lag like Clapton'.* But most of the press were supportive – even the tabloids were uncritical – and the comments tended to be effusive. For most of those present, inspired by the sight of a reformed addict and alcoholic quipping with the heir to the throne, it was a moving moment. 'Some of them were actually *crying*,' notes the same musician. Forrester was also present. The triumph of perseverance and reconstruction that had, almost incredibly, led to this scene had begun ten years earlier when he took over Clapton's career.

Extending his role as a model supporter of causes, Clapton next appeared, alongside Dire Straits, at the Nelson Mandela birthday tribute

* The Princess of Wales was a Clapton fan.

at Wembley. (In 1976 Clapton's comments had prompted the formation of Rock Against Racism; in 1988 he headed the bill at a concert organized by Artists Against Apartheid.) He gave money to Alcoholics Anonymous and clothes to the Sharp Shop (a charity for alcohol and drug addicts); he played a benefit concert at Wintershall in aid of the King Edward VII Hospital. He even salvaged the career of Andy Fairweather-Low, the otherwise forgotten pop singer who in time assumed the role, vacated by Gary Brooker in 1982, of Clapton's aide-de-camp.

For all the recycling that went on of Clapton's career, this was among the most depressing times of his life. His health, after years of alcoholic excess and wolfed-down meals, had begun to suffer: a diet of curries, hamburgers and baked beans, washed down by lemonade and coffee, had given him a fuller face and the beginnings of a pot belly. He had unhealthy skin and a smoker's cough. For all his refound fame and success, he led a notoriously chaotic private life. The affair with Del Santo had cooled by 1988. Everything suggests that Clapton was, in modern parlance, dysfunctional in his relationships. So far as he had recognizable feelings about women they were nostalgic. 'Holy Mother' had had a literal application to Pat. 'Miss You' was a parting salvo at Clapton's defecting lovers. 'Old Love', which he wrote in 1989, was the last and most important of these laments over the failure of past liaisons, a song of rage and self-pity.

Clapton was always professing his respect and admiration of women. Yet the relationships tended to progress along distressingly familiar lines: the gift of a designer dress; the expensive meal; the sex (in which, according to one of them, 'the woman was expected to take the precautions'), after which Clapton would sit for hours in his upholstered chair, brooding or strumming the guitar. 'There was no dialogue,' says a visitor to Hurtwood Edge in 1988. 'Just this moody, lonely guy who couldn't relate to women. Of course, it was quite different *before* he had you. I remember Eric telling me the music was his soul and the lyrics were his conscience – anything to get those knickers off.'

All things considered, it was striking how many fans believed that Clapton's charitable works existed outside his main career. One of the characteristics of the tyrannical mind has always been to erect opportunism to the status of a principle. To describe the behaviour of Clapton and his manager as tyrannical might sound extreme. But it is wishful thinking to suppose that tyrannical impulses and a supposedly liberating art form like rock are incompatible. It showed a notably deft touch to raise a cash-generating figure like Clapton, on account of his charitable deeds, to a point where he could no longer be criticized with impunity; one might as well carp at the Queen Mother. No one doubted that Clapton's involvement with a myriad causes was deeply heartfelt (even though, as with Artists Against Apartheid, he seems to have come to them relatively late in life). Equally, no one could have denied that the resulting exposure seemed not to have harmed his career. As a direct result of his appearance at the Mandela concert, *The Cream of Eric Clapton* climbed in the charts. Interest in Clapton's back catalogue increased. Marshbrook paid its principal director £461,740 in 1988, almost twice the sum shown the previous year. For the first time since 1984 Clapton's publishing business, E. C. Music, recorded a net profit. (Duck Records, for the fifth year running, turned over £2000.) It is stressed that no suspicion of anything underhand attaches itself to Clapton's business affairs. His appearances at events like Live Aid, the Prince's Trust and Wintershall may have been entirely due to a sense of personal empathy with the beneficiaries. At the same time, Marshbrook's own description of its principal activity, 'the exploitation of the services of an artiste in the entertainment industry', may, almost uniquely for a company, convey a trace of irony. 'From the mid-eighties onwards,' says Pete Brown, 'it became all about identifying Eric with causes. There may have been a degree of self-interest, but Clapton gave back more than he took.'

The word 'still', inevitably marking the process of national or artistic decline (as in, 'Britain is still the third largest producer of cars in Europe'; 'the Rolling Stones are still the greatest rock and roll band in the world') was widely used to promote Clapton's tour of North America that autumn. The group – Clapton, Knopfler, Ferrone, East, the keyboardist Alan Clark, Jody Linscott on percussion and the backing singers Katie Kissoon and Tessa Niles – opened at the Starplex Amphitheater, Dallas, on 1 September. According to the local press, they were 'still' the best, Clapton 'still' divine, the ticket 'still' the hottest in town. Somehow the word 'still' reeked of the need for reassurance and comfort. There was a feeling that Clapton's more credulous fans (and that included elements of the press) outdid in enthusiasm those who judged the music in its own right. Thus Clapton's appearance in New Orleans was trailed excitedly in the *Picayune* (whose classified columns offered front-row seats at five times face value) whereas, two days later, the same title gave merely 'grudging respect' to the actual concert. A longer review was filed by Joel Selvin in the San Francisco *Chronicle*, the paper that first canonized Clapton in America in 1967:

> [Clapton's] concerts have become increasingly ritualized, never delving too deeply into the mountainous catalog of recordings that produced [*Crossroads*], but sticking to tried and true stalwarts like 'After Midnight', 'Cocaine', 'Layla' and all the others . . .
> Nevertheless, he has attained a stature with his following that goes far beyond a simple rock guitar figure, but some kind of monument to sixties rock guitar styles. With a simple elegance and a cunning gift never to let his reach overextend his grasp, Clapton etched a style that burrows down the middle of the popular fancy . . .
> It is the role of the pop musician to extract a palpable essence of the adventurous and make it play in Peoria, so to speak, a skill at which Clapton excels and that which truly sets him apart.

The climax of Clapton's tour, an impromptu one, came when he played with Jack Bruce in New York's Bottom Line Club; the two combined on 'Sunshine Of Your Love' and a sixteen-minute version of 'Spoonful'. Based on recent evidence – this, their collaboration on *Willpower* and a cameo by Bruce on the *South Bank Show* – the prospects for a Cream reunion remained uncertain. Relations between Clapton and Bruce were still brittle. Periodically, as often as once every five or ten years, one of the trio would be quoted as pining for the company of the others. Clapton and Baker became friendly again in the late 1970s. A decade later it was Clapton and Bruce (the triangular relationship, two members of the group combining to upset the third, being a Cream forte) before Bruce and Baker came together in 1990. By then, Bruce was back to his previous tack on Clapton. 'We haven't really talked in years,' he told *You* magazine. 'Eric and I were always on different paths. I was interested in the music but he was always very ambitious, very intent on becoming a big star . . . He and Robert Stigwood joined together to push him as the star of Cream.'

Clapton returned from a Japanese tour in November 1988. As he settled into Hurtwood Edge for Christmas, he was aware that his status in the public view had changed, that he was now not just a star but a celebrity. His response was curious. While Clapton's public image became more polished and urbane, in private he sank into a deeper, more consciously constructed anonymity. He continued, as always, to lead an intricate social life. After briefly trying to live with Del Santo and their son as a family Clapton had abandoned the experiment, a decision he later blamed on

> My inability to settle down ... It seems to be almost impossible for me to find myself in a relationship without wanting to get away at some point, wanting to run away and go and be a little boy again and play the guitar and misbehave. I don't know whether I'll ever grow up.

In fact, even before he made the admission, Clapton and Del Santo had parted. While he undoubtedly continued to see Conor, responsibility for the boy's upbringing fell on his mother. For a time the two commuted between Milan, their home in London and a condominium Clapton bought on their behalf in the Galleria building in New York. In 1990 Del Santo met an Italian industrialist named Silvio Sardi with whom she in turn had a child. It would be quite wrong to suggest that she and Clapton never provided a stable family background for their son. Both adults, in their different ways, contributed to Conor's welfare. But in his voluntary taking of divorced-father status – elaborate gifts and special treats tending to replace the day-to-day business of parenthood – glimmerings of Clapton's lifelong fear of commitment could be seen. The result was a man who, at the very height of his commercial and popular powers, showed few signs of subduing his own internal demons. It was still possible to see Clapton twice in the same day and leave with the unsettling feeling of having met two different men. The figure who smiled and waved at his annual charity concert at Dunsfold was the same one who cut his old friend Jim McCarty dead when the two met that winter in London.

A charge of sameness had been raised against Clapton's Albert Hall concerts in 1988. An overpowering sense of *déjà vu* greeted his performances there in 1989. After warm-up nights in Sheffield, Newcastle and Edinburgh, Clapton opened a season of twelve concerts in London on 20 January. Not only did the material* largely duplicate the running-order of

---

* 'So strong in depth,' said *The Times*, 'it could hardly go wrong,' a point echoed by Phillinganes, who describes Clapton's available repertoire as 'awesome'.

1988, by now there was a sense of routine or ritual attached to the event, something Clapton himself recognized when he said, 'I'm a very habitual person, and I like nothing more in my life than to have a routine, even if it's only a yearly project at the Royal Albert Hall. I don't see any reason for it to end. To me it's like setting up a new proms . . . I tend towards delusions of grandeur.'

The idea that Clapton, for all his knowledge and experience, might be a kind of journeyman (the title he gave his next album), more comfortable in the shadow of a strong musical figure, was lent credence by the increasing number of guests with whom he worked. In 1989 alone he appeared live with Pete Townshend, the Womacks, Carl Perkins, Tina Turner, Steve Winwood, Elton John, the Rolling Stones, Harrison and, almost inevitably, Knopfler and Collins. While most were one-off collaborations and none damaged his professional standing, they led in time to an inevitable weakening of Clapton's own stature. For nearly thirty years the guitarist had sold himself as a loner, someone whose musical integrity exceeded that of other performers. Now, that claim appeared patently false, and it was clear, as Clapton jigged onstage or pulled faces with Mick Jagger, that he no longer believed in it himself. As the eighties ended, those artists who counted their careers in decades rather than years began to coalesce in the public mind, constants like Clapton, Jagger and Harrison who were appreciated for merely existing rather than anything they said or did. It might be natural for these archetypes of British rock to band together, appearing on the same stages and surfacing on each other's albums. Inevitably, it also meant that each sacrificed a portion of his own identity with every cameo played or guest performance given. Clapton's most precious asset – independence – died in 1989.

Clapton spent much of that spring in New York, recording tracks eventually released as *Journeyman*, showing, says Phillinganes, 'remarkable devotion to the job at hand'. A second musician also confirms that 'Eric was more focused than on previous albums'. He continued, none the less, to engage in the fruitful business of soundtracks, writing themes for *Licence To Kill* (held up by a dispute between Forrester and the Bond film's producers), *Lethal Weapon 2* and *Communion*. The spirit of solidarity with his fellow sixties' originals was continued when, in a single month, Clapton played alongside Keith Richards in New York; received an award from the same guitarist; recorded Elton John's 'Border Song' for the compilation album *Two Rooms*; attended Bill Wyman's wedding reception; and appeared with Winwood and Fairweather-Low. The last were present

245

when Clapton played at Wintershall that July in support of Macmillan Nurses. (No one commented on the irony of a concert financing cancer relief being fronted by a man who chain-smoked his way through it.)

For the hundreds of thousands who bought *Two Rooms* or the remixed *Layla*, who watched profiles on TV or attended charity concerts like Wintershall, this was the image Clapton now presented. The effect of his exceptional period of activity was to consolidate his position as a stalwart of British rock: a figure of fun and nostalgia; and, above all, a survivor.

Survival for what? Though a 'slave of the blues', Clapton had long since put his servitude to good advantage. In 1959, even in 1969, there had been a mission; in 1989 there was, at best, a formula for generating cash and keeping Clapton from getting bored. The increasingly insipid songs and ritualistic concerts continued to be bought and attended in record numbers. Clapton having survived, it seemed, was enough in itself. He needed merely to turn up, guitar in hand, to send his fans home ecstatic. Having gone from cult to star to celebrity, Clapton was on the fringe of becoming something else: an institution. For several years there had been no more threats to his financial security of the kind that plagued him in the 1970s. Clapton was able, within reason, to make the kind of music he wanted. Forrester ensured that the concerts were suitably timed, and few enough in number, that sell-outs were guaranteed. The overall effect was that, barring some unpardonable lapse or public scandal – and it was hard to see what that might be – Clapton was secure, unassailable; he might continue to make anaemic records and give self-parodying performances, but the fans clung to him as an act of faith. 'By then', as George Terry says, 'it must have seemed to Eric that he'd cracked it. The only thing lacking was any challenge.'

The niche Clapton occupied as a kindly, sympathetic and above all English personality was nowhere better demonstrated than in his adoption of cricket. This sport, briefly played as a boy, returned to Clapton's attention in 1984, when there was a ritual exchange of guitar and cricket bat with Ian Botham. In the following two years Clapton attended a variety of matches, supported cricketers' charities and even founded his own team. He recorded a song called 'Fight', an agreeable piece of foolery largely composed by Botham and David English. When the Eric Clapton XI first took the field in 1986 it seemed to set the seal on a career that, having gone some way in its espousal of more exotic habits, had triumphantly returned to its roots.

The job of managing the side fell, from 1989, on David Rees. Rees remembers Clapton as a 'lousy' cricketer, fired by 'enthusiasm rather than talent', even that waning when Clapton injured a finger while batting in a charity match in 1989. More pertinently, he found 'Eric . . . a strange sort of character, withdrawn, aloof', for whom the 'shared camaraderie of cricket' ended the second stumps were drawn. Rees had the impression that the on-field ritual of the sport meant more to Clapton than its playing. 'He loved putting on accents and dressing up* – you could see him playing the part of the eccentric squire.' That Clapton valued cricket for its Englishness, bracketing it thus with fishing, was confirmed by an interview he gave at the time:

> My ideal fantasy of England when I'm away from home is going to Lord's or being by the river with a fly rod. Those are the things that sum up England for me more than anything. The fact that it rarely happens because of the weather is another matter.

The suspicion was that, whatever Clapton's feelings for the sport, the organization of his team ran, like every other part of the empire, to Forrester's direction. Rees recalls a number of 'highly businesslike' meetings in Harley House 'which clearly demonstrated Roger's keenness that the image be right'. A former Test player involved with the side also believes 'promoting Eric-the-cricketer was good for business', though 'that didn't preclude a genuine interest in the matches', which did, after all, raise thousands of pounds for charity. In a way cricket also afforded Clapton a harmless kind of relaxation – Rees states it as certain that 'Eric screwed a barmaid in the shower after a match in Northampton' – and provided an outlet for his lifelong love of play-acting and disguise. In later years he frequently checked into hotels under the alias 'Denis Compton'.

The idea that sex, drink and cricket had replaced sex, drugs and rock and roll in Clapton's affections was only partly true. In the three years he managed the team, Rees 'never once saw Eric with anything stronger than a mug of coffee'. Nothing suggests that Clapton touched alcohol again after the Michelob débâcle and his return to Hazelden. 'Whatever he was on,' says Rees, 'and he could appear almost drunk in his behaviour,

---

* Clapton's 'dressing-up' extended to commissioning a crest – a crossed bat and guitar – for the team. He wore a blazer with the emblem to a single event that summer: the Songwriters Hall of Fame dinner in Los Angeles.

it wasn't booze. Eric seemed to go from the depths of despair to a sort of giddy high, all to his own thought process. I remember him laughing aloud one day in the field at Worcester. Nothing remotely funny was happening.' Andy Peebles also recalls Clapton as 'unnerving in his mood swings'. Both men believed his involvement with cricket to have been genuine, if selective, Peebles comparing him to the England player David Gower, 'two enigmas who seemed to march to the sound of their own drums'. Rees, too, thinks there was something 'unpredictable and wilful' about Clapton – he went out of his way to do favours to people in no position to return them, handing out tickets to the Albert Hall, but shying from personal friendships – and that 'even then it was clear cricket was only a passing phase'. By 1991 Clapton had replaced the sport with an addiction to Nintendo, which, along with fly-fishing and vintage cars, proved that the consuming passions of his life were solitary.

Clapton began a European tour on 6 July 1989. Resisting the temptation to trade on recent labour, the songs recorded in New York were eschewed in favour of more trusted material: 'Crossroads', 'White Room', 'Badge' and 'Sunshine Of Your Love' were all retained, as were 'Cocaine', 'Layla' and 'Bell Bottom Blues'. The only change was the addition of Phil Palmer, a guitarist Clapton had met in the studio in 1985, who filled the role, previously undertaken by Terry, Lee and Renwick, of laying the musical foundation under Clapton's embellishments.

There was, however, a notable departure from the standard itinerary. Clapton played a series of concerts in southern Africa, ending with a charity event in Maputo, Mozambique, on 30 July. While ecstatically received in the local press, there were mutterings from at least one musician who remembered events in Birmingham about 'the rehabilitation thirteen years provided'. Clapton later told a cricketer that he was both 'affected' and 'appalled' by conditions in Africa, though he reserved his most critical judgement for the return flight to London, during which he trapped a nerve in his back.

The event, trivial in itself, seemed to confirm the intimations Clapton had made in 1986 about ageing. As has been seen, there were other problems troubling him – his smoker's cough and recurrent toothache – not to mention his vampire's complexion and changeable weight. Though enjoying generally fair health – miraculously fair, for someone of his lifestyle – Clapton still experienced the usual ailments. At about the time he returned from Africa, his eyesight began to deteriorate. His hearing, after years of exposure to pain-threshold noise, was indifferent. A new beard, restored after Clapton's clean-shaven interlude, was noticeably flecked with grey. To his credit, Clapton accepted all the familiar and tedious rituals of middle age, commenting on them wryly in the press and cheerfully admitting that his fingers, the tools of Clapton's trade, now 'took time to get loose'. As Dave Markee says, 'Being a guitarist, not a singer, he could look forward to a career in his fifties and sixties ... Even so, Eric was sensitive to ageing. He felt insecure playing with people younger than he was.' Coincidentally or not, Clapton appeared that autumn with Townshend, Elton John and the Rolling Stones, all of a vintage comparable to, or greater than himself.

The Stones connection came about when Clapton rang Jane Rose, Keith Richards's manager, asking for tickets to the group's concert in New York. Rose in turn invited him on stage. The result was a rousing version of 'Little Red Rooster' and, according to a partner at Peat Marwick, the auditors for the tour, 'a *Satyricon*-like scene backstage where Eric and Bill [Wyman], in particular, rooted themselves silly', the two events both reprised eight weeks later on the Stones' closing night in Atlantic City.

It was not only by immersing himself with other sixties musicians that Clapton showed signs of age. In 1989 he appeared on both *Wogan* and Sue Lawley's *Saturday Matters*, continuing or even completing the process of becoming a family entertainer, while, on 18 November, he returned to the Albert Hall alongside Billy Connolly, Pamela Stephenson and members of the Royal Ballet in a concert sponsored by Parents For Safe Food.

All this activity preceded the release of *Journeyman*, Clapton's first new album in three years. In claiming to have been 'firm in making sure the record was for me . . . that I was going to be singing it and that you were [just] going to be accompanying me if you were in the studio', Clapton implied a more cohesive work than the sprawling stylistic hybrids of *Behind The Sun* and *August*. For one, Collins was replaced as producer by Russ Titelman. Jerry Williams, the songwriter called in by Warners to salvage *Behind The Sun*, returned; he, Harrison, Daryl Hall, Robert Cray, Chaka Khan and the Womacks ensured that, however unified in concept, *Journeyman* was at best motley in performance. The first track, 'Pretending', was typical: an elaborately played rocker with impeccable guitar, vocals in exquisite taste, neither of which diminished the song's strong resemblance to one of Clapton's film soundtracks. 'Anything For Your Love' was the aural equivalent of designer fashion, a seamlessly executed blues pastiche wholly devoid of passion. At this stage, eighteen years after it was first entered, Clapton finally succumbed to the plea for 'another "Layla"'. 'Bad Love' began, as that had, with anthemic guitar tapering into a first verse addressing, as had 'Layla', a woman; the hard-rock drums, rippling piano and gritty vocals were all present. For good measure the middle section of 'Badge' was thrown in. All that separated 'Bad Love' from 'Layla' was the experience of two decades. In 1971 Clapton had sung of despair, of begging, of going insane; in 1989 he declared himself 'one of the lucky people'. If ever there was proof that energy expended as an entertainer and social worker was energy forfeited as a songwriter and performer, this was it. Where once Clapton's light-weight music had been at odds with the *angst*-ridden lyrics, the opposite was true of 'Bad Love'. The raucousness of the opening guitar raised expectations never fulfilled by the message. It may be unfair to single out the words for special attention, but there was something about the lines 'And now I see that my life has been so blue/With all the heartaches I had till I met you' that was almost satirically inept. 'Running On Faith', at least, had music and lyrics written by the same man (Williams); the result was exactly the kind of soft-focus, undemanding ballad at which Clapton excelled. The side ended with a convincing version of Ray Charles's 'Hard Times' and the laughable rock and roll flummery of 'Hound Dog', complete with growling effects by Forrester.

Side Two opened with 'No Alibis', more from the same pop landscape covered by everyone from Elton John to Hüsker Dü. Harrison guested on the forgettable 'Run So Far', seguing tactfully into 'Old Love', Clapton's latest effort to rationalize his feelings about Boyd. If musicians, like the rest of us, rarely cast off the behavioural patterns of their youth, it was fitting for Clapton to strike a lachrymose note in writing about his ex-wife. Boyd, it seemed, had left him nonplussed, bewildered, 'angry/ To know that the flame still burns'. These were the lyrics that more properly belonged to 'Bad Love'. Instead, welded to a sepulchral, down-beat tempo, they came across as maudlin – Clapton had *had* Boyd and lost her – an effect one reviewer described as 'cravenly self-indulgent'. 'Old Love' was, at least, recognizably Clapton's. The next song, 'Breaking Point', would have fitted more easily on a Huey Lewis album. It gave way to the absurdly, almost wilfully banal 'Lead Me On' before sprinting to the finish with 'Before You Accuse Me', a back-to-the-roots rave-up by Bo Diddley.

With the recent spate of guest appearances, film scores, awards and repackaged collections of old glories – taken to new depths by Polygram's release of a CD of, among other titles, *Time Pieces*, making an anthology of a compilation – it was easy to forget how long it was since Clapton had last written a decent song. Of *Journeyman*'s twelve tracks his name appeared on just two, and even then linked to that of a collaborator. On the other hand, as a commercial venture the album was a substantial if unexceptional success. It gave innocent pleasure to over a million fans. Its failure was, in the end, a failure of Clapton's nerve; there was some high-brow stuff, but for the most part he shunned altitude in favour of the sleepy-time ballads and old-fashioned rock singalongs for which *Journeyman* is remembered. While no one doubted the sincerity of his efforts, the hard truth was that Clapton was not best placed to re-create either the lush production values or naïve, rough-and-ready feel that made these styles relevant to their times. With little or no effort to interpret the songs, he simply pasted the occasional guitar solo on to the basic arrangements. As a painless and sometimes impressive medley of the rock, pop, jazz and blues working practices of the last thirty years, *Journeyman* was a respectable effort. As an Eric Clapton album it was a nonentity.

Clapton's remuneration from Marshbrook in 1989 was £629,763, a nearly 40 per cent increase on the previous year. E. C. Music turned over a total of £153,576 and paid Clapton £95,000. He needed the money, since in his years at the top he had acquired some expensive tastes. As well as maintaining Hurtwood Edge, Clapton bought a holiday home in Antigua and a duplex apartment – occupied by del Santo – in New York. He continued to collect fast cars and designer clothes. At the same time, he could affect a notably unostentatious, almost commonplace appearance in public. On 5 November 1989 Clapton attended a Guy Fawkes celebration on Ripley Green, where he was seen by Noel Chelberg, 'alone, wearing a battered green coat and exuding the opposite of rock star chic'. He still enjoyed near hallowed status in the local community. Clapton compensated for his relative decline on the international stage by taking up constituency causes more diligently than ever. This was one area, as Duncan Caine observes, 'where Eric stood head and shoulders above any other star'. Money was still donated, generously and without fuss, to local charities. Clapton still gave unstintingly of his time to the Cranleigh Round Table. Anyone could approach him in Ewhurst or Ripley high street and be rewarded with an autograph or a friendly word. Within four days of performing with the Rolling Stones in Atlantic City, Clapton was on stage for a charity Christmas show at Chiddingford Ex-Serviceman's Club, happily playing to a few hundred villagers and assuring them it was 'the night of [his] life'.

When Clapton had discovered cricket in 1984 he also characteristically discovered a liking for the sport's attractive female spectators. If 1989 was the year in which Clapton became a British way of life, it was also the year in which another domestic institution, the tabloid press, developed an interest in his private life.

The gossip columnists' gaze had first fallen on Clapton at the time of his separation from Boyd. The self-fulfilling roles sometimes acted out by those in the public eye was something he recognized: 'When it got into the papers . . . it really did hurt, because it hadn't occurred to me up until that point that it was really anyone else's business. And when you see it all in black and white it tends to become almost a little too real. You start believing what you read.'

That was in 1985. Four years later, when the couple's divorce was aired, cuttings files were ransacked and photo libraries scoured to dramatize what was, by any standards, a remarkably civilized parting. Clapton had in fact some significant support, mainly from middlebrow titles like the *Daily Mail* and *Express*. But he regarded most journalists as basically hostile – 'animals', he once called them – and recorded, but never released, a song for *Journeyman* called 'Murdoch's Men'. Clapton himself was at his best with the correspondents of the music press, especially the Americans, who concentrated largely on the professional life and not at all on the private.

The reverse was true, in particular, of the *Sun* and *Daily Mirror*. By the end of the decade, both of these publications regularly included gossip about Clapton's love-life. Among the rumoured relationships, the most notorious was said to be with Grace Jones (with whom Clapton had a social friendship). The most serious was with the Italian model Carla Bruni. Clapton and Bruni – in whom there was a passing resemblance to the svelte, dark-haired Del Santo – spent much of that autumn together in Europe, Hurtwood Edge and America. The relationship ended at Christmas, by which time Clapton had introduced Bruni to Mick Jagger. There, matters might have rested but for the claim by Jerry Hall, seized on by the press, that the model had promptly transferred her affections from one rock star to another. The business came to a head in July 1992, when Jagger was reported as living with Bruni in, variously, London, Rome, Milan, New York, Los Angeles and, most colourfully, the Amanpuri Hotel, Phuket. The event, briefly revived when Hall made a commercial referring archly to her husband's liking for 'Italian pasta', was already forgotten by the time the couple reconciled three months later.

Jagger, at least, was an old hand at dealing with the personal scrutiny of the media. For Clapton it was a relatively new experience. He responded with a mixture of fear, loathing, indifference and occasional winning goodwill. He took a keen interest in his public image. At heart, says Markee, Clapton 'had a longing to speak direct to people without the distorting influence of Fleet Street'. It hardly needs saying that those vehicles approved by Forrester – *The South Bank Show*, for instance – were selected for the flattering light they were likely to shed on Clapton's career. It was the rogue elements of the media (the gossip columnist or unauthorized biographer) whose motives were suspected. On his own terms, and sufficiently prepared for the ordeal, Clapton could be a relaxed and fluent interviewee. He bridled only when the questioning became intrusive or personal. No one blamed him for that. It was perhaps unfortunate that, in so successfully raising his profile since 1985, Clapton ran the risk of attracting a correspondingly raised interest from the press.

A sidelight on Clapton's ability to 'speak direct to people' is given by Steve Judson, a fan present at the Metropole Hotel, Birmingham, in January 1990. Clapton appeared on the evening of the 14th, 'very friendly, open and unassuming', though complaining of having trapped a finger in his bedroom door. The difference between Clapton-the-household-name and Clapton-the-man was striking. Nothing could have better symbolized the contrast than his willingness, having confirmed Judson was alone, to speak 'quite candidly and at length' about his music, access that would have taken months, or an eternity, to arrange through management channels. Judson came away with the sense of a 'quiet, genuinely modest' person 'chronically shy of back-slappers', happier to talk about 'stagecraft, rather than personal matters' and bitterly convinced that elements of the media were biased against him.

Clapton's fourth season at the Albert Hall confirmed that familiarity had bred, if not contempt, at least a sense of *ennui* among the press. According to *The Times* and the *Guardian*, the only two broadsheets to send reviewers to the concerts, he was, respectively, 'the grand old man of British blues' and 'one of rock's sixties legends who has never quite lived up to his nickname of "God"'. Clapton could, of course, be an articulate and even engaging speaker, particularly to journalists to whom he could open his mind frankly on a musical level, without fear of being distorted. But he had a low opinion of entertainment and diary writers, and did not bother to hide it; the result was that Clapton came into disfavour with many of the columnists in whose territory he most naturally fell. By becoming a theatrical figure while clinging stubbornly to his own self-image as a serious musician, he risked alienating or at best irritating the powerful showbusiness critics' lobby, who retaliated by either ignoring Clapton or referring disparagingly to his 'sameness'.

In the event, the word was singularly inapt for the series of eighteen concerts that opened that January. The season was divided into four separate formats: six nights each with Clapton in a four-piece and thirteen-piece group; three blues nights; and three backed by the National Philharmonic Orchestra. (Clapton had warmed up by playing an orchestrated version of *Edge of Darkness* at a concert the previous November.) For the first time in three years the running order of the shows was significantly altered, with generous helpings of *Journeyman* inserted at the expense of songs like 'Forever Man' and 'Behind The Mask'. Finally, Clapton himself took a noticeably more robust, stage-front approach, apparently relishing the glamorously exalted image his fans foisted on him, smiling broadly, encouraging the musicians, and informing *Guitar World*, 'I don't want to get out of the fucking way. I want to be in the front row. Maybe I didn't [in the sixties], but I do now.'

The resulting music was either likeable and inspired or likeable but uninspired, according to Clapton's whim. Rock-bottom was touched on the orchestral nights. This particular conceit, entered into by Clapton and Michael Kamen, proved for all time the incompatibility of rock and classical music played live. There was a complete lack of counterpoint in the melody, not to mention the matter of playing in a different time scale. The four- and thirteen-piece nights also saw Clapton on variable form. On standards like 'Layla' he could give the impression of losing interest in the material, his voice lapsing into a heavily mannered, strangulated growl, almost as if he were using the lyrics as a mouthwash. His guitar-playing often had the same perfunctory quality. It was only on the blues nights, in the company of men like Robert Cray, Buddy Guy and Chuck Berry's pianist Johnnie Johnson, that Clapton invariably excelled. Cray in particular had a salutary effect, transforming him from the grey-bearded, beloved family entertainer into something approaching the raunchy R&B merchant of old. (Cray, too, came to the blues as a convert.) True, the vast majority of the material pre-dated 1960 and leant heavily on the writers, producers and performers of the previous era, but there was no denying the panache Clapton brought to the arrangements. There was particular praise for 'Have You Ever Loved A Woman' and Cray's own 'Same Thing'.

If the blues nights, relaxed but emotionally charged, were the height of Clapton's season, the depths were reached on the evenings he stood in his dinner jacket and floppy bouffant, seemingly lost among the props of his self-confessed delusions of grandeur – the xylophones, piccolos and French horns – glancing uncertainly in Kamen's direction and giving the impression, according to the *Guardian*, of having 'wandered capriciously onto the wrong stage'. A double live album of the eighteen nights, to be called *Four Faces Of Eric Clapton*, was later scrapped. Fans had to content themselves with *Journeyman* and the accompanying single, 'Bad Love', the latter in a collector's edition including two colour postcards and an impression of Clapton's family tree.

The tour moved to Scandinavia, Europe and America, where Clapton opened at the Omni, Atlanta, on 28 March. There was a guest appearance on *Saturday Night Live*; Clapton was presented with a Living Legend Award at a ceremony in New York; Harrison materialized on stage in Los Angeles. Those were the highlights of a tour successful in that, though Clapton was better on some nights than others, the audience was never bored. The group, notably the excitable Ray Cooper, saw to that. Those who tended to listen to Clapton's playing and singing in isolation – critics, for instance – detected, in the *Weekly*'s phrase, 'an almost folkish atmosphere, as Clapton made up in melodic finesse anything lacking in guitar heroics'. It might seem churlish to comment, as the paper did, on the 'thinness' of a single instrument within the overall mix. Yet Clapton had not dispelled the notion of being a one-man band; on the contrary, as he told *Guitar World*, he encouraged it. No single musician, *Rolling Stone* suggested, had ever been the focus of so much attention within a supposedly collective group. It was only natural that the concerts would be seen as successes or failures as Clapton himself succeeded or failed, or the work of Cooper and the rest as the necessary dirt from which exquisite flowers grew.

The two halves of the tour were separated by a month's holiday in Antigua. Clapton was seen there in June, though the press never successfully learnt the names of the women or woman who accompanied him. The affair with Bruni had ended; a relationship with Michelle Pfeiffer lay in the future. A bodyguard of gigantic proportion, whose jacket bulged significantly by one armpit, discouraged further speculation. All that was known was that 'someone' had joined Clapton in his home outside St John's, eating lobster in the beachside hotel, though eschewing the local rum, and that he himself enjoyed a 'weakness for women', a preference for women to men and a press campaign he characterized as 'people trying to marry me off'.

Clapton certainly continued to seek out female company (though not, he insisted to Sue Lawley, necessarily extending that into sex). His motives for doing so may not have been those he mentioned. Clapton had famously ambivalent feelings about women. Pete Brown was only one in a long line of friends who formed the opinion 'Eric felt threatened by the opposite sex'. Clapton was not far into his teens when Matthew Wood concluded 'he pathologically hated his mother'. According to Philip Solly, 'he always drew your attention to her shortcomings'. In later years Clapton's treatment of both Martin and Ormsby-Gore was almost old-fashioned in its advancement of the man over the woman. Boyd herself noted him as a chauvinist. It is not stretching belief to say that Clapton needed women to make good a crippling lack of self-confidence. Pat's defection was a blow that helped to shape his personality, making him more lonely, single-minded and suspicious than a Wood or Solly. The sense of maternal love which nourished other children was closed off entirely. Clapton compensated, first by shunning women altogether, then, as a rock star, by accumulating them as trophies. He collected girlfriends in the same way he collected anything. He adopted a policy of safety-in-numbers. Although Clapton was rarely without a blonde or an Italian model in tow, the relationships still acted out the rites, manners and forms of language he learnt as a boy. This meant a permanent apparatus of self-containment and the putting of distance, only breached by Boyd, between himself and the woman. So far as Clapton ever let himself go, it was with a series of animals and household pets – his best friend as a child had been his dog – with whom he abandoned himself in a carefree display of emotion, an uninhibited effusion of irresponsibility, happiness and love.

In short, Clapton presented a vulnerable, lost and irresistible image to women, many of whom saw it as a personal challenge to penetrate his formidable reserve. It was one of the peculiar paradoxes of his life that while everything got better, he experienced it as having worsened. Never had Clapton been wealthier, more admired or better cared for; never had he looked so woebegone. Clapton had never been so free; never had he

256

seemed so trapped. Sympathy for him even extended to the media. 'I think journalists probably feel sorry for me,' he told *Rolling Stone*. On other occasions he spoke of the eternal desire of girlfriends to mother him, or, failing that, to bear his children. One woman, the strikingly named Baroness Manga-Moarea Cefalu, took this to unnatural lengths in claiming to be pregnant by Clapton, briefing a lawyer to bring proceedings while she traversed Europe with a cushion in her skirts.

Clapton returned from Antigua in time to play at the year's major rock event, the Nordoff-Robbins benefit concert at Knebworth. Starting with Bangladesh, nearly twenty years before, Clapton was always ready to lend his name to causes, even those in which his personal involvement was tenuous. It may be harsh to question the motives of someone who was often generous, but there were those, like Jonathan King, who detected melodrama in Clapton's near-annual effusions on behalf of one charity or another. According to them, Clapton's lachrymose statements or outpourings of love could be seen as emotion for its own sake, deliberately willed and partial, whipped up and played for, self-dramatized, and gratuitously linking his name with the fashionable causes of the day.

Another explanation is that Clapton both wanted and needed the chance to perform, the central relationship of his life being that between himself and the audience. It is worth noting that, at a time when other sixties musicians had restricted their appearances to the occasional gala or set-piece event, Clapton continued to play and tour with the relish of a teenager. He gave 112 concerts in 1990. No sooner had Clapton left the stage at Knebworth than he was rehearsing for the second leg of the American tour, opening on 23 July in Miami.

It was after a show in Alpine Valley, East Troy, a month later that the guitarist Stevie Ray Vaughan, along with three members of Clapton's entourage, Bobby Brooks, Nigel Browne and Colin Smythe, were killed in a helicopter crash. While much was made in the headlines of Clapton's brush with death – the more imaginative versions had him declining a seat on the flight due to a premonition – a more reliable account was the one he gave to James Henke:

There was a convoy of helicopters, about five of them, and they had to go back through this very thick fog up to about a hundred feet above the ground. And once we came out of that, we just took off for Chicago. And when I got back, I went straight to bed. And I was woken about seven in the morning by my manager saying that the helicopter with Stevie Ray and our chaps hadn't come back. And then a bit later, someone discovered the wreckage. That was it.

After a meeting chaired by Clapton and Forrester it was agreed that the tour would go on.* When the initial shock had worn off – the loss of Vaughan, recently recovering from alcoholism, was especially harrowing – the press were left to ruminate on Clapton's strange propensity to attract violence and death. From Hendrix and Allman, through to Relf, Radle and Grech, to say nothing of Jim Gordon, the casualty rate among his friends and colleagues was remarkable. Bobby Whitlock strikes a nerve when he speaks of 'the shadow over Eric's life . . . It seems he was born for suffering like a bird for the air or a fish for the sea.' George Terry also notes that the loss of so many partners 'hardly sweetened' a character already prone to melancholy. No one, not even the most credulous believers in the black arts, suggested that close association with Clapton was in itself invariably harmful (though Radle's final illness could be attributed to the lifestyle he led under his friend's influence); being forced to witness and then brood on fate's implacable malice was, however, Clapton's lot. He could have been forgiven his moments of introspection. He *had* had a harder life than some. When, a year after Vaughan's death, Clapton's old friend Bill Graham was killed in identical fashion, it seemed to be of a piece with an ominously fated existence. As has been seen, there were other reasons for Clapton's generally gloomy view of life – 'Every day I find something I'm going to suffer about', he told a magazine – and it was arguable that his maudlin side more than once lapsed into self-pity. Even so, to maintain as he now did that 'I've survived, and therefore I've got some kind of responsibility' showed a welcome advance from the egotistical and self-indulgent character of old. When Hendrix had died in 1970 Clapton promptly surrendered to a 'terrible, lonely' feeling that accelerated his own retirement and near-fatal decline. Twenty years later, when a man with whom he had stood on stage minutes earlier was also killed, Clapton would only say that 'Life is fragile, and . . . if you are given another twenty-four hours, it's a blessing.' A journalist who knew him well in both periods adds simply: 'Eric grew up, in the sense of accepting grief without personal paranoia, in his mid-forties. It took him longer than most, but he did it.'

* Clapton attended Nigel Browne's funeral in London.

258

From the US, Clapton went on to tour South America, Australia, the Far East and Japan, culminating in a deliriously received concert in Yokohama on 13 December. He also took the opportunity to re-record 'Bad Love' for a commercial selling Hondas. (It joined 'Layla' and 'I Feel Free' in being used to advertise cars. Pete Brown is still fuming about the latter.) The benefit of all this activity – the touring, soundtracks, commercials and the royalties from *Journeyman* – was impressive. If a man is known by the company that keeps him, Clapton prospered dramatically from his directorship of Marshbrook. In 1990 he earned a total of £5,097,553, a nearly tenfold increase on 1989, making him one of the highest-paid executives in Britain. Marshbrook, of which E. C. Music became a wholly owned subsidiary, turned over £11,253,343, of which £8 million came from North America, recording a gross profit of £6,459,133. Clapton, after years of being rich, had entered the realms of the Rolling Stones and ex-Beatles.

Of all the many ironies of Clapton's life, his achieving millionaire status was probably the most noteworthy, if only because of the exquisite timing. It occurred just at the moment that, after years of dressing up, Clapton announced himself 'no longer obsessed by clothes' and again stressing his egalitarian, working-class credentials. While outstandingly modest in some ways and lavish in his support of working-class values, Clapton was particularly adept at pretending to be the opposite of what he was. When a musician friend met him in London that Christmas he found 'Eric claiming to be broke and talking in a put-on Gorblimey accent'. David Rees also remembers the 'humble artisan' as one of the masks Clapton carried in his sizeable internal wardrobe. Bobby Whitlock confirms that inverted snobbery was at work as early as Derek and the Dominos. As the year ended, Clapton was again in Hurtwood Edge, charming villagers and kissing babies like a campaigning politician. He denied being well-off, yet owned a company whose turnover was that of a small conglomerate. Clapton's unpretentious instincts did him credit. Journalists who interviewed him came away genuinely impressed by his diffidence; profiles invariably referred to his modesty and reserve. Less convinced was the woman living in Newark Lane, Ripley, for whom Clapton, whose sole purpose in talking to people 'was to see his own reflection in their eyes', continued to compensate aggressively for the insecurity instilled in him as a boy. The rich, famous and fulfilled man whom the world saw still considered himself a victim maimed for life by that early catastrophic shock.

10

Legend

In the fifties Bill Haley and the rest, whose rebelliousness may have been more proverbial than real, redefined pop as teenage music; it was inconceivable that anyone in their twenties, let alone over thirty, could be part of the audience. The music business itself was an *ad hoc* affair, employing none of the marketing and PR techniques so prevalent later. Forty years on, the trade had become mature and sophisticated in its machinations, the embodiment rather than the opposite of mainstream commerce, in which the 'oldie', AOR or New Age trouper was likely to be dusted off and repackaged at the expense of the caterwauling new-comer. What was once all youthful defiance was now civilized and even adult industry, dominated, as Adam Sweeting says, 'by back-catalogue reissues, nostalgic monthly magazines replete with car and hi-fi ads, and the systematic watering-down of rock's golden years with institutions such as the soporific *Unplugged* concert series'.

Clapton and his management understood this and played on it brilli-antly. Somewhere after Live Aid it seems to have dawned on Forrester that a steady supply of repackagings, anthologies, compilations and live LPs could sustain a career just as well as the tedious business of releasing new material. From 1966 to 1976 there were eleven Clapton albums recorded all or in part in the studio; in the next decade, six. Since 1986 the audience had had to make do with the forty-odd minutes of *Journey-man* and bizarre special offers such as a drawing of Clapton's family tree. Whatever the merits of his live performances, and, to his credit, he continued to tour voraciously, it was difficult to escape the impression that Clapton had run out of creative steam. His career now was a matter of smart reshuffling of familiar formulae. 'The grand old man' welcomed by *The Times* to the Albert Hall was just that: a beloved and staid senior professional whose choice of a Victorian concert-hall as his second home seemed more fitting with each passing year.

Clapton opened a season of twenty-four nights at the venue on 5 February 1991. The four formats of the previous year were retained (the thirteen-piece group pared to nine); the orchestral nights were doubled to six. At his best, in a band supported by East, Ferrone, Phillinganes, Palmer, Cooper and the pianist Chuck Leavell, Clapton was impressive, his guitar buzzing and soaring over the rhythm section like a stunt pilot. At his worst – the orchestral nights – he seemed tired and listless, as though the actual performance was no more than a soundcheck. Clapton's most reliable asset was his voice, a rich and full-bodied instrument improved since 1990 and unrecognizable from the wheedling twang of his youth.

The inevitable live album, *24 Nights*, was released that autumn. While much was made of the apparent spontaneity of the work ('This is an all live recording,' read the sleeve-notes. 'No overdubbing or fixes') *24 Nights* was, in fact, a medley of Clapton's 1990 and 1991 seasons: thus 'Badge' and its neighbour 'Running On Faith', separated only by Clapton's 'Good evening', actually spanned an interval of thirteen months. The audience calling for a song was not necessarily the same one applauding it later. Having said that, there were satisfying and even outstanding moments on *24 Nights*, such as the solo on 'White Room' or Clapton's vocals on 'Bell Bottom Blues'. There was even a stripped-down and surprisingly moving version of 'Wonderful Tonight'. Too often, though, the album bore little trace of the irresistible rock spirit with which Clapton had first achieved chart success; instead, its flat and downbeat mood seemed guaranteed to confuse listeners hoping for another dose of Cream-like chords. At the Albert Hall, before admittedly adoring crowds, Clapton proved stubbornly unwilling to take the easy path to success, relying on tastefully arranged but insipid versions of standards and the *folie de grandeur* of the orchestral nights over the true spirit of invention.

Among the reviews of *24 Nights* was one in *Musician* calling it 'ill-conceived and sluggishly executed . . . the product of a bored and lack-lustre band, redeemed by moments of mild inspiration'. According to the *Guardian*, it was 'whimsical and contrived'. Clapton himself hastened to join such consensus. 'In hindsight, I can see that I was tired,' he told James Henke. 'I'd done a whole year of touring, and I wasn't really up to it . . . We had to scrape the barrel a lot to come up with a good selection.' As the first Clapton album in two years – and the first live offering in a decade – 24 *Nights* made precarious sense. Five of the songs were merely lifted from *Journeyman*; two others had been present on Clapton's last concert LP, *Just One Night*; incredibly, 'Layla' was again missing. The idea that 24 *Nights* might have been a barefaced effort to boost profits, a cashing-in on the uncritical loyalty (and disposable income) of older Clapton fans, was underlined by the 'limited edition' comprising two CDs, a scrapbook of drawings and 'items of memorabilia pasted in by hand', a commentary by Derek Taylor and sundry badges, backstage passes and guitar picks – the whole signed by Clapton – on sale for £225. The income from this, the accompanying video and Clapton's back catalogue contributed to a payment of £3,867,124 from Marshbrook (exclusive of £115,971 from E. C. Music), a substantial drop from 1990, but enough to keep Clapton on the list of Britain's best-paid directors.

Clapton repaid the favour to Buddy Guy and Johnnie Johnson, two of his sidemen at the Albert Hall, by making guest appearances on their albums. He followed them, in mid-March, by playing on Richie Sambora's LP *Stranger In This Town*. The process by which these cameos came about was revealed by Clapton to *Rolling Stone*:

> [Sambora] really put me on the spot. It was a nightmare. I got a very sweet, dedicated letter from him, and I was deeply touched, my ego was pumped up . . . I showed up at the studio, and he gave me a gift, which was a massive twelve-string Taylor guitar with my name on it . . . And then he put the tape on, and I realized instantly that I was completely out of my depth. The song wasn't what I expected it to be, and I had to sit down and go down to the bottom of my socks and pull up whatever I had to make it work . . . So there goes your reputation right out the window.

(Sambora himself is more sanguine, saying of Clapton, 'I told him the chance to talk to him was like him getting the chance to talk to Robert Johnson.')

The rest of the year was supposed to be a holiday for Clapton. Since June 1989 he had toured America, Europe, Scandinavia, the Middle East, Japan and Africa, appeared live with Elton John and the Rolling Stones, performed benefits and charities and completed two record-breaking seasons at the Albert Hall. It was a widespread, and probably valid, complaint that he took too much on himself, constantly lobbying Forrester for work when even the latter would have been happy with a period of royalty-counting and relaxation. On the other hand, the risk that Clapton might glut the market was avoided by the careful choice of venues and halls – few of which, with the exception of London, were ever repeated – and the nucleus of fans who would travel anywhere within distance to see Clapton play, no matter how small the interval between concerts. It was rather in Forrester's favour that, despite managing a man who made Frank Sinatra seem stage-shy by comparison, the performances invariably sold out, inevitably to respectful popular (if not always critical) notices. Clapton since Live Aid had been outstandingly successful, and there was a great deal of which he and his manager could fairly boast. If a performer is assessed by the simple measure of popularity, then Clapton from 1985 to 1991 scores remarkably well. Although many of the best reviews depended on the nostalgic forgiveness of the reviewer, Clapton was by any definition a famous, highly esteemed and treasured entertainer, few of whose fans would have begrudged him the nine-month break he now planned.

All that came to a tragic end on 20 March 1991 when Clapton's son Conor fell to his death from the fifty-third floor of the Galleria Building in New York. Clapton himself was in New York; he and Conor had been to the Ringling Brothers circus the previous day. According to a family friend, Ed White, the plan had been for 'Eric to take a year off work to spend time with his son'; a neighbour of Clapton in Ewhurst also says, 'He was worrying about Conor constantly, whether he was doing enough for the boy.' It was among the most sorry ironies of a life not untouched by shadow that Conor's death should have occurred at the very moment his father, after four and a half years of relative neglect, should have decided to narrow the gap between them.

As 1991 began, Clapton's feelings of curiosity and love for his son continued to grow. Where once Conor had been the cause of only guilt-ridden expressions of regret, now he loomed large and weighty in Clapton's letters and conversation. Relations with Del Santo, who maintained custody of the child, also improved. She, Conor and the Italian tycoon Silvio Sardi were ensconced in the duplex on East 57th Street purchased by Clapton for £3 million; she retained homes in Milan and London. When Clapton flew to New York in mid-March it was for the express purpose of seeing Del Santo and the mop-haired youngster whom neighbours recall capering in the Galleria's chrome and marble lobby, dressed in an Armani sweatshirt and looking, in the words of one resident, Evelyn de Maria, 'like the sort of child who could break your heart'.

The cause of the accident, breathlessly aired in the tabloid press, was later established as a mixture of negligence and childlike curiosity. According to New York police, a housekeeper cleaning the apartment had opened a picture window in order to air a bedroom. The child wandered into the room in his pyjamas, climbed on to the ledge – there was speculation that he was apeing the trapeze artists at the circus – overbalanced and fell 750 feet on to the roof of an adjacent building.

A contributory factor, it emerged, was the absence of protective window guards, mandatory in New York State in apartments housing children under twelve. Among the more excitable reports of the accident was one in the *Sun* claiming, 'Shattered rock star Eric Clapton could be JAILED after his little son fell to his death . . . Clapton could face up to a year in prison, a fine or both . . . But a City Hall official said: "It is highly unlikely we would want to capitalize on a tragedy such as this." ' Legal proceedings were never brought against Clapton. He did, however, record a public safety film some weeks later, warning other parents of their responsibility and speaking movingly of his own loss.

Contacted by Del Santo, Clapton had arrived at the scene minutes after Conor's death. His own description, given six months later to James Henke, is both affecting and direct. Clapton kept his emotions guarded, persuading himself to 'go inside (him)self', disguising one kind of feeling as well as ventilating another:

> I didn't believe it . . . I was here in this hotel when it happened, only about ten blocks down the road. And the phone rang and I picked it up and Lori was on the other end, and she was hysterical. She said that Conor was dead. And I thought, 'Well, this is ridiculous. Don't be silly.' I said, 'Are you sure?' . . . And then I just went off the edge of the world for a while. I ran down there, and I saw paramedic equipment everywhere, and ambulances and police cars . . . Somehow I went into another mode. I took charge. And then right after that I started going to a lot of AA meetings and talking about it.

Conor Clapton was buried in the churchyard of St Mary Magdalen, Ripley, on 28 March. Among the mourners were Clapton, in dark suit and sunglasses, Boyd, Harrison and Phil Collins. Uninvited but also present were members of the press who brawled and shouted behind barricades erected immediately beside the grave. The Reverend Christopher Elson, a man fiercely protective of Clapton's privacy, read St Mark 10: 13–16, before remonstrating violently with the *Sun* photographer and the stringer from *Hello!* 'A lot of people were upset and insulted by the lack of respect,' says Clapton. 'But it didn't impinge on my own grief in any way.' As the cortège made its way to Hurtwood Edge Clapton stopped and thanked a local woman who offered her condolences. She had the impression from the exchange that 'Eric didn't want to show how much he missed Conor. It was business-as-usual. The feeling [in the village] was that he'd lost the person who had shaped his life more than anyone else.'

Among those who sent sympathy were Keith Richards, Mayall, Bruce and Baker, and (testifying to Clapton's social assimilation) Prince Charles and members of the Kennedy family.* Hate mail also came in – anonymous and frequently rambling accusations that Clapton had contributed to his son's death. Finally, there was a substantial and sometimes crudely sexual correspondence from women, a gigantic repository of maternal, marital and compassionate instincts of which Clapton said, 'There [was] a kind of woman I think that saw it as a fantastic opportunity for either gain or, maybe, even to give me something. I had letters from women who wanted to be surrogate wives with families. I had letters from women who said I have got a girl who is four and we would love to move in with you and help you start your life again.'

Almost all Clapton's correspondents, elements of the press, and above all his fans and public agreed, in the words of Linda Chandler, that 'fate seemed to pick on Eric unfairly'. In the matter of losing friends or loved ones, Clapton was certainly unfortunate: in the past year alone Rick Grech, Vaughan, Brooks, Browne, Smythe and now Conor had all met sudden deaths; on 21 March, the day after Conor's accident, Leo Fender, the designer whose guitar Clapton made famous, also died. It said volumes for his new sense of maturity that Clapton eschewed drink or drugs in the months following his losses. Now, in spite (and because) of the listless mood which descended as soon as he stopped working, he became gradually more susceptible to the idea of company at Hurtwood Edge. Anyone making the transition from the outside world to Clapton's home knew they were crossing the Rubicon which divided his public image from

---

* Dave Markee also wrote. He notes without bitterness that 'nothing was ever heard from Eric' after January 1983.

more truthful ways of talking. A woman who did so remembers 'Eric seeming very calm and relaxed, which was his way of dealing with it'. Clapton himself later spoke of '[being] scared that I wasn't suffering enough, and [having] to go into analysis to sort that out a bit'.

By the middle of the summer, Clapton had begun venturing back into the public eye. He was photographed at Wimbledon with Tatum O'Neal (fuelling rumours of a romance) and at dinner with Cher (ditto). In September, six months after Conor's death, Clapton returned to New York. Despite giving one observer the impression of being 'steely, rather than elegiac' about his fate Clapton was sufficiently moved to put Hurt-wood Edge, his home of twenty-two years, on the market. At £2 million (fifty times the amount Clapton had paid in 1969) the house attracted only passing interest; after nine months it was withdrawn from sale. Clapton did, however, commission a wholesale refurbishment of the property and meanwhile bought a six-bedroomed house in Old Church Street, Chelsea, described by Tim Rice, who also viewed it, as 'tasteful, but a shade steep at £1.5 million'. In New York Clapton stayed with friends, in hotels or at the Galleria, where his neighbours included Domingo, Pavarotti, Sinatra, and, closer to home, Billy Joel and Bob Dylan.

Clapton had started to write as a form of therapy in the days immediately following Conor's death. That was for his own sake. A more commercial outlet was his acceptance of a commission to write music for *Rush*, the film version of Kim Wozencraft's novel dealing with a narcotics agent who becomes addicted. ('I saw the movie and was impressed by the low-key documentary style of it,' he says.) A total of fifteen pieces were recorded in Los Angeles, including in late September a song which came to epitomize Clapton's latter-day output just as 'Crossroads' or 'Layla' had embodied his earlier work. When 'Tears In Heaven' first appeared on the soundtrack of *Rush*, it proved for all time that Clapton's voice and ability to fashion a memorable hook were as integral to his popularity as his guitar-playing.

24 Nights earned mixed reviews when it was released that October. The competent but over-familiar feel of the *Rainbow Concert* and *E.C. Was Here* – of which the best that could be said was that Clapton's head was higher than his feet when he made them – continued. In the same month he announced plans to tour Japan with Harrison and, in a not unrelated move, appeared on the cover of *Rolling Stone*. According to the magazine Clapton seemed 'healthy and relaxed', 'chain-smok[ing] cigarettes and sipping coffee' and answering 'every question without hesitation'. 'Healthy', 'relaxed' and 'coffee', the buzzwords of recovery therapy, all foretold an interview in which Clapton would play on his methodical present rather than his tumultuous past. In the event the most revealing moment came when he was asked about his friendship with Harrison:

> 'We always talked. Some of it was very LSD-type conversation and very esoteric, sort of cosmo-speak, especially from George. And he would show up from time to time, when Pattie and I were living together. He came around once, and it was all very trippy. It got quite hostile . . .'
> 'So will you be playing "Layla" on the tour?'
> 'Yeah. [Laughs] That's always been a bone of contention.'

Clapton may have been being disingenuous in saying that the Japanese tour was 'certainly not for business'. The receipts from the five concerts in Osaka and Tokyo were excellent for business. Nor did the events exactly proceed in the improvised, let's-put-the-show-on-right-here manner suggested in *Rolling Stone*. Steve Judson was present at Bray Studios when Clapton, Harrison and an extended group of musicians and backing singers arrived to rehearse that November. According to Judson, there was a 'friendly but highly organized' structure in the studio, with Clapton dominant over the 'shrinking' Harrison. Having made the same discovery in 1990, Judson was again struck by how 'friendly and natural' Clapton was when allowed to relax. While rehearsals proceeded chaotically around him, he was a source of calm and reassurance. Judson was told he would be 'provided access' in Japan, and in time duly found himself chatting with Clapton over breakfast, reviewing the previous night's performance and discussing the strange tendency of the Japanese audience to treat rock concerts like a religious service.

The choice of venue owed everything to this sense of adoring, uncritical respect, conspicuously absent when Harrison had last toured America in 1974. For over ten years Forrester had watched the annual winter tours of the Orient as an Indian fakir watches a snake. It was the ideal location for two stalwarts like Clapton and Harrison to greet their fans – at the airport they were mobbed like members of the Beatles – and gently cash in on past glories, playing a set heavily loaded with old favourites.* The

---

* Despite Clapton's assurance, there was no 'Layla'. 'Something', 'Wonderful Tonight' and 'Old Love' were, however, all included.

concerts themselves were received euphorically by the public and never less than respectfully by the press. Even critics like Ben Elliott who had written disparagingly of Clapton's recent output were forced to admit that the events were 'amply rabble-rousing, containing some of the best-crafted pop ever committed to vinyl'. In 1979 Clapton had gone to Tokyo to record the live LP *Just One Night*, a welcome return to form at a time when his career was, at best, erratic. Twelve years later Harrison performed the same trick with *Live In Japan*, like Clapton's a creatively deceptive album, relying on note-for-note reproductions of standards, but showing the same exceptional control over its audience.

Among the projects and half-formed ideas in Clapton's repertoire were a seemingly infinite number of remastered and live LPs, including threatened sequels to the *Rainbow* and *E.C. Was Here* albums. With those, *24 Nights* and concert versions of 'Wonderful Tonight' and 'Edge of Darkness', Clapton's profile was as high as ever. It seemed a churlish technicality to insist it should be related to a newly recorded album.

Yet the genius of Clapton and his manager lay in their updating of a single selling-point in unusual ways. No one else could have contrived the same mix of guest appearances, one-off collaborations, nostalgic reworkings of old hits and *ad-hoc* projects for which Clapton was famous. Whether he had a new record to plug or not, he was continually changing the musical menu. Sooner or later, it was inevitable that his sights would come to rest on the *Unplugged* concert series.

On 16 January 1992 Clapton and his group duly arrived at Bray Studios – an audience was found by Johnnie Walker of Radio 1 – and played a selection of numbers from *Journeyman*, the Dominos ('Layla' and 'Nobody Knows You') and throwbacks like 'San Francisco Bay Blues', first performed thirty years earlier on Richmond Green. 'Tears in Heaven' was also included. After being aired on Sue Lawley's programme later in the month, the song was released (backed by a live version of 'White Room') as a single, eventually reaching number two in the chart.

'Tears In Heaven', simultaneously released on *Rush*, was Clapton's requiem for his son. It does nothing to diminish the song to say that at least part of its appeal was sentimental rather than musical. All of the ingredients – the lyrics, the understated tune, Clapton's appearances on BBC and MTV – were a tribute to his talent for forging new material which seemed to have been familiar for years. No one hearing 'Tears In Heaven' could fail to recall it. The song, in some views a simple elegy, in others an angry anthem to Clapton's own survival, was judged a masterpiece of craftsmanship. The letter columns of the press blossomed with laudatory epithets. Rabbis and vicars began preaching sermons on Clapton's text. Clapton himself averaged over a hundred letters a day from well-wishers. Sales and reviews were impressive enough, but Clapton was struck even more, if possible, by the effect the song had on ordinary listeners. Among the mail coming into Hurtwood Edge and Harley House were appreciative messages from other parents. At least one woman wrote to *The Times* saying the loss of her own son had been made easier by the 'symbols and allegories' of the work. And Richard Putt, head of a firm of undertakers, reported that 'Tears In Heaven' was the most popular choice of music to be requested at funerals.

There were other opinions. In spite of the song's subject matter and evident sincerity, 'Tears' was received by some critics with suspicion and dismay. Reviews by Clapton's ex-colleagues bristled with such adjectives as embarrassing, distressing, tasteless, tawdry and cynical. A former member of the Yardbirds says bluntly that 'writing it was understandable. Recording it was logical. But releasing it as a single was self-indulgent beyond belief.' Those with long memories made the link to 'Layla' – another occasion on which an intensely personal experience was made public – and suggested that, now as then, a general disintegration of Clapton's personality was taking place. 'Someone took the decision to release it while Eric was still disorientated,' says Chris Dreja. 'In my view, it should never have happened.'

Unplugged itself was a popular and critical success, though that underestimates Clapton's achievement in selling six million copies in a year. Fans might have had to wait until the last moment for the crowning triumph of Clapton's career, but in *Unplugged* they found it: from the raucous interplay on 'Rollin' and Tumblin'' to the vocal on 'Running On Faith' to the slight but haunting refrain of 'Lonely Stranger', Clapton, hunched with his acoustic guitar, dragged back his best songs from the archive to live performance. 'Layla' was ingeniously recast as a half-angry, half-affectionate homage to old love. There was a nostalgic rendering of 'Nobody Knows You' in the style in which Clapton might have sung the song in 1961. The arrangements, if not old-fashioned, recalled the best of the original rock groups in bringing a brash enthusiasm to the task at hand, and keeping it brief. It was true, as critics pointed out, that Clapton, unlike a Stephen Stills or Richard Thompson, was a guitarist whose authority depended on the sort of sonic assault denied by *Unplugged*. His modest acoustic work was a mere shadow of his electric virtuosity. But for verve and sheer, unadorned simplicity (Clapton appearing in a dark suit and, for the first time in public, glasses), the songs ranging from the dirge-like to the full-moon howl of 'Nobody Knows You', few records communicated with such spirit. It was hard to avoid the feeling, as Clapton introduced a song like 'Circus Has Left Town', of eavesdropping on private therapy.

That left the question of Clapton's motives in releasing *Unplugged* commercially. The disc jockey Johnnie Walker reports that Forrester promised only to 'think about' issuing the session after the original MTV broadcast. Since seven months passed before *Unplugged* appeared in the shops, it can be assumed that Forrester considered the matter thoroughly. (It was coincidental that, when the album did appear, it was shortly before the deadline for inclusion in the 1993 Grammys.) Clapton himself would say only that, 'My audience would be very surprised if I didn't make some reference to [Conor's death] . . . I didn't want to insult them by not including them in my grief' and, less guardedly, that 'The opportunity [*Rush*] gave me was excellent, because it meant I could write ['Tears in Heaven'] . . . express my own feelings, and have it come out soon so that there was an audience for it.' The third member of the triangle, Warner Brothers, needed no encouragement: reversing the premise of its title, *Unplugged* was ruthlessly promoted on television in America. In its energy and directness, its conveying of the abyss under every life, its tapping the anxieties that fuelled Clapton's best work, *Unplugged* was a welcome and even striking return to the basics. In its packaging of the confusion and vulnerability of a man under emotional stress, there must be a suspicion that those responsible for the record intruded on Clapton's grief.

A sold-out tour of Britain followed, culminating in Clapton's sixth season of concerts at the Albert Hall. Continuing the *Unplugged* format, a total of five acoustic numbers were included, proving how much life there remained in the well-worn theme of reinvention. The idea that Clapton, for all his willingness to appear raw and unadorned before an audience, retained an eye for the commercial chance was strengthened by his choice of musical collaborations in 1992. In March he recorded 'Runaway Train' with Elton John; in April 'It's Probably Me', and other material for *Lethal Weapon 3*, with Sting; there were also five live appearances with John in London and America, for the last of which Clapton boasted less abundant hair than that of the pianist.

The main business of the year was a two-part tour of America. Reviews for Clapton were largely admiring and never less than affectionate. It only states the obvious to say that to his other considerable assets Clapton now drew a ground swell of sympathy. Even those who had previously ignored him responded with a mixture of approval and goodwill. It was surprising how perfect an image of the lonely artist Clapton projected when one had never heard a note by him. The public saw him as a tragic reclusive figure, which was a small part of what Clapton really was; the press suspended judgement. The tour which began in Dallas on 25 April gave evidence of his more enduring appeal: the depth of the old masters absorbed as a teenager and Clapton's own finely honed ear for a tune combined in a two-hour set of superior rock, blues standards and for-mulaic pop. By the time the first half of the tour ended in Miami more than quarter of a million fans had gone home happy.

After European dates, including the Montreux Jazz Festival, Clapton was back in America in August. His cropped hair, unsmiling face and air of separateness from his musicians reminded some of the Bluesbreakers. Indeed it seemed that Clapton, acting the chameleon he was, physically changed appearance between the continents. His way of dress and speech in Pittsburgh or Chicago was as American as, in Birmingham or London, it was English. At the Albert Hall the humour tended to be sneaked in surreptitiously rather than rehearsed; at the Tacoma Dome, where the writer was present on 6 September, Clapton seemed to deliver jokes as if from an autocue. The emphasis was on unreconstructed power-pop, professional, sometimes indulgent, often inspired, invariably gripping. There was a bedrock seriousness to Clapton's face which suggested that, for him, a venue like Tacoma was best viewed from the remove of a concert stage. One was left with the impression of a performer extending his sense of irony into detachment (looking, according to one critic, as though 'he'd been wound up and aimed at the stage') but who delivered a competent and satisfying greatest-hits collection along with a smattering of new material.

Clapton was present in Los Angeles three days later to receive an MTV 'best video' award for 'Tears In Heaven'. He played the song live. Visitors backstage at the Pauley Pavilion were surprised and even shocked by Clapton's appearance: he arrived in the hall in an electric golf cart wearing his glasses and tweed jacket and looking, according to a stagehand, Alan Wineberg, 'about ten years older than the year before' (when Clapton had made a cameo appearance). It was true that Clapton, nearing his forty-eighth birthday, was no longer young; his haircut, glasses and eccentric schoolmaster's jacket were only befitting a man approaching, in professional terms, late middle age. In the ruthless currency of market research, Clapton's fans were now shepherded into predetermined patterns of behaviour. They were ABC1, income-earning, equity-owning adults for whom the boxed-set CD was admired as much for its packaging as its contents. In acquiring a kind of bitter wisdom and growing with his audience, Clapton was only doing what the Warners promotion department would have asked of him. Then again, ageing had been in Clapton's game plan from the start. The music which first inspired him was written by sixty- and seventy-year-old men by comparison to whom even the bald, unprepossessing Ray Cooper looked like a teenager. It may be that Clapton had only recently approached the true maturity of the originals.*

From the perspective of two years, the MTV ceremony can be seen to have begun the process of Clapton's beatification, reaching a level not far short of his status as 'God', in which trophies and awards outnumbered even his concert appearances and occasional albums. It was true that he commanded an unusually respectful and loyal audience. He touched on universal themes in *Unplugged*. Even so, to speak of him, as one guest did, as a 'saint' was stretching belief. Clapton was freely compared to other great tragic artists – Robert Johnson was mentioned – though it was pointed out that, unlike Johnson's, his work now showed that tragedy could have its share of levity. As Clapton stood beaming and waving in the Pauley Pavilion it was possible to suppose that he bore his grief with equanimity and that the adoring audience would have forgiven him anything. (Their tolerance did not, however, extend to buying, in sufficient numbers, the reissued 'Layla', given its usual ten-yearly release that October. It reached only number 45 in the chart.)

Clapton was present that autumn at the twenty-fifth anniversary party for *Rolling Stone*, where he spent a long, some thought inordinately long, time alone with Yoko Ono. More significantly, he played at the gala tribute to Bob Dylan in Madison Square Garden. Something of the universal appeal of Clapton's playing emerged in his versions of 'Don't Think Twice' and 'Love Minus Zero'. According to Pete Brown, who watched the live broadcast in London, 'Not one of the other musicians, including Dylan, could touch him. It was amazing . . . Just when you thought he'd settled on a life of terminal blandness, there was Eric playing like Freddie

---

* Even so, says Wineberg, 'It was a shock to hear him talking about arthritis.'

King. The two operative words to describe it were "intelligent" and "dignified". The effect was startling because it was so unexpected.' Dick Heckstall-Smith, who also watched the televised event, says only that, 'it made you wonder why he couldn't sustain it. That was the riddle of Clapton.'

The same week that Clapton was thrilling audiences in New York he attended the Chelsea Arts Club ball at the Albert Hall, wandering distractedly about the floor and striking one guest, Terry Gill, as 'out of it'. The two events epitomized the contrasts in Clapton's life: the ascetic artist vying for attention with the dedicated partygoer and celebrity. It does not stretch credulity to say that Clapton sought distraction from private disappointments by immersing himself in work. The corollary was that he remained, and remains, addicted to the company of women. Diners at the Chelsea Arts Club became used to the sight of Clapton and his latest companion – never the same one twice – arriving from Old Church Street and making for the bar, where, according to Gill, 'they existed on mineral water and cigarettes'. Clapton, who could use the club in the reasonable hope that his privacy would be respected, became almost a nightly fixture. News of his arrival was only sporadically leaked to the press. By and large his appearances in Chelsea were low-key and unobtrusive, although memories remain of the night a waiter, overcome at serving his childhood hero, dropped a heavy plate on Clapton's lap; after the fuss had died down, Gill had the feeling that both parties were 'mutually unimpressed' by the encounter.

As the year ended Clapton was seen opening a drug rehabilitation centre with the Duchess of York. It would be tempting to trust in the usual skeleton of royal narratives ('a friend says', 'a Palace source reveals') to suggest a liaison between Clapton and the woman recently separated from her husband. No such suggestion exists. The idea that Clapton included the Duchess of York among his long list of social partners is preposterous. He was, however, on notably friendly terms with the Princess of Wales, a known Clapton fan since his appearance at the Prince's Trust in 1986 and a fellow diner at Clapton's favourite restaurant, San Lorenzo. The relationship between the two was sexual in that it could only have existed between a man and a woman. The reason why in San Lorenzo some people thought it was also physical was because of the way she treated him. The Princess was seen to tease Clapton. There was a reversal of the usual roles of the impish rocker and demure royal in much of what they did. 'She used to tell him off while Eric stood there blushing like a schoolboy,' says one witness to their meetings. 'It wasn't impossible to imagine an intimate friendship.'

One reason for Clapton's growing affection for royalty was the obvious nostalgia he felt for the Britain of his youth. It was part of his longing for tradition and roots. It also appealed to him to meet a woman like the Princess of Wales who, whatever her own problems, was almost alone of his partners in not fighting a secret battle against breakdown. To know a normal adult who admired him was an uplifting experience. The Princess in turn must have enjoyed the attentions of someone who amused and flattered her. An army officer who knows both parties is adamant that 'this is one close friendship the press totally missed. There really was something going on between them with Lorenzo's as a rendezvous. You could see it was so, just looking at their faces.'

Among the roll-call of actresses, models and other women with whom Clapton was more openly friendly were Patsy Kensit, Annie Mayhew, Stephanie Beacham, Valerie Golino, Kathy Lloyd, Julia Smith (now married to England rugby captain Will Carling), Marie Helvin, Davina McCall and Susannah Doyle. He was photographed dining with Del Santo and walking through Chelsea with a woman named Francesca Amfitheatrof. The idea that Clapton, within two years of his fiftieth birthday, might continue to enjoy an exotically full life was highlighted by the eccentric figure of Baroness Cefalu, still bitterly complaining of having been deflowered by the guitarist in 1987. While rumours persisted that, at least in his youth, Clapton had not been averse to experiment (as well as John Dunbar's claim that Clapton and Mick Jagger were found in bed together, there was Chrissie Shrimpton, herself linked to Jagger, who calls Clapton 'decidedly camp' and 'the first man to paint his nails and backcomb his hair'), the more conventional view was that he was enthusiastically heterosexual. Certainly Clapton displayed what Gill calls an 'old-fashioned attitude' to women at the Arts Club and – reversing a lifelong preference for fast food – San Lorenzo. The actress Diana Rigg was greeted by Clapton on a transatlantic flight with a 'warmth' she found striking. Shrimpton's sister Jean calls him 'completely attractive' to the opposite sex. A woman whose business it was to service the needs of rock stars in the 1960s confirms that Clapton was 'aggressive in bed and passive out of it – a rare combination for those days'. A more recent companion describes him as 'a romantic, candlelight-and-music type' who 'liked women in black lace underwear', a view supported by Janet Reger's report of Clapton's 'horrifying' lingerie bill at her shop.

Sex was one thing. In terms of emotional fulfilment Clapton continued his generally unhappy track record. For some months he escorted the actress Michelle Pfeiffer, among those thought to have visited him in Antigua, a relationship at least one Clapton watcher considered 'promising'. The press, attracted by Pfeiffer's recent incarnation as Catwoman, were intrigued. Since Clapton's divorce the gossip columns had eagerly watched every feminine social liaison. At least one photographer was on permanent standby outside Clapton's homes. Enthusiasm waned only when Pfeiffer, adopting a baby on the grounds of wanting to be a mother without recourse to a man 'who's driving me nuts', married the television producer David Kelley.

Clapton's affair with Pfeiffer proceeded with unusual caution. A more public romance took place with Naomi Campbell. On 11 October 1992, under the headline RED HOT ERIC'S PLAYING IT COOL, the *People* reported the couple as 'determined to stay out of the limelight while they get to know each other', a process believed to have been rapid. By the time Cream were inducted to the Rock and Roll Hall of Fame in January, Clapton and Campbell were dining together at Bill Bouquet's, a restaurant described by one Hollywood guide as 'a place couples go to see and be seen'. Next morning's *Tribune* duly reported on the liaison between the 'King of Rock' and the 'Catwalk Queen'. No one was certain at what point during the spring the breakdown took place. In later months both monarchs tended to disclaim their own roles in the affair. By May the media watch was reporting on yet another mystery beauty shuffling up the steps of San Lorenzo with Clapton, while Campbell announced her engagement to Adam Clayton.

Making every concession possible, there was a lingering suspicion that Clapton, for all his 'attractiveness' and 'warmth', was unhappily accident-prone when it came to women. The man who by his own admission had 'laid over a thousand groupies' approached his half-century without a steady partner. Clapton always said he preferred the company of women to men. But that was only half the story. What he meant was that he preferred women in their traditional roles, happy to take second place to the one insuperable rival, the ruling passion of Clapton's life, his work. It was also true that the sort of commitment expected by most wives and lovers was deeply repugnant to one of his naturally reserved temperament. Clapton's emotional barriers remained. The impossibility to which he admitted of 'finding [himself] in a relationship without wanting to get away' meant that all such affairs were conducted at arm's length. Looking at Clapton's life in full, it would seem that he never escaped from the overpowering sense of desertion by his mother. In Clapton's mind the end result of any relationship was to exacerbate his feelings of loneliness and self-doubt. It is a plausible and adequate explanation of his difficulties that, feeling let down by the first woman he knew, he never again abandoned himself to a woman. On this reading, Pat Clapton's treatment of her son resulted in his growing up emotionally stunted.

Clapton saw in 1993 by fronting an impromptu group, the Character Defects, in a concert in aid of Alcoholics Anonymous. The thousand invited guests included names like Anthony Hopkins. Opening the ninety-minute set with the traditional but startling, 'Hello, I'm Eric. I'm an alcoholic', he gave a performance notable for its spirit and sense of audience participation. According to an unnamed friend in the *Daily Mail*, 'Eric knows that without AA he may not have been around today. He wanted to give something back.' Other observers felt that, in bringing honesty, frankness and self-revelation to bear in a crusade, Clapton devalued his own virtues. Appearing on behalf of drug- and drink-related charities had become a consuming passion. It was almost inevitable that before long Clapton would blame 'government cuts' for threatening an organization like the Chemical Dependency Centre (in reality funded by a Conservative minister). One result was that a number of Clapton's older fans, while admiring the quality and enthusiasm of his music, became wary of his periodic outbursts on behalf of causes more familiar to him than themselves. Another result was much-needed publicity for the causes.

One of the most curious episodes of an already singular year for Clapton was the reformation of Cream. This event, announced only forty-eight hours beforehand but planned by Forrester for months in advance, took place at the Rock and Roll Hall of Fame in Los Angeles. The selected audience queued in the rain outside the Crown Plaza Hotel to see Clapton, Bruce and Baker play together for the first time since 1968. Reviews of their performance of 'Sunshine Of Your Love', 'Politician' and 'Born Under A Bad Sign' were fulsome. Bruce calls the evening 'great – as good as when we first rehearsed at Ginger's house'. There was inevitable speculation that the reunion would become permanent. Again Bruce's reaction – 'Don't count on anything. Don't count anything out' – may be significant: as recently as 1990 mere mention of Cream was high on the list of Bruce's pet hates. If doubts about the group's intentions remained, there was evidence in Los Angeles that Cream's appeal came not only from the sense of reliving the past but from the songs and their sound. As Clapton's guitar weaved over the gigantic beat one was reminded of just what the group meant in the first place: a tightly played fusion of blues-rock which, until improvisational excess took over, marked one of the few truly distinctive sounds of the sixties.

American fans were content to see Cream on stage again. A more critical approach was taken in England, where the *Sun* described the group as 'old fogeys' and *The Times* asked, 'Is it possible for them to play "Sunshine Of Your Love" with its necessary verve? And how much are people willing to pay to see bits fly off the ancient Ginger Baker, as his stiff joints stretch the forty-minute drum solo on "Toad" into a mind-contracting hour-and-a-half?' (Between $700 and $1500 a ticket, was the answer in Los Angeles.)

Cream's induction into the Hall of Fame was an indication of the way the rock zeitgeist was going. When the industry came to decide on its favourite son for 1992 there were not many entries, and the verdict was quickly reached. Clapton had already won an MTV award for 'Tears In Heaven'. In February he was named 'outstanding recording artist' by the Royal Variety Club. Finally, even as the closing notes of 'Born Under A Bad Sign' died away, Clapton was nominated for a total of nine Grammys, ranging from 'album of the year' (*Unplugged*) to 'best rock song' ('Layla') to 'best composition for a motion picture' (*Rush*). It was twenty years since Clapton had won his first Grammy for *Bangladesh*. While, as Walker says, 'there was undoubtedly a sympathy vote involved', most of Clapton's friends felt the recognition to be well earned and overdue, as for an elderly and respected actor winning a lifetime achievement award. 'I felt genuinely proud of him,' Bruce remembers.

Some of the simple appeal of *Unplugged* was retained for Clapton's 1993 Albert Hall concerts. The season, which opened on 20 February, turned out to be a sort of master-class on the blues. No one questioned Clapton's credentials to play the music he described in the programme notes as '[having] given me so much inspiration and pleasure in life'. The objections came from fellow professionals, like Paul Jones, who says that 'by playing it in a safe, comfortable setting, Eric may have thought he was popularizing the blues. Unfortunately, it's an unsafe, dangerous kind of music. The two things collided.' The other complaints were from ordinary concertgoers who, despite advance warnings to the contrary, expected Clapton's usual repertoire of rock standards and ballads. According to this view there was something perverse in Clapton paying tribute to his heroes from Chicago and the Mississippi Delta while favourites like 'Layla' and 'Wonderful Tonight' went unheard. 'Only Eric' – a phrase heard fairly often in the foyer – could play twelve concerts so genuinely unheeding of public expectations (and lacking in commercial relevance) as these.

If it was true that not all Clapton's chosen material – songs dealing with wayward women and freight trains tending to dominate – suited the venue, it was equally true that he commanded an unusually forgiving audience. They cheered as soon as he settled on to a chair and picked up his acoustic guitar. After opening with Leroy Carr's raw, uninhibited 'How Long Blues' Clapton played half a dozen songs accompanied only by Chris Stainton. There was a steady upbeat progression as more musicians came on stage. Finally, on Robert Johnson's 'Walking Blues', Clapton switched to electric guitar. After an hour of monumental forbearance, the crowd were rewarded with a volley of dramatic solos, the best of which came during Freddie King's 'Love Her With A Feeling'. This was music beyond even the reviewers' reproach. The critics looked on sentiment as the rope at which they could clutch to save them from drowning. According to *The Times*, Clapton was 'relaxed, yet utterly impassioned'; in the *Express*'s view 'it was impossible not to be won over by the emotionally charged performance'; while for the *Telegraph*, 'the blues [were] safe in Eric Clapton's hands'. The only reservations were about Clapton's voice, described as 'not coarse enough' and 'neither sufficiently melancholy nor languid' to convey basic blues properly.

Clapton's decision to devote twelve concerts to the blues was both brave and quixotic. Much of the material was unfamiliar to the inexpert ear. Most of the supporting group, with the exception of Stainton and Dunn, were anonymous, and, as always, Clapton was sadly lacking in stage presence. It was to his credit that he held and finally captivated his audience. The climax of the concerts was a song that enraptured the crowd, made a profound impact on the press and was widely quoted as Clapton's favourite. The theme of 'Nobody Knows You' was uncompromisingly stark: when Clapton sang of pain, loss, abandonment and despair it was possible to imagine that he put more than usual heart into the lyrics. As the house lights came up even the most gnarled and sceptical pundits felt moved to join the applause. Clapton himself blinked, raised an arm, nodded to where, on successive nights, Naomi Campbell and Yvonne Kelly sat in the audience – and left.

The irony, of course, was that the very opposite of the song's title applied to Clapton. 'Nobody Knows You' *was* effective. It was also affected; affected in that Clapton's implied identification with the lyrics rang false. As awards and recognition came for *Unplugged*, even he may have been struck by the contradiction. Clapton continued to talk of himself as directionless, 'never, ever in a permanent situation', someone outside the musical mainstream. Yet the particular attention both he and Forrester gave to *Unplugged* suggests that they were well aware that it would become one of Clapton's major commercial triumphs. If manager and client really thought they were unknown, neither was paying attention to the *Billboard* singles and albums charts or to the panegyrics issuing from the Academy of Recording Arts and Sciences in Los Angeles.

On 24 February, between the fourth and fifth nights at the Albert Hall, Clapton and Forrester arrived in America. Despite mutterings by Peter Jackson, Clapton's tour manager, about the logistics of interrupting a residency in London in order to collect awards in California, the party were safely ensconced at the Shrine Auditorium. As Clapton accepted his first Grammy for 'Tears In Heaven' he told the audience, 'I don't think I deserve to win this. There were better songs.' He also performed on the show and, after picking up his sixth and final trophy to a standing ovation, admitted: 'I feel incredibly guilty. I don't know why I feel so guilty about taking so many of these. I don't know what to say. I'm very moved and very shaky, and very emotional . . . I want to thank a lot of people but the one person I want to thank is my son for the love he gave me and the song he gave me.' His final words to the 15,000 crowd were, 'I have received a great honour but I've lost the one thing I truly loved.'

Clapton's Grammys were for Record of the Year, Album of the Year, Song of the Year, Best Pop Vocal, Best Rock Vocal and Best Rock Song ('Layla'). He failed to win only for his film and television scores. Clapton had initially been nervous about his reception in Los Angeles – two Grammys were his total from the previous thirty years – but his first trip to the podium allayed his fears. Half-way through the night it became clear that this was one of those occasions of communal goodwill towards a given artist. ('If you're up against Eric Clapton in any other categories,' said the host, Garry Shandling, 'I'd go home now.') Clapton's final appearance on stage, clutching all six of his awards, was the signal for overwhelming enthusiasm. The press was eulogistic. 'Rarely has there been a more obvious winner' was the fell phrase used in *Variety*. 'Whatever we experienced tonight,' said the *Tribune*, 'it was unique.' 'Sheer heaven,' breathed *Billboard*.

Earlier in the week Clapton had spoken about the child who, as he put it, became 'famous overnight'. 'I still don't truly accept Conor is dead,' he told CBS News. 'I still don't believe that I won't see him in a couple of weeks. Losing him was unbelievably devastating . . . But as a recovering alcoholic, my philosophy tells me I was lucky to have him because he got me sober.' Del Santo was also quoted. Bizarrely, she was said to have heard 'Tears In Heaven' for the first time in a shopping mall. 'The sound of Eric's voice, the music – it made me weep,' she said. 'I know [Clapton] is saying those words in "Tears In Heaven" because he is worried that they didn't spend enough time together . . . Eric is frightened that if he met Conor in heaven, our son might not recognize him.' As Clapton returned to London and the Albert Hall his final word was on the logic behind releasing *Unplugged* in the first place ('I really didn't want [the album] to come out and I finally agreed to it in a limited edition . . . And then it sold a few, and a few more, and I thought, well, why not give it a try?'), a process richly illustrative of Forrester's role as manager.

Clapton's achievement is not lessened by saying there was a sympathy vote at work; sympathy for the loss of his son and for the relative indifference of the Academy in the past. With the best will in the world it was hard to avoid a sense of compensatory recognition for a song like 'Layla', released over twenty years before. It was also noted that 1993 was Clapton's thirtieth anniversary as a professional. While Little Richard, not he, won the Lifetime Achievement Award, at least one musician present thought the event 'a crude effort to place Eric on the same list of approved entertainers as Elton and Tina Turner'. According to this view, Clapton was being recognized as much for having endured as for the unrivalled quality of his recent work.

Critics now rushed to lavish praise on him. In Philip Norman's words, Clapton was 'rock's most extraordinary survivor, a 48-year-old whose constitution must be little short of Churchillian to have withstood all the abuses', a man who 'by reaching into the depths of his heart has at last touched the sky'. Like Norman, Melvyn Bragg referred to Clapton's past and exotic love-life ('There were complications with women that made *Dallas* look like *Playschool*'), while finding symbolic value in him as 'late twentieth-century man, some sort of survivor-hero having the nerve to twist out of his guts music which moves our hearts whoever we are'. To Phil Collins, Clapton was 'not the sort of chap who seeks recognition

... He is a quiet man, who likes to get on with his life and his job. But I know these awards are special to him.' The enduring impression was of a shy, reclusive figure, sensitive and intelligent, who accepted even praise with reluctance; an ordeal for which Clapton was rewarded by seeing his weekly album sales triple in the seven days after the Grammys.

The world competed to heap honours on him. On 29 April Clapton made the cover of *Rolling Stone* again; in June he received a Nordoff-Robbins Music Therapy award (smiling through Pete Townshend's speech claiming 'Eric abuses impressionable young Italian women'); there were gold and platinum discs for *Unplugged*. Clapton's kudos, and assimilation into the mainstream, reached new heights when Annie Leibovitz, the celebrity photographer, arrived to take portraits of Bill Clinton in the White House. 'We've never had music in the Oval Office,' a functionary told her as she plugged in a tape recorder. 'No problem,' interjected the new President. He happily posed to the sound of 'Layla'.

As Clapton's stock rose so did his attractiveness to women. With the revelation that there was no permanent fixture in his life there was keen competition amongst actresses and models to secure the prized place at Clapton's table. On 4 July he was present at a reception for Molly Parkin, Clapton's sponsor at the Chelsea Arts Club, a self-confessed 'powerhouse of sexuality' with whom he seemed on strikingly good terms. A fortnight later Clapton appeared dressed as the Invisible Man – some thought an unconscious metaphor for his life – with the Duchess of York. A cricketer who met him that summer was prepared to find 'Eric, as usual, surrounded by beauties'. In the event Clapton struck 'a rather morbid figure, alone, unhappy' and admitting to having had his 'recurrent row' with a woman.

The fact was that Clapton had spent much of the day on the phone with the Princess of Wales.

Among the girlfriends appearing almost weekly with Clapton in the tabloids or the pages of *Hello!* were Charlotte Weston, Yelitza Negrete, Susannah Constantine, and, reviving a friendship thought to have ended in 1989, Carla Bruni. Those were passing affairs. More substantial were Clapton's liaisons with Paula Hamilton, resuming a modelling career after her own long struggle with alcoholism, and Christopher Reeve's ex-wife, Gae Exton, who playfully informed the press, 'If the right man comes along and the circumstances were right, I would happily get married and have more children.' Despite the *Daily Mail*'s puckish headline, 'Eric, It's Over To You', Exton, too, joined the list of former lovers.

That Clapton was susceptible to female company is certain, but he was also a realist. 'I've been with many different types of partner and a lot of the problems have been to do with me trying to get the answers about myself from someone else,' he told *Q*. That he feared commitment and inclined to short if intense liaisons is also certain, but is not a weakness confined to rock stars. That most of his attitudes to women were old-fashioned and boorish is also true; and that he was a romantic rather than a pragmatist in love is self-evident. It does not take a genius to see that Clapton compensated for his low self-esteem by accumulating girlfriends and mistresses. His was an addictive personality. Clapton's strange mix of ego and insecurity was what led him to acquire lovers in the same way he bulk-bought suits or became hooked on prescription painkillers. He might, as he put it, 'like beautiful things, be it clothes, jewellery, cars, paintings [or] women', but Clapton believed in quantity as much as quality. The impression remains of a man who failed to maintain a steady sense of direction to preserve his aim. Dogged as he was all his life by melancholy, Clapton needed – almost a pathological need – to ensure that his numerous affairs broke down in order to confirm his own jaundiced views about women. The process was self-fulfilling. The lessons Clapton drew – of the unreliability of any relationship – were largely untainted by bitterness or self-pity. He continued to speak and write affectingly about love while remaining someone (he told Rees) whose 'one and only chance had been blown'. It is hard to avoid the conclusion that Clapton valued Boyd more as the years without her went by. As late as 1993 he was still dedicating songs to his ex-wife from the stage.

That October Clapton gave three concerts in Birmingham and Sheffield to raise funds for the Chemical Dependency Centre. The events themselves were anodyne ('I shall count the termination of the need to listen to "Wonderful Tonight" among the compensations for death,' wrote one critic); irony was supplied by the sight, once again, of Clapton and Joe Cocker drinking orange juice backstage. Steve Judson was also present at Birmingham. 'The security was terrific,' he says. 'Officials from [the Centre] were literally pleading to be photographed with Clapton. Peter [Jackson] and Alphi [O'Leary] saw that they weren't.' By rock music standards, where even fledgeling figures have enjoyed the limelight and sung their own praises audibly, Clapton was a modest man. He still relished the publicity afforded his status; although unpretentious, he had a streak of vanity. But compared to certain colleagues, he was almost morbidly retiring. Anyone backstage at a Clapton concert could anticipate not only Jackson and O'Leary but an entire phalanx of assistants and bodyguards barring their way. Access to Mick Jagger was simple by comparison. No one would have questioned Clapton's right, as Judson puts it, 'not to be hassled before or after a gig'. But the entourage surrounding Clapton did more than just protect him. There were complaints of high-handed and threatening behaviour. Clapton placed enormous importance on the loyalty engendered in his staff. The corollary was that they became protective – some said over-protective – of their employer. A sort of court developed around Clapton wherever he played. At its centre were Forrester, Jackson and O'Leary, at its fringes the aides and officious 'security advisers' so obtrusive in Birmingham. It was difficult to avoid the comparison between the accessible community VIP and the man who enjoyed near-imperial status on tour. In consequence, certain 'friends of Eric', turned away from their idol backstage, began to speak of the contradictions between the private and the public man. This contrast did not happen overnight; it had long been recorded. But it came as a shock to realize that Clapton's concerts proceeded like those of the average rock star.

Nineteen ninety-three closed with two final tributes. In December Clapton appeared on *Curves, Contours And Body Horns*, a television special on Leo Fender. Clapton himself was the subject of a thirtieth anniversary feature in *Billboard*. Remarkably free of musical detail, the interview by Timothy White revealed a more polished personality than the bellicose football-supporting hoodlum of old. The impression was of a relaxed, middle-aged Renaissance figure, a man who quoted Steinbeck and Hemingway, spoke of himself with wry objectivity – literally as an object of sympathy and nostalgia – and insisted, 'We have to refer to my sobriety to find a context to talk in.' As part of the feature Clapton's colleagues and suppliers were invited to take out advertising space. Among those doing so were Reprise, Virgin, Polydor, Warner Brothers, Creative Artists, Clapton's accountants and solicitors and two hotels, in one of which his welcome had, at some time in the past, been uncertain. Among those failing to appear was any original member of Clapton's groups with the exception of Jack Bruce (who referred obliquely to their taking LSD at the time of *Disraeli Gears*).

On that note, after a short tour of Japan, Clapton's *annus mirabilis* ended.

He was on stage, for the eighth consecutive season at the Albert Hall, on 20 February 1994. When Clapton had picked up his Martin acoustic to record *Unplugged* two years earlier, even he may not have known that the event would mark yet another stage in his circular career. Continuing the stark format of 1993 and making good his promise, after years of doing the opposite, to 'rough up' the performance, Clapton appeared at the Albert Hall – in patched jeans and for the first time without his trademark cigarette – to act out his boyhood fantasies by opening with sixty minutes of blues standards. Now released from the irksome task of travelling around the world, having hit rock albums and generally being a global superstar, Clapton was happy to sit with his guitar and play duets with old friends like Chris Stainton. In 1993 there had been mild unease in the crowd as their hero plucked one acoustic number after another and tangible relief as the signature Stratocaster was handed up by Lee Dickson. The same reactions were evident in 1994 as Clapton eked out an hour of Muddy Waters and Freddie King covers and then announced 'White Room', respectively. The second half of the concerts stayed close to the Cream and Derek and the Dominos songbooks, with a rousing version of Hendrix's 'Stone Free'. Perhaps the evening's only disappointment was 'Crossroads', stripped of its original beat and, in a curious decision of pacing, reduced to an aimless shuffle.

If, yet again, a charge of sameness could be levelled against the material – despite the claim in the 1993 programme that 'Following these blues nights, Eric will be going into the studio to start recording some of the many songs he has written over the last year and a half', nothing had appeared twelve months later – it was equally true that the audience was there as much to celebrate Clapton himself as any particular aspects of his music. The event on 28 February was a case in point. Clapton's hundredth appearance at the Albert Hall was a charity concert attended by the Duchess of York. No one would have criticized his decision to make a speech from the stage or to donate the proceeds from the night to Children In Crisis. But it had to be said that, for pomp and circumstance, Clapton's season at the Hall was rapidly assuming the characteristics of the proms he liked to compare it to. The ritual of the performance was something seized on in the press. 'Much as it is an achievement in itself to create such a feeling of cosy well-being, there was a worry that this was not to be a night of fresh horizons,' wrote Paul Sexton. 'It was good to visit Clapton on his annual vacation, [but] it begins to look as though he should go somewhere else for his holidays next year.'

Sexton's comments were typical of a generally reserved, though never less than respectful attitude to Clapton. It was not always so. In the sixties Clapton's public image was fitful and erratic. Never a naturally gifted speaker, he tended to leave press relations to Stigwood or to let his music do the talking. That only opened up more questions. Because Clapton was the virtual equivalent of a method actor – no one else pushed himself so deep into techniques or delved so far into roles – a clear picture never emerged. No sooner cast as a purist, he was playing mainstream rock and miming on *Top of the Pops*; praised to absurd levels as a soloist, he retreated into bland communal anonymity and then retired altogether. It hardly needs saying that everything could have ended for Clapton then: ended by death; decay; or simply the desertion of his long-suffering fans. That things turned out as they did was due to Clapton's keen intuitive feel for an audience, better expressed in concert than on record, and Roger Forrester. Between them they devised the hectic work schedule and generally benign public persona responsible for the goodwill on which Clapton drew so heavily at moments of crisis. By the time the last emergency was reached in 1987 Clapton's public standing was, once again, so formidable that unless he or Forrester made some fatal mistake it would be irresistible.

Forrester did not make fatal mistakes. Methodical, icily efficient, he made other managers look hopelessly negligent by comparison. Among Forrester's numerous achievements was changing the whole status of the impresario into that of a serious and even respected figure while not conspicuously raising his own profile. Whereas managers had once been almost as much part of rock mythology as the performers – Colonel Parker, Larry Parnes, Brian Epstein, Andrew Oldham and Allen Klein epitomize their eras as much as their clients do – Forrester was content to abide in the shadows, rarely quoted, never interviewed, a master of organization and logistics, the bedrock on which Clapton's whole career was founded.

The charge against Forrester is that he became over-possessive. In the matter of controlling Clapton's infrequent utterances to the press; in granting access to some and aggressively rebuffing others; in his high-handed and sometimes arrogant treatment of Clapton's ex-colleagues; above all, in his assuming of day-to-day responsibility for his client's life, Forrester effected a relationship in which, as Jack Bruce says, 'Eric wouldn't sneeze without Roger's say-so.'

Set against this, Forrester showed impressive nerve in taking on

Clapton at a time at which even the latter says, 'I was a gibbering wreck. I didn't have one saving grace . . . There wasn't one thing that redeemed me.' That was at the low point of Clapton's drug addiction. It may be that Stigwood, who describes himself today as 'Eric's very good friend' never visited Hurtwood Edge in the period 1971–3, whereas Forrester was one of the few to get past Clapton's door. It took a man of unusual resilience to rescue and in time revive a career hell bent on self-destruction. Perhaps it was not surprising that Forrester decided a robust management style was the best one. The results were self-evident. In 1973 Clapton was reduced to pawning guitars and considering selling his cars. In 1993 he was worth £30 million. Colleagues were startled, and some upset, not just by the aggressive shielding of client by manager, but also by the apparent role-reversal. Clapton seemed to be seeking his adviser's approval, rather than the other way round. There was something childlike in the way he deferred to Forrester and risked offending, by association, some of his staunchest fans. (A contributor to *Where's Eric*, a newsletter of innocuous views, speaks of the 'paranoid' attitude taken by management.) There was criticism, too, of Forrester's 'wilful' marketing of Clapton's name: some sponsors were rejected and others, no less arbitrarily, seized on, leading to at least one endorsement Jack Bruce considers 'unfortunate'. (Clapton was never the innocent in selling his wares, some believed. As early as 1967 Cream were involved in an enthusiastic though unsuccessful effort to advertise Falstaff beer.) Over the years Forrester became an increasingly controversial figure, and a source of fascination to Clapton watchers, as many of whom feared as admired him. Some of the attributes which irritated ordinary fans were counted as virtues by the music industry: above all, Forrester's intellect and renowned coolness at times of crisis, qualities thought crucial in handling Clapton. 'Roger was the last man in the world to panic,' says George Terry. 'Whatever you think of him, and two views are possible, he kept Eric on the road when no one else could have done it.'

Here was a new phenomenon in the rock business: a man at home in the boardrooms and corridors of power, yet so completely assimilated into his client's life that his influence stretched even to arranging for Clapton's marriage. Rarely in the whole history of such relationships has one man been so fully identified with another. Epstein, Oldham and Klein had all lasted for years; Forrester had survived for decades. Part of the reason was his intelligence and commendable calmness under fire. But Forrester's real strength lay in his unrivalled grasp (one not always shared by Clapton) of his client's interests; his ability to reverse the usual roles of employer and assistant; and his taking responsibility for literally everything that it was not vital for Clapton to do himself. If Forrester's reward for all this – the elegant office suite, the country home, the Bentley – was impressive, equally impressive were his tenacity, his loyalty and above all his willingness, as Dave Markee puts it, to 'go to the wall for Eric'. As a boy Clapton had craved attention; as a man he looked for support. Forrester gave them to him. It was as simple as that. Looking at Clapton's life as a whole it is possible to see a kind of immaturity of which his need for a dominant father-figure was characteristic. It is greatly to Forrester's credit that he identified the role and stuck with it even at a time when other parents might have considered infanticide.

From the illegitimate, morbidly shy child to the family entertainer and favourite of royalty, it is tempting to see Clapton's journey as that of a misfit into a pillar of the establishment. He cuts a jaunty and studiously affable figure these days, certainly compared to other sixties' survivors. Mick Jagger, for all his own vaunted assimilation, remains a spiky and unpredictable character; Townshend and McCartney limit themselves to the occasional epigrammatic quote; Harrison and Starr are virtually silent. Next to them Clapton seems like a paragon of sociability. One of his greatest strengths lies in his embodying the most threatening of music in a thoroughly unthreatening way – as Pete Brown puts it, 'keeping one foot in the Delta and the other planted firmly in Guildford high street'. Relatively few fans might have stuck with him over thirty years, and Clapton had found a way of exasperating most of them. But to survivors, and the millions who came later, he gave impressive and sometimes inspired schooling in the blues, heavily dependent on the suspension of disbelief and never requiring the listener's identification with the message. Clapton's fans related less to the missionary work of his youth than to the expert craftsman of recent pop standards. Provided he was prepared to co-operate with them on these, they never challenged his wider musical context. As with Forrester, Clapton enjoyed a perfect symbiotic relation-ship with his audience: he promised them anything so long as they listened.

In the past, when other artists talked about the self-revelatory nature of live performance, Clapton had insisted merely that the crowd 'have a good time'. As he got older he grew more serious. In 1990 he told Q that 'One of the reasons I can sell out the Albert Hall for so many nights is because people know it can go either way.' According to this reading Clapton in his late forties was a man on the move, living dangerously, never content to play the same thing twice. When he insists, 'Every time I pick up a guitar and play, it's the last chance I've got', the enthusiast is stirred by the intoxicating thought that he might be afforded a glimpse of the inner man.

A more likely prospect is of a seasoned, endlessly polished entertainer, spent of artistic vision, whose distinctive voice has become just another pleasant, and at times ploddingly obvious, pop sound. None of this is likely to concern the fans who, so far from expecting Clapton to go 'either way', admire him for exactly the opposite reason: his predictability. The odds are lengthening that Clapton will advance his guitar-playing beyond the point to which he took it twenty-five years ago. That is not to preclude the chances of his continuing to perform, year after year, at least a pastiche of his own primary sources. Anyone buying a ticket to the Albert Hall can look forward to an unusually full medley of the century's major musical trends. That only leaves the question of Clapton's motives. It may be that he betrays a sense of ego in constantly exposing himself to an audience; arguably he enjoys the routine; he may even appreciate the money. The last is an argument that pulls heavily with Clapton's critics. Along with the successes of the last twenty (mainly the last ten) years, Clapton has developed some expensive tastes. He may not need as much as welcome the income, but it weighs powerfully as an incentive to tour and perform at a time when his contemporaries have taken voluntary retirement.

Perhaps the most compelling reason of all, however, is that Clapton feels he still has important things to say, and needs a more prominent platform than his occasional albums from which to say them.

This sense of mission, of being born to perform, was one Clapton grasped early on: from the time he mimed to Gene Vincent records with his plastic guitar, or sang 'I Belong To Glasgow' standing behind the curtains in his grandparents' front room. As in the transmission of certain diseases, there seems in Clapton a strong genetic element – undoubtedly gleaned from his father – binding him to the artistic side of life. Every parent knows that there is an innate character in children which cannot be changed by education or family influence. As has been seen, Clapton's youthful instincts tended to the withdrawn, the sensitive, the morose. They were qualities he never lost. In so far as he learnt anything else during his early years it was a deep and abiding distrust of women. Making whatever allowance one will, there is something odd about Clapton's constant protestations of respect for the opposite sex. The intended note of self-awareness rings false. The number of Clapton's lovers does not detract from his place in history – it may even add to his stature. Compared to others of his calling he might be said to have led a sheltered life. But it remains a fact that, until recently, Clapton's relationships tended to be conducted generally through a miasma of drugs and drink, and almost entirely on his own terms.

There are different views and different constructions of Clapton's tortured personality. Through analysis, therapy and his own soul-searching remarks to the press, he seems to have studied the matter thoroughly. Clapton's tragedy conceivably lies in his being sufficiently intelligent to diagnose his condition, but not intelligent enough to think of a remedy. There may not be one. Some people build prisons for themselves from their own self-loathing, and then resentfully anticipate the suspicion and disapproval of others. The remark of his Hollyfield schoolmaster about Clapton 'permanently carrying . . . a slightly querulous look, as if daring you to challenge him' comes to mind. That was in 1958. Nearly three decades later – 1987 was the year Clapton assumed his modern perspective – there was evidence that he remained a bitter, occasionally fractious figure, an essentially weak character prone to compensatory bursts of aggression. Or, as Clapton himself puts it, 'I'm a very good blamer.'

The truth is that, for much of his adolescence and early adulthood, Clapton had no distinctive personality outside his music. He barely existed without a guitar. Pattie Boyd was only the most compelling witness when she told Coleman, 'On a one-to-one confrontation, as one human being to another, he sometimes can't or won't express himself without the instrument.' The guitars themselves became love-objects to Clapton; it is not exaggerating to say that he related to them almost as humans. The appliances were given nicknames. During the recording of *Behind The Sun* Clapton screamed 'as if someone had taken a dagger and plunged it into my arm' when Stephen Bishop idly picked up his friend's Stratocaster. Clapton himself refused to touch Muddy Waters's guitar on the grounds that 'it had an aura and demanded special treatment'. Other musicians took the attitude that they were journeymen experimenting with pieces of wood and string. Pete Townshend's act was to destroy the very instruments of his trade. Compared to theirs, Clapton's relationship with his guitar was such that, some nights, the presence of the audience was almost like a messy *ménage à trois*.

*   *   *

289

What was Clapton – at least until 1987 – like?

It says something to conclude that in most respects he was a Tory, almost even a Thatcherite. Clapton welded a broad streak of libertarianism to a generally conservative view of life. His constant assertion of his 'roots', his love of peculiarly English habits and customs and his ambivalent attitude to foreigners all suggest a man more than usually motivated by tradition. The charade of living within a fixed weekly wage and Clapton's views on the hierarchical nature of society ('I'm getting twenty quid more than you,' he once told O'Leary. 'I'm the guitarist') would also commend themselves to the monetarist. Personally capricious, he could be demanding of others. (Clapton 'won't tolerate inferiority,' notes Forrester.) Finally, as has been seen, in translating the sound working-man's values, including those of bluntness and intolerance, on to the concert stage, Clapton betrayed the unacceptable face of his personality. For all his vaunted identification with blacks, it was clear he had no such convictions.

Clapton has been widely praised for daring to show his more vulnerable side in public. 'When I lost my son,' he told Adrian Deevoy, 'I didn't run off and hide . . . I wrote a song and I gave it to the world because I wanted to share it with them and I think people respected that.' Clapton is less candid on the subject of his temperamental failings and leans heavily on an impressionistic reading of the past. He continues, for instance, to downplay the final days of Derek and the Dominos. According to Bobby Whitlock, Clapton's first choice of drummer had been not Gordon but Jim Keltner. Consequently, 'there was a terrible scene between them,' he remembers; an impression confirmed by the guitarist's choice of words in disbanding the group. Here, some discrepancy exists between Clapton's account ('I put my guitar down and walked out') and Whitlock's ('I'll fucking get you, you bastard'). On another occasion he screamed at Gordon for the provocative remark: 'Hello, Eric. How are you today?' Whitlock, who remains friendly with Clapton, describes him as 'a basically kind but sometimes touchy guy', with a strong capacity for both melancholy and nostalgia. When the Dominos were living at Hurtwood Edge in 1970, Whitlock was intrigued to find that 'Eric kept everything, I mean *everything*, he ever owned. There were kids' clothes, old T-shirts and caps, school reports and drawings, including one from 1958 labelled "Eric Clapton, King Of The Guitar".' Richard Drew, who visited the house at about the same time, confirms that 'Eric was sentimental about possessions, the older and more beaten-up the better. He had a kind of banal retentiveness.'

Previous hagiographies of Clapton have been inclined to use his artistic temperament as an excuse for what was, even by rock music standards, some outstandingly churlish behaviour. Stripped of this defence, not all of Clapton's characteristics bear the most cursory inspection. His personal opinions were suspect, but how much more suspect when imparted to an adoring audience? In this amended view, Clapton played on the susceptibilities of his youthful fans, exploited their known fads and tastes and affected a public image startlingly at odds with his pinched, introverted personality. 'He simply wasn't very pleasant when I knew him,' says Chris Dreja. 'There were mitigating factors, but I remember someone who was tense, uptight and at war with the world'; someone who found that fame and money simply exacerbated his unhappiness. The central enigma of Clapton's life is how such a personality, described by a second musician as 'fractured', evolved into the global icon it became.

And yet: however many ironies can be made to surface, however great the disparity between Clapton's private life and public utterances, disapproving of him is a curiously empty experience. One might as well disapprove of a child. There was, until his forties, something weak and half formed about Clapton. Stubborn on detail, he was famously easily led. Both Clapton's life and career have lurched from one fad and infatuation to another, his youthful – juvenile – capacity for change surviving into middle age. That is to say his strengths and his weaknesses are essentially the same. Clapton is young at heart. The extension of this is that his character seems almost a case of arrested development, the childlike virtues marred by the childish vices. When Clapton praised ('Freddie King was my first choice' . . . 'I think the world of Robert Cray' . . . 'He [Springsteen] is fabulous' . . . 'Mark Knopfler is totally unique' . . . 'Sting has that same quality') he did so with indiscriminate enthusiasm. When Clapton criticized he could be almost infantile in his anger.

His own view of himself was of someone detached, apart, one man and his guitar versus the world. In that Clapton's opinion was self-fulfilling – he made a habit of offending his friends – he became in time someone supremely qualified to play the blues. Clapton's personality and music are more than usually linked. It is possible to connect his manner with his matter. Dismaying as they were in some respects, the obstacles that Clapton built round his dealings with others unquestionably suited him. He knew that both his mind and his music were sharpened by adversity. Clapton acknowledged as much when he told a journalist, 'My strength in "peacetime" . . . is almost negligible. My strength, as a human being able to live happily in a peaceful situation, is not there. I'm only strong if I'm in a bind.' It was 1991, when real tragedy overcame him, before Clapton revised his gloomy, fatalist's view of life, informing a magazine, 'I try to look on every day now as being a bonus.' Sense was knocked into him by unhappiness.

'Eric was a thoughtful man,' Whitlock insists; but he had no storyline in his head for how his life should progress. His comment to Markee about 'the improbable [becoming] inevitable' will be remembered. Clapton's thirty-year career has included a brief R & B group, blues purism, Carnaby-Street-Swinging-London pop, self-effacing gospel and soul, drink-fuelled cockney nostalgia, self-effacing country and reggae, anthemic rock and, most recently, healthy but wistful revivalism. Between transformations, he has written for television and films, recorded with everyone from the Beatles to Ian Botham, rescued the careers of Gary Brooker and Andy Fairweather-Low, espoused philosophies from near-fascism to total anarchy, supported charities and had a cause formed against him. Eric Clapton, therefore, is not one to make a virtue of consistency. Vanity and play-acting are always occupational hazards for anyone in the performing arts. Even so, Clapton's track record bears comparison to the great transients like Bowie and Dylan. Three distinct phases emerge, each separated from the other by a crisis.

In the first, 1963–71, Clapton arrived, dragging the guitar out of its footling years, and found himself pushed to stardom. Of this period Pete Brown's comment is telling: 'Eric was scared shitless of fame . . . On the other hand, he loved the goodies that Cream brought. The need for success vying with contempt for those who bestow it.' It is reasonable to see Clapton in 1970 or 1971 as a man whose career ran independent of his happiness. ('Fear and loneliness' were the reasons he later gave for taking drugs.) To be left floundering at home at the very apogee of his fame required self-destructive skills of a high order. During his seclusion Clapton's reputation gained from the theory that he had cracked under the pressure of his epic – Godlike – status. Interest focused on Clapton's habits, his foibles and the apparently wilful streak that led him to break up or abandon groups at their very moment of triumph. Something heroic and self-denying was inferred and Clapton was given the status of a latter-day saint of rock legend. That the tragic view of Clapton was something of a simplification the preceding pages have, perhaps, shown; and in the seventies a reaction set in which portrayed Clapton as an ephemeral figure – a musicologist rather than a musician, devoid of any distinguishing principle. This, too, was an inadequate picture of the man.

There were, however, some notably low points to Clapton's thirties, a decade he admits to having 'hated'. Clapton's flirtations with alien musical styles were ineffectual; his own songs were patchy and unconvincing, with none of the bitter wit of a Lennon or the joyous derangement of a Dylan. By the mid-1970s Clapton was reduced to imitating his imitators, asserting his fame by beery denunciation of his critics, a Lear-like figure who had given up his kingdom but still wanted to be king. He seemed, in his detractors' eyes, not to stand for anything. From his lying comatose on stage in Buffalo to his racist outburst in Birmingham to his 'blandly unobtrusive' performance at Blackbushe, Clapton's career became little better than a joke. (It was, however, as Marshbrook's records confirm, a singularly practical joke.) The crisis, first reached in 1981–2, was not finally overcome until 1987, when Clapton pledged to give up drinking. Any contemporary study of his life opens then.

The beloved family entertainer is, therefore, a relatively recent creation. Until his forties Clapton's elastic music and brittle personality set new standards in risking chaos and succumbing to it. With the release of *August* and fatherhood, the Albert Hall and sobriety, Clapton seemed to scale down if not vanquish his furies. Where once there were drugs, now there was cricket. Where once a mission, now a formula. Clapton remained capable of surprising, just as his music remained capable of dramatic, bravura touches; in summer 1994 he was recording an album described as 'almost purely blues'. Perhaps this – his ability to recycle himself so fully, and so without embarrassment at the circle formed – is Clapton's greatest legacy. There are not many artists whose gestures, habits, clothes, moods, even their moments of blindness and self-deception, so perfectly evoke their times. As Pete Brown says, 'Consider the changes Eric has seen. Consider the disappointment and the loss. Consider the achievement and the despair. Consider the magic.

'Consider the madness.'

Epilogue

As well as selling six million copies in a year, *Unplugged* was an attempt by Clapton to come to terms with the death of his son. *From The Cradle*, the all-blues record he had been promising to make for years, was part of his recovery. The album, released in September 1994, went to number one on the *Billboard* chart. It earned glowing reviews. *From The Cradle* celebrated Clapton's reason for being: transcendent, fundamental blues with few overdubs or edits and fewer stylistic departures. It was the formula pieces like 'Five Long Years' and 'I'm Tore Down' that revealed an essential truth: Clapton soared higher off clever imitation than off original expression. The notice in *Rolling Stone* struck a nerve when it spoke of *Cradle's* 'facsimiles' of Elmore James and Willie Dixon standards. To the *Weekly* there was a sense in which Clapton 'uses the blues as a prop, not a springboard'. These were isolated voices in an otherwise unanimous outpouring of praise. *From The Cradle* sold 400,000 copies in a week. It was heavily promoted on television and radio. In March 1995 the record won a Grammy for Best Traditional Blues Album. Clapton was nominated for a Brit Award in the category of best male solo artist.

He followed the album by playing on the season premiere of *Saturday Night Live* and undertaking his first full American tour since 1992. Clapton performed at arenas for a month, then returned to smaller clubs in some cities, including New York and Los Angeles. They were all blues shows, no matter how many people screamed for hits like 'Cocaine' or 'Layla'. At the Albert Hall, where Clapton began his ninth annual season on 19 February 1995, there was open muttering and at least one walk-out in protest at the repertoire. According to David Cheal, 'This was a show that didn't quite live up to standards ... It

294

seemed [Clapton] and his band spent too long limbering up with light-weight acoustic tunes, so that by the time he finally strapped on his white Stratocaster and was doing the business with heart-stopping songs like "Have You Ever Loved A Woman", the show was nearly over.' In the *Daily Mail's* view, 'One was torn between admiration for his skills, sincerity and emotional engagement and wondering why he should ignore all his own body of work.' As his starched jeans and baggy sweater suggested, Clapton was growing older, drawing less heavily on inspiration than on habit, and becoming, with each passing year, more of an institution.

On 1 January 1995, in a move widely predicted in the media, Clapton was awarded the OBE for services to music. His salary for the previous twelve months was £13.4 million, making him one of Britain's highest paid company directors.

In the seventies and eighties heroin had given way to brandy as Clapton's drug of choice. By the mid-nineties he had learned a better method of dealing with his problems: sharing them. Of his weekly sessions with a family therapist, Clapton told the *New York Times*, 'I have such a strange, deluded idea of what the world is about that if I'm left to my own resources, I would go insane.' Despite his more mature, life-affirming attitude, Clapton did little to encourage the notion that he might, at last, be settling down. In April 1994 he began a relationship with the actress Susannah Doyle (described by Clapton as 'the most fascinating woman' he had ever met), left her for Francesca Amfitheatrof, and was visited in New York by *Pulp Fiction's* Uma Thurman. By the summer of 1995 Clapton was once again shuffling up the steps of San Lorenzo with a parade of starlets and models, and complaining in private of his 'recurrent row' with his women.

Besides the guitar and the blues, Clapton's only other long-term relationship has been with tragedy. In December 1994 Clapton's grandmother, Rose Clapp, died and was buried in the churchyard at Ripley's St Mary Magdalen. And then, on 8 April 1995 Alice Ormsby-Gore, the woman who went through heroin addiction with Clapton, was found dead at home in Boscombe, a rundown district of Bournemouth. It would be difficult to imagine a more harrowing end for the heiress brought up on an 8000-acre estate than the twilight years as an alcoholic and recluse. According to her neighbours in Boscombe, she rarely left her ground-floor bedsit. Nicola Jones, who lived opposite, said she had been oblivious to Ormsby-Gore's background: 'I saw her occasionally walking across to the shops. Once I noticed her eyes were closed and she looked asleep . . . She was shuffling along and was a pathetic sight. She always looked shabby and her flat was in a disgusting condition.' She said she had heard Ormsby-Gore had been found 'with a syringe stuck in her arm.'

Clapton responded as he always did. He immersed himself in his work. The Albert Hall was followed by concerts in Birmingham and Glasgow, a tour of Europe, guest appearances, and a televised tribute to Stevie Ray Vaughan. The rest of Clapton's 1995 projects, to give them their due, were triumphantly intelligent choices. He lent his name, or cash, to a number of blues albums. As before, he raised money for Alcoholics Anonymous and the Sharp Shop. And, in an astonishingly liberated insight, Clapton cleaned house, literally. Out went 32 of his paintings because, he said, he'd had enough of the 'snobbish and hypocritical' art world. There were other instances of letting go, of simplification. *From The Cradle* was just the latest hint that, for Clapton, the future lay in going backwards. Everything, from now on, would be figuratively or musically unplugged.

He was back at the Albert Hall, for the tenth straight year, in February 1996. Yet again, most of the crowd-pleasing workouts were deep-sixed for vague, mid-paced pop odes and the usual blues suspects. Left *in situ* were only a handful of Cream hits. That June, Clapton closed the show at the Prince's Trust (formally known as the Mastercard 'Masters of Music' concert) in Hyde Park. The challenge of animating 200,000 fans in sub-zero weather was too much for Alanis Morissette, Dylan, and the other sacrificial warm-ups. But it was impossible not to be moved by Clapton's emotionally charged set. This, after all, wasn't some postmodern ironist at work. Clapton had *lived* the blues as much as a white Englishman ever can. All the familiar formulae were made fresh again by the soul-grabbing poignancy of his slow tunes, the joyful snap of his belters, and the raw-throated vocals. A gospel choir bopped from foot to foot during the dire 'Holy Mother'. Even at this sorry low, in a foggy and dripping park, Clapton got the middle-aged fans dancing in the dark. I don't know how he did it, and I was there, I still am.

His reinvention of house epics like 'Crossroads', the spring-cleaning and even the crewcut all cast a wry sideways light on Clapton. The deconstruction continued apace in 1997. For the first time since the days of *August* and *Journeyman*, he was missing from the Albert Hall.

While, bizarrely, Clapton blamed a booking glitch, the truth was more complex. He pulled out because, bluntly, he was turning into a human fixture of the English season. As a friend says, 'it scared Eric shitless he'd become a kind of pop equivalent of Lords or Wimbledon.' In a typically perverse move, Clapton then released an album called *Retail Therapy* under the alias TDF. It was unregenerate white noise, devoid of charm, warmth, or anything resembling a tune. Since Eno's well-touted farragos of whistles and bells, ambient music's more obstreperous drones have been filched by everyone from Bowie to Oasis. Each, in their different way, has gazed deep into rock's role as shop-floor clatter. Even so, it was a shock when Clapton joined the industrial nation.

The scaling-down of his life and legend did Clapton no harm financially. According to the *Sunday Times*, he was worth £75 million in 1997. (The 32 pieces of art added precisely £41,665 to Marshbrook's books.) Based on his back catalogue and an income stream that netted £50 million in royalties from 1991 to 1996, Clapton was one of the 200 richest men in Britain. Over thirty years this dour, emotionally stunted 'Loony', with his phenomenal ear, his *savoir-vivre*, his vigilant manager, even that unusual thing, a sense of doubt, had given his soul to the blues. But, predictably, it was only when Clapton recast himself as a Survivor that he got rich,

His love life wasn't, however, flourishing. There were still innumerable affairs, alleged affairs, girlfriends, friends, and dates, Clapton went out with the singer Sheryl Crow. Tongues wagged about a woman called Anne Vance, a former head of the Betty Ford Clinic. He still saw Yvonne Kelly. Clapton's policy on remarriage, though, bowed increasingly to the law of diminishing returns. 'I value my solitude and privacy and boundaries...I've learnt more about respecting my own needs. I probably could [marry]. But she'd have had to have done the same amount of work in this area as me.'

Clapton again nixed the Albert Hall in 1998. Proving the sheer range of his capriciousness, he told British fans he'd 'rung in' a booking, but too late. They settled instead for three nights at Earls Court that fall.

Meanwhile Clapton released *Pilgrim*, his first studio album of new material in nine years, Advance PR copies were stamped with the warning 'For security purposes, all review CDs of this title bear an individual number', evidently to fend off bootleggers. In the event, there was no wild rush to lay hands on *Pilgrim* ahead of time. 'She's

Gone' turned a fragile, *461*-era riff into a full-length rocker; 'River of Tears' was alternately obsessive and depressive, again mining Clapton's stock theme, love-gone-awry'; 'Fall Like Rain' doffed its hat, like half the cuts on *No Reason To Cry*, to Don Williams. The reference points for 'My Father's Eyes', meanwhile, were Steve Winwood via Curtis Mayfield. Those were the highs of an album which clearly saw its first duty as education, and was only rarely willing to slip in a little entertainment like ice in one of Stigwood's dry Martinis. *Pilgrim* flopped on the chart.

There was, though, a sub-plot. Clapton had had one of the most dysfunctional, and talked-of, childhoods even in rock. At 53, he was still writing about his father's eyes. In one cynic's view 'a sad example of pop gods' self-parody, Eric could shock us now only by revealing that actually he was quite a well-adjusted, happy guy.' Whatever its already limited chances, that prospect was torpedoed by the media's 'discovery' of Edward Fryer in April 1998. According to the *Daily Mail*, which splashed its scoop over four pages, 'Clapton's dad was a pianist, crooner and drifter who lived his life on the road, performing Nat King Cole songs in hotels and bars across his native Canada. He was also a supreme ladies' man, who fell in love and married at least twice, in the same way that his son has a reputation for dating scores of beautiful women . . . Sadly, Clapton will never be able to meet his father, who died of leukaemia aged 65 on May 15 1985.'

Oddly enough, all the above, and more, appeared in *Edge Of Darkness* on its first publication in 1994.

One of the strangest sights of a life not untouched by whim came that spring, when Clapton wielded a golden shovel to break ground on the Crossroads Centre, a 36-bed drug-treatment facility on Antigua. He put up more than $2 million to pay construction costs. Clapton also found time and money to help recovering addicts and alcoholics closer to home. He spent 'several days' working alongside full-time counsellors at a London rehab clinic. 'Because of having survived a pretty disastrous journey through my life,' he says, 'there seems to be something vital about me being able to participate in this, and give something back . . . It's now much more vital to me than sitting in my bedroom and playing.'

Bluntly, music had ceased to be his top priority. According to *The Times*, Clapton now put it at number three. 'I had to make that decision in order to stay away from my past life. I'd come to think that rock and roll was my saviour, but it doesn't quite work that way.' Left unanswered was the *Source*'s rhetorical query of *Pilgrim*. 'Slowhand doesn't give a fuck anymore. Why should we?'

On that note, Clapton hit the road. The 1998 tour wound through 35 American cities, complete with a five-piece band, three backing singers and a full orchestra. Perhaps his relentless smoothing-down of the music was inspired by his new sponsor, Lexus (Clapton traded to Volkswagen in Europe); or it may just have been the latest in an easy-listening continuum that began in 1974. Whatever the cause, Clapton took his lumps from the critics, though money rained down at the box office. For the most part, the gigs featured flawless guitar, staging in exquisite taste, neither of which made up for what Clapton once routinely had: raw, ungilded power. 'Nice' was the fell word used by the *Mail*.

Clapton rounded off 1998 by playing home-town concerts in London. Then he was back on his longest road trip of all, the one leading to what Blake calls the palace of wisdom. After wrapping sessions for his seventeenth solo album, Clapton was hard at his volunteer work in London and Antigua. To some, this appeared to be a modern version of the King's Evil, whereby it was widely believed that the royal touch could cure scrofula, and sufferers went mad for it. According to Macaulay in his *History of England*, the practice hit its peak under Charles II, who touched over 100,000 people during his reign. 'In 1680, the throng was such that six or seven of the sick were trampled to death,' Macaulay wrote. Given his fanatical popularity, and the fact that dozens of women would rush him whenever he strolled down King's Road, there was always the danger that mob rule might suddenly recur. In his mid-fifties, Clapton was still swarmed over the instant he set foot in the street. Ironically, it may be only now that his fame has matched his starting ambitions. Equally perversely, he no longer wants it.

Tempus fugit, Pattie Boyd thinks the last thirty years have gone by 'like a flash'. They've gone by like a mushroom cloud for her ex, and in the boom and smoke of them Clapton must have taken consolation from his self-image, no less true today than ever, as 'one man and his guitar versus the world'.

Appendix 1
Chronology

30 March 1945	Eric Patrick Clapton born at Ripley, Surrey
1950–56	Attends Church of England First School
1956–8	St Bede's School
1958–61	Hollyfield School
1958	Given first guitar, a £14 Spanish acoustic
1961	To Kingston Art College
1962	Expelled from Kingston. Given a Kay 'Red Devil' electric guitar, Clapton practises at home, in Kingston, and in L'Auberge coffee bar in Richmond
February–August 1963	Joins Tom McGuinness in the Roosters
Autumn 1963	Plays with Brian Casser (Casey Jones), performing a bizarre mix of pop, folk-rock and cabaret
November 1963–March 1965	The Yardbirds
April 1965–June 1966	John Mayall's Bluesbreakers
Autumn 1965	Goes missing with the Glands – a kind of musical equivalent of the Goons – in Greece
April 1966	Joins one-off studio group including Jack Bruce. Begins rehearsing with Bruce and Ginger Baker
11 June 1966	Confirmatory 'ERIC, JACK AND GINGER TEAM UP' headline in *Melody Maker*

July 1966	*Blues Breakers With Eric Clapton* released
29 July 1966	First public appearance by Cream at the Twisted Wheel, Manchester
22 March 1967	Cream arrive in New York
29 October 1967	Meets Pattie Boyd at the Saville Theatre, London
November 1967	*Disraeli Gears* released
11 May 1968	*Rolling Stone* review describing Clapton as 'a master of blues clichés' and 'a virtuoso at performing other people's ideas'
May 1968	Clapton decides to leave Cream
August 1968	*Wheels Of Fire* released
26 November 1968	Farewell concerts at the Royal Albert Hall
Spring 1969	Takes possession of Hurtwood Edge, Ewhurst
April 1969	The 'Eric Clapton, Stevie Winwood, Ginger Baker Band' announced in *Melody Maker*
7 June 1969	World première of Blind Faith in Hyde Park, London
November 1969	Begins recording first solo album, backed by Delaney and Bonnie Bramlett and members of their group
Spring 1970	Blind Faith disband. Première of Derek and the Dominos
August 1970	*Eric Clapton* released
9 September 1970	'Layla' recorded at Criteria Studios, Miami
December 1970	*Layla And Other Assorted Love Songs* released to indifferent world
May 1971	The Dominos disband
1 August 1971	Clapton comes out of semi-retirement to play at the Concert For Bangladesh in New York
13 January 1973	Two comeback performances at the Rainbow Theatre, London

10 April 1974	Formally announces comeback, after successful treatment for heroin addiction
July–August 1974	A distinctly upbeat Clapton tours America
August 1974	*461 Ocean Boulevard* released
10 September 1974	Clapton becomes company secretary of Marshbrook Limited
5 December 1974	Clapton plays at Hammersmith Odeon and turns down yet another offer to join the Rolling Stones
June–August 1975	Tours America
February–April 1976	Records at Shangri-La Studios, Malibu, with Bob Dylan, Robbie Robertson, Van Morrison, Pete Townshend, Ronnie Wood and Billy Preston
5 August 1976	Invites audience at the Birmingham Odeon to vote for Enoch Powell to 'stop [Britain] becoming a colony'
September 1976	Rock Against Racism formed in protest at Clapton's remarks
7 September 1976	Writes 'Wonderful Tonight' for Pattie Boyd
26 November 1976	Performs at The Band's farewell concert, later released as *The Last Waltz*
November 1977	*Slowhand* released
15 July 1978	Appears as support for Bob Dylan in front of 250,000 crowd at Blackbushe – a performance Ray Coleman describes as 'blandly unobtrusive'
20 February 1979	Clapton admits himself to be a 'very nervous and bitter man'
27 March 1979	Marries Pattie Boyd in Tucson, Arizona
August 1979	Clapton fires Carl Radle, Dick Sims and Jamie Oldaker from his group. Radle dies in 1980
17 October 1979	Riots at Clapton's concert at Katowice,

	Poland. Clapton flees the country in tears while the authorities threaten his manager with arrest and impound his money
May 1980	Tour of Britain
February 1981	Clapton tells the *Daily Mirror* he lives on a weekly wage-packet and 'Go[es] down the pub in Ripley on Fridays'
14 March 1981	Clapton rushed to hospital in St Paul, suffering from ulcers. Remainder of American tour cancelled
9–13 September 1981	Clapton joins charity concerts for Amnesty International
7 January 1982	Starts treatment for alcoholism at the Hazelden Foundation
September 1982	Fires Dave Markee, Gary Brooker, Henry Spinetti and Chris Stainton (later reprieved) from his group
February 1983	*Money And Cigarettes* released, the first album on Clapton's own label
September–December 1983	Plays eleven concerts in support of ARMS (Action Research into Multiple Sclerosis) in Britain and America
January 1984	Records theme music for *The Hit*, beginning a long and outstandingly successful career writing for film and television
June–July 1984	Tours as part of Roger Waters's *Pros and Cons of Hitch-Hiking* revue
11 January 1985	Ruth Kelly, Clapton's first child, born in Doncaster Maternity Hospital
March 1985	*Behind The Sun* released
15 May 1985	Edward Fryer, Clapton's father, dies
13 July 1985	Clapton performs at Live Aid in Philadelphia
November 1985	*Edge of Darkness* broadcast
20 June 1986	Appears at Prince's Trust 10th birthday party

21 August 1986	Conor Loren Clapton born in St Mary's Hospital, Paddington
November 1986	*August* released
6 January 1987	Clapton's first season at the Royal Albert Hall opens
November 1987	Clapton re-enters Hazelden at the same time as he advertises Michelob beer on American television
April 1988	*Crossroads* released
12 May 1988	Clapton divorces Pattie Boyd
30 July 1989	Clapton draws 102,000 people to a concert in Maputo, Mozambique
November 1989	*Journeyman* released
30 June 1990	Clapton performs at the year's major rock event, the Nordoff-Robbins benefit concert at Knebworth
26 August 1990	Stevie Ray Vaughan and three members of Clapton's entourage – Bobby Brooks, Nigel Browne and Colin Smythe – killed in a helicopter crash
September 1989–September 1990	Clapton earns £5,097,553 through Marshbrook, which turns over more than £11 million
20 March 1991	Conor Clapton dies in New York
September 1991	Clapton records soundtrack for *Rush* in Los Angeles, including 'Tears In Heaven'
December 1991	Tours Japan with George Harrison
16 January 1992	Clapton records *Unplugged* at Bray Studios, Berkshire
9 September 1992	Clapton receives MTV 'best video' award for 'Tears In Heaven'
16 October 1992	Appears at the 30th anniversary tribute to Bob Dylan in New York. According to Pete Brown, 'the two operative words to describe [Clapton's performance] were "intelligent" and "dignified"'

12 January 1993	Cream re-forms to play three numbers at the annual Rock and Roll Hall of Fame
24 February 1993	Clapton wins six Grammys in Los Angeles During the year he also collects an 'outstanding recording artist' trophy, gold and platinum discs for *Unplugged* and a Nordoff-Robbins music therapy award
7 February 1994	Wins 'top male artist' American Music Award
20 February 1994	Opens eighth annual season at Royal Albert Hall
16 June 1994	Clapton tells David Frost, 'I'm still trying to unravel my childhood' and 'I don't really know who I am.'
July–August 1994	Records album described as 'almost purely blues'
12 September 1994	*From the Cradle* released. The album sells 400,000 copies in a week
October–November 1994	Clapton plays on the season premiere of *Saturday Night Live* and undertakes his first full American tour since 1992
20 December 1994	Clapton attends his grandmother Rose Clapp's funeral in Ripley. The triumph of perseverance that had led him to the top of the charts had begun thirty-six years before, when she bought him his first guitar
1 January 1995	Clapton is awarded the OBE
19 February 1995	Begins ninth annual season at the Albert Hall, followed by dates elsewhere in Britain and Europe
1 March 1995	Clapton wins a Grammy for Best Traditional Blues Album
10–11 May 1995	Appears alongside Buddy Guy, B. B. King and Robert Cray in a televised tribute to Stevie Ray Vaughan

306

Summer 1995	Clapton returns to the Studio
1995-96	He cleans house, literally, selling 32 paintings at auction and adding £41,665 to Marshbrook's books
February 1996	Clapton's tenth—and, as it turns out, last—straight season at the Albert Hall
29 June 1996	Closes the show at the Prince's Trust concert in Hyde Park
July 1997	*Retail Therapy*, unregenerate white noise, released under the alias TDF, out on Warners
1997	The *Sunday Times* fixes Clapton's wealth at £75 million, making him one of the 200 richest men in Britain
February 1998	*Pilgrim* released
March 1998	Clapton wields a golden shovel to break ground on the Crossroads Centre, a 36-bed drug clinic on Antigua. He puts up more than $2 million to pay construction costs
April–June 1998	Plays in 35 American cities, complete with a five-piece band, three backing singers, and a full orchestra. The tour is sponsored by Lexus
15–17 October 1998	Clapton finally does hometown gigs, in Earls Court, London
Winter 1998–1999	The studio
April 1999	Clapton ends his business relationship with Roger Forrester—and rounds off an era

Appendix 2
Eric Clapton's Groups
1963–99

THE ROOSTERS (*1963*)

Clapton, Tom McGuinness (guitar bass), Ben Palmer (piano), Terry Brennan (vocals), Robin Mason (drums)

CASEY JONES AND THE ENGINEERS (*1963*)

Clapton, Tom McGuinness (bass), Brian Casser (vocals), Dave McCumisky (guitar), Ray Stock (drums)

THE YARDBIRDS (*1963–5*)

Clapton, Keith Relf (vocals), Chris Dreja (guitar), Jim McCarty (drums), Paul Samwell-Smith (bass)

JOHN MAYALL'S BLUESBREAKERS (*1965–6*)

Clapton, John Mayall (vocals, keyboards), Hughie Flint (drums), John McVie (bass)

THE GLANDS (*1965*)

Clapton, Ben Palmer (piano), Jake Milton (drums), Bernie Greenwood (saxophone), John Baily (vocals), Bob Ray (bass)

CREAM (*1966-8*)

Clapton, Jack Bruce (bass, vocals), Ginger Baker (drums)

BLIND FAITH (*1969-70*)

Clapton, Steve Winwood (keyboards, vocals), Rick Grech (bass), Ginger Baker (drums)

DELANEY AND BONNIE AND FRIENDS (*1969-70*)

Clapton, Delaney Bramlett (vocals), Bonnie Bramlett (vocals), Rita Coolidge (vocals), George Harrison (guitar), Carl Radle (bass), Bobby Whitlock (keyboards), Jim Gordon (drums), various others

DEREK AND THE DOMINOS (*1970-71*)

Clapton, Carl Radle (bass), Bobby Whitlock (keyboards), Jim Gordon (drums), with assistance from Duane Allman and Dave Mason (both guitar)

THE PALPITATIONS – ERIC CLAPTON'S RAINBOW CONCERT (*1973*)

Clapton, Steve Winwood (keyboards, vocals), Pete Townshend, Ronnie Wood (both guitars), Rick Grech (bass), Jim Capaldi, Jimmy Karstein, Reebop (all drums/percussion)

ERIC CLAPTON AND HIS BAND (*1974-8*)

Clapton, George Terry (guitar), Carl Radle (bass), Dick Sims (keyboards), Jamie Oldaker (drums), Yvonne Elliman and Marcy Levy (both vocals), Sergio Pastora (occasional percussion)

ERIC CLAPTON AND HIS BAND (*1978–9*)

Clapton, Carl Radle (bass), Dick Sims (keyboards), Jamie Oldaker (drums)

ERIC CLAPTON AND HIS BAND (*1979*)

Clapton, Albert Lee (guitar), Carl Radle (bass), Dick Sims (keyboards), Jamie Oldaker (drums)

ERIC CLAPTON AND HIS BAND (*1979–82*)

Clapton, Albert Lee (guitar, vocals), Gary Brooker (piano, vocals), Dave Markee (bass), Chris Stainton (keyboards), Henry Spinetti (drums)

ERIC CLAPTON AND HIS BAND (*1982–4*)

Clapton, Albert Lee (guitar, vocals), Chris Stainton (keyboards), Donald 'Duck' Dunn (bass), Roger Hawkins, replaced by Jamie Oldaker (drums)

ERIC CLAPTON AND HIS BAND (*1984*)

Clapton, Chris Stainton (keyboards), Jamie Oldaker (drums), Donald 'Duck' Dunn (bass), Peter Robinson (synthesizer), Marcy Levy and Shaun Murphy (both vocals)

ERIC CLAPTON AND HIS BAND (*1985*)

Clapton, Tim Renwick (guitar), Chris Stainton (keyboards), Jamie Oldaker (drums), Donald 'Duck' Dunn (bass), Marcy Levy and Shaun Murphy (both vocals)

ERIC CLAPTON AND HIS BAND (*1986*)

Clapton, Greg Phillinganes (keyboards, vocals), Nathan East (bass), Phil Collins (drums, vocals)

ERIC CLAPTON AT THE ALBERT HALL (*1987*)

Clapton, Greg Phillinganes (keyboards, vocals), Nathan East (bass), Steve Ferrone (drums), with assistance from Mark Knopfler (guitar) and Phil Collins (drums)

ERIC CLAPTON AT THE ALBERT HALL (*1988*)

Clapton, Greg Phillinganes (keyboards, vocals), Nathan East (bass), Steve Ferrone (drums), supported by Mark Knopfler (guitar) and Tessa Niles and Katie Kissoon (vocals)

ERIC CLAPTON AT THE ALBERT HALL (*1989*)

Clapton, Greg Phillinganes (keyboards, vocals), Nathan East (bass), Phil Collins (drums), with assistance from Steve Ferrone (drums), Alan Clark (keyboards), Ray Cooper (percussion), Tessa Niles and Katie Kissoon (vocals)

ERIC CLAPTON AT THE ALBERT HALL (*1990*)

Clapton with a variety of formats, in which the main group was Greg Phillinganes (keyboards, vocals), Nathan East (bass), Steve Ferrone (drums)

ERIC CLAPTON AT THE ALBERT HALL (*1991*)

Clapton with a series of bluesmen, associates and classical musicians, in which the basic group was again Greg Phillinganes (keyboards, vocals), Nathan East (bass), Steve Ferrone (drums). Others featured were Phil Palmer, Jimmy Vaughan, Albert Collins, Robert Cray, Buddy Guy (all guitar), Johnnie Johnson, Chuck Leavell (both keyboards), Jamie Oldaker (drums), Ray Cooper (percussion), Joey Spampinato (bass), Jerry Portnoy (harmonica)

ERIC CLAPTON WITH GEORGE HARRISON (*1991*)

Clapton, Harrison, Andy Fairweather-Low (all guitar), Greg Phillinganes (keyboards, vocals), Chuck Leavell (keyboards), Nathan East (bass), Steve Ferrone (drums), Ray Cooper (percussion), Tessa Niles and Katie Kissoon (vocals)

ERIC CLAPTON AT THE ALBERT HALL (*1992*)

Clapton, Andy Fairweather-Low (guitar), Nathan East (bass), Steve Ferrone (drums), Chuck Leavell (keyboards), Ray Cooper (percussion), Tessa Niles and Katie Kissoon (vocals)

ERIC CLAPTON AT THE ALBERT HALL (*1993*)

Clapton, Andy Fairweather-Low (guitar), Chris Stainton (keyboards), Donald 'Duck' Dunn (bass), Richie Hayward (drums), Jerry Portnoy (harmonica), Tim Sanders, Simon Clarke (both saxophones), Roddy Lorimer (trumpet)

ERIC CLAPTON AT THE ALBERT HALL (*1994*)

Clapton, Andy Fairweather-Low (guitar), Dave Bronze (bass), Chris Stainton (keyboards), Richie Hayward (drums), Jerry Portnoy (harmonica)

ERIC CLAPTON AND HIS BAND (*1994–95*)

Clapton, Andy Fairweather-Low (guitar), Dave Bronze (bass), Chris Stainton (keyboards), Jim Keltner, Richie Hayward (both drums), Jerry Portnoy (harmonica), Tim Sanders, Simon Clarke (both saxophones), Roddy Lorimer (trumpet)

ERIC CLAPTON IN HYDE PARK (*1996*)

Clapton, Andy Fairweather-Low (guitar), Dave Bronze (bass), Chris Stainton (keyboards), Steve Gadd (drums), Jerry Portnoy (harmonica),

Tim Sanders, Simon Clarke (both saxophones), Roddy Lorimer (trumpet), Tessa Niles and Katie Kissoon (vocals), the East London Gospel Choir

ERIC CLAPTON AND HIS BAND (*1998–99*)

Clapton, Andy Fairweather-Low, Alan Darby (guitars), Nathan East (bass), Steve Gadd (drums), Katie Kissoon and others (vocals), various orchestral formats

Sources and Chapter Notes

The author has a great many debts. The following notes indicate the principal sources used in writing each chapter of the book. Formal interviews and on-the-record conversations are listed by name. Inevitably, many requested that their comments remain anonymous and therefore no acknowledgement appears of the enormous help, encouragement and kindness I received from a number of quarters. Where Eric Clapton himself is quoted, the sources are his own published interviews or the memory of those who spoke to him.

CHAPTER 1

A full account of Cream's farewell performances is available in books, magazines and on film. Personal comment was supplied by Pete Brown, Dick Heckstall-Smith and Jack Bruce, all of whom attended – and in Bruce's case played at – the concerts. For the account of Clapton in 1993, newspaper reports and my own memory are entirely responsible.

CHAPTER 2

Various accounts of Clapton's childhood have been previously published, most notably in Ray Coleman's *Survivor* (Sidgwick & Jackson, 1985). They tell one part of the story. Further comment and analysis on the years 1945–63 was supplied by Mary Wild, headteacher of Ripley Church of England First School; Jan Jameson, headteacher of St Bede's Church of England Middle School; the staff of Hollyfield School; and Robert Simonson of the Surrey Record Office. Additional interviews were conducted with Matthew Wood and Anne McDowell, with Clapton's classmates Jenny Dolan, Chris Dreja and Philip Solly, and with his former masters Goronwy Gealy and Peter Strachan. Clapton's poem was contributed by Richard Drew.

The work of charting Clapton's early musical career was made possible with the help of Dick Heckstall-Smith, Ben Palmer, Tom McGuinness and the late Alexis Korner.

Public records were obtained from the National Archives of Canada (Government Records Branch), the General Register Office and both the British Library and the British Newspaper Library, Colindale.

CHAPTER 3

Major sources for the period 1963–66 included Chris Dreja and Jim McCarty, and Hughie Flint, of the Yardbirds and John Mayall's Bluesbreakers respectively. Mayall himself spoke to me by telephone. A number of new facts about Clapton's early career were supplied by Geoff Bradford, Georgie Fame, Chris Farlowe, Dick Heckstall-Smith, Pete Hogman, Paul Jones, the late Alexis Korner, Tom McGuinness, Ben Palmer, John Platt and Dick Taylor. Additional material was provided by Pete Brown, Tom Keylock, Gary Lawson, Kay Munday, Sally Prescott, Chris Rea and Pamela Wynn (formerly Mayall). Research was also conducted in the Ship and Half Moon pubs, Ripley, and Dobell's Music Shop, the latter, alas, now closed.

Published source material included Harry Shapiro's *Slowhand*, reprinted as *Lost In The Blues* (Guinness, 1992); Marc Roberty's *Clapton: The Complete Chronicles* (Pyramid, 1991) and *The New Visual Documentary* (Omnibus, 1990), Steve Turner's *Conversations With Eric Clapton* (Abacus, 1976) and, again, Ray Coleman's *Survivor*.

CHAPTER 4

Pete Brown, lyricist of some of Cream's most enduring numbers, was a major source for this chapter. Jack Bruce, while not going as far as a formal interview, allowed himself a number of veiled opinions about Clapton, as did Robert Stigwood through his assistant Gary Patterson. Ben Palmer, given the unenviable job of transporting Cream and their equipment around the world, also provided invaluable help.

Additional sources included Elaine Akalovsky, Martin Forbes, Anthony Haden-Guest, Dick Heckstall-Smith, the late C. L. R. James, Tom Keylock, Nick Parkinson and John Platt. Returns for Marshbrook and Clapton's other financial holdings can be seen at Companies House. The previously referred-to published sources, as well as Marc Roberty's *Eric Clapton: The Complete Recording Sessions 1963–1992* (Blandford, 1993), were all consulted.

Pattie Boyd returned my telephone call.

CHAPTER 5

Among the sources consulted were Pete Brown, Ray Connolly, Richard Drew, Dick Heckstall-Smith, Tom Keylock, Ben Palmer, Don Short, the late Ian Stewart, Rob Townsend and Bobby Whitlock. Both Dave Markee and Scott Ross were invaluable in locating the exact chronology of Clapton's finding, losing and refinding religion. Keith Richards's comments to me in February 1977 were also noted.

Acknowledgement is again made to Ray Coleman, who interviewed Meg and George Patterson, to Harry Shapiro and to Marc Roberty's various works, recently joined by *Eric Clapton In His Own Words* (Omnibus, 1993).

'Presence of the Lord' (Clapton) © 1969, Throat Music Limited.

'Layla' (Clapton, Gordon) © 1970, Throat Music Limited.

CHAPTER 6

Clapton's life on tour of America was vividly recalled by Tim Rice, George Terry, Steve Turner's *Conversations* (Abacus, 1976) and my own research in the Warwick Hotel, New York. Reference should also be made in that context to *Rolling Stone* and to the Egyptian and Moore Theatres, both of Seattle.

Sources on Clapton's role as a community celebrity included Duncan Caine, Linda Chandler and Christopher Elson; as a celebrant of Alexis Korner's fiftieth birthday party, Chris Farlowe, Dick Heckstall-Smith and Paul Jones; and as a football fan, John Evans, secretary of West Bromwich Albion F.C.

An interpretation of Clapton's outburst at Birmingham in August 1976 was supplied by the late C. L. R. James. Clapton's own letter on the subject was originally published in *Sounds*.

'Wonderful Tonight' (Clapton) © 1977, Throat Music Limited.

CHAPTER 7

Invaluable help was given by Chris Thacker, who introduced me to Dave Markee and reported the comments of Henry Spinetti, both formerly of Clapton's group.

Other sources included Pete Brown, Jack Bruce, Peter Cockwill, Chris Dreja, Gary Glitter, Jim McCarty, Tom McGuinness and Cliff Richard. Research on Clapton's activities in Seattle was carried out by Jim Meyersahm and John Prins IV; Noel Chelberg provided details of the Hazelden Foundation.

Documentary material was again obtained from Companies House and The General Register Office.

'Hold Me Lord' (Clapton) © 1981, Throat Music Limited.

CHAPTER 8

Musicians interviewed included Chris Dreja, Jim McCarty and Dave Markee. Other material was obtained from Pete Brown, Linda Chandler, David Evans, Jeff Griffin, Anthony Haden-Guest, the late Sir Leonard Hutton, Andy Peebles and Pamela Wynn.

Details on Edward Fryer were supplied by the National Archives of Canada; on the birth of Clapton's children by the General Register Office; and on Clapton's finances by Companies House.

A source at the American Lung Association also – trenchantly – put that organization's view of Clapton at my disposal.

'The Shape You're In' (Clapton) © 1983, EC Music Limited.

CHAPTER 9

Comment on Clapton in and around his Surrey home was provided by Duncan Caine, Linda Chandler, Sylvia Clapton and Matthew Wood. Acknowledgement should also be made to Christopher Elson and the staff and customers of the Windmill Inn, Ewhurst.

A summary of Clapton-the-cricketer was supplied by David Rees, formerly manager of the Eric Clapton XI, as well as by Godfrey Evans,

Andy Peebles and Tim Rice. Other interviews were conducted with Pete Brown, Noel Chelberg, Steve Judson, Colin Longmore (illuminating on Clapton in Antigua), Dave Markee and Anthony Phillips. Companies House was again consulted.

A useful but by no means comprehensive profile of Clapton in 1987 can be found on the LWT video *The Man And His Music*.

'Old Love' (Clapton, Cray) © 1989, EC Music Limited/Chappell Music Limited.

'Bad Love' (Clapton, Jones) © 1989, EC Music Limited/Chappell Music Limted/Warner Chappell Music Limited.

CHAPTER 10

Sources included Steve Judson and, in America, Evelyn de Maria and Jim Meyersahm. CBS News made a number of quotes available.

An idea of Clapton's social life in the 1990s was supplied by Terry Gill and others associated with the Chelsea Arts Club; Dick Heckstall-Smith was instructive on Clapton's appearance at the gala tribute to Bob Dylan; the offer of the 'limited edition' *24 Nights* is included in the programme for Clapton's 1993 season at the Albert Hall – I am grateful to Elise Moore-Searson for getting me there.

Summaries of Clapton's career were provided by Pete Brown and Tim Rice and, again, his former colleagues Chris Dreja, Hughie Flint, Jim McCarty, Dave Markee, George Terry and Bobby Whitlock.

EPILOGUE

Sterling research on Clapton's closing the show at the 1966 Prince's Trust was done by Terry Lambert, Malcolm Galfe and Belinda Lawson. The *Sunday Times* put their record of his finances at my disposal. Much of the rest of the data was collated by Amanda Ripley, to whom many thanks.

Index